Get the eBook FREE!

(PDF, ePub, Kindle, and liveBook all included)

We believe that once you buy a book from us, you should be able to read it in any format we have available. To get electronic versions of this book at no additional cost to you, purchase and then register this book at the Manning website.

Go to https://www.manning.com/freebook and follow the instructions to complete your pBook registration.

That's it!
Thanks from Manning!

Quarkus in Action

Quarkus in Action

MARTIN ŠTEFANKO
JAN MARTIŠKA
FOREWORD BY MARKUS EISELE

MANNING
SHELTER ISLAND

| Manning Publications Co.
20 Baldwin Road
PO Box 761
Shelter Island, NY 11964 | Development editors: Bobbie Jennings and Dustin Archibald
Technical editor: Dani Cortés
Review editor: Dunja Nikitović
Production editor: Kathy Rossland
Copy editor: Alisa Larson
Proofreader: Olga Milanko
Technical proofreader: Raphael Villela
Typesetter: Dennis Dalinnik
Cover designer: Marija Tudor |

ISBN: 9781633438958
Printed in the United States of America

To the Quarkus community,
for making Java so cool and for being so open and helpful.

brief contents

contents

foreword

It is an honor to introduce you to *Quarkus in Action*, a book I have searched for since I began my personal Quarkus journey. Even if Java wasn't my first programming language, it is the one that has stuck with me the longest—from the early days, when server-side Java began to power the largest enterprise applications, all the way to today's distributed, service-oriented architectures. What continues to surprise me is not only the power of the language itself but also the solid ecosystem of tools and frameworks that makes developers' lives easier and working with Java even more enjoyable. With the advent of smaller runtimes like WildFly and adaptable packaging for container-based JVM applications, developers need to handle a lot more moving parts and configuration elements. The inherent complexity overwhelmed me quickly, and there is little that made me forget about it as much as Quarkus does. With its very effective convention over configuration approach that not only uses sensible defaults but also allows for the necessary flexibility in various environments to high-performance native executables, extended by an ever-growing universe of available extensions, it is the Swiss army knife a Java developer always dreamt of. This makes it a true developer companion that boosts everyone's productivity.

Martin Štefanko and Jan Martiška masterfully capture the essence of Quarkus's developer-centric approach and are your cruise directors, explaining every stop on the tour, from the fundamentals to the development of a real-world application. And there's hardly a better duo for this. Martin has worked on the fundamentals of Quarkus as an engineer for more than seven years now and knows the ins and outs of long-running transactions and application health. Jan has shaped the Quarkus project since the beginning and holds a special love for metrics and GraphQL. Their knowledge and experience with various real-world applications shine through every chapter of this amazing book.

Let's take a look at the cruise plan. The cruise directors begin by setting sail to explore the core principles of Quarkus and how they help you navigate the development of modern, cloud-native applications. You'll disembark at your first port, creating a REST-based application and compiling it into a GraalVM native image. Along the voyage, you'll discover what distinguishes Quarkus from alternative Java frameworks and how important developer productivity is.

Next, the cruise directors will chart a course toward building a complete car rental system. This onboard project will serve as a practical demonstration of how to meet the requirements of modern cloud-native applications. You'll explore various communication protocols, database integrations, and security measures, each with a concrete example of how it fits into the car rental system.

Finally, the cruise will reach the shores of cloud deployment. You'll learn how to containerize your applications and disembark them seamlessly to Kubernetes or OpenShift. The cruise directors will also guide you through serverless deployments, showcasing the flexibility and power of Quarkus in the cloud.

Quarkus in Action is not just another technical manual; it's an engaging and insightful excursion of Quarkus's capabilities. The authors' clear explanations and practical examples, enriched with hands-on exercises, make learning Quarkus an enjoyable adventure.

—MARKUS EISELE
Java Champion and Developer Tools Evangelist at Red Hat
@myfear

preface

We (Martin and Jan) are both software developers with a long-lasting passion for Java, open source software, and creating tools and frameworks that other developers will enjoy using. As employees of Red Hat, the main company behind Quarkus, we have been involved with Quarkus since its very early stages, and it has made us very happy to see how Quarkus has been pushing boundaries, making Java still highly relevant for development despite its very long history—the first Java version was released in 1995. People have proclaimed Java dead countless times, but it's still here and going strong, not just out of inertia, but it's still developing and adopting modern practices, especially the move toward cloud-native and serverless computing. Quarkus is one of the main catalysts that help Java (and JVM languages in general) keep moving forward, and we strongly believe in its potential to become a ubiquitous tool in the enterprise Java ecosystem. So, apart from promoting it in various ways online and at conferences, we decided to write a book about it, and it is the first such endeavor for both of us. It was daunting at first, but working together daily with many of the minds behind Quarkus was a great asset that made it easier.

In this book, we want to share a selection of the best stuff that has recently come out of the Java ecosystem, and Quarkus is a pivotal example of that. We want to debunk a lot of myths about Java being slow, cumbersome to use, and ill-suited for the requirements of the modern cloud-focused world. It was a real pleasure to write this book despite it taking a lot more time and effort than we had initially thought. We learned a great deal in the process and hope that you will learn a lot while reading it, too.

acknowledgments

We would like to thank everybody who has helped us by providing feedback and answering our questions. This includes our colleagues at Red Hat, specifically Max Rydahl Andersen, Clément Escoffier, Phillip Krüger, Andy Damevin, and Bruno Baptista, among others.

A special thanks goes to Georgios Andrianakis and Ioannis Canellos, who were with us for the initial stages of the book before they, unfortunately, had to switch and focus on different priorities.

We also want to thank everyone at Manning Publications who helped to create this book with the relentless reviews and feedback cycle. We thank both our original and current acquisitions editors, Troy Dreier and Michael Stephens, without whom the book wouldn't exist. Specific thanks go to both our development editors Bobbie Jennings and Dustin Archibald whose feedback made the book into what it is today. We also want to thank our technical proofreader, Raphael Villela, who caught many issues in the coding parts.

Special thanks to technical editor Dani Cortés. Daniel is a computer and telecommunications engineer, and master in cybersecurity. He has over 25 years of experience in the field of programming, in various languages and frameworks such as Java, Python, and Golang.

To all the reviewers: Alessandro Campeis, Anthony Staunton, Antonio Gagliardi, Balakrishnan Balasubramanian, Carles Arnal, Christopher Kardell, Conor Redmond, Cosimo Damiano Prete, Dániel Ágota, Dušan Odalović, Fernando Bernardino, Geoff Newson, Harro Lissenberg, Hugo Cruz, Jérôme Bâton, Josip Bilandzija, Marc-Oliver

Scheele, Mikkel Arentoft, Mladen Knežić, Najeeb Arif, Ozan Günalp, Paul Snow, Richard Meinsen, Robin Coe, Ronald Haring, Sergio Britos, Simeon Leyzerzon, Simona Russo, Srinivas Nagulapalli, Surendra Pepakayala, and Theo Despoudis, your suggestions helped make this a better book.

I would like to express a huge thank you to my wife, Megi, who supported me through the struggles and long nights of writing.

—MARTIN

A big thanks goes to my wife, Magdalena, for all her patience and securing a quiet environment for me despite the difficulties of working at home with two little kids.

—JAN

about this book

Quarkus in Action is intended to teach readers how to use Quarkus, a modern cloud-native Java stack that puts a lot of emphasis on developer productivity and ease of use. While Quarkus has a vibrant community and lots of resources available online and this book doesn't claim it will teach you all aspects of Quarkus, it attempts to provide a concise learning path to demonstrate the key features of Quarkus to get you started. After reading the book, a reader should be well-equipped to become part of the Quarkus community, start exploring more and more extensions in the Quarkus eco-system that might be useful for their programming projects, contribute to existing Quarkus extensions, or even extend the ecosystem by starting their own extension and making it available to others.

Who should read this book

Quarkus in Action is chiefly for Java developers who want to learn about the latest and greatest in modern Java. General knowledge of programming in Java is assumed. However, developers who aren't active Java users might find it interesting, too, because it debunks a lot of myths about Java being slow, cumbersome, and inefficient.

How this book is organized: A road map

The book has three parts that cover 12 chapters. Part 1 introduces the basics of Quarkus and why you should care about it:

- Chapter 1 explains what Quarkus is, what problems it tries to solve, and what it offers compared to its alternatives.

- Chapter 2 lets you get started with Quarkus by creating your first application.
- Chapter 3 takes you on a guided tour of the developer productivity enhancers that Quarkus boasts and shows how easy and fun it is to develop with it.

Part 2 includes most of the practical exercises. It delves deeper into the various frameworks and libraries that you can use with Quarkus and walks you through building a set of microservice projects—the Acme Car Rental system. Each chapter in this part focuses on a different aspect of application development and makes further progress with building the Acme Car Rental project:

- Chapter 4 focuses on remote communication between microservices and teaches you to build REST, GraphQL, and gRPC services with Quarkus—both the server and client sides.
- Chapter 5 introduces the testing toolset that Quarkus provides for developing automated tests with ease.
- Chapter 6 delves into the frontend world and shows the basics of securing Quarkus applications.
- Chapter 7 discusses what Quarkus has to offer related to working with databases, transactions, and persistent data.
- Chapter 8 describes the concept of reactive programming, why you might want to learn it, and how Quarkus supports it.
- Chapter 9 describes the concept of Quarkus messaging for robust and scalable asynchronous communication among microservices.

Part 3 focuses on the cloud-native and operational aspects of Quarkus. It explains how to make your application suitable for deploying in cloud environments and takes you through deploying the car rental system in OpenShift. The book finishes with a chapter about how you can extend Quarkus with support for new technologies:

- Chapter 10 introduces the patterns that modern cloud-native applications should follow, namely observability (health checks, metrics, tracing) and fault tolerance.
- Chapter 11 takes you through containerizing your application and deploying it in the cloud (Kubernetes and OpenShift).
- Chapter 12 discusses how you can extend Quarkus with your own extensions, adding support for new libraries, and when it makes sense to do so.

About the code

This book contains many examples of source code both in numbered listings and in line with normal text. In both cases, source code is formatted in a `fixed-width font like this` to separate it from ordinary text.

In many cases, the original source code has been reformatted; we've added line breaks and reworked indentation to accommodate the available page space in the book. In rare cases, even this was not enough, and listings include line-continuation markers (➥). Code annotations accompany many of the listings, highlighting important concepts.

You can get executable snippets of code from the liveBook (online) version of this book at https://livebook.manning.com/book/quarkus-in-action. The complete code for the examples in the book is available for download from the Manning website at https://www.manning.com/books/quarkus-in-action, and from GitHub at https://github.com/xstefank/quarkus-in-action.

liveBook discussion forum

Purchase of *Quarkus in Action* includes free access to liveBook, Manning's online reading platform. Using liveBook's exclusive discussion features, you can attach comments to the book globally or to specific sections or paragraphs. It's a snap to make notes for yourself, ask and answer technical questions, and receive help from the authors and other users. To access the forum, go to https://livebook.manning.com/book/quarkus -in-action/discussion. You can also learn more about Manning's forums and the rules of conduct at https://livebook.manning.com/discussion.

Manning's commitment to our readers is to provide a venue where a meaningful dialogue between individual readers and between readers and the authors can take place. It is not a commitment to any specific amount of participation on the part of the authors, whose contribution to the forum remains voluntary (and unpaid). We suggest you try asking the authors some challenging questions lest their interest stray! The forum and the archives of previous discussions will be accessible from the publisher's website as long as the book is in print.

Other online resources

To learn about Quarkus, you may find these resources useful:

- *The official Quarkus website*—https://quarkus.io
- *Official Quarkus documentation*—https://quarkus.io/guides/
- *Stackoverflow*—https://stackoverflow.com/questions/tagged/quarkus
- *Zulip Chat*—https://quarkusio.zulipchat.com (where most Quarkus developers can be found)
- *Red Hat build of Quarkus*—https://developers.redhat.com/products/quarkus/ overview (the enterprise version of Quarkus)

about the authors

 **MARTIN ŠTEFANKO** has been working on Red Hat's middleware portfolio for the last nine years. He started with WildFly and JBoss EAP application servers, where he got a lot of hands-on experience with many technologies and libraries that were included in these distributions (these libraries eventually came to be also included in Quarkus through WildFly Swarm and later Thorntail), to name a few, for instance, SmallRye, RESTEasy, or Narayana. Martin has been contributing to Quarkus since version 0.12.0. He is responsible for the SmallRye Health and LRA extensions but is also contributing to several other core extensions mostly around MicroProfile integration.

 **JAN MARTIŠKA** has been a Red Hatter for over 10 years and spent most of this tenure working on open source, Java-based application platforms. Starting out working on JBoss Enterprise Application Platform (WildFly), he gained lots of exposure to various technologies in the Java (Jakarta) EE platform and the surrounding landscape. Jan furthered Quarkus's observability capabilities by leading the MicroProfile Metrics specification and taking care of the relevant Quarkus extension. He is a major contributor to the GraphQL capabilities of Quarkus, and a contributor to the LangChain4j project and its integration into Quarkus.

about the cover illustration

The figure on the cover of *Quarkus in Action*, titled "Roussillonnaise," or "A woman from Roussillon," is taken from a book by Louis Curmer published in 1841. This illustration is finely drawn and colored by hand.

In those days, it was easy to identify where people lived and what their trade or station in life was just by their dress. Manning celebrates the inventiveness and initiative of the computer business with book covers based on the rich diversity of regional culture centuries ago, brought back to life by pictures from collections such as this one.

Part 1

Getting started
with Quarkus

What is Quarkus? Why and how should I start developing applications with it? How does it compare to the countless other frameworks in the Java and JVM landscape? Will it actually make my life easier, or is it just another framework that one has to learn? Is it just for server-side stuff, or can I use it on the client side as well? What about the cloud? Can I use it there?

In the first part of the book, we will take a look at all these questions. We will have a look at the basic philosophy of Quarkus and what makes it different from other frameworks. Then we will jump straight into some basic examples and get our hands dirty with some code. It's going to be a fun ride!

What is Quarkus?

This chapter covers
- Introducing Quarkus
- Understanding the Quarkus principles
- Analyzing Quarkus architecture
- Evaluating Quarkus alternatives

With a vast ecosystem of libraries, frameworks, standards, runtimes, and experienced developers, Java is a great choice for building modern, robust, and scalable software. In today's data-oriented, cloud-first, cost-sensitive world, Java is also sometimes viewed as mature, slow, and resource-intensive. Quarkus changes this perception, offering a fast, lightweight, and flexible Java framework perfect for modern enterprise applications.

Quarkus combines popular libraries, Java standards, and best practices with an innovative approach to building and running applications, delivering both great user experience and developer productivity. Its build processing-oriented architecture results in smaller and faster runnable artifacts, perfect for contemporary designs like microservices and serverless as well as more traditional monolithic applications. It's also great for specialized use cases like CLI apps, edge, GitHub actions, and Kubernetes operators.

In this book, we'll show you how to build Java applications using Quarkus from the ground up, gradually working toward an enterprise system consisting of multiple Quarkus microservices. Along the way, we will explain the main concepts, tools, and features of Quarkus to help you understand where and how Quarkus can be a good fit for your next projects.

1.1 Why Quarkus?

It's natural to ask, "Why do I need to learn a new framework when we already have framework X?" Java frameworks like Spring have been around for years and have extensive public documentation, problem solutions, and user stories, as well as massive legacy codebases. When these frameworks were designed—in some cases, 20+ years ago—the Java world was very different.

Java was originally designed for big, long-running applications, which created a perception that it didn't fit particularly well into modern computing environments. With the move to the cloud environments, application startup times and memory/CPU utilization became the prominent application metrics. Long starts and the high memory use of Java applications are no longer acceptable since such processing translates directly into cloud costs.

Quarkus was created to address these challenges. It defines a very lightweight framework that splits the application processing into the build-time and runtime phases. Any Java stack needs to do a lot of processing once the application starts—for example, reading and processing the application's code, annotations, configuration, injection points (inversion of control), or generating dynamic code to initialize the application within the framework properly. And all of this processing repeats with every application start.

Quarkus moves as much processing as possible to the build-time phase (application build/packaging) to save resources at runtime. The packaged application carries only the results of these initial framework operations, which makes it not only faster to start since they don't need to be executed at startup but also smaller in size because any code that is needed only in this initialization phase is never included in the final packaged artifact.

While performance benefits are very important, Quarkus also puts enormous effort into the developer experience when using the framework. It provides the *Dev mode*, which is a continuous execution of the Quarkus application, allowing live reloads of code and configuration changes. By just saving our changes in the editor and invoking the application, Quarkus dynamically applies those changes so we can see the results of our modifications in mere milliseconds. The development flow doesn't need to stop to recompile and rerun the application, which closes the reevaluation loop in a continuous experience similar to scripting languages while we still work with the Java virtual machine (JVM). Dev mode bundles a lot of productivity boosting features that we dive into in this book.

Quarkus also exposes all these features for integrations, which makes it very popular among library developers too. With its over 700 *extensions* (pluggable pieces of functionalities) that integrate different popular libraries (e.g., Hibernate, Jackson, or LangChain4j), Quarkus proves that it stands out as a framework where the Java ecosystem wants to be.

1.2 *Introducing Quarkus*

The name Quarkus consists of two parts—quark and us. A *quark* is an elementary particle that constitutes matter aligning with the very small resource footprint that Quarkus aims to provide. The second part, *us*, comprises us developers, engineers, and operations who utilize various software development processes where Quarkus creates an environment as useful as possible.

Quarkus is defined as a "Kubernetes Native Java stack tailored for OpenJDK HotSpot and GraalVM, crafted from the best of breed Java libraries and standards" (https://quarkus.io). But what does this really mean? Let's break down the definition and describe in depth what Quarkus is, what problems it tries to solve, and why you should care about learning it.

1.2.1 *A Kubernetes native stack*

We use the term *Kubernetes native* to describe tools and frameworks specifically targeting Kubernetes as the target deployment platform. Does this label imply that the stack of tools that Quarkus provides is exclusively related to Kubernetes? No, it's mostly a way to communicate that the development team has taken the extra effort to ensure a positive user experience on Kubernetes (or cloud in general).

Since not everyone may be familiar with the Kubernetes platform, let's do a quick Kubernetes (https://kubernetes.io) introduction. As enterprise applications and services started to move from physical servers to the cloud, the need to encapsulate the application with its execution environment (i.e., the operating system and dependencies) became prominent. This led to the evolution of container technologies made mainstream by Docker (https://docker.io). With containers becoming increasingly popular, the need for container management appeared, and that's precisely what Kubernetes is: the de-facto standard container management platform.

> **NOTE** You don't need to understand Kubernetes in detail to use Quarkus. However, it puts some of the driving design decisions of Quarkus into perspective so it's beneficial to understand the basic concepts even if you don't intend to use Quarkus in Kubernetes.

Figure 1.1 visualizes the relationships between applications, containers, and the management platform. The user-provided containers lifecycle and resourcing are delegated to the Kubernetes platform. The technologies that run inside the containers might differ. Kubernetes treats the container as a unit without knowing the container's internals.

Kubernetes operates containers in the units called pods. Each pod usually consists of one and sometimes even more containers (also known as sidecars—for instance,

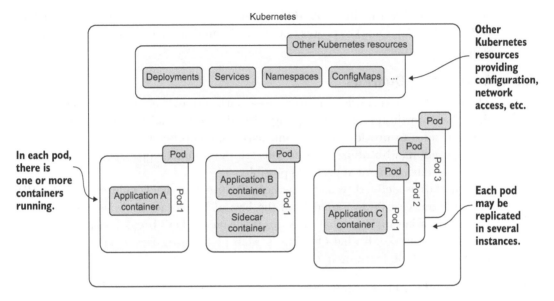

Figure 1.1   Kubernetes architecture and some types of Kubernetes resources. Pods are the most important resource; applications run in them.

for logging). Figure 1.2 depicts a standard JVM container in a pod, which, except for the user application, also packages the actual JVM on which the application runs. In turn, the JVM requires some other dependencies, for instance, `glibc`, which the container also needs to include.

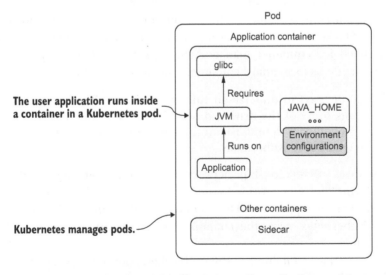

Figure 1.2   Visualizing the relationships between the application, container, and Kubernetes

Delegating management of the application lifecycle to Kubernetes also requires a way to make dynamic decisions in terms of configuring our application. The configuration of the individual containers might be different even for the same application replicated in different instances (e.g., a unique identifier). For this reason, Docker containers and consecutively, the Kubernetes platform allows us to override the configuration values inside the respective containers with environment variables. These can be implicitly deduced from the container specification as, for instance, the JAVA_HOME shown in figure 1.2, or we can manually pass them to the container (or pod) when it's starting.

So, in what ways is Quarkus Kubernetes native? By being designed for containers as the main packaging format utilized in the cloud and by providing a toolset that allows you to build and deploy containers in a single step. Additionally, Quarkus supports a series of features that promote integration with the cloud platforms (e.g., exposing health-related information, external configuration options, etc.), which are integral to a positive user experience in the cloud environment.

DESIGNED FOR CONTAINERS

The software industry has been skeptical about the use of Java inside containers. Containers need to start quickly, consume few resources (CPU, memory), and be small because these performance metrics directly translate to the cost of applications in the cloud. Java generally doesn't have a good reputation in this area. But this is no longer true with Quarkus, as we will see throughout this book.

SINGLE-STEP DEPLOYMENTS

Many developers despise writing configuration files, deployment manifests, or anything else expressed in a markup language. However, Kubernetes deployments do require writing such manifests. Some feel it's not part of their role, and others find it boring. Still, all these developers might be relieved to learn that Quarkus comes with its own tools that allow your application to be packaged into a container, which can then be shipped to Kubernetes as part of your application build without requiring developers to compose the manifests themselves. This feature saves time, limits errors, and guarantees that the experience is optimized for each application. In other words, the framework understands the needs of your application and fulfills them by tuning the deployment process accordingly.

1.2.2 OpenJDK HotSpot and GraalVM

OpenJDK HotSpot (https://openjdk.org/groups/hotspot/) refers to the JVM, the most common runtime for Java applications. GraalVM (https://www.graalvm.org) is a JVM and development kit distribution that brings improved performance, support for multiple languages, and native image (binary) compilation to the table. GraalVM is composed of a set of different layers that, compared to the traditional JVM, provides a way of also supporting non-JVM languages (e.g., JavaScript, Python). The complete overview of GraalVM functionality is beyond the scope of this book. We will, however, focus on the GraalVM compiler and the native image compilation, which are the main parts of GraalVM that Quarkus utilizes.

Native compilation allows users to build a standalone binary executable that runs without requiring a JVM. It represents simplified application distribution and provides an execution environment where the application no longer has to wait for the JVM to start, which decreases the application startup time. Such native executables start in 10s of milliseconds, which is incredibly fast for any Java application (we will get more into this in chapter 2). We can thus create binaries written in Java that start as fast as the ones produced by Go code, without the need to learn a new language.

So why don't we compile all our Java code into native binaries? The main problem is that the process of creating a native image is often tedious as it requires a lot of configuration and tuning. Quarkus helps significantly on this front, as we demonstrate throughout this book.

The important decision applications developers need to make is whether they should stick to JVM (OpenJDK) or make a move to the GraalVM native compilation. The correct answer is that there is no "one size fits all" solution. Services that need to optimize the startup time (e.g., serverless) prefer native compilation, while the ones that need to optimize the throughput (microservices) might perform better on JVM.

For Quarkus, it is essential to provide a framework that can work equally well in both scenarios. It provides almost all required configurations for the successful GraalVM compilation of your application, which makes it very easy to switch between the Java archive (JAR) and native. The build of a native executable is then trivial as it only requires using a flag at build time without needing additional code changes or configuration files.

1.2.3   *Libraries and standards*

The last part of the definition is the best-of-breed Java libraries and standards, which refers to the wide range of popular libraries and enterprise Java standards supported by Quarkus both in JVM and native modes. As we mentioned before, compiling applications into native binaries is a tedious process. Adding third-party libraries to your application makes it even more complex. Quarkus provides native compilation support for the most popular libraries and standards implementations available in the Java ecosystem. Furthermore, this support is not limited just to the native mode. Even in the JVM mode, Quarkus defines sensible configuration defaults (convention over configuration) and provides innovative features improving the manipulation and ease of use of the library in your code that you'll discover in the chapters to come.

Quarkus uses standards like MicroProfile (https://microprofile.io) and Jakarta EE (Enterprise Edition; https://jakarta.ee) and popular open source frameworks such as Hibernate (https://hibernate.org), Vertx (https://vertx.io), Apache Camel (https://camel.apache.org), or RESTEasy (https://resteasy.dev). This allows developers to reuse their expertise and years of practice with these libraries when they start working with Quarkus.

Open source standards alleviate the need for applications to be tightly coupled to a single vendor since multiple vendors implement the standard. Practically, this means that teams can move from other frameworks supporting MicroProfile or Jakarta EE standards to Quarkus without the need to reimplement everything from scratch. This is not just because the users utilize the same application programming interfaces (APIs) they already know but also because the utilization of the standard APIs presents easier migration paths of existing modules. For instance, if the application already uses standards like MicroProfile, the migration might not even require code changes.

What if we told you that you could even port chunks of code written using Spring Boot APIs? Quarkus also provides limited support for a few Spring APIs (e.g., dependency injection, data, or web) to ease the migration paths for developers that need to adjust to the MicroProfile and Jakarta EE APIs, which might be new to them.

1.3   Principles of Quarkus

Now that we've broken down the definition of Quarkus, let's discuss two more important principles that Quarkus builds upon which are not included in the main definition:

- Seamlessly connecting imperative and reactive programming
- Making developers' lives easier

1.3.1   Imperative and reactive programming seamlessly connected together

Most Java developers are used to writing code in an imperative model, which involves writing a sequence of statements that describe how the program operates. However, there is also an alternative paradigm called *reactive programming*. Reactive programming utilizes asynchronous data streams that allow your software to be performant, scale dynamically, sustain heavy load, and react to events declaratively.

Quarkus has excellent support for both imperative and reactive programming. Under the hood, Quarkus has a reactive engine. However, it doesn't force you to use the reactive programming model. Users can still program imperatively or even combine the two paradigms (even in the same application). Using "just enough reactive" is helpful for developers and teams that are new to the reactive programming model and need to ease into it.

Reactive programming has become an important alternative to the imperative paradigm that needs to be considered when the developed application is expected to be responsive and scalable also under heavy user traffic. This is why we demonstrate the use of reactive programming in the example application developed throughout the book.

With Java Development Kit (JDK) 21, Project Loom (or virtual threads) became a supported feature that aims to solve the complexity of reactive programming. Quarkus fully supports executions of the user code on virtual threads, and it allows easy switching between blocking, reactive, and virtual threads. However, there are some limitations to virtual threads that users should be aware of, which is why we think that covering reactive programming in this book is important even if you decide not to use it.

1.3.2   *Making developers' lives easier*

We could devote whole chapters to talking about performance characteristics, programming paradigms, and standards, but what good are they for if you, the developer, can't enjoy what you are doing? People may argue about the importance of developer experience. Still, if you take a moment to think about it, you'll realize that many software stacks and even programming languages have been created with the sole purpose of improving the developer experience.

Quarkus brings to the table a pleasant development model that boosts developers' productivity with features that make tedious and repetitive software development tasks obsolete. Quarkus provides a feedback loop that allows developers to test their code as they develop it without having to restart the actual application or perform any other kind of ceremonial tasks. Throughout this book, we refer to this loop as the *Dev mode*. This feedback loop not only makes the development processes faster but also serves as an essential learning tool. Developers get to see what works and what doesn't very fast and free of repetitiveness, which helps them fix bugs, implement features, and learn things more quickly.

This kind of feedback loop is pretty common among interpreted languages (e.g., JavaScript). It allows developers to write code and see their changes take immediate effect without rebuilding or reloading. However, that is not common in compiled languages like Java. With all Quarkus features encompassed in this development loop, Quarkus provides a unique development experience similar to scripting languages. But it does this with compiled JVM languages like Java or Kotlin.

1.4   *The Quarkus architecture*

Let's take a closer look at the key components of the Quarkus architecture visualized in figure 1.3.

At the base of the figure are the components representing the execution environment. *HotSpot* refers to the JVM and its just-in-time (JIT) compilation mechanism. *GraalVM* is the tooling responsible for compiling Java code into native binaries.

On top of this layer are the critical components used in the Quarkus build tooling. The *Jandex* (https://github.com/smallrye/jandex) library provides the indexing of Java classes to a class model representation that is memory efficient and fast to search. It also allows the build tool to do all the heavy lifting related to code metadata extraction so that it doesn't have to happen at runtime.

Gizmo (https://github.com/quarkusio/gizmo) is a bytecode manipulation library. Bytecode is the output of the Java compiler the JVM executes. Tools and frameworks that need to generate code either generate source code that is then compiled into bytecode or generate the bytecode directly later during runtime. Gizmo is the library used by the Quarkus build tools to generate bytecode during build time. An example of using Gizmo is producing code needed by *ArC* (Quarkus extension, see section 2.7), the dependency injection framework of Quarkus. ArC implements the *CDI* specification (https://www.cdi-spec.org), but all the dependency resolution and

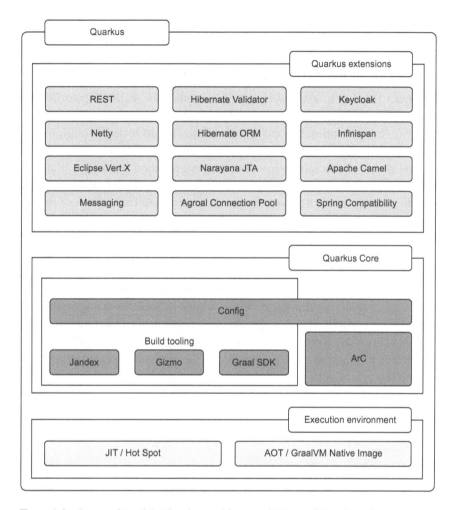

Figure 1.3   An overview of the Quarkus architecture in layers. Extensions that provide support for various frameworks are built around the core layer.

wiring are processed at compile time, following the general philosophy of Quarkus tooling.

The *Graal SDK* (Software Development Kit) provides integration for the native image builds. The last remaining component of the core layer is related to the configuration. Quarkus presents a unified configuration model for everything that the application might require, including both the platform and user-specific configuration properties.

The extensions are pluggable pieces of functionality that can extend either the build-time or the runtime features of Quarkus and cover a wide area of different functionalities, including integration, automation, security, and more. There are hundreds of Quarkus extensions available. Individual applications are free to pick and choose only the functionalities that they require, which has a direct impact on the application size and processing speed.

1.5   *Building the Acme Car Rental application using Quarkus*

Throughout this book, we build a real-life application called *Acme Car Rental*. Most chapters will contribute some parts of the functionality, bringing everything together by the end. An application like car rental is realistic and broad enough to cover all the different technologies explained in this book. And it is a change from the to-do apps, blogs, and shops, which software stacks often use for their examples. It also lends itself to being architected using microservices. Microservice architecture is not a panacea, but it simplifies the teaching process as it cleanly separates different parts of the system.

You can find the code of the Acme Car Rental application at https://github.com/ xstefank/quarkus-in-action. The repository subdivides the content into directories per chapter. Each directory contains subdirectories for the individual sections of the respective chapter that contain the final code after the particular section. The final version of the Acme Car Rental is provided in the `acme-car-rental` root directory. If you have any problems, you always know where to look. You might also analyze the commit history, where you can see the respective code differences. We wanted to make this process as easy to consume as possible, so we also provide links to the relevant commits for each section right next to the particular section directory as shown in figure 1.4.

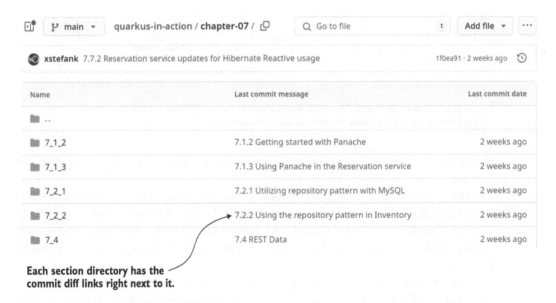

Figure 1.4   The book's GitHub source code repository structure with the commit diffs. The solution to each practical section is in the corresponding directory.

The provided code is excellent reference material. However, we chose to write this book so that you, the reader, can follow the development of the car rental system with us. Coding along with us isn't required, but it can give you a very different experience. You may decide for yourself what your preferred practice is.

1.5.1 Use cases

To get an idea of the car rental application's essential features, let's evaluate the primary use cases that cover user management, billing, fleet management, and integration areas. It is important to understand the problems we are solving before diving into the actual solutions.

The car rental system requirements include an interface that employees can use to look up inventory and perform bookings. A modern interface must also expose this functionality to its customers via the web or mobile so that customers can browse, book, and pay for cars. Figure 1.5 visually represents the interface.

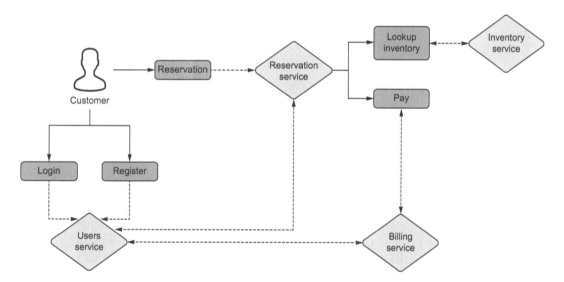

Figure 1.5 Modeling actions performed by customers in the Acme Car Rental system

By analyzing how the customer utilizes the system, we can differentiate two use cases: user management and reservation making. User management relates to user login and register options provided by the Users service. This service acts as the user entry API that separates the rest of the services. Making the reservation is a more complicated process for which the customers need to log into the system. The Reservation service then provides cars received from the Inventory service filtered to only the available cars for the customer-selected time period. If the user decides to make the reservation, the Reservation service calls the Billing service to proceed with the payment.

What about employees? What is their interaction with the system now that most of the functionality is passed directly to the customers? Figure 1.6 provides a visual representation of the employee use cases and how they tie into the core system services.

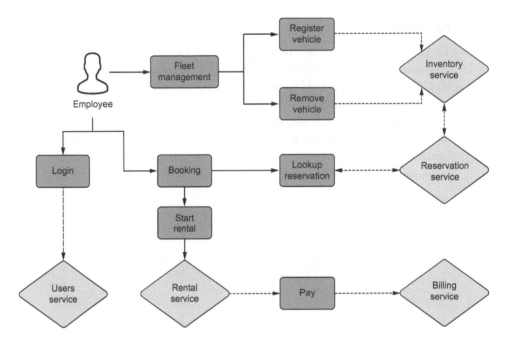

Figure 1.6   Modeling actions performed by employees in the Acme Car Rental system

Since renting a car requires interaction with an employee to verify the validity of the reservation, employees must have access to the system. An employee also performs other tasks, such as fleet management. Employees can register and remove vehicles through the Inventory service. They can also perform bookings, a multistep process that involves looking up the reservation, starting the rental in the Rental service, and paying through the Billing service.

The Acme Car Rental system is relatively simple on purpose. It represents an adequate complexity problem to solve, providing real-world examples of what developers may come across. We want to focus on explaining the Quarkus features without the need to provide genuine business value. However, we surely don't mean that such a system wouldn't make it in the real world.

1.5.2   Architecture

The previous section identified core actors, use cases, and potential services. If we are to embrace the microservices architecture, we compose the car rental system as a set of standalone applications. Each application represents an independent service and uses a decentralized data store. Services communicate using multiple channels, including REST, GraphQL, gRPC, RabbitMQ, and Kafka. Figure 1.7 shows how the services communicate with each other.

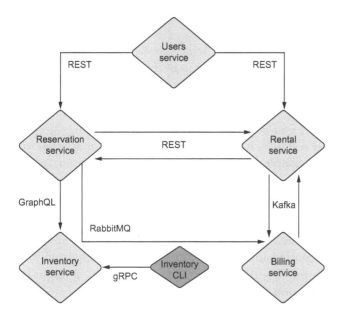

Figure 1.7 Car rental architecture and the various remote protocols that services use to communicate

Real-life applications usually limit themselves to just a couple of different communication technologies, depending on their needs. However, we designed the car rental application for teaching purposes, and thus, it does not have such limits. It covers as many communication technologies as possible. The same applies to database technologies. Each service utilizes different data store, ranging from traditional relational to NoSQL (non-SQL) databases.

Since microservices systems rarely consist of only business services, our car rental also contains a few third-party services (not demonstrated in figure 1.7) that provide some functionality for the whole system. Apparent examples would be the Kafka and RabbitMQ brokers that will propagate the messages between our services. But our car rental system also includes other services—for instance, the metrics registry (Prometheus) or the traces collector (Jaeger) integrated with the business microservices to collect their metrics or call traces, respectively.

We need to point out the Inventory CLI application at the bottom part of the architecture diagram. It represents a standalone command line Quarkus application employees can use to group operations over cars in the Inventory service. All other services composed together as Quarkus microservices are expected to run simultaneously to provide the overall car rental system functionality. We also need to mention that the Users service provides a simple user interface that allows users to log in and make reservations.

Acme Car Rental represents a small but coherent system. For a real-world application, it might be too complex since it relies on many software stacks that are quite different. However, since our goal is to explain how Quarkus integrates with all these technologies, car rental serves as an excellent learning material.

1.5.3   *Implementation*

For the implementation of the services of Acme Car Rental, we fix the Quarkus version to 3.15.1, which is the latest released version by the code freeze for this book. Feel free to experiment with the newer versions, but obviously, we cannot guarantee that everything will still work.

> **TIP** If you decide to try a newer released version of Quarkus by the time of your read, Quarkus also ships a built-in update mechanism that often works with even older versions. Simply run `./mvnw quarkus:update` (Maven), `quarkus update` (CLI), or `./gradlew quarkusUpdate` (Gradle) to update your project.

Quarkus also provides the Long-Term Support (LTS) releases that are supported for a longer time than regular releases. It is valuable to users who don't want to follow regular Quarkus updates that come very quickly. Fortunately for us, the 3.15 release stream is an LTS release! It was started in September 2024, and it's supported for the next year. If you want to experiment with the latest Quarkus versions, it might be safer to use the latest LTS 3.15.x version, which is considered more stable.

We develop in Java as our primary language. However, we need also to point out that Quarkus supports two alternative JVM languages—Kotlin and Scala (detailed in appendix A). We use JDK version 21, which is the latest JDK LTS release version available at the time of this writing.

> **NOTE** Quarkus 3.15.1 requires a minimum of JDK version 17.

The primary build tool we use in car rental is Maven (if you prefer to work with Gradle, see appendix A). The required version of Maven is 3.9.8+. Nevertheless, Quarkus comes with Maven integrated into the projects (Maven wrapper), which handles Maven versioning for you.

Since each chapter examines a particular technology, we want to prioritize the teaching of its software stack and its Quarkus integration in each respective chapter. Nonetheless, for the completeness of your Quarkus learning, we explain the use of Kotlin and Scala together with the Quarkus application building on top of Gradle in appendix A.

1.6   *Alternative frameworks*

As we mentioned previously, the Java ecosystem includes many tools and frameworks. If you're considering Quarkus, it's helpful to understand how it compares to established tools like Spring as well as newer entrants like Micronaut and Helidon. Let's take a quick look at these frameworks to see how they stack up against Quarkus. The intent here is not to provide a side-by-side benchmark but rather to call out the relevant differences in their designs and uses.

1.6.1 Spring Boot

Spring Boot (https://spring.io/projects/spring-boot) is a framework for creating standalone Java applications. It extends and modernizes the Spring Framework, which was originally created as an alternative to slow-moving J2EE (nowadays, Jakarta EE). It comes with many sensible defaults out of the box, reducing the amount of the needed boilerplate code (convention over configuration), which allows users to override only the required functionality provided by the framework. This is often referred to as an opinionated approach. This approach affects not only the configuration but also the selection of APIs that Spring supports. For example, Spring doesn't support many MicroProfile specifications, and it usually isn't the recommended approach for the few that it does. The most prominent example is REST support. While Jakarta RESTful Web Services (i.e., JAX-RS, a specification under Jakarta EE and MicroProfile) is optionally supported, Spring suggests to use the Spring-specific REST controller API.

The Spring ecosystem has been around for over 20 years now. This aging comes with its pros and cons. It has matured, and it has a great and vibrant community around it. On the other hand, it has been designed around techniques that take a toll on runtime performance (e.g., reflection). So, compared to the new generation of frameworks like Quarkus and others discussed in this section, it is sometimes harder for it to align with recent trends such as native compilation.

Spring Boot is probably the most popular Java framework on the market right now. Still, no other framework was able to convince as many Java developers to migrate their Spring Boot applications as Quarkus did. Since its inception in 2019, Quarkus's approach to performance and an incredible development experience detailed throughout this book made Quarkus skyrocket to take over second place. And Quarkus's adoption is still actively growing.

As already mentioned, Quarkus also provides a set of extensions with Spring APIs like web, data, and security. These extensions significantly help with the transition from Spring Boot to Quarkus. However, the intended use of these extensions is only for the fastest possible adoption, not for long-running application maintenance. When you get to the migration point, automation tools also help with the actual individual migration tasks (e.g., Migration Toolkit for Applications; https://mng.bz/2yom).

Spring provides support for native images with GraalVM since Spring Framework 6 and Spring Boot 3. The native compilation can, however, be problematic. Quarkus was created with GraalVM in mind from the start, so the problems that Spring still faces regarding GraalVM compilations are often resolved in Quarkus (e.g., reflection). Additionally, Quarkus extensions are also able to provide any GraalVM native compilation specific information because they know what kind of code the user writes. This eliminates the need for users to provide this information themselves, which makes their native compilations seamless.

1.6.2 *Micronaut*

Micronaut (http://micronaut.io) is a modern Java-based application framework that emphasizes microservice architectures and serverless deployments. Micronaut is very similar to Quarkus as it also focuses on modern software trends. Similar to Quarkus, Micronaut also uses ahead-of-time (AOT) compilation, which limits the memory footprint and speeds up the startup time of user applications. It also provides a live run mode that restarts the application when it detects changes. However, this mode restarts (not reloads) the application, meaning the application is not responding when the restart is in progress. Conversely, Quarkus handles the restart through classloader swapping, so it continues to serve the old version of your application until the new version is ready. Quarkus's Dev mode also provides the so-called instrumentation-based reload that doesn't even restart the application; it just dynamically replaces the bytecode (without losing the state of your application) unless the restart cannot be avoided.

Quarkus's Dev mode also provides a lot of additional features that we dive into in chapter 3. For instance, the automated management of third-party services for development and test purposes. These kinds of integrations need to be manually configured by users in Micronaut while Quarkus configures and runs everything automatically.

In terms of native support, Micronaut has decent support for native images. The image can be created by specifying a build flag or a separate Gradle task, similar to Quarkus. It provides configuration options that users can specify to tweak the native compilation. However, as of this writing, Micronaut doesn't guarantee native image compatibility for third-party libraries, which Quarkus does if the library is integrated as an extension (we will learn about extensions in chapter 2).

1.6.3 *Helidon*

Helidon (https://helidon.io) is a project for building Java-based microservices. Helidon feels more like a library and less like a framework. This stems from the fact that developers can use it without the inversion of control. Still, inversion of control is possible if the user decides to use it. These options create two distinct flavors of the Helidon, the standard edition (SE) and the MicroProfile edition (MP), with the former being more of a library and the latter more of a framework. The user has to decide on project creation as the two flavors are quite different in terms of dependencies and style.

> **NOTE** Inversion of control is a design principle in which the framework manages the user code—for instance, CDI, as previously mentioned.

Helidon's Dev mode (`helidon dev`) provides a similar experience as Micronaut: it restarts the application when it detects changes in the watched resources without additional functionalities.

Likewise, as with Quarkus or Micronaut, the native compilation can be enabled by the build time property, and it is available with both Helidon SE and MP. Creating native images with third-party libraries is supported for the libraries for which Helidon provides integrations.

1.6.4 Framework summary

The direction and goals that all modern frameworks take are pretty clear— helping developers write resource-efficient applications with fast startup times optimized for cloud deployment. In our opinion, compared to the competition, Quarkus delivers top performance and the most concise story around the native image compilation. In addition, it's faster to develop and explore Quarkus features due to its Dev mode. Quarkus brings a sense of fulfillment and confidence for any productive developers because they can quickly see the fruit of their labor, free of the overhead of traditional Java development workflows.

1.7 Next steps

Now it's time to get ready to code! We have a good idea of what Quarkus is by now, so naturally, the next step is to try it. We start by creating our first Quarkus application in the next chapter. From there, we plunge into the amazing productivity enhancements that Quarkus provides. In the rest of the book, we then utilize this knowledge and all the available tools to create our (unnecessarily complex :)) car rental system!

We want you to learn Quarkus by using it. So let's see Quarkus in action!

Summary

- Quarkus is a full-stack Java framework for developing modern cloud-native enterprise applications (monolithic, microservices, serverless, etc.).
- Quarkus was built from the ground up with containers and Kubernetes in mind.
- Since Quarkus supports many well-known standards and popular libraries, the learning curves are often short as users can utilize well-known APIs.
- Quarkus provides excellent support for building native binaries with GraalVM.
- The new development workflow—Dev mode—introduced in Quarkus, improves user productivity and can be a great learning tool.
- The Acme Car Rental application is an example system we will build throughout the book to demonstrate Quarkus features.
- Quarkus integrates various frameworks and libraries through extensions. There are hundreds of extensions available in the ecosystem.

Your first Quarkus
application

This chapter covers

- Creating Quarkus applications
- Analyzing the content of Quarkus applications
- Demonstrating the packaging and running of Quarkus
- Explaining Quarkus extensions

Imagine being asked to evaluate Quarkus for your current company. Your boss asks you to get acquainted with the tools required to run and package Quarkus applications, different strategies for easing the learning curve for your colleagues, and, of course, a small performance measurement that can prove that Quarkus is the right choice. You should evaluate the extensibility and usability of the Quarkus by demonstrating a simple application deployment on your computer and be able to state the reasons why you would choose Quarkus as your application runtime.

Any first contact with every new technology represents an interesting experience—either positive or negative. After the previous chapter, you should have a good idea of what Quarkus is and what it aims to achieve. Now it's time to get our hands dirty.

In this chapter, we will learn how easy and fast it is to get started with Quarkus development. Following several easy steps, we will generate, package, and run a working Quarkus application. Exploring what the Quarkus development tools generate for us out of the box will also allow us to take this experience one step further: we will package the application not only into an executable Java archive (JAR) format, which can be run with `java -jar`, but also into a native executable built with GraalVM. As a small bonus, Quarkus also generates Dockerfiles, allowing us to build Docker images for all available packaging formats. This is just what Quarkus generates out of the box. If you add more extensions, it can generate even more useful files (e.g., Kubernetes resources). So, let's dive right in and create your first Quarkus application.

2.1 Generating Quarkus applications

Quarkus is a very developer-focused framework. It tries to provide developers with a number of options to generate a starting application depending on user preference. In this section, we explore different choices available for generating a new Quarkus application. You can easily apply these options to start building your business application as demonstrated with the Acme Car Rental services.

We can create Quarkus applications in three distinctive ways:

- Quarkus Maven plugin
- Quarkus CLI (command line interface)
- The website's graphical starter interface

You may ask why there are three different options available for the same task. Quarkus chose this path because the target developer audience differs broadly in inclinations to various technologies. For instance, some programmers don't like to click-configure anything, so using a graphical interface is probably impractical. Conversely, Quarkus CLI requires additional steps to get the CLI installed. The Maven plugin is a good alternative because Maven is also broadly used as the build tool for Quarkus projects. However, there is an evenly large community of engineers who prefer to use Gradle as the build tool of their choice. And, in that case, they probably don't have Maven installed.

In the following sections, we will establish how Quarkus integrates with these tools to create new Quarkus applications that generate Java projects based on the Apache Maven. If you prefer the Gradle build tool, we mention the necessary flags that tell Quarkus to create Gradle-based projects after each command (appendix A provides more details about Gradle usage).

> **NOTE** Quarkus applications can also be generated through other means (e.g., integrated development environments [IDEs]) that provide wrappers around the tooling mentioned in this chapter.

2.1.1   *Generating Quarkus applications with Maven*

To generate the Quarkus application with Apache Maven, we utilize the Quarkus Maven plugin (`io.quarkus:quarkus-maven-plugin`) and its `create` goal. The following `mvn` command invocation will create a new Quarkus project generated in the `quarkus-in-action` directory.

```
$ mvn io.quarkus.platform:quarkus-maven-plugin:3.15.1:create \
    -DprojectGroupId=org.acme \
    -DprojectArtifactId=quarkus-in-action \
    -Dextensions="quarkus-rest"
```

The `quarkus-maven-plugin` invocation on the first line requires the full Quarkus Maven plugin GAV (`groupId`, `artifactId`, and `version`) because we are creating a new Maven project without any initial setup. We have to set the generated project Maven `groupId` and `artifactId`. Otherwise, we would be prompted for these values interactively. Lastly, we specify the optional extensions list to be included in the generated project. This command generates a Maven project in the `quarkus-in-action` directory.

By default, Quarkus uses the latest available Quarkus platform version. So, if you want to continue with the version we use in this book, you need to set this version explicitly with the `-DplatformVersion=3.15.1` system property. The command to generate Quarkus application with version 3.15.1 is

```
$ mvn io.quarkus.platform:quarkus-maven-plugin:3.15.1:create \
    -DplatformVersion=3.15.1 \
    -DprojectGroupId=org.acme \
    -DprojectArtifactId=quarkus-in-action \
    -Dextensions="quarkus-rest"
```

Feel free to continue with the latest version, as the starting Quarkus content we focus on in this chapter isn't changing much. However, for the next chapters, we will fix the Quarkus version to 3.15.1.

The `quarkus-rest` extension represents a default REST layer implementation. It implements the Jakarta RESTful Web Services (JAX-RS) API used in Quarkus. This extension is included even if you don't specify any extension parameters. The snippets include this extension explicitly to provide an example of defining extensions.

If you wish to generate a project utilizing the Gradle build tool, you can add the `-DbuildTool=gradle` system property. If you want to find more, feel free to jump to appendix A. You can continue with Gradle even if we focus on Maven.

If you don't specify the project's `groupId` or `artifactId` with the system properties, the `create` goal prompts you for this information during its invocation. Don't worry about the extensions if you don't know them yet. We will cover them in detail later in this chapter. This is all you need to do to get the base project code generated with the Quarkus Maven plugin.

TIP   You can use the `mvn io.quarkus.platform:quarkus-maven-plugin:3 .15.1:help -Ddetail=true -Dgoal=create` command to check all available parameters of the `create` goal.

2.1.2   Generating Quarkus applications with CLI

Quarkus CLI is an intuitive command-line program called `quarkus` that allows users to utilize basic Quarkus operations like generating application code, managing extensions, and launching Quarkus.

The installation of the `quarkus` CLI is optional; however, installation is preferred as it is utilized throughout this book. The installation instructions are available in appendix B or at https://quarkus.io/guides/cli-tooling.

To generate a Quarkus application with the same setup as with the Maven plugin but utilizing the Quarkus CLI `quarkus`, you need to run the following command:

```
$ quarkus create app org.acme:quarkus-in-action --extension quarkus-rest
```

Similarly, as with Maven, we can use the `-P 3.15.1` parameter (or its long version `--platform-bom`) to fix the Quarkus platform version to 3.15.1. To generate a project utilizing the Gradle build tool, you can add the `--gradle` flag.

This command generates the same application as the previous Maven command. The result is again available in the `quarkus-in-action` directory. One difference from the Maven plugin invocation is that when you run this CLI command without arguments (just `quarkus create app`), the generated application will not ask you to provide them. It will use preconfigured defaults (for instance, the code is generated in `code-with-quarkus` directory).

TIP   To get more information about what the `quarkus` CLI can do, you can run commands with a `-h` or `--help` flag, as, for instance, in `quarkus create app -h` or just `quarkus -h`.

2.1.3   Generating Quarkus applications from code.quarkus.io

Next, we analyze the graphical user interface (GUI) of the Quarkus application generator available at https://code.quarkus.io. This website, detailed in figure 2.1, specifies all parameters of the generated Quarkus application through a sophisticated graphical form. This UI is very useful as many users prefer to click-configure new Quarkus applications. However, this Quarkus online generator also provides a REST API that users might utilize to generate a ZIP file with the new Quarkus application remotely. Note that to open the full UI, you need to click MORE OPTIONS button.

This GUI provides the same project configuration capabilities of the generated Quarkus applications as the Maven plugin or the `quarkus` CLI. Starting with the setting of the Quarkus platform version at the top of the page, you then need to set up the project GAV and build tool (or you can use the default values). Next, you can choose the JDK version and decide whether to generate some starting code or an empty Quarkus project (starting code is implicitly enabled with the plugin and CLI).

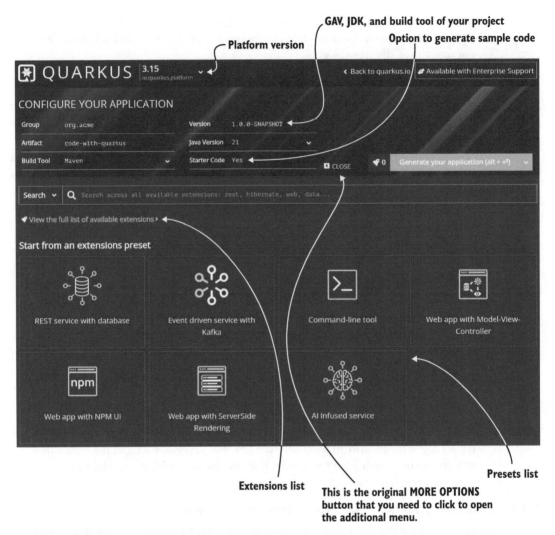

GAV, JDK, and build tool of your project

Option to generate sample code

Platform version

Figure 2.1 Quarkus generator interface at code.quarkus.io that you can use to generate project scaffolding and customize it by adding Quarkus extensions from its catalog

At the end of the page, you can browse and choose individual Quarkus extension presets you want to include in your application. Presets represent a group of extensions that are commonly used for a particular type of application (microservices, Kafka, CLI, etc.). If you click the View the full list of available extensions button, you can browse and choose individual extensions you want to include in your project. Figure 2.2 shows the configuration that generates the same project as the one we generated in the previous sections.

Finally, after you click the Generate your application button, you are provided with an option to download a ZIP file containing your application. If you check just

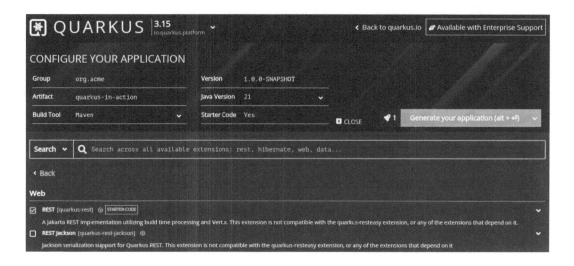

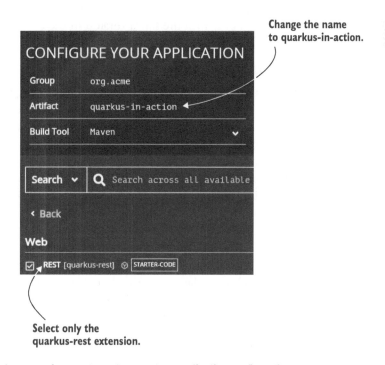

Figure 2.2 Quarkus generator example `quarkus-in-action` application configuration

the `quarkus-rest` extension and change the artifact to `quarkus-in-action`, you will generate the same application as we did with Maven and with the CLI. If you prefer Gradle, you can easily choose it from the Build Tool dropdown menu.

2.1.4   *code.quarkus.io REST API*

The generator also provides a REST API exposed at https://code.quarkus.io/api API root (this URL is not callable, but its subpaths are). Furthermore, it provides an OpenAPI document together with the corresponding Swagger UI that you can use to investigate available calls and options at https://code.quarkus.io/q/swagger-ui. Utilizing this REST API, we can generate the same quarkus-in-action application with the following HTTP GET request:

```
$ curl "https://code.quarkus.io/api/download?
  g=org.acme&a=quarkus-in-action&e=quarkus-rest"
  --output quarkus-in-action.zip
```

Unzipping the downloaded ZIP file from both the GUI and REST API download creates the same application in the quarkus-in-action directory, which contains only the quarkus-rest extension.

> **NOTE**   The platform version can be set with "S=io.quarkus.platform:3.15" query parameter. However, both the generator UI and this API create Quarkus projects only with the latest version in the 3.15 release stream which will not be 3.15.1 but some newer 3.15.x.

2.2   *Contents of the generated application*

No matter which way you prefer to generate the starting Quarkus application, if you add the quarkus-rest extension, you see the same results as we analyze in this section. Remember that we are focusing on the Maven project structure, so if you generated a Gradle project, the result is different.

When you learn about new technology, it is best to start with a general overview. If you list the files of the generated quarkus-in-action application, the directory structure appears as shown in figure 2.3. Depending on your background, this might seem like a lot or maybe not that much. But rest assured that it is everything you need to get working with Quarkus.

The generated content follows the standard structure of the Java Maven project. The pom.xml file represents the Maven build configuration file. In the directory src/main/java, we develop the Java source code files (.java). In src/main/resources, we place other non-source code–related files as properties (configuration) or HTML pages. Quarkus also creates the src/main/docker directory (not typically included in Maven projects) in which it provides generated Dockerfiles. The test source code is composed in the src/test/java directory.

The remaining set of files located in the root directory of the generated Quarkus project is either related to the Maven wrapper that is included within the generated application or represent useful configuration files used in common environments that Quarkus applications usually utilize.

The Maven Wrapper is a set of files (e.g., mvnw or mvnw.cmd, .mvn directory) that allow you to build the project even if you don't have Maven installed. You can invoke

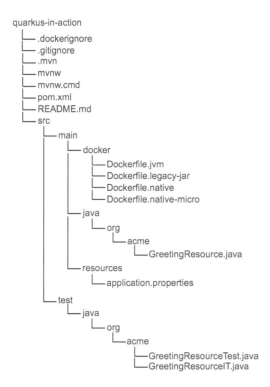

```
quarkus-in-action
  └── .dockerignore
  └── .gitignore
  └── .mvn
  └── mvnw
  └── mvnw.cmd
  └── pom.xml
  └── README.md
  └── src
       └── main
            └── docker
                 └── Dockerfile.jvm
                 └── Dockerfile.legacy-jar
                 └── Dockerfile.native
                 └── Dockerfile.native-micro
            └── java
                 └── org
                      └── acme
                           └── GreetingResource.java
            └── resources
                 └── application.properties
       └── test
            └── java
                 └── org
                      └── acme
                           └── GreetingResourceTest.java
                           └── GreetingResourceIT.java
```

Figure 2.3 Quarkus application directory structure for Maven-based projects

them instead of your normal mvn commands. They also freeze the particular version of
Maven, which is typically guaranteed to work for the project where the wrapper is bundled. If you don't have the correct version of Maven installed, the wrapper downloads
it and unpacks it into your home directory and then invokes it whenever you work
with this particular project.

The rest of the configuration files are utilized in various deployment environments. For instance, files like .gitignore or .dockerignore list files that are not
included in the Git or Docker build, respectively.

> **NOTE** The structure might differ if you didn't set the option to generate sam-
> ple code when you were generating the Quarkus application.

Let's analyze individual parts in detail step by step. We do not explain all the files that
you can see in figure 2.3 as they are not required for our purposes.

2.2.1 *Maven pom.xml file*

The primary build descriptor of Maven projects is available in the pom.xml file. Maven
defines the standard structure of this XML file, which is why we focus only on the
Quarkus-specific parts.

DEPENDENCIES

The most important part of the generated `pom.xml` is the `<dependencies>` element mostly containing the Quarkus extensions, all represented as Maven artifacts. The following listing details this part of the `pom.xml` file.

> **Listing 2.1   Quarkus `<dependencies>` element (including extensions)**

```
<dependencies>
  <dependency>
    <groupId>io.quarkus</groupId>
    <artifactId>quarkus-rest</artifactId>          ◁─── quarkus-rest
  </dependency>                                          extension that we
  <dependency>                                           added explicitly
    <groupId>io.quarkus</groupId>
    <artifactId>quarkus-arc</artifactId>           ◁─┐  The extensions providing the
  </dependency>                                        dependency injection (arc) and testing
  <dependency>                                          (junit5) implicitly added by Quarkus
    <groupId>io.quarkus</groupId>
    <artifactId>quarkus-junit5</artifactId>
    <scope>test</scope>
  </dependency>                                        Normal Maven dependency
  <dependency>                                          (not an extension because it's
    <groupId>io.rest-assured</groupId>            ◁─┐  not in io.quarkus groupId)
    <artifactId>rest-assured</artifactId>
    <scope>test</scope>
  </dependency>
</dependencies>
```

If you examine the contents of this element a little closer, you can identify the `quarkus-rest` extension that we explicitly added to our application when it was generated. However, two other Quarkus extensions are implicitly included, as shown in listing 2.1. You can identify them by the `groupId` `io.quarkus` and the `artifactId` starting with the `quarkus-` prefix. If you are familiar with Maven, you might notice that the versions of these Quarkus artifacts are not defined. This is because they are all defined in the Quarkus BOM (Bill of Materials) specified in the `<dependencyManagement>` section of the `pom.xml` file. The BOM is always versioned per a specific Quarkus platform version and contains the correct versions of all platform extensions and other useful artifacts (e.g., for testing). Using the BOM also ensures that all utilized extensions are guaranteed to work together.

> **NOTE** Some Quarkus extensions, particularly those not available in the Quarkus core platform (e.g., Quarkiverse, see 2.7.5), do not need to be versioned with the same version as the Quarkus platform. The versions of these extensions need to be specified explicitly.

MAVEN PLUGINS

In the `<build>` section of the generated `pom.xml`, we can also locate the definition of the `io.quarkus.platform:quarkus-maven-plugin`—the same plugin we use to generate the Quarkus application. Listing 2.2 details its definition. The main purpose of this plugin is to package the application into the correct target artifacts and manage the Dev mode's lifecycle (we will detail the Dev mode in chapter 3). Because it is included in the `pom.xml` build descriptor of our project, we can refer to it simply as `quarkus` without the need to also specify the full GAV as when we generated the application in section 2.1.1 (e.g., `./mvnw quarkus:help`). The version of this plugin also aligns with the platform version of Quarkus specified for this project. The individual goals are specific to the Quarkus lifecycle, and users don't need to modify them.

> **Listing 2.2   Quarkus Maven plugin declaration**

```
<plugin>
  <groupId>${quarkus.platform.group-id}</groupId>
  <artifactId>quarkus-maven-plugin</artifactId>
  <version>${quarkus.platform.version}</version>
  <extensions>true</extensions>
  <executions>
    <execution>
      <goals>
        <goal>build</goal>              ◁─┐  Generates the final
        <goal>generate-code</goal>        │  application artifacts
        <goal>generate-code-tests</goal>  │  (e.g., the executable JAR)
        <goal>native-image-agent</goal>
      </goals>                          ◁─┐  Source code that generates
    </execution>                          │  before the source compilation
  </executions>                           │  (e.g., gRPC proto files)
</plugin>
```

The other three defined plugins in the `<build>` section—`maven-compiler-plugin`, `maven-surefire-plugin`, and `maven-failsafe-plugin`—allow Quarkus to pass some additional configuration parameters to the Java compiler and the test execution, respectively. Feel free to check the official documentation at https://maven.apache .org if you want to learn more about these plugins.

PROFILES

The `<profiles>` section of the `pom.xml` contains the definition of the `native` Maven profile. Listing 2.3 contains the declaration of this profile as it is defined in `pom.xml`. This profile modifies Quarkus's build to also package your application as a native GraalVM executable file that we will learn about in section 2.4. The important part is the property `quarkus.native.enabled`, which is set to `true`. This tells the Quarkus Maven plugin to package the application into a native executable. The `skipITs` configuration is connected to the execution of the native tests run as integration tests (the native executable is started separately, and the test calls the exposed API).

> **Listing 2.3   Quarkus `native` Maven profile**

```
<profile>
  <id>native</id>
  <activation>
    <property>
      <name>native</name>    ◁─┐  Allows to run the profile
                               │  also with -Dnative (in
                               │  addition to -Pnative)
```

```
        </property>
      </activation>
      <properties>
        <skipITs>false</skipITs>                    The system property that
        <quarkus.native.enabled>true                controls whether a native
        </quarkus.native.enabled>          ◁────┘   build will be performed
      </properties>
    </profile>
```

2.2.2   *Generated code and resources*

If you create your Quarkus application with the enabled option to generate sample code, you can locate the generated code in the `src/main/java/` directory. Listing 2.4 contains the generated `org.acme.GreetingResource` class, which is created because we included the `quarkus-rest` extension (every individual extension may contribute some of its own sample code to the generated projects).

> **Listing 2.4   `GreetingResource` class: generated sample JAX-RS endpoint**

```
package org.acme;

import jakarta.ws.rs.GET;
import jakarta.ws.rs.Path;
import jakarta.ws.rs.Produces;
import jakarta.ws.rs.core.MediaType;         The HTTP path on
                                             which this resource
                                             is exposed
@Path("/hello")
public class GreetingResource {         ◁──┘

                                             The HTTP method (GET) used
    @GET                                ◁──┘ to invoke this method
    @Produces(MediaType.TEXT_PLAIN)     ◁──────────   The media type for the
    public String hello() {                            Content-Type HTTP header
        return "Hello from Quarkus REST";   ◁──┐
    }                                           Returns a Hello from
}                                               Quarkus REST text for GET
                                                /hello HTTP requests
```

This class composes a sample Jakarta RESTful Web Services (JAX-RS) server that exposes a single endpoint at the `/hello` path. The server is defined by a few annotations specified in the JAX-RS specification (`jakarta.ws.rs.*`). The `GreetingResource` exposes a single HTTP GET `/hello` call by its API.

> **NOTE**   This is the simplest possible HTTP GET method. We will see many examples of different REST APIs throughout the book.

Moving on to the `src/main/resources` directory, we discover a very important file called `application.properties` that contains our Quarkus configuration (chapter 3 details the configuration options of Quarkus applications). The `application.properties` file is the default location of the Quarkus's configuration. However, the configuration locations are also configurable if you need to add different locations where Quarkus looks for configuration files.

NOTE Quarkus also reads configuration from environment variables and system properties. More information in chapter 3.

The last subdirectory under the `src/main` directory, `docker`, separates four different Dockerfiles for building Docker images for various Quarkus packaging types. Here you can choose to build your Docker images based on the different distributions and different Quarkus's packaging types. We will go over individual Dockerfiles in detail in section 2.6.

The test subdirectory (`src/test/java`) contains the Java test source files. The sample code includes two Java classes generated in the same package `org.acme` as the class they test (`GreetingResource`). The `GreetingResourceTest` class provides a sample of the Quarkus test class. Its source code is available in listing 2.5.

Listing 2.5 Quarkus test example with REST Assured

```java
package org.acme;

import io.quarkus.test.junit.QuarkusTest;
import org.junit.jupiter.api.Test;

import static io.restassured.RestAssured.given;
import static org.hamcrest.CoreMatchers.is;

@QuarkusTest
public class GreetingResourceTest {

    @Test
    public void testHelloEndpoint() {
        given()
            .when().get("/hello")
            .then()
                .statusCode(200)
                .body(is("Hello from Quarkus REST"));
    }
}
```

Verifies that the GET /hello HTTP request is successful (200 OK)

Verifies that the GET /hello HTTP request actually returns Hello from Quarkus REST

The test class is annotated with `@QuarkusTest` annotation that denotes it as a Quarkus test. It calls the JAX-RS endpoint exposed by the `GreetingResource` with JUnit 5 and REST Assured APIs. It then asserts that the server responded successfully (200) and that the response's content is equal to the String `Hello from Quarkus REST`.

The second test class, `GreetingResourceIT` (listing 2.6) extends the first test class `GreetingResourceTest` and is annotated with the `@QuarkusIntegrationTest` annotation to mark it for execution with the packaged build artifacts—either the executable JAR, native image, or container (if built with Quarkus).

Listing 2.6 Quarkus integration test

```java
package org.acme;

import io.quarkus.test.junit.QuarkusIntegrationTest;

@QuarkusIntegrationTest
public class GreetingResourceIT extends GreetingResourceTest {
```

```
    // Execute the same tests but in packaged mode.
}
```

As demonstrated in figure 2.4, with integration tests, the test execution JVM runs separately from the Quarkus application artifact. The test only calls the application's exposed API. This is also the only way to execute tests with the native image or container. By extending the `GreetingResourceTest` we aim to execute the same tests for both traditional (Java unit tests in the same JVM) and integration test executions. The integration test isn't required to extend a unit test if the tests don't apply to both modes.

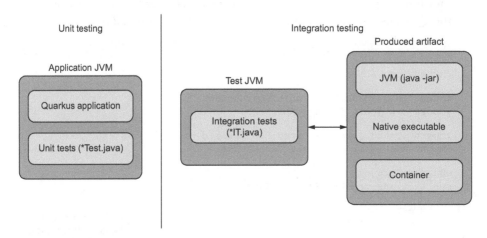

Figure 2.4   Unit versus integration testing with Quarkus. Unit tests run in a single JVM, integration tests run separately from the application under test.

2.3   *Running the Quarkus Application*

We have learned how Quarkus functions and what the Quarkus application contains. Now it's time to run the Quarkus application we generated in the previous sections and investigate where Quarkus excels.

If you are not already in the generated `quarkus-in-action` directory, change your working directory to it. Before running any Maven (or Gradle) project, you need to package it. But does this need to be done with Quarkus too? The answer is both yes and no. One of the best Quarkus features, which makes the development with Quarkus such an enjoyable experience, is called the Development mode (also called *Dev mode*). In short, Dev mode is a continuous run of your Quarkus application that allows you to change your application code dynamically. With just a simple browser refresh (or any HTTP request), it recompiles and reruns the whole application to display the results of your changes in mere milliseconds. The point here is to demonstrate that Quarkus applications can run without manual building/packaging operations commonly required for Java applications.

To start the Quarkus application in Dev mode, you can run the command available in the following snippet, where we invoke Quarkus Maven plugin goal `dev`. We reference `quarkus-maven-plugin` only as `quarkus` this time. This is possible because our Maven project configuration, namely the `pom.xml` file, contains the Quarkus plugin definition.

```
$ ./mvnw quarkus:dev
```

If the Quarkus application builds on top of the Gradle tool, then you can run this command instead:

```
$ ./gradlew --console=plain quarkusDev
```

The same result can be achieved with the `quarkus` CLI. The invocation is simply run as:

```
$ quarkus dev
```

You might choose one of the previous tooling-specific commands depending on your preference. However, the `quarkus` CLI gives you the benefit of working with both Maven and Gradle projects in the same way.

If you run the Dev mode for the first time, you will see the following question:

```
---------------------------
--- Help improve Quarkus ---
---------------------------
* Learn more: https://quarkus.io/usage/
* Do you agree to contribute anonymous build time data to the Quarkus
➥ community? (y/n and enter)
```

You can decide yourself whether you want to contribute the build time statistics from your local machine or not, but we recommend you answer this question when you're asked because otherwise it times out after 10 seconds, and you will be asked again next time you start the Dev mode.

> **TIP** When you answer this question, Quarkus creates a new file `io.quarkus` `.analytics.localconfig` in your `$HOME/.redhat` directory where you can change this setting if you change your mind.

When you execute the `quarkus-in-action` application in Dev mode, you will see the output similar to the one in listing 2.7 in the console.

Listing 2.7 The output of the Quarkus application started in Dev mode

```
$ quarkus dev
...

__  ____  __  _____   ___  __ ____  _____
 --/ __ \/ / / / _ | / _ \/ //_/ / / / __/
 -/ /_/ / /_/ / __ |/ , _/ ,< / /_/ /\ \
--_____/_/ |_/_/|_/_/|_|\____/___/
2024-09-26 16:56:43,710 INFO  [io.quarkus] (Quarkus Main Thread)
➥ quarkus-in-action 1.0.0-SNAPSHOT on JVM (powered by Quarkus 3.15.1)
➥ started in 1.250s. Listening on: http://localhost:8080
```

```
2024-09-26 16:56:43,712 INFO  [io.quarkus] (Quarkus Main Thread) Profile
⟹ dev activated. Live Coding activated.
2024-09-26 16:56:43,712 INFO  [io.quarkus] (Quarkus Main Thread) Installed
⟹ features: [cdi, rest, smallrye-context-propagation, vertx]
```

You might notice that we have two additional extensions listed in the "Installed features" list at the end of the output, `smallrye-context-propagation`, responsible for correctly passing contexts between threads and `vertx`, the underlying reactive engine of Quarkus. These extensions are implicitly added to the `quarkus-in-action` application as dependencies of `quarkus-rest`.

Our project is now up and running in the Quarkus Dev mode. You can now open `http://localhost:8080` in your browser that redirects you to `http://localhost:8080/q/dev-ui/welcome` which is a generated welcome page of your first Quarkus application. It will look like the one in figure 2.5. It contains some basic information about different resources in your application (we learned about them in the section 2.2) and pointers to the documentation.

Figure 2.5 Quarkus welcome page that is included in generated projects by default

Additionally, you can access the exposed endpoint at `http://localhost:8080/hello` in your browser or with any similar tool able to make HTTP GET request as cURL (`curl http://localhost:8080/hello`) or HTTPie (`http :8080/hello`). However, if you want to use these command line tools, they need to be installed separately.

> **NOTE**   Throughout the book, we prefer to use HTTPie versus cURL because it is more compact. If you want, you can install it from https://httpie.io/download.

Opening the URL in a browser or running any of the previous commands gets `200 OK` HTTP response with `Hello from Quarkus REST` content from our JAX-RS method `GreetingResource#hello` as we demonstrate in the following snippet:

```
$ http :8080/hello
HTTP/1.1 200 OK
Content-Type: text/plain;charset=UTF-8
content-length: 23

Hello from Quarkus REST
```

You can stop the Quarkus Dev mode by pressing Ctrl+C or `q` in the terminal where it is running.

Quarkus Dev mode is very useful for the development cycles, but when you are ready to run your application in production, you need to package it for shipping it to your platform. Quarkus packages with the build system you defined your project with, i.e., either with Maven or Gradle. The package goal is executed with one of the commands in the following listing. The CLI again has the advantage of abstracting from the actual build tool in use.

> **Listing 2.8   Quarkus package commands in Maven, CLI, and Gradle**

```
# Maven
./mvnw package

# CLI
quarkus build

# Gradle
./gradlew build
```

Quarkus package goals produce several output files in the `./target` (or `./build` for Gradle) directory which follow the standard Maven build artifacts. The output of the application's code and resources compiled from the `quarkus-in-action` project is included in the `quarkus-in-action-1.0.0-SNAPSHOT.jar` JAR. This JAR is standard Maven output. In this sense, it is not runnable.

> **TIP**   It is often also useful to clean your packaged artifacts, meaning removing the `./target` (or `./build`) directory because the build tools sometimes might not fully remove/repackage all artifacts correctly. Thus, you can very

often see the builds run as ./mvnw clean package, quarkus build --clean, and ./gradlew clean build.

The main Quarkus artifacts are located in the quarkus-app directory. This directory contains the executable quarkus-run.jar, which you can run with java -jar. It also includes the lib directory into which Quarkus copies the application's dependencies. This is purposely done because quarkus-run.jar is not a fat JAR (also known as über JAR) that packages the application together with all its dependencies like you might be familiar with from other frameworks (however, Quarkus can be configured to be built this way). Instead, the dependencies are externalized and referenced in the quarkus-run.jar's MANIFEST.MF file. For instance, this is useful in the Docker image where you might want to put application dependencies—which don't usually change that often—into a separate layer beneath the application layer, which, in turn, would contain your quarkus-run.jar. In fact, this is already done for you in the generated Dockerfiles (you can check, for instance, the src/main/docker/Dockerfile.jvm file). This means that if you are to move your executable JAR quarkus-run.jar, you are also required to move the lib folder with it to move its dependencies.

Listing 2.9 demonstrates how you can run your packaged application as an executable JAR. The output looks similar to the one in the Dev mode, but notice that the application now runs in the prod (production) mode.

> **Listing 2.9   Running Quarkus with java -jar**

```
$ java -jar target/quarkus-app/quarkus-run.jar
 __  ____  __  _____   ___  __ ____  _____
 --/ __ \/ / / / _ | / _ \/ //_/ / / / __/
 -/ /_/ / /_/ / __ |/ , _/ ,< / /_/ /\ \
 --_____/_/ |_/_/|_/_/|_|\____/___/
2024-09-26 17:00:34,488 INFO  [io.quarkus] (main) quarkus-in-action
➥ 1.0.0-SNAPSHOT on JVM (powered by Quarkus 3.15.1) started in 0.456s.
➥ Listening on: http://0.0.0.0:8080
2024-09-26 17:00:34,492 INFO  [io.quarkus] (main) Profile prod activated.
2024-09-26 17:00:34,492 INFO  [io.quarkus] (main) Installed features: [cdi,
➥ rest, smallrye-context-propagation, vertx]
```

You can now access the application in the same way as we did in the Dev mode at http://localhost:8080/hello in your browser or the terminal. The welcome page is no longer included since it is available only in Dev mode.

2.4   *Native compilation with GraalVM*

Now that you understand how to run Quarkus with normal JDK (java -jar), it is time to take it one step further and investigate the native executions with GraalVM.

2.4.1   *GraalVM*

GraalVM is defined as "a high-performance JDK designed to accelerate the execution of applications written in Java and other JVM languages" (https://www.graalvm.org).

It covers a lot of functionalities with its rich feature set. The main feature interesting for Quarkus is called the *native-image*. Native-image represents "a technology that allows compiling of Java code ahead-of-time to a binary—a native executable. A native executable includes only the code required at run time—that is, the application classes, standard-library classes, the language runtime, and statically-linked native code from the JDK" (https://www.graalvm.org). The native executable follows the closed world assumption: it statically analyzes the execution paths of the application to provide a platform-specific, self-contained, small, and, most importantly, performant executable binary. Such binaries usually start in 10s of milliseconds, making Java usable in very restrictive environments such as serverless architectures.

NOTE Ahead-of-time compilation refers to the process of compiling Java byte-code into a native binary specific to a CPU architecture and operating system.

2.4.2 *How does the native execution compare to JVM execution?*

Figure 2.6 demonstrates the difference between the JVM and native binary compilations and executions.

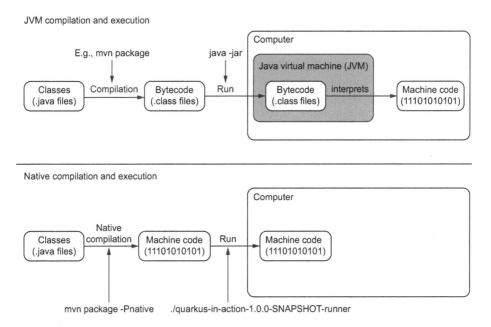

Figure 2.6 JVM and native binary executions comparison. In native mode, the application doesn't need the JVM.

When we compile Java program (.java) files, we get the bytecode. Bytecode is a portable, platform-independent set of instructions that lies somewhere between the source code that we write (Java) and the machine code that the computer can interpret.

It represents an intermediary that the JVM compiles into the different particular machine codes depending on where the bytecode runs. This is what makes Java so portable. We can write our programs once and run them anywhere the JVM runs.

The artifacts produced by GraalVM represent a binary (0s and 1s) executable programs. They are already compiled into the machine code the computer understands and can directly execute. Of course, that means the JVM is no longer needed since we don't have any bytecode to process. However, this also means that the produced machine code is specific to the platform for which it was built, so if you build the native binary for Linux, you can't run it on Windows.

2.4.3 *GraalVM distributions*

There are three distributions of GraalVM available:

- Oracle GraalVM Community Edition (CE)
- Oracle GraalVM Enterprise Edition (EE)
- Mandrel (https://github.com/graalvm/mandrel)

GraalVM EE is an enterprise (paid) distribution of GraalVM CE with better performance than GraalVM CE. Mandrel is a downstream (forked) distribution of the Oracle GraalVM CE with the main goal of providing a way to build a native executable specifically designed to support Quarkus. Thus, it is the GraalVM distribution which is preferred for creating Quarkus native executables. Mandrel focuses mainly on the `native-image` build tool. It doesn't provide a full GraalVM toolset.

But before we move on, there is one more thing: if, for any reason, you are not able to install Mandrel or GraalVM, don't worry. Quarkus also provides a way to create your native executable in a container runtime build that embeds your Maven build with integrated GraalVM inside a Docker or Podman container. But this method can only build Linux-based native binary that you can't directly run on different operating systems (but it can run in a container). This process is detailed in section 2.4.5. So, if your operating system is Linux, you don't need to install GraalVM. But in every other case (Windows or Mac), you need to install GraalVM to produce native executables that are compatible with your platform.

If you need to install GraalVM locally, the instructions on how to install and configure GraalVM or Mandrel are available in the appendix B. If you installed and configured Mandrel or GraalVM correctly, you can run the commands used in listing 2.10 to verify your configurations. The GRAALVM_HOME environment variable should be pointing to your installation of Mandrel/GraalVM. If you also use GraalVM directly, you should verify that you installed the `native-image` binary correctly.

> **Listing 2.10 Verifying a Mandrel or GraalVM installation**

```
$ echo $GRAALVM_HOME
/path/to/graalvm
```

```
# only for GraalVM CE/EE
$ $GRAALVM_HOME/bin/native-image --help

GraalVM Native Image (https://www.graalvm.org/native-image/)
...
```

2.4.4 Packaging Quarkus as a native executable

To demonstrate the native builds, we utilize the same `quarkus-in-action` application we generated earlier in this chapter. You may remember that the generated `pom.xml` contains a Maven profile called `native` (listing 2.3). To package your application into a native executable, you can run one of the commands available in the following listing depending on the build tool used and preference.

Listing 2.11 Quarkus native compilation commands

```
# Utilizing Maven profile
$ ./mvnw package -Pnative

# Gradle needs to use the system property
$ ./gradlew build -Dquarkus.package.type=native

# Or quarkus CLI for a general approach
$ quarkus build --native
```

The build takes longer (usually several minutes), as producing a native executable requires a lot of processing. It also requires a notable portion of memory. For reference, on one author's computer, the native build of `quarkus-in-action` project takes around 1 minute (including tests) and uses about 2.8 GB of memory. But that is it.

Listing 2.12 shows how you can now run your Quarkus application by directly running the generated binary. If you check the generated output in the `target` directory, you will find a new artifact called `quarkus-in-action-1.0.0-SNAPSHOT-runner`. Of course, this might differ if you run this build on a different platform (`.exe`, for instance).

Listing 2.12 Running Quarkus native executable binary

```
$ ./target/quarkus-in-action-1.0.0-SNAPSHOT-runner

__  ____  __  _____   ___  __ ____  _____
 --/ __ \/ / / / _ | / _ \/ //_/ / / / __/
 -/ /_/ / /_/ / __ |/ , _/ ,< / /_/ /\ \
--_____/_/ |_/_/|_/_/|_|\____/___/
2024-09-26 17:04:48,328 INFO  [io.quarkus] (main) quarkus-in-action
   1.0.0-SNAPSHOT native (powered by Quarkus 3.15.1) started in 0.010s.
   Listening on: http://0.0.0.0:8080
2024-09-26 17:04:48,328 INFO  [io.quarkus] (main) Profile prod activated.
2024-09-26 17:04:48,328 INFO  [io.quarkus] (main) Installed features: [cdi,
   rest, smallrye-context-propagation, vertx]
```

Did you notice how fast it started? Very impressive, right? Getting this kind of performance out of the box is undoubtedly not standard for most projects. At least not in Java.

2.4.5   *Native executable with a container build*

It is also possible to build a GraalVM native executable *without* GraalVM or Mandrel installed. Quarkus delegates the build and packaging of your application to a Docker (or Podman) container that contains the appropriately configured GraalVM.

> **WARNING**   The installation of Docker (or Podman) is outside the scope of this book.

But why do we then need to configure Mandrel/GraalVM at all? Because building native executables this way can only produce a Linux-specific executable application. Even if you don't run on top of Linux, you can still utilize this binary in your Docker images. However, since most of the targeting platforms—like production, continuous integration (CI) systems, containers, clouds, and similar—usually run on top of some Linux distribution, this functionality is very appreciated in cases where installing GraalVM presents a problem. These environments often try to limit the amount of installed software. So Quarkus provides this option if you just want to produce an executable application that you can then easily package and run in a containerized environment (e.g., Kubernetes).

Quarkus executes the native build inside the Docker container in two cases: either on user request (in that case, it needs to be explicitly specified by a configuration property `-Dquarkus.native.container-build=true`) or as a fallback, in case it is not able to find a valid GraalVM environment (e.g., `GRAALVM_HOME` is not set).

To explicitly request a build in a container, you can run the build with the system properties as defined in listing 2.13.

> **Listing 2.13   An explicit request for a Docker native build**

```
# Maven
$ ./mvnw package -Pnative -Dquarkus.native.container-build=true

# Gradle
$ ./gradlew build -Dquarkus.package.type=native \
  -Dquarkus.native.container-build=true

# CLI
$ quarkus build --native -Dquarkus.native.container-build=true
```

Quarkus detects which container runtime (Docker or Podman) you have, but you are also allowed to override this manually with the configuration property `-Dquarkus .native.container-runtime=docker|podman`. If you do not want to repeat these properties every time you build your native executable, you can also specify them in the `application.properties` file (more information about Quarkus configuration is available in chapter 3). In the output of the build, you see the following information (the messages can mention `podman` in case that is your container environment):

```
[INFO] [io.quarkus.deployment.pkg.steps.NativeImageBuildContainerRunner]
➥ Using docker to run the native image builder
[INFO] [io.quarkus.deployment.pkg.steps.NativeImageBuildContainerRunner]
➥ Pulling builder image
➥ 'quay.io/quarkus/ubi-quarkus-mandrel-builder-image:jdk-21'
```

In the second (implicit) case, when you do not have a GraalVM environment, you can see the following message in addition to the same build information as above.

```
[WARNING] [io.quarkus.deployment.pkg.steps.NativeImageBuildStep] Cannot
➥ find the `native-image` in the GRAALVM_HOME, JAVA_HOME and System PATH.
➥ Attempting to fall back to container build.
```

The produced Linux binary `quarkus-in-action-1.0.0-SNAPSHOT-runner` is available in the `target` directory. So essentially, if your platform is Linux, you do not need to install GraalVM or Mandrel to produce a native compatible with your system. In every other case (Windows and Mac), you must install one of them to produce a native compatible with your platform. Later on, we look into how you can integrate a creation of the Docker image that can utilize this Linux binary within your Maven (or Gradle) build. Then, in one step, it creates a runnable image with your application that you can easily run on any of the previously discussed platforms.

2.5   Unequaled performance

Probably all of us have been asked to optimize applications for performance at least once in our careers. The metrics, such as startup time, typically don't fall into the most optimized category. However, in the move to a cloud environment managed by Kubernetes where you don't control when precisely Kubernetes decides to restart your application, or in the architectures with rapid scale-downs, such as serverless, the startup time is essential. You probably don't want to waste time starting your application for several minutes during the rush hour to keep your customers waiting until you can process their requests.

As you probably noticed, Quarkus starts really fast, and that's not the only performance benefit Quarkus provides. So, how does Quarkus achieve such a great performance? Quarkus utilizes a concept of build-time processing. This means that Quarkus aims to move as much processing as possible to build time (when your application is being compiled) rather than doing them during runtime, as is typically the case with Java runtimes. Figure 2.7 provides a visual representation of this processing.

In traditional Java frameworks, packaging your application is the first and only thing done at build time. These frameworks package all the classes and configurations needed for your application to run into the produced artifacts. They also include everything that is needed by the framework and any libraries that your application utilizes. However, a lot of the packaged classes will only be used once for the runtime initialization, and then they will just be left there, unused, for the whole application run.

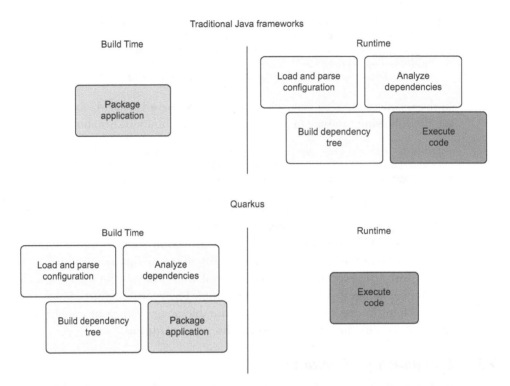

Figure 2.7 Quarkus build time vs. runtime processing. Quarkus moves as much processing as possible to build time.

Build time processing or ahead-of-time compilation means that a lot of tasks that are usually done when your application first starts (which is why it typically takes a long time for Java applications to start) can be executed during the application compilation; the results can be recorded and then utilized when the application is started.

In Quarkus, preprocessing, including class loading, annotation scanning, configuration processing, and more, are all executed during the application build. Classes only used for the application initialization are never loaded into the runtime (production!) JVM, resulting in very low memory usage and unquestionably faster startup times.

Surely, Quarkus cannot perform all preprocessing tasks and record them at build time. For instance, hardcoding the HTTP port on which the application runs during compilation might be problematic (since we might want to run the application on different ports in different environments). For this reason, Quarkus provides a mechanism that gives the developer an option to move as much processing as needed to build time while still integrating it with potential required runtime processing. The extensions framework directly accommodates this mechanism, as we will learn in section 2.7.

NOTE As a consequence of the build time initialization architecture, built-in Quarkus configuration properties are split into two groups: those applied at build time and those applied at runtime. Build-time properties generally define things like enabling various optional features. Runtime properties are used for things that are unknown during the build or would be impractical to fix during the build, like the already mentioned HTTP port for listening (because if Quarkus took that property into consideration already at build time, then you wouldn't be able to change the HTTP port when actually starting your application). If you're unsure whether a particular configuration property is fixed at build time or overridable at runtime, you can check the Quarkus documentation that lists all available properties (https://quarkus.io/guides/all-config).

If you are evaluating Quarkus, you might also be asked to demonstrate some real performance benefits. Let's take a look at some numbers, namely detailing the startup times and memory utilization (representing the main cloud requirements for your application) that you can present to your management.

Let's start by looking at the artifacts we created in the previous sections. GraalVM is often described as the main driver for these performance enhancements. Still, in Quarkus, both JAR and native formats certainly demonstrate the value that Quarkus processing brings to the table. By starting the `quarkus-in-action` application in the JVM mode (listing 2.14), we can analyze the startup time logged when the application is starting.

> **Listing 2.14 Running Quarkus in JVM mode as a runnable JAR**

```
$ java -jar target/quarkus-app/quarkus-run.jar

 __  ____  __  _____   ___  __ ____  _____
 --/ __ \/ / / / _ | / _ \/ //_/ / / / __/
 -/ /_/ / /_/ / __ |/ , _/ ,< / /_/ /\ \
 --_____/_/ |_/_/|_/_/|_|\____/___/
2024-09-26 17:14:26,698 INFO  [io.quarkus] (main) quarkus-in-action
➥ 1.0.0-SNAPSHOT on JVM (powered by Quarkus 3.15.1) started in 0.397s.
➥ Listening on: http://0.0.0.0:8080
2024-09-26 17:14:26,702 INFO  [io.quarkus] (main) Profile prod activated.
2024-09-26 17:14:26,703 INFO  [io.quarkus] (main) Installed features: [cdi,
➥ rest, smallrye-context-propagation, vertx]
```

Wow! Starting any Java application in just 0.397 seconds is incredibly fast! Of course, this number can differ depending on your environment, but the starting time for typical Quarkus REST applications rarely exceeds 2 seconds.

Let's also look at memory utilization as another critical performance driver for cloud-native applications because the less memory service consumes, the more services we can run in the same amount of allocated memory (for which we pay in the cloud). Listing 2.15 illustrates the memory usage of our Quarkus application started in JVM mode using the `ps` command. We use Resident Set Size (RSS) for our measurements, which outputs the amount of RAM used by the individual programs.

> **Listing 2.15 Quarkus JVM memory utilization**

```
ps -eo command,rss | grep quarkus
java -jar target/quarkus-ap 132864
```

Again, a JVM application utilizing only 132 MB of RAM is a great result, especially since we just started it. So Quarkus in the JVM mode is already very performant, and this mode is suitable for production deployment in a lot of use cases. But let's take this one step further and follow the exact measurements for the generated GraalVM native executable. The following listing indicates both the startup time and the RSS usage of the generated Quarkus native binary.

Listing 2.16 **Quarkus performance measurements of the native executable**

```
$ ./target/quarkus-in-action-1.0.0-SNAPSHOT-runner

 __  ____  __  _____   ___  __ ____  _____
 --/ __ \/ / / / _ | / _ \/ //_/ / / / __/
 -/ /_/ / /_/ / __ |/ , _/ ,< / /_/ /\ \
 --_____/_/ |_/_/|_/_/|_|\____/___/
2024-09-26 17:16:29,597 INFO  [io.quarkus] (main) quarkus-in-action
➥ 1.0.0-SNAPSHOT native (powered by Quarkus 3.15.1) started in 0.009s.
➥ Listening on: http://0.0.0.0:8080
2024-09-26 17:16:29,597 INFO  [io.quarkus] (main) Profile prod activated.
2024-09-26 17:16:29,597 INFO  [io.quarkus] (main) Installed features: [cdi,
➥ rest, smallrye-context-propagation, vertx]

# in a new terminal
$ ps -eo command,rss | grep quarkus
./target/quarkus-in-action- 47632
```

Now, this is really impressive! Just 9 ms to start and only 47 MB of RAM used? These values make Java comparable with generally faster (scripting) languages like Node.js or Go. Adding 10 ms to the request handling is essentially negligible. This is a significant milestone for Java developers since it allows teams to migrate to, for instance, the serverless architecture without the need to learn a different programming language.

The continuous growth of cloud migration and, in addition, serverless environments make the low memory footprint and fast startup very valuable metrics when choosing the application framework. Quarkus, with its build time processing, presents an excellent choice in this regard. So it is not only about how easy and enjoyable the work with Quarkus is for you during the development. You can simply demonstrate the practical production value as well.

2.5.1 *When to use JVM and when to compile to native*

With Quarkus, the compilation into the native executable image for users represents only a simple switch of a build time parameter. It makes sense to consider compiling a native executable once the development cycle is done to get this kind of performance benefit. So, does it always make sense to compile native binary? Well, not really.

Native compilations with GraalVM in Quarkus, one of the first frameworks that embraced native images, are often misunderstood as the primary performance benefit and, thus, the required last step before the application deploys to production. However, this is not the case. As we have already learned, Quarkus utilizes a concept of build-time processing, which is the main reason for achieving better performance. Native images take it to another level, but does that mean we should use them everywhere?

The answer is no. Using a native image or a runnable JAR should always depend on the target use case. Why? Because the main metric of your application in production is throughput (the number of requests per unit of time). With the way that the JVM JIT (just-in-time) compiler optimizes your code when the application runs (depending on the execution paths of your application), it can eventually outperform the native image's great performance. Remember that native compilations work statically, ahead of time, before any code is actually run. In this sense, they cannot know which paths will be utilized in which way and thus cannot apply the best optimizations.

> **NOTE** GraalVM Enterprise Edition also provides Profile-Guided Optimizations that allow providing profiling data taken from the running application to the native image compilation, which helps with this limitation.

If we imagine the application's execution in time (figure 2.8), we can analyze the JVM throughput performance when all optimizations take place. When the JVM application reaches peak performance, it can outperform the native image performance, which is already high from the beginning. However, it is static for the whole run of the application.

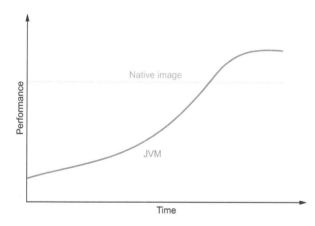

Figure 2.8 A comparison of JVM and native image performance over time. JVM usually outperforms native for long-running processes, but it takes time to reach peak performance.

Typically, in an environment where the startup time is not critical and the application is expected to be running for some time (classic microservices), the JAR can outperform the native executable. However, if the startup time is critical and we don't expect the application to run for a long time (serverless environments), the native executable is the better choice.

2.6 *Building container images with Quarkus*

With the continuous push on the workloads to move to the cloud, building Docker
(https://www.docker.com) or Podman (https://podman.io) container images is now an
integral part of our everyday work for almost all of us. As we learned in section 2.2, the
generated application contains the included Dockerfiles that we can use to create
Docker images. However, Quarkus was built with Kubernetes (or cloud in general) in
mind. This means that it is not mandatory to use these files directly, and there is possibly a better way to create (and also deploy) your images, which is represented by a
set of extensions discussed in chapter 11. Nevertheless, you might still run into a use
case requiring a Dockerfile. So let's take a look into what Quarkus created for us out
of the box.

In the `src/main/docker` directory, you can see four Dockerfiles:

- `Dockerfile.jvm`—For the Quarkus ran in the JVM mode as a fast JAR (default).
- `Dockerfile.legacy-jar`—For the Quarkus ran in the JVM mode as the legacy
  JAR format. Quarkus used the legacy JAR format before the team came up with
  the idea of fast JAR, which is now the default. You can find more information
  about the available JAR formats at https://mng.bz/VV7O.
- `Dockerfile.native`—For the Quarkus ran as a native executable.
- `Dockerfile.native-micro`—Similarly, packages the native executable but utilizes a custom micro base image that is tuned for Quarkus native executables,
  which results in a smaller size of the resulting image. More information about
  this micro image is available at https://mng.bz/xKOY.

Quarkus describes how you can create an image from each Dockerfile directly in the
respective Dockerfile's comments. Each of these files contains instructions on how to
package your Quarkus application and how to utilize Docker commands to build the
image and run the container. Let's take a closer look at the last Dockerfile from the
list `Dockerfile.native-micro` in the following listing.

> **Listing 2.17 `Dockerfile.native-micro` Dockerfile**

```
####
# This Dockerfile is used in order to build a container that runs the
# Quarkus application in native (no JVM) mode.
# It uses a micro base image, tuned for Quarkus native executables.
# It reduces the size of the resulting container image.
# Check https://quarkus.io/guides/quarkus-runtime-base-image for further
# information about this image.
#
# Before building the container image run:
#
# ./mvnw package -Dnative          ⟵──┐  Instructions on how to
#                                      │  package your Quarkus
# Then, build the image with:          │  application
#
```

```
# docker build -f src/main/docker/Dockerfile.native-micro
# -t quarkus/quarkus-in-action .                    ◁────┐  Instructions on how to build
#                                                          │  a Docker (Podman) image
# Then run the container using:                            │  using this Dockerfile
#
# docker run -i --rm -p 8080:8080
# quarkus/quarkus-in-action              ◁────┐  Instructions on how to
#                                              │  run the created image
###
FROM quay.io/quarkus/quarkus-micro-image:2.0     ◁────┐  The actual
WORKDIR /work/                                         │  Dockerfile content
RUN chown 1001 /work \
    && chmod "g+rwX" /work \
    && chown 1001:root /work
COPY --chown=1001:root target/*-runner /work/application

EXPOSE 8080
USER 1001

ENTRYPOINT ["./application", "-Dquarkus.http.host=0.0.0.0"]
```

The file starts with a short description of the produced image. Next, it demonstrates the individual instructions needed to package your Quarkus application and to build a Docker image utilizing this Dockerfile. It also illustrates how you can start a container utilizing the created Docker image. The actual content of the Dockerfile is at the end of the file.

The following snippet details the produced container image. The interesting part is the image size, which is only 78.4 MB:

```
$ docker image ls quarkus/quarkus-in-action
REPOSITORY                  TAG        IMAGE ID       CREATED          SIZE
quarkus/quarkus-in-action   latest     dadb7bda8ebc   31 seconds ago   78.4MB
```

For comparison, `Dockerfile.native` is around 143 MB. So the micro image saves ~45% of the image size. The JAR Docker image built with `Dockerfile.jvm` is about 448 MB. This might seem like too much; however, because of the way the Quarkus is packaged in the JVM mode, splitting the application JAR into a separate artifact (`quarkus-run.jar`) and the dependencies into an independent directory (`lib`, see section 2.3), the image is built with dependencies in the layer before the layer that contains the runnable JAR. In this way, every time you rebuild this image, if you do not change the dependencies— which would result in also recreating the `lib` layer—your build will be very small, containing only your application, which needs to be recompiled due to the changes you are making. This strategy can also be utilized in a remote repository (cloud, Kubernetes) where you can push the base image layers, which do not change that often, and push only the smaller application layers through the network on changes.

> **TIP** If you use Podman, we recommend you adjust your installation according to the information provided in https://quarkus.io/guides/podman to allow Podman to handle all Quarkus scenarios correctly.

2.7   *Extensions*

Extensions are an integral part of the Quarkus architecture. They represent the mechanisms that allow users to pick and choose only the functionality that is absolutely necessary for their particular Quarkus application. This means that each Quarkus instance only packages the indispensable dependencies required for its correct behavior. In this way, Quarkus packages less (only required) code and resources, meaning less processing and, in turn, faster startup times and better memory utilization that your application brings into production.

2.7.1   *What is an extension?*

From a developer's point of view, Quarkus extensions are simply modules that provide additional functionality by integrating a library or a framework with the Quarkus core—an integral Quarkus code base that provides wiring code, including all what the extensions need. A couple of prominent examples of extensions are those for Hibernate (database management) and RESTEasy (REST server/client). By providing such a modular system, Quarkus allows you to choose whatever functionality you need in your individual applications without delivering everything in a single monolithic package, thus achieving a better runtime footprint.

> **NOTE**   In this section, we focus on how to use existing extensions, but we will also develop our custom extension in chapter 12!

If we break down the `pom.xml` of the `quarkus-in-action` application we generated, we see the `quarkus-rest` extension, which implements the JAX-RS specification for running REST Services. It is located in the dependencies section, as shown in listing 2.18. In Quarkus projects, the extensions are managed as Maven dependencies. The `io.quarkus:quarkus-rest` Maven dependency represents the `quarkus-rest` extension.

Listing 2.18   Quarkus REST extension Maven dependency

```
<dependency>
    <groupId>io.quarkus</groupId>
    <artifactId>quarkus-rest</artifactId>
</dependency>
```

From the architectural point of view, the integration of extensions into Quarkus is demonstrated in figure 2.9. The extensions are the top layer users interact with the most. You can integrate only the needed functionality, which differs per application. Some extensions are further divided into more extensions where some parts of their functionality vary. For instance, if you need to use JSON with REST, you can choose from two different JSON serialization libraries (Jackson and JSON-B), meaning Quarkus offers two additional extensions that provide correct wiring for REST and the respective JSON library.

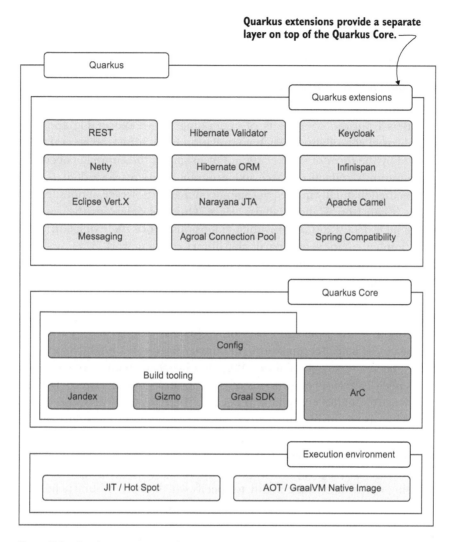

Figure 2.9 Quarkus component view and some examples of extensions

The ArC extension (also available in `pom.xml` in the `<dependencies>` section) is listed beneath other extensions because it is unique. ArC implements the dependency injection framework. If you are familiar with Java EE, ArC implements the Contexts and Dependency Injection (CDI) specification. This extension provides an integral functionality that almost all other extensions and the Quarkus core rely on. However, some applications (e.g., the command line applications) might not require such functionality, so you can remove it if needed.

Some extensions are also added to Quarkus applications implicitly, typically as dependencies of other already-added extensions. You probably noted that when you run the `quarkus-in-action` application (e.g., listing 2.9), there are four extensions in the list: `cdi` (ArC), `quarkus-rest` that we included explicitly and two implicit extensions, `smallrye-context-propagation` and `vertx`.

2.7.2 *Native compilations and build-time processing*

Another important benefit of the extensions approach in Quarkus is their ability to shield users from the complexity of generating native executable applications with GraalVM-based compilations. Such compilation must adhere to several rules that are mandated by the form of its execution. For example, the compiler needs to know all the application's reflectively accessed program elements ahead of time, meaning often specified manually in the packaging command (however, it does try to deduct as much as it can from static analysis). Here, Quarkus delegates the responsibility of knowing such details to the individual extensions. Since the extension provides integration/implementation of a particular library or framework, it knows what kind of code the user writes. Therefore, it can help to denote this kind of information to the GraalVM compiler automatically, without any user intervention. To compile into a native executable, you can simply add a command-line flag, as demonstrated in section 2.4.

As long as your application uses only Quarkus extensions, Quarkus guarantees almost seamless native compilation (of course, edge cases might happen). In a Java runtime, this is a very useful feature. Why? For instance, many popular Java enterprise libraries need to access components of your application reflectively. This is problematic for GraalVM native compilations because the reflectively accessed classes need to be explicitly listed during the native build. The integration code provided by the extension can do that for you. Using extensions is thus always the preferred way of adding additional functionality to your Quarkus application.

Something that your application also benefits from, but what you can't directly see when using extensions, is the ability to specify which parts of library/framework integration execute during the build time and which need to be relayed to the runtime. It can also define which parts of the code compile during the build to produce the bytecode that can be included in the packaged application for execution during runtime. Since the extension developer knows the details of the integrated code, it is often straightforward to define these respective areas. It is also possible to directly scan the user application in which the extension is added to get the information about available user classes and resources, so the extension can make dynamic decisions depending on the code you typed in your Quarkus application. This mechanism allows the integration of the libraries to take the full advantage of the build-time principle of Quarkus.

Surely, you can still add any Java dependency to your Quarkus application. It will generally work in the JVM mode as in any other Java runtime. However, you might notice problems when compiling into a native executable with GraalVM or Mandrel. Many users or maintainers of popular libraries thus choose to implement the Quarkus integration with their respective libraries in custom Quarkus extensions that they can easily expose to all Quarkus users. If you are interested in writing your custom extensions, we dedicate all of chapter 12 to this subject.

2.7.3 *Working with Quarkus extensions*

The number of available Quarkus extensions is enormous. Nevertheless, the Quarkus extensions management tooling can compose a coherent experience of finding, adding, and removing Quarkus extensions. For better clarity, the examples utilized in this chapter will focus on the commands available in the `quarkus` CLI tool. However, all presented commands are also available in the Quarkus Maven plugin goals and Gradle tasks.

> **TIP** To get all available goals of the Quarkus Maven plugin, you can invoke `./mvnw quarkus:help`, and to get available Gradle tasks, you can use `./gradlew tasks`.

To list all extensions already installed in the Quarkus application, run the command in listing 2.19. If you execute it in the `quarkus-in-action` application directory, it correctly outputs the `quarkus-rest` extension we installed at the project creation. If you run this command from a directory that is not a Quarkus project, it lists all extensions.

Listing 2.19 Listing extensions installed in the Quarkus application

```
$ quarkus extension list
Current Quarkus extensions installed:

* ArtifactId                              Extension Name
* quarkus-rest                            REST

To get more information, append `--full` to your command line.
```

As an application grows over time and it needs to provide additional business value, it will use more and more of Quarkus's built-in capabilities. If you want to list all available installable extensions (which is a very long list since we currently have only one extension installed), you might run the command detailed in the following listing.

Listing 2.20 The installable extensions list

```
$ quarkus extension --installable
Listing extensions (default action, see --help).
Current Quarkus extensions installable:

* ArtifactId                              Extension Name
* blaze-persistence-integration-quarkus-3 Blaze-Persistence
* camel-quarkus-activemq                  Camel ActiveMQ
...
```

NOTE If you prefer a graphical interface, https://quarkus.io/extensions/ also lists all available Quarkus extensions with instructions for how to add them to your Quarkus projects.

As browsing and searching in this long list might be difficult, the capabilities provided by extensions are grouped into categories to make it easier to select the desired ones. You can list the categories by invoking the `extension categories` command.

Listing 2.21 **Listing Quarkus extensions categories**

```
$ quarkus extension categories
Available Quarkus extension categories:

alt-languages
business-automation
cloud
compatibility
core
data
integration
messaging
miscellaneous
observability
reactive
security
serialization
web
grpc

To get more information, append `--full` to your command line.

To list extensions in given category, use:
`quarkus extension list --installable --category "categoryId"`
```

Note the `--full` flag is available for all these commands. With this flag, the output contains more information about available categories (or extensions) to help you if you are unsure what category or extension you are looking for.

Say that you need to interact with Kafka from your Quarkus application. Based on the previous output, you might have already guessed that you need to look into the `messaging` category, but if not, you can still invoke the `quarkus extension categories --full` command to find that the `messaging` category directly mentions Kafka in its description. To find what extensions would suit this use case, you can invoke the following command to get installable extensions from the `messaging` category.

Listing 2.22 **Listing all extensions in the messaging category**

```
$ quarkus extension list --installable --category "messaging"
Current Quarkus extensions installable:

✱ ArtifactId                            Extension Name
  citrus-quarkus                        Citrus
```

```
    quarkus-artemis-core                    Artemis Core
    quarkus-artemis-jms                     Artemis JMS
  ✱ quarkus-google-cloud-pubsub            Google Cloud Pubsub
    quarkus-hivemq-client                   Quarkus - HiveMQ Client
  ✱ quarkus-kafka-client                    Apache Kafka Client
  ✱ quarkus-kafka-streams                   Apache Kafka Streams
    quarkus-kafka-streams-processor         Kafka Streams Processor
  ✱ quarkus-messaging                       Messaging
  ✱ quarkus-messaging-amqp                  Messaging - AMQP Connector
  ✱ quarkus-messaging-kafka                 Messaging - Kafka Connector


...

To get more information, append `--full` to your command line.

Add an extension to your project by adding the dependency to your pom.xml
➥ or use `quarkus extension add "artifactId"`
```

> **TIP** We purposely use the long forms of the parameters for the `quarkus` CLI.
> However, most commands have shorter aliases so users don't need to type full
> names. The command `quarkus extension list --installable --category`
> `"messaging"` can thus be shortened to `quarkus ext list -ic "messaging"`. The
> CLI also comes with autocompletion that you can integrate with your Bash or
> ZSH shell. You can find all available options with `quarkus extension -h`.

From this output, we can summarize that the `quarkus-messaging-kafka` extension is
appropriate for the Kafka integration. The output also makes it clear which command
we need to invoke to add this extension to our project:

```
$ quarkus extension add "quarkus-messaging-kafka"
[SUCCESS] ✓  Extension io.quarkus:quarkus-messaging-kafka has been installed
```

This means that `pom.xml` has been modified, and a new Maven dependency has been
added to the dependencies section. The new `quarkus-messaging-kafka` extension is
detailed in the following listing.

Listing 2.23 `quarkus-messaging-kafka` **extension in the** `pom.xml` **dependency**

```
<dependency>
    <groupId>io.quarkus</groupId>
    <artifactId>quarkus-messaging-kafka</artifactId>
</dependency>
```

Removing Quarkus extensions is done similarly. The `pom.xml` is again modified by
removing the previously mentioned Maven dependency. Analogous to adding an
extension, you can locate the success message in the build's output:

```
$ quarkus extension remove "quarkus-messaging-kafka"
[SUCCESS] ✓  Extension io.quarkus:quarkus-messaging-kafka has been
➥ uninstalled
```

Using the `quarkus` CLI (or Maven plugin, Gradle tasks) represents a better utilization of Quarkus extensions—namely, in browsing and searching for available extensions to achieve a particular task. However, Quarkus only modifies the `pom.xml` dependencies section in the background. So you are free to directly modify `pom.xml` if you already know what you need to do.

2.7.4   Quarkus guides

So far, we have learned how to manage the Quarkus extensions in your projects. However, knowing where to find the official documentation about what a Quarkus extension offers is often beneficial. For most extensions, Quarkus documentation provides a guide that offers the most helpful information about the extension and how to use it. It also usually contains some sample code for getting started with the extension and lists all available configuration properties applicable to the respective extension.

The Quarkus guides are hosted at https://quarkus.io/guides/. The website has an intuitive UI that allows users to search for available guides and, thus, extensions that they might want to use in their Quarkus applications. Furthermore, the `quarkus` CLI conveniently provides a link to an official guide for the extension (if a guide exists) when used together with `--full` flag. You can see this in action in the last column of listing 2.24. Because the output of this command is too long, we display only the Kafka extension we used previously with columns split per line.

> **Listing 2.24   Quarkus messaging category list with the `--full` flag**

```
$ quarkus extension list --installable --category "messaging" --full
Current Quarkus extensions installable:

* ArtifactId quarkus-messaging-kafka
  Extension  Messaging - Kafka Connector
  Version    3.15.1
  Guide      https://quarkus.io/guides/kafka-getting-started

  ...
```

The structure of the Quarkus guide generally consists of a set of step-by-step instructions that build a small Quarkus application utilizing the described extension and showing its functionalities. It also provides a final solution in the form of a final built application available in the Quarkus quickstarts repository. At the end of each guide, there is a list of feasible configuration properties that can configure the mentioned extension. These guides provide concise documentation for respective extensions and are the best place to retrieve information about different functionalities that your Quarkus applications can utilize.

2.7.5 *Quarkiverse*

Since initially introduced in 2019, Quarkus has grown at an unprecedented rate. With its frequent releases, robust support, and innovation, the community around Quarkus expands rapidly still today, moving Quarkus even further. Naturally, when more and more developers try Quarkus, they want to integrate their libraries with Quarkus to provide a custom extension that would make the use of their library easier. However, the Quarkus repository started to grow more than expected, and such a considerable number of extensions in the core Quarkus repository became unmaintainable.

For this reason, the Quarkus community created the Quarkiverse (Quarkus + Universe). Quarkiverse is a GitHub organization maintained by the Quarkus team that provides hosting of community extensions. The extensions in Quarkiverse are fully integrated into all the tooling we learned about in this chapter. Quarkus users can get all the benefits of the community extensions in the same way as with the core Quarkus extensions. The only difference is in the GAV definition of the Quarkiverse extensions, which typically includes different `groupIds` and versions.

When a developer wants to create an extension in Quarkiverse, the Quarkus team creates a new repository in the Quarkiverse organization with full administration rights given to the developer. The continuous integration (CI) and build/publish setup is already provided in the created repository. Developers publish their extension code as they see fit. Quarkiverse infrastructure takes care of validating it with the core Quarkus platform and possibly publishing it for the end users to consume.

Quarkiverse extensions are fully integrated extensions that can be used in Quarkus applications. The only thing to remember is that since they are versioned separately, users should check whether updates are available manually. You can find all available Quarkiverse extensions at https://github.com/quarkiverse.

2.8 *Next steps*

In this chapter, we created our first Quarkus application. We analyzed the project structure and described the application packaging into both runnable JAR and native executable formats. We then explained running Quarkus in these various formats and built Docker or Podman images from them. Lastly, we learned what Quarkus extensions are and how to utilize them for Quarkus development. All these concepts are the essential building blocks on which we later start developing the Acme Car Rental microservices. Hopefully, you now have a running Quarkus application, and you can't wait to learn more about what you can do with it.

This chapter is just the tip of the iceberg. Quarkus's extensions provide a vast ecosystem of possibilities, which we will be diving into throughout the rest of this book. In the next chapter, we will start by learning what functionalities make Quarkus development such an enjoyable experience.

Summary

- You can generate Quarkus applications in three distinct ways, using: Maven plugin, command-line interface, or web starter `code.quarkus.io`.
- Quarkus applications follow a standard Maven (or Gradle) content structure. Quarkus also contains many useful additional files you can utilize in development and production.
- Compilations produce either runnable JAR of user applications, but can also utilize GraalVM or Mandrel to create native executable applications.
- Quarkus extensions represent optional modules containing integrations with different libraries and frameworks that can be dynamically added to and removed from the Quarkus application. They also provide integrations that allow straightforward native (GraalVM) compilation with minimal additional effort from the developer.
- Quarkus extensions can be managed through the `quarkus` CLI tool, which provides a simple way to list, add, and remove extensions from a project (whether it is based on Maven or Gradle).
- Quarkus guides offer detailed documentation about the extensions and their functionalities. This documentation also contains a sample code for getting started with the extension.
- Quarkiverse is a community-driven organization that provides hosting for community extensions. It is fully integrated into the Quarkus ecosystem.

Enhancing developer productivity with Quarkus

This chapter covers

- Speeding up application development with Quarkus's Dev mode
- Configuration mechanisms of Quarkus applications
- Experimenting with Dev UI to get insights into a running application
- Automatically running development instances of remote services using Dev Services
- Adding continuous testing into your application development workflow

As you recall from previous chapters, Quarkus offers several tools that make application development much faster, smoother, and the developer's life easier. In fact, developer productivity is one of the central ideas of Quarkus design. It is possible to develop in Java in a way where you simply make a change to your source file, hit the `Refresh` button in your browser, and all the changes you did are immediately visible! Gone are the days when you had to manually stop the application, run a Maven build, and start it again. You can enjoy the quick redeploy that is more common to dynamic languages like JavaScript but still use a statically typed compiled language—Java or Kotlin.

To give you a sneak peek before diving into it, Dev Services is another feature that you will surely enjoy. If you've worked on real-world projects, you've probably used databases a lot. In that case, you're probably familiar with the tediousness of managing databases for development—spinning them up, tearing them down, and controlling the schema/data. This is where Dev Services come into play. By using Dev Services, Quarkus can spin up disposable database instances for the application in a matter of seconds, fill them with some basic data, and automatically provide the wiring between the application and the database.

Databases are not the only feature offered by Dev Services. Quarkus can provide instances of many other types of remote services, like messaging brokers, for example. And you can write support for your own Dev Services too (however, it would require writing a custom extension, which we will touch on in chapter 12).

> **NOTE** The majority of Dev Services implementations use the Testcontainers upstream library, but it's not the only supported way.

We also introduce the concept of continuous testing, where your tests execute automatically in the background on each code change while you can continue working with the application. This is another massive improvement over the classic workflows where you have to run tests separately and wait for them to finish, and you immediately notice how much time you can save.

This chapter focuses on the features Quarkus offers to make your life much easier as a developer. In each section, we'll explore one of them, along with hands-on examples based on further experimenting with the `quarkus-in-action` application from the previous chapter. Because these examples modify the source code of the `quarkus-in-action` application, you can find the updated sources in the directory `chapter-03`.

3.1 Development mode

Quarkus's development mode, often referred to as *Dev mode*, radically changes how we develop Java applications. Traditionally, the development loop workflow has looked something like the one in figure 3.1. Generally, to test your changes, you need to manually hit recompilation, run tests (at least once in a while), and restart the application. Of course, the exact workflow varies depending on what kind of application you're writing. If you're using a traditional Jakarta EE application server, the "Restart the application" part becomes the "Redeploy the application."

With Quarkus development mode, all this gets simpler, as shown in figure 3.2. When you make changes to your application and then hit the `Refresh` button in your browser, you immediately see the changes because the application gets recompiled and reloaded in the background within milliseconds.

This reload loop happens without the need to start a new Java virtual machine—the original one is reused to host the new version of your application.

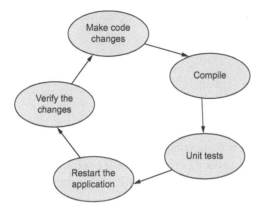

Figure 3.1   Traditional development workflow with Java that requires a lot of manual steps to see the changes

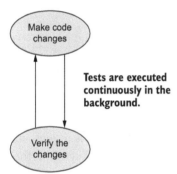

Tests are executed continuously in the background.

Figure 3.2   Simplified development workflow with Quarkus: no need to manually recompile and redeploy the application

And even better, your unit tests are executed automatically in the background, without you having to do anything or without interfering with your application, which allows you to work with your application while the tests are still running (if they take a long time to complete). We will talk more about continuous testing in the section 3.5.

3.1.1   Trying live coding with the Quarkus project

Let's try some live coding and play around with the `quarkus-in-action` project that we created in the previous chapter. Open a terminal, go to the directory containing the project, and start it in Dev mode:

```
$ quarkus dev
```

> **NOTE**   If you prefer using Maven directly instead of the CLI, use `mvn quarkus`
> `:dev` (or `./mvnw quarkus:dev` if using the Maven wrapper).

We already know that we can verify that our application runs by opening http://localhost:8080/hello in a browser, which shows a greeting. Now, try changing that greeting a little. In your IDE of choice, open the `GreetingResource` class that implements our application's REST resource available in the source file `src/main/java/`

org/acme/GreetingResource.java and change the string returned from the greeting method to something else, for example:

```
@GET
@Produces(MediaType.TEXT_PLAIN)
public String hello() {
    return "Hello Quarkus";
}
```

Now save the file (that might not even be needed because your IDE does it automatically), go back to your browser, and press F5 (refresh). After refreshing, you should see the updated greeting right away. Quarkus did the work to recompile and redeploy your application in the background transparently, and it probably took only a few hundred milliseconds after it received the HTTP request from your browser. You can verify that a reload occurred by looking into the console logs in your terminal. In particular, it relates to these two lines (omitting the timestamps):

```
INFO  [io.quarkus] (Quarkus Main Thread) quarkus-in-action stopped in 0.014s
(...)
INFO  [io.qua.dep.dev.RuntimeUpdatesProcessor] (vert.x-worker-thread-0)
   Live reload total time: 0.350s
```

These lines tell you that the application was stopped and then reloaded and how long the reload took. By the way, it's not always necessary to send a request to trigger a reload—you can also trigger it at any time by pressing the s key while the terminal window with your running application is in focus.

> **NOTE**   If you run a full build ./mvnw package that includes tests, you probably have a failing test now because the included GreetingResourceTest asserts that the greeting is Hello from Quarkus REST. You can either update the test or skip it with -DskipTests when running a Maven build. We will experiment with tests in section 3.5. We haven't yet enabled the continuous testing feature, so tests only run as part of the full build with ./mvnw package.

You might also be asking what happens if you introduce a syntax error in your code. In the traditional Java development world, this would result in a failed build, depending on your build tool. With Quarkus Dev mode, it's different. Try deliberately injecting a syntax error. For example, remove the semicolon after the return statement we changed previously. Then, refresh again (F5).

Instead of the GreetingResource showing you a text greeting, you should now see an error page (and the HTTP response code is 500). A shortened version of the included exception looks something like the following listing.

Listing 3.1   Compilation failure in Dev mode

```
java.lang.RuntimeException: Compilation Failed:
/quarkus-in-action/src/main/java/org/acme/GreetingResource.java:14:
```

```
➥ error: ';' expected
        return "Hello Quarkus"
                               ^

(stack trace omitted...)
```

A very similar snippet appears in the console log, too. So, instead of not being able to build and run your application at all, Quarkus is still running, and it can handle requests. It also returns information about the error instead of serving the application itself. If you now fix your error by adding the missing semicolon and refresh again, the application gets back up.

This concludes the hands-on example of the Dev mode. If you want to exit the application running in Dev mode, bring focus to the terminal window where it is running, and then either press q, which is the built-in command for quitting, or send the process a signal to terminate itself by pressing Ctrl+C.

3.1.2 How does it work?

Live coding and automatic reloading work not only for changes in your Java code. Changes to resource files, such as HTML files with the frontend code, or the main configuration file (`application.properties`) trigger a reload, too. When you add a new dependency, it even works for changes in your build descriptor, `pom.xml` or `build.gradle`.

Reload does not happen immediately when a change is detected. Instead, the application waits for an HTTP request to arrive (or for the user to trigger a reload manually). When Quarkus detects a change after an HTTP request comes, it triggers the reload. The request is held for a while to be then handled by the "new" version of your application. Of course, this means that your application takes a bit longer to respond than usual, but unless the change is something that slows down the reload substantially (like adding a new dependency that is not present in the local Maven repository and has to be downloaded), it should finish within a few hundred milliseconds, which is hardly noticeable.

All of this is possible thanks to a unique class loader architecture that allows reusing a single Java virtual machine for running multiple versions of the application in parallel in an isolated manner. The architecture is an advanced topic that we won't dive into here, but if you're interested in details about how it works, review the official documentation at https://quarkus.io/guides/class-loading-reference.

It's important to mention that the application loses any state it had before the reload. All application classes get loaded again in a new class loader, and the garbage collection processes the previously created (now released) objects. The so-called instrumentation-based reload can partially mitigate this. It can be enabled using the `quarkus.live-reload.instrumentation` property set to `true` (inside the `application.properties` file, which we describe in the next section) or by pressing i inside the terminal window or the Dev UI. When enabled, some specific minor changes can be applied to the source code without a full reload, only by replacing the relevant bytecode dynamically, without dropping the affected objects along with their state. However, due to various technical reasons, this is possible only for changes that update just bodies of methods. Changes such as adding new classes, methods, fields, or configurations still trigger a full reload and lose the application's state. After a reload, the console log tells you whether a full or instrumentation-based reload occurred. Instrumentation-based reload is disabled by default because it can sometimes lead to confusing behavior and should be used carefully. Experiment with it if you want. You will notice that an instrumentation-based reload is even quicker than the full one.

3.2   *Application configuration*

One challenge that developers of enterprise Java applications face is configuring their applications. Every framework you use might have its own configuration style, be it an XML or YAML file, system properties, or specific configuration models that Jakarta EE application servers have (`persistence.xml`, `web.xml`, etc.). Quarkus put much effort into making application configuration as easy as possible. In fact, in most cases, all you need is a simple file that contains a set of properties (unless you need to, for example, dynamically obtain configuration values from a remote service). In that file, you can configure all aspects of your application, regardless of which extensions you are using, because each Quarkus extension that you add to your project contributes a set of properties that you can use for configuring the application behavior related to that extension. That single file is usually named `application.properties`, and by default, it resides in the `src/main/resources` directory (for both Maven and Gradle projects).

> **NOTE**   Quarkus also supports an equivalent YAML-based configuration style with the `quarkus-config-yaml` extension. In this case, config property names are mapped to YAML keys, and everything is expected to be in an `application.yaml` file instead. In this book, we focus on using `application.properties`, but we can also map all configuration properties into YAML if needed. Each configuration property can also be overridden with an environment variable or a system property with a name that is derived from the configuration property name. We will touch on that later, too.

The `application.properties` file is used not only for configuring the built-in behavior related to Quarkus extensions, but any of your application-specific configurations can also make use of it. The application's code can access each property listed in this file. To make this possible, Quarkus tightly integrates with the MicroProfile Config API (see https://microprofile.io/specifications/microprofile-config/).

> **NOTE**   Built-in configuration properties (those that control the behavior of Quarkus itself and define data sources, thread pools, etc.) have names starting with the `quarkus.` prefix. You must name your application-specific configuration properties so that they start with a different word or unexpected behavior may result. Quarkus logs a warning if it encounters a defined property in the `quarkus` namespace that it doesn't recognize as a built-in property (such log entry can also help you notice that you've made a typo).

3.2.1 Experimenting with application configuration

Let's now externalize some application-specific configuration into properties in the application.properties file. We will do this to improve the quarkus-in-action application so that the configuration defines the returned greeting rather than a hard-coded string.

With the application still running in Dev mode, open the application.properties file in the src/main/resources/ directory. It should be empty for now. Add the following line:

```
greeting=Hello configuration
```

Then, change the GreetingResource to look into the configuration instead of using a hard-coded greeting. Inject the value of the greeting property as shown in the following listing.

Listing 3.2 Injecting a configured greeting message

```
import org.eclipse.microprofile.config.inject.ConfigProperty;

...

public class GreetingResource {

    @ConfigProperty(name = "greeting")
    String greeting;

    @GET
    @Produces(MediaType.TEXT_PLAIN)
    public String hello() {
        return greeting;
    }

...
```

Refresh the http://localhost:8080/hello page in your browser and verify that the greeting is Hello configuration.

3.2.2 Configuration profiles

In many cases, you need the configuration values to be different depending on the lifecycle stage your application is running. For example, you usually need to connect to a different database instance when developing (or testing) the application than the one used during production. For that reason, Quarkus introduces the concept of configuration profiles.

By default, there are three configuration profiles:

- prod—Active when the application is running in production mode.
- dev—Active when application runs in Dev mode.
- test—Active during tests.

NOTE It is also possible to define additional custom user profiles, which can be activated with the `quarkus.profile` configuration property.

Each of these profiles can use a different set of configuration values. To declare a property value for a particular profile, the property name in your `application.properties` file needs to be prepended with a `%` character followed by the configuration profile's name and then a dot, after which comes the regular property name and value. For example, a `quarkus.http.port` property defines the port on which Quarkus listens for HTTP traffic. By default, it's 8080. If you want to change this HTTP port specifically when running in Dev mode, add this to your configuration file:

Listing 3.3 Example of a property declaration only applicable in Dev mode

```
%dev.quarkus.http.port=7777
```

NOTE Another alternative for declaring properties for different profiles is to use a separate file for each profile. In the previous example, you could also create a file named `application-dev.properties` and type `quarkus.http.port=7777` in it. The result would be equivalent.

When determining the set of values that will be active, Quarkus gives preference to the lines that declare a value specific to a particular profile if this profile is active. If there is no declaration specifically for this profile, Quarkus looks for a general declaration (without a profile prefix). If there is no such declaration, the property resorts to its default value if the application requires it.

3.2.3 *Overriding application.properties*

Some deployment environments (e.g., Kubernetes) require you to tweak the configuration values dynamically, which is not possible to do with the `application.properties` since this file is included in the compiled artifact. Out of the box, Quarkus provides two ways of overriding configuration—JVM system properties and environment variables.

The configuration values are read in the following priority: system properties, environment variables, and only then `application.properties` (potential additional configuration sources have their own custom priority). We can easily experiment with the `quarkus-in-action` application to demonstrate that. Stop the application (or Dev mode) if it is running and then run the application as demonstrated in the following listing.

Listing 3.4 Config override with system property

```
$ GREETING="Environment variable value" quarkus dev \
-Dgreeting="System property value"
```

This command sets the GREETING environment variable to Environment variable value and system property -Dgreeting to System property value when the application runs in Dev mode. Remember that in the application.properties, we still define the greeting config value as Hello configuration. Notice also that we need to capitalize the environment variable name. This is the standard way of defining environment variables. So, to define a config property as an environment value, the name of the property needs to be capitalized, and the dot delimiters (.) need to be replaced by underscores (_). For instance, config property my.greeting would be defined as MY_GREETING. The exact rules for mapping environment variables are described in the documentation (https://mng.bz/KG1n).

Invoking the http://localhost:8080/hello endpoint now correctly outputs "System property value" since the system property override took precedence. If you now restart the application like shown in listing 3.5—that means without the system property definition—and repeat the call to the /hello endpoint, you will see that, as we have just learned, the environment variable takes precedence, and the returned value is "Environment variable value".

Listing 3.5   Config override with the environment variable

```
$ GREETING="Environment variable value" quarkus dev
```

Of course, if you don't define either of them, Quarkus picks the application.properties configuration value, as we have already seen in listing 3.2.

application.properties is thus the main configuration file that includes most of the configuration of the Quarkus applications. However, in cases where some values need to be changed dynamically depending on different factors, you can override configurations by specifying either the system property or the environment variable when running the Quarkus application.

> **NOTE**   The example that we showed for overriding a property was for an application-specific property (meaning that it's not a built-in property from a Quarkus extension, and thus, its name doesn't start with quarkus.). If you apply this to built-in Quarkus properties, keep in mind that such overriding doesn't work for properties that are fixed at build time; these were briefly explained in chapter 2.

3.3   *Dev UI*

Dev UI is a browser-based tool that allows you to gain insights into your application running in Dev mode and even interact with it (change its state). It further facilitates application development by visualizing some framework-level abstractions that your application is using. In some cases, you might find that the insights gained by using the Dev UI can even substitute using a debugger. To gain an idea of what you can accomplish with the Dev UI, here is a list of notable examples:

- List all configuration keys and values (this can be invaluable, especially if you have multiple sources of configuration that supply different values for the same keys).

- List all CDI beans in the application, and for each of them, list their associated interceptors and priorities.

- List CDI beans detected (during the build) as unused and, therefore, not included in the resulting application.

- List Jakarta Persistence (JPA) entities along with their mapping to database tables.

- Wipe data from a development database to start from scratch.

- If you are using the Scheduler extension to schedule periodic tasks, you can manually trigger a task's execution outside the schedule.

- Rerun unit tests with a single click.

- View reports from completed test runs.

The architecture allows each Quarkus extension separately to plug its own tools into the Dev UI, so the complete list of options depends on which extensions the Quarkus application includes.

3.3.1   *Experimenting with Dev UI*

Run the `quarkus-in-action` application again in Dev mode. To open the Dev UI, you have two options. One of them is to open http://localhost:8080/q/dev-ui in your web browser manually. The easier way is to press the d key while the focus is on the terminal window where your application is running. This should open your browser automatically.

The landing page is named Extensions (see the menu on the left side of the page). On the Extensions page, you see cards, and each card represents one Quarkus extension active in your project. Some extensions have Dev UI features, which are then available via buttons inside the extension's card. Some extensions don't offer any Dev UI features, so their card only shows a short description of the extension. For extensions that have user guides, the top-right corner provides a link to that guide (the link looks like a book icon) when you hover your mouse over them. At the bottom of the page, you should see the server log.

The `quarkus-in-action` application does not use a lot of extensions. In fact, you probably see only a few cards, as shown in figure 3.3: The most prominent ones are REST and ArC, where ArC is the extension that handles contexts and dependency injection (CDI). You might see more cards if you've added some other extensions to your project.

CHANGING THE CONFIGURATION

But before we play with the ArC extension, let's briefly explore the Config Editor. Click the `Configuration` panel in the menu on the left. You should then see a very long table

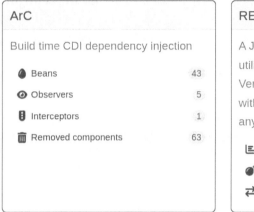

Figure 3.3 Examples of Dev UI cards. Each extension has its own card and can contribute various pages to the Dev UI.

containing all the configuration properties your application can understand either because they are built-in `quarkus.*` properties relevant to an extension you're using or because you have defined them as an application-specific property. If you scroll down, you will also see pure JVM system properties and environment variables.

All configuration properties understood by Quarkus (by the extensions that you're using) are listed here, even those for which you didn't specify any value. For those, you see their default value. All properties are writable. The `application.properties` file reflects any changes you make here to make them persistent. If you change the value of a property not listed in your `application.properties` (or `application.yaml` if you use YAML instead), it gets added to the file.

> **NOTE** Even if you override something in the bottom part (which contains system properties and environment variables), a new configuration property of the same name will also appear in the `application.properties` file. Note that it doesn't mean that your application will see this new value of such system property or environment variable when calling `System.getProperties()` and `System.getenv()`. Contents of `application.properties` are not automatically translated to system properties. You need to use the MicroProfile Config API to read these values from your application.

To test out a change to a Quarkus built-in property, let's change the `quarkus.log.console.darken` property that controls the color of log messages in the terminal. The table should list it relatively high. If you can't find it, start typing its name into the search bar (filter) at the top of the page. The default value of this property is 0, so change it to 1, and then either click the corresponding `save` icon on the right or press `Enter`. After doing this, several things happen:

- Your application gets automatically reloaded because the configuration has changed.
- A new line containing `quarkus.log.console.darken=1` appears in your `application.properties`
- The configuration update also causes the new log messages (since the reload) in the terminal to be darker.

NOTE   If you're running Quarkus inside an IDE, the color change might not be visible, depending on the terminal's capabilities. In that case, you might want to run the application in a regular shell terminal. Similarly, it might not be visible in the log view that is shown in the browser, so you might have to look at the actual terminal window.

To revert this change, change the value back to `0` and press `Enter` (or click the `save` icon) again. Note that the new entry in `application.properties` stays there even if you change the value back to the default, so you might need to remove the line manually if you don't want it there.

LISTING THE APPLICATION'S CDI BEANS

Next, let's look at the card of an extension that offers Dev UI features, and that is ArC. It allows you to introspect things related to the CDI container. Go back to the `Extensions` page of the Dev UI (using the left-side menu) and find the card titled `ArC`.

If you click the `Beans` link, it takes you to a table that contains the list of all CDI beans in your application. In our case, most of them are built-in beans created by Quarkus, but there is one application bean, and that is our REST endpoint, `org.acme.GreetingResource` (every REST endpoint is a CDI bean even if you don't add any CDI annotation to it). The table shows the application beans first, so it is the first entry (see figure 3.4).

- You can see that its CDI scope is `@Singleton`, the default one for REST endpoints.
- Notice that the class name is a clickable link. If you click it, Quarkus will do its best to detect what IDE you use, open it if it's not running, and open the source code of that class! Only application beans have clickable names.
- The second column tells you the type of bean. In this case, it's a bean created from a class.
- The last column provides an optional link to the Bean Dependency Graph, which constitutes a visual representation of bean dependencies.

The Bean Dependency Graph presents a very useful depiction of bean dependencies which looks like the one in figure 3.5.

Bean	Kind	
`@Singleton` `org.acme.GreetingResource`	Class	
`@Singleton` `io.quarkus.resteasy.reactive.server.runtime.exceptionma`	Class	
`@Singleton` `io.quarkus.resteasy.reactive.server.runtime.exceptionma`	Class	

`@Singleton`
`@BossEventLoopGroup`
`io.netty.channel.EventLoopGroup`
	Synthetic	

`@Singleton`
`@MainEventLoopGroup`
`io.netty.channel.EventLoopGroup`
	Synthetic	

`@Dependent` `io.smallrye.config.SmallRyeConfig`	Producer method `ConfigProducer.getConfig()`	

Figure 3.4 **List of the application's CDI beans in the Dev UI, including beans added through the application code and auxiliary beans generated by Quarkus**

Figure 3.5 **The Bean Dependency Graph of the** `GreetingResource` **class**

3.4 *Dev Services*

When developing enterprise applications, dealing with remote resources like databases and message brokers is one of the most annoying aspects that slows you down. To be able to run your application and verify your changes, you need to have a development instance of them running somewhere, and most of the time, you have to manage it yourself. That's where Quarkus comes in. Quarkus can handle that for you by using the so-called Dev Services. This means that Quarkus will automatically run and manage an instance of such a resource for you. Generally, if you add an extension that supports Dev Services and you don't provide configuration for the remote service, Quarkus attempts to run an instance of that service and supply the wiring between it and your application.

> **NOTE** Dev Services are designed to work only in Dev mode and during tests. You can't use them in production. To run your application in production

mode, you have to provide the actual connection configuration of a remote service instance.

The extensions listed in table 3.1 provide support for Dev Services. This list serves as an example reference. It is not exhaustive and will probably contain more extensions when you read this book.

Table 3.1   **List of extensions that support automatic management of remote services via Dev Services**

Service	Extension that supports it	Description
AMQP	`quarkus-messaging-amqp`	AMQP message broker
Apicurio Registry	`quarkus-apicurio-registry-avro`	API registry
Databases	All SQL database drivers, including reactive ones, excluding Oracle	JDBC drivers and reactive database clients
Infinispan	`quarkus-infinispan-client`	Distributed key-value store
Kafka	`quarkus-kafka-client`	Kafka message broker
Keycloak	`quarkus-oidc`	Keycloak server as an OpenID Connect provider
Kubernetes	`kubernetes-client`	Kubernetes testing instance
MongoDB	`quarkus-mongodb-client`	Document-based database
Neo4j	`quarkus-neo4j`	Graph database
RabbitMQ	`quarkus-messaging-rabbitmq`	RabbitMQ broker to be used with Reactive Messaging
Redis	`quarkus-redis-client`	In-memory data structure store
Vault	`quarkus-vault`	HashiCorp Vault for storing secrets

For documentation about how to use Dev Services with each supported extension and a list of all related configuration properties, refer to the official documentation of Dev Services at https://quarkus.io/guides/dev-services.

Dev Services generally require Docker (or Podman) to be available because they use containers to run the underlying services. There are some exceptions, for example, the H2 and Derby databases; these are run directly inside the JVM of your application.

3.4.1   *Securing the Quarkus application using OpenID Connect and Dev Services*

Let's learn how to use Dev Services to easily add an OpenID Connect (OIDC) authentication layer to your application. Similarly, we could add a connection to a database, but since the application is so simple that it doesn't need a database, showcasing some basic security features is more fitting.

The authentication workflow works like this:

- Quarkus Dev Services automatically spins up an instance of *Keycloak*, an OIDC provider. This requires a working Podman or Docker runtime, because the instance runs as a container.
- Then, we will use the Dev UI to obtain a security token from the embedded Keycloak instance.
- Finally, we will use that token to send an authenticated request to the application and verify that we can log in to it and print the name of the currently logged-in user.

Start by adding the `quarkus-oidc` extension to the application (you can do this while Dev mode is still running or after shutting it down). For example, using the CLI:

```
$ quarkus extension add oidc
```

It adds the extension and triggers a reload of our application (if you did this while Dev mode was running). The reloading will take longer than usual because Quarkus has to use your container runtime to spin up an instance of Keycloak. This message appears in the log when the reload finishes:

```
INFO  [io.qua.oid.dep.dev.key.KeycloakDevServicesProcessor] (build-11) Dev
➥ Services for Keycloak started.
```

You can also verify that a container for Keycloak is running. For example, if you are using Docker, see the following listing.

Listing 3.6 Verifying that Keycloak is running in a Docker container

```
docker ps
CONTAINER  ID  IMAGE  COMMAND  CREATED  STATUS  PORTS  NAMES
d89a92d83c7a  quay.io/keycloak/keycloak:25.0.6  "/opt/keycloak/bin/k..."
2 minutes ago  Up 2 minutes  8443/tcp, 9000/tcp, 0.0.0.0:32768->8080/tcp,
[::]:32768->8080/tcp  epic_dhawan
```

Another way to show information about the Keycloak container is to press the c key in the terminal where your Dev mode application is running. This shows information about all running Dev Services containers, as shown in the following listing.

Listing 3.7 Listing running Dev Services containers

```
== Dev Services

keycloak
  Container:         d89a92d83c7a/epic_dhawan
➥ quay.io/keycloak/keycloak:25.0.6
  Network:           bridge - 0.0.0.0:32768->8080/tcp ,:::32768->8080/tcp
  Exec command:      docker exec -it d89a92d83c7a /bin/bash
  Injected config:   - client.quarkus.oidc.auth-server-url=
➥ http://localhost:32768/realms/quarkus
```

```
            - keycloak.realms=quarkus
            - keycloak.url=http://localhost:32768
            - oidc.users=alice=alice,bob=bob
            - quarkus.oidc.application-type=service
            - quarkus.oidc.auth-server-url=
➡ http://localhost:32768/realms/quarkus
            - quarkus.oidc.client-id=quarkus-app
            - quarkus.oidc.credentials.secret=secret
```

NOTE   From now on, whenever you run the application in Dev or test mode, it spins up an instance of Keycloak. Because the project's tests don't touch Keycloak, this unnecessarily slows down test execution. If you want to avoid that, add the `%test.quarkus.oidc.enabled=false` configuration line to your `application.properties`. This configuration completely disables the OIDC extension when running tests, and tests won't start a Keycloak instance anymore.

Now, to verify that we can log into the application, we need an endpoint that prints the currently logged-in user's name. Open the `GreetingResource` class and add the following code as demonstrated in listing 3.8.

Listing 3.8   Source of the `GreetingResource#whoAmI` method

```
// import jakarta.ws.rs.core.Context;
// import jakarta.ws.rs.core.SecurityContext;
// import java.security.Principal;

@GET
@Path("/whoami")
@Produces(MediaType.TEXT_PLAIN)
public String whoAmI(@Context SecurityContext securityContext) {
    Principal userPrincipal = securityContext.getUserPrincipal();
    if (userPrincipal != null) {
        return userPrincipal.getName();
    } else {
        return "anonymous";
    }
}
```

From now on, when you invoke the `/hello/whoami` endpoint, the response contains the username of the authenticated user or `anonymous` when invoked without authentication. Try opening `localhost:8080/hello/whoami` in your browser. It shows `anonymous`. You didn't specify the token, but you can still open the page because we didn't configure authentication to be mandatory. Beware that if you send an HTTP request with an invalid access token (rather than not specifying any token at all), the server will return a `401 Unauthorized` response instead of the message `anonymous`.

  To obtain an authentication token, go to the Dev UI (press d with a focus on the Quarkus terminal window), and you will see a new card, OpenID Connect, as shown in figure 3.6.

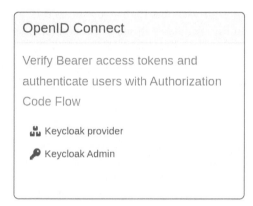

Figure 3.6   OpenID Connect card in the Dev UI

Click the `Keycloak provider` button, and then the big green button saying `Log into Single Page Application`. It takes you to Keycloak's login page shown in figure 3.7.

Figure 3.7   Login page of Keycloak

Use `alice`, both as the username and as the password. This username–password pair automatically exists in Keycloak instances started through Dev Services, so don't worry—this combination won't work on a production instance! After logging in, Keycloak takes you back to the Dev UI, now as an authenticated user. To view your token, click the `View Access Token` link. The right column (`Decoded`) shows the raw token as a JSON document, while the left column (`Encoded`) shows its Base64-encoded version, a long alphanumeric string. This is what you need to attach to your HTTP request when calling the JAX-RS endpoint. Click it and copy it to your clipboard or save it into a text file. There is also the copy button in the top-right corner, which will copy the token directly to your clipboard.

> **NOTE**   By default, the access token is only valid for 10 minutes, so you need to do the next step within that timeframe. If 10 minutes is not enough, you can extend it in the administration console of Keycloak (there is the `Keycloak Admin` link in the top-right corner, and the credentials are `admin:admin`) by switching to the `quarkus` realm in the dropdown menu in the top-left corner and then changing the `Access Token Lifespan` value in the `Realm settings ->Tokens` tab. You must log in again if the token expires to obtain a new token.

Now try invoking the endpoint while supplying the token. In the following snippet, replace `$AUTH_TOKEN` with the Base64-encoded version of Alice's token. We pass it to the `Authorization` header of the HTTP request. Since many readers might not be familiar with HTTP headers passing to HTTPie, we also provide an example using `curl`. You can also use any other tooling that allows you to add custom HTTP headers to requests:

```
http :8080/hello/whoami "Authorization:Bearer $AUTH_TOKEN"
```

```
curl -H "Authorization: Bearer $AUTH_TOKEN" localhost:8080/hello/whoami
```

The response says `alice` since the token corresponds to this user.

3.5   *Continuous testing*

We can all agree that automated tests are essential to any real-world software project. Every application platform should provide tools to enable writing tests for projects using that platform, and Quarkus is no different. It defines a unique testing framework that tightly integrates with JUnit. This test framework allows you to quickly spin up an instance of your application (of course, with the possibility to change some parts of it, replace real remote services with mocks, etc.) and perform tests by working with individual parts of your application (by injecting them into the test, for example). For instance, it can take it to a higher level and communicate with the application as a black box by sending HTTP requests. Nevertheless, features of the testing framework are not what we focus on in this section—we will cover something more exciting—the capability to run tests continuously. Chapter 5 contains a deeper dive into the testing framework and its capabilities.

Now, what do we mean by continuous testing? We already know the Dev mode and live reloading of your application. To take it one step further, Quarkus doesn't only quickly reload your application upon every change, but it can also rerun your tests along with it! Every reload generally triggers a test run if continuous testing is enabled. That's another tremendous improvement to the developer's workflow because the tests can

run parallel with any other tasks you do while developing, without spending time starting their execution or waiting for them to finish. Even though tests execute within the
same JVM where your development instance lives, you don't have to worry about affect-
ing the application's state. This is because tests are run in a separate class loader so they
have their isolated application instance on which they run. If your tests take a long time
to complete, you can safely interact with your application while tests are still running!

3.5.1 *Testing the Quarkus in Action project*

Once again, run the Quarkus in Action application in Dev mode (quarkus dev). Look
into its src/test/java directory. You will notice that there are two test classes, Greeting-
ResourceTest and GreetingResourceIT. The latter is specifically for testing in native
mode and is not relevant to this example, so we're going to ignore it for now and only
look at GreetingResourceTest. The source code of the only testing method looks like
the following listing.

Listing 3.9 Source code for a simple test

```
@Test
void testHelloEndpoint() {
    given()
        .when().get("/hello")
        .then()
            .statusCode(200)
            .body(is("Hello from Quarkus REST"));
}
```

The test uses the RestAssured library, which is a toolkit for running tests against REST
endpoints. The code is relatively easy to read. It verifies that when you send an HTTP
GET request to the /hello endpoint of your application, then the result has a status
code 200 (meaning success), and that the response body contains the string Hello
from Quarkus REST. Let's try to run our test now. Bring focus to the terminal with your
running Dev mode and hit the r key, which starts continuous testing.

> **NOTE** To have continuous testing enabled automatically at application start,
> you can set the quarkus.test.continuous-testing property to enabled.

If you followed the previous exercises and are continuing from there, it is very likely
that the test fails because we have changed that response from Hello from Quarkus
REST to Hello Quarkus in the Dev mode section and then to Hello configuration in
the configuration section.

  If the test failed, you see a red failure report (including a stack trace) in the log.
This is in the status line at the bottom.

Listing 3.10 Status line in the terminal showing a failure in continuous testing

```
1 test failed (0 passing, 0 skipped), 1 test was run in 1773ms. Tests
➥ completed at 17:14:43.
```

NOTE This time, the test took a relatively long time to finish (almost 1.8 seconds in our case). This only occurs the first time you run tests after starting Dev mode. Subsequent runs will be faster, which you can verify immediately by hitting the r button to rerun tests. In our case, the time drops to about 300 milliseconds.

If the test passed, you see a green status line.

Listing 3.11   Status line in the terminal showing a successful run of continuous testing

```
All 1 test is passing (0 skipped), 1 test was run in 256ms. Tests
⇒ completed at 17:18:08.
```

If your test failed, fix it by changing the response back to `Hello from Quarkus REST` (either directly in the `GreetingResource` class or, if you changed it to read the configuration, by updating the `greeting` configuration property in the `application.properties` file). If your test passed, try the opposite, and deliberately change the response to make the test fail.

After performing your change in the source code (or `application.properties`), save the source file. Notice that the tests get rerun immediately! When continuous testing is enabled, the behavior of Dev mode changes so that a live reload triggers by merely detecting a source file change (otherwise, it is when an HTTP request or some other specific event is received). Can you already see how much of a time saver this is for developers?

NOTE You don't have to worry about breaking the running application or the testing pipeline by saving a source file that contains a syntax error. If you do, then instead of running your tests and showing you the results, Quarkus will offer you an error message in the terminal to help you fix that.

CONTROLLING TEST OUTPUT

You can use the o key in the terminal window to control the test output. If the test output is disabled (it is by default), you only see the failure stack traces after a test run. If you hit o to enable test output, your terminal will start showing logs produced by the testing instance of your application, including logs produced by the test itself. For example, they will look like the ones in listing 3.12. You can tell that these logs come from the testing instance by the name of the thread executing them. It is the `Test runner` thread. Notice that the testing instance binds to a different HTTP port (8081 as opposed to 8080) and uses the `test` config profile.

Listing 3.12   Logs produced by running a test when test output is enabled

```
2024-09-11 17:25:05,153 INFO  [io.qua.test] (Test runner thread) Running
⇒ 1/1. Running: org.acme.GreetingResourceTest#GreetingResourceTest
2024-09-11 17:25:05,385 INFO  [io.quarkus] (Test runner thread)
⇒ quarkus-in-action 1.0.0-SNAPSHOT on JVM (powered by Quarkus 3.15.1)
```

```
⇒ started in 0.230s. Listening on: http://localhost:8081
2024-09-11 17:25:05,386 INFO  [io.quarkus] (Test runner thread) Profile
⇒ test activated.
2024-09-11 17:25:05,387 INFO  [io.quarkus] (Test runner thread) Installed
⇒ features: [cdi, oidc, rest, security,
⇒ smallrye-context-propagation, vertx]
```

USING THE DEV UI FOR TESTING AND VIEWING TEST REPORTS

So far, we have used the terminal window to control your application's testing. You might prefer a graphical interface, though, especially for reviewing test reports because a bunch of stack traces lying about in the terminal log is probably not something you want to see when diagnosing failures resulting from running your test suite.

This is where the Dev UI comes in again. Everything test-related that the terminal controls can do, the Dev UI does too. Open the Dev UI (press 'd' in the terminal) and choose Continuous Testing in the left-side menu. If you haven't enabled continuous testing yet, you will need to click the Start button to enable it and run the whole set of tests. Shortly after that, you should see the results, as shown in figure 3.8 if the tests are passing or figure 3.9 in case of failures.

Figure 3.8   Dev UI continuous testing in case of success

Figure 3.9   Dev UI continuous testing in case of failure

To rerun tests, click the Run all button. To view details of failing tests, click the name of the test.

NOTE As a Java developer, you might be used to HTML or XML test reports generated by Maven or Gradle plugins. Because our tests are JUnit-based and continuous testing embedded in the Quarkus process is just a special way to run them, of course, they also get executed the "normal" way during a Maven build (by the Surefire or Failsafe plugins during the `test` or `verify` Maven goals) and produce traditional reports in the `target/surefire-reports` and `target/failsafe-reports` directories. The reports that you can find in the Dev UI try to mimic them, but they might not include all the information that you would get after running the tests manually.

3.6   *Next steps*

We learned about the features of Quarkus that improve the lives of application developers and save a tremendous amount of time. You can enjoy the quick development turnaround time known from dynamic languages but still use a static language like Java and Kotlin. The concept that a single properties file can store all necessary configurations for the application is another improvement. You don't have to deal with several bloated XML configuration files like in the old times of working with Java EE. Most of the tedious work in managing database instances for development is now gone, with Quarkus managing them automatically (we will explore databases in chapter 7). The Dev UI provides invaluable insights into running application for troubleshooting purposes, and it can save you from using a debugger. Another time saver is getting your tests executed automatically in the background after each source code change without preventing you from further experimenting with the application while the tests are still running.

These features together make up the productivity boosts and development experience improvements that Quarkus provides. Now that we've learned about the general benefits of using Quarkus, this book's part 2 will focus on particular frameworks and libraries that Quarkus supports. We will start by examining the parts related to remote communication (various protocols for communicating with other applications and services).

Summary

- The development mode of Quarkus significantly improves the development process and saves a lot of time when writing applications.
- Live reloading happens in the background automatically after changing the source code and interacting with the application. It is also very fast.
- If the developer introduces an error, be it a syntax error or invalid usage of a library, Dev mode will still continue running but will respond to HTTP requests with details about the error instead of serving the actual application content.
- In most cases, one properties file is enough to contain all configurations related to the application (both the configuration of Quarkus built-ins and application-specific properties). Usually, the file is `src/main/resources/application .properties`.

- Dev UI is a browser-based tool that provides insights into applications running in Dev mode, facilitating troubleshooting during development. Different Quarkus extensions contribute different features available in the Dev UI if that extension is active.

- Dev UI also allows manipulating the application, for example, by changing the configuration values, triggering scheduled events out of schedule, wiping databases, etc.

- Dev Services is a tool that further simplifies development by automatically managing instances of remote resources such as databases or message brokers and providing the wiring between the application and the resource. It works by spawning containers with these resources, automatically shutting them down when Dev mode is stopped.

- Quarkus is tightly integrated with JUnit 5 to allow a smooth experience for writing and executing tests.

- Continuous testing is a way to quickly run your application's tests after each source code change in a fully automated fashion. The developer can continue experimenting with the application without interruption and only check the test results as they appear in the console or in the Dev UI.

Part 2

Developing Quarkus applications

By now, you have gained at least a basic understanding of what Quarkus is and how it can help you build applications easily and painlessly. But yeah, writing real-world applications in Java requires using Java frameworks. And with Quarkus, you have a lot of them at your disposal. In the second part of the book, we will look at some of the most important frameworks that you will probably need to use when actually using Quarkus in the real world. But don't worry. Quarkus does not invent a bunch of new frameworks and force you to learn them. Instead, it integrates with the most popular Java frameworks and libraries that you are probably already familiar with.

We will start by looking at frameworks related to remote communication because microservices have to talk together. Then we will move on to testing because software needs to be tested before it can be put to production. Then we will move on to frontend because you might need to create a web application that users will access via a browser. We will also look at security, because you don't want unauthorized users to do bad things to your application. After that, we will look at database access, because all applications need to store data somewhere. Then we will make an excursion to the world of reactive programming and explain why you might or might not need it.

After part 2, you will be able to really claim to be a Quarkus developer. Let's go!

Handling communications

This chapter covers

- Exposing and consuming APIs using the REST paradigm
- GraphQL as an alternative to the REST paradigm
- gRPC and Protocol Buffers as yet another way to expose and consume APIs

Microservices applications require a lot of network communication between the various parts. Recall that we plan to develop a system comprising the Users, Reservation, Rental, Inventory, and Billing services. All of these services need to exchange information between them. This communication can be synchronous, where an application that requires some data from another system makes a network call and waits for the result, or asynchronous, where the requesting service receives a notification of the result when it completes. In this chapter, we focus on synchronous communication since it still is the primarily utilized method of network communication in the microservices architecture. Specifically, we will learn how Quarkus makes it very easy to develop client and server applications that produce and consume data over the following protocols:

- Hypertext Transfer Protocol (HTTP) with representational state transfer (REST)
- GraphQL
- gRPC

REST is a ubiquitous paradigm that probably doesn't require a long introduction. Quarkus makes it easy to design your own REST API with a simple annotation-based model. We also learn how to write the client side—it's just as easy since you can use the same annotations on the client.

GraphQL may be new to some developers. It's an alternative to REST that gives the client more control over what data exactly it wants to receive. Unlike REST, it also allows the client the flexibility to request multiple types of data in a single HTTP request, making it a good fit for constrained environments where limiting the number of requests and the amount of transferred data is important. Just like with REST, Quarkus uses annotations to define your GraphQL API as well as to consume it. It also offers a UI, which we can use to manually test our GraphQL APIs.

gRPC is a high-performance, open source universal remote procedure calls (RPC) framework that provides support for multiple languages. As you might have guessed, Quarkus also provides a simple annotation-based programming model for creating gRPC services and clients and UI support to manually experiment with them.

The high-level view of the Acme Car Rental system is presented in figure 4.1. This diagram shows all the services comprising the system and the remote protocols utilized for communication among them. In this chapter, we develop several of these services to demonstrate, compare, and explain the applicability of the analyzed network protocols.

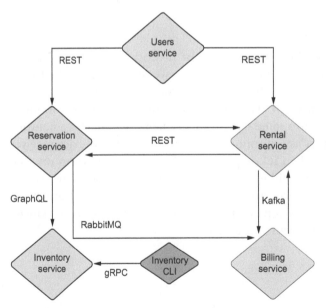

Figure 4.1 The Acme Car Rental system architecture and the utilized remote protocols

This is a lot of microservices to run on a single machine simultaneously, even for development. Therefore, we must distinguish different ports on which the individual services run. For simplicity, we will use the predefined port mapping for our local development environments, detailed in table 4.1. It also helps categorize different services when we talk about them. For instance, if we call an application running on port `8081`, you can deduce that we called the Reservation service.

Table 4.1 The port mapping of the car rental services for local development

Service	Port
Users	`localhost:8080`
Reservation	`localhost:8081`
Rental	`localhost:8082`
Inventory	`localhost:8083`
Billing	`localhost:8084`

The code of all services is available in the public code repository at https://github .com/xstefank/quarkus-in-action. Individual directories split the book's content per chapter. Each chapter is further split into directories per section, which contain the code developed in the particular sections. Additionally, all commits are composed gradually to provide even greater detail (diffs) on all individually developed parts throughout this book. The final version of the developed system is also available in the `acme-car-rental` directory.

4.1 *Developing REST-based Quarkus applications*

REST (representational state transfer) is the most common architectural style to communicate between services, mainly because it relies on the universal and well-understood HTTP protocol and because it's relatively easy to use. Especially in the Java ecosystem, REST services are very popular. Quarkus makes developing such services straightforward via an annotation-based model utilizing a set of extensions. The `quarkus-rest` extension is used for the server side and implements the Jakarta RESTful Web Services specification, while the `quarkus-rest-client` is used for developing clients and implements two client-side specifications: MicroProfile REST Client and Jakarta REST Client API. As we will see later on in this chapter, Quarkus also offers a bunch of tools for easily invoking REST endpoints manually.

Table 4.2 gives a brief overview of the most important JAX-RS annotations. We will put these annotations to good use shortly.

Table 4.2   List of the most important JAX-RS annotations and their descriptions

Annotation	Description
@Path	Identifies the relative URI path that a resource class or method will serve requests for
@GET	Indicates that the annotated method handles HTTP GET requests
@POST	Indicates that the annotated method handles HTTP POST requests
@Consumes	Defines the media types that a resource class or method accepts
@Produces	Defines the media types that a resource class or method produces

4.2   *Car rental Reservation service*

Let's start coding the first service. We now develop a simplified version of the Reservation service. This service exposes a REST endpoint for working with car reservations, which is what we need to implement first.

We begin by creating a new Quarkus application by executing the following command. The `--no-code` flag specifies that we don't want any example code generated:

```
$ quarkus create app org.acme:reservation-service -P 3.15.1 \
--extension quarkus-rest-jackson,quarkus-rest-client-jackson,\
quarkus-smallrye-openapi --no-code
```

We choose the `quarkus-rest-jackson` extension because we want to use the *Jackson* library to handle JSON serialization and deserialization of requests and responses of the REST services that the Reservation service exposes. The `quarkus-rest` extension, which provides the core REST functionality, is a dependency of `quarkus-rest-jackson` (which adds just the Jackson support to it), so we don't have to add `quarkus-rest` explicitly.

We use the `quarkus-rest-client-jackson` extension because we want to use Jackson to handle JSON serialization and deserialization of the downstream REST requests that the Reservation service creates. Again, the core REST client functionality is brought in transitively as the `quarkus-rest-client` extension.

The `quarkus-smallrye-openapi` extension adds the ability to generate an OpenAPI document, which documents our exposed REST API. It also creates a simple UI that we can use to test the REST endpoints that we develop.

To avoid port conflicts when running multiple services together, open the `application.properties` configuration file in the newly generated `reservation-service` project and add the property `quarkus.http.port=8081`.

For this part of our journey, the Reservation service needs to do two things:

- For user-provided start and end dates, return a list of cars that are available for rent.
- Make a reservation for a specific car for a set of dates.

Before creating any code, make sure to launch Quarkus Dev mode, which can be done, as you might remember, by running the Quarkus CLI:

```
$ quarkus dev
```

4.2.1   Checking car availability

First, we need to define a model for cars, which, in our case, is very simple. This car model contains information about the license plate number of the car, its manufacturer, and the model name. It will also contain an ID field to identify each car uniquely. To create this model, add a new `org.acme.reservation.inventory.Car` class into the `src/main/java` directory containing the code in the following listing.

Listing 4.1   The `Car` class, representing a car available for rental

```java
package org.acme.reservation.inventory;

public class Car {

    public Long id;
    public String licensePlateNumber;
    public String manufacturer;
    public String model;

    public Car(Long id, String licensePlateNumber,
            String manufacturer, String model) {
        this.id = id;
        this.licensePlateNumber = licensePlateNumber;
        this.manufacturer = manufacturer;
        this.model = model;
    }
}
```

In this example, we used public fields instead of regular properties (a private field with a getter and setter) because it's shorter, and we wanted to show that it's possible. We know this may stir up some heated discussions about code style—if you prefer private fields along with getters and setters, you may use them instead; it will work the same way.

> **NOTE**   You can use the Lombok library to make your code shorter through its `@Data` classes. Java record classes and Kotlin data classes are also supported.

As you might recall from our architecture diagram, the list of available cars will be provided by the Inventory service, so we need to model that communication. We do so by creating an interface abstracting these calls named `InventoryClient` in the package `org.acme.reservation.inventory` that contains one method: `allCars`, used to obtain all cars. The code for this interface is shown in the following listing.

Listing 4.2   The `InventoryClient` abstracts calls to the Inventory service

```java
package org.acme.reservation.inventory;

import java.util.List;

public interface InventoryClient {

    List<Car> allCars();
}
```

As we have not written the Inventory service yet (we will do this when we discuss GraphQL), we will, for the time being, use a simple static list as a stub for the calls of the Inventory service. Create a new `InMemoryInventoryClient` class that implements the `InventoryClient` interface in the same package with the code shown in the following listing.

Listing 4.3   The source code of the `InMemoryInventoryClient` class

```java
package org.acme.reservation.inventory;

import java.util.List;
import jakarta.inject.Singleton;

@Singleton
public class InMemoryInventoryClient implements InventoryClient {

    private static final List<Car> ALL_CARS = List.of(
            new Car(1L, "ABC-123", "Toyota", "Corolla"),
            new Car(2L, "ABC-987", "Honda", "Jazz"),
            new Car(3L, "XYZ-123", "Renault", "Clio"),
            new Car(4L, "XYZ-987", "Ford", "Focus")
            );

    @Override
    public List<Car> allCars() {
        return ALL_CARS;
    }
}
```

This annotation is part of the Context and Dependency Injection (CDI) specification. It allows us to use this class as the implementation of InventoryClient wherever the application needs such implementation.

It goes without saying that we need a way to model reservations, so we keep it simple by adding only the necessary fields—the ID of the car relevant to the reservation, the start and end dates, and a unique ID for the reservation. Create a new class, `org.acme.reservation.reservation.Reservation`, with the code in listing 4.4. We also include the `isReserved` method, which checks whether the reservation overlaps with any of the days in the duration passed as arguments.

Listing 4.4   The code of the `Reservation` class which models reservations

```java
package org.acme.reservation.reservation;

import java.time.LocalDate;
```

```
public class Reservation {

    public Long id;
    public Long carId;
    public LocalDate startDay;
    public LocalDate endDay;

    /**
     * Check if the given duration overlaps with this reservation
     * @return true if the dates overlap with the reservation, false
     * otherwise
     */
    public boolean isReserved(LocalDate startDay, LocalDate endDay) {
        return (!(this.endDay.isBefore(startDay) ||
            this.startDay.isAfter(endDay)));
    }
}
```

With this model in place, we now turn our attention to persisting these reservations, as a reservation system that does not persist reservations makes little sense in practice! Following good object-oriented design principles, we model the interactions with the persistence layer via an interface named `ReservationsRepository`. We only need this layer to do two things: save a reservation and retrieve all reservations. The new interface, `org.acme.reservation.reservation.ReservationsRepository`, can be written as shown in the following listing.

Listing 4.5   The `ReservationsRepository` interface abstracting persistence

```
package org.acme.reservation.reservation;

import java.util.List;

public interface ReservationsRepository {

    List<Reservation> findAll();

    Reservation save(Reservation reservation);
}
```

As we are not using a full-blown database just yet, we can use a simple list as a stub created in the `InMemoryReservationsRepository` class created in the same package. It represents a very simple implementation of `ReservationsRepository`. The code is shown in the following listing.

Listing 4.6   The source code of the `InMemoryReservationsRepository` class

```
package org.acme.reservation.reservation;

import java.util.Collections;
import java.util.List;
import java.util.concurrent.CopyOnWriteArrayList;
```

```
import java.util.concurrent.atomic.AtomicLong;
import jakarta.inject.Singleton;

@Singleton
public class InMemoryReservationsRepository
                    implements ReservationsRepository {

    private final AtomicLong ids = new AtomicLong(0);
    private final List<Reservation> store =
        new CopyOnWriteArrayList<>();                    ◄─┐ This (thread-safe) list
                                                            │ is essentially our
                                                            │ data store.
    @Override
    public List<Reservation> findAll() {
        return Collections.unmodifiableList(store);
    }

    @Override
    public Reservation save(Reservation reservation) {
        reservation.id = ids.incrementAndGet();         ◄─┐ Assigns a unique ID
        store.add(reservation);                            │ to the reservation we
        return reservation;                                │ are about to save
    }
}
```

We can now turn our attention to creating a REST endpoint handling the HTTP
GET requests under the /reservation/availability path, which returns all available cars for the given start and end date (supplied as query parameters). Let's create a new class representing our REST resource in the org.acme.reservation.rest
package called ReservationResource using the code in listing 4.7. If there's a generated GreetingResource class, you may remove it (but it shouldn't be there if you
used the --no-code flag when creating the project).

The implementation of the availability method isn't complicated. It retrieves
all the available cars from the inventory, checks which are already reserved for the
dates in question, and returns the remaining ones.

Listing 4.7   The source code of the `ReservationResource` REST resource

```
package org.acme.reservation.rest;

import java.time.LocalDate;
import java.util.Collection;
import java.util.HashMap;
import java.util.List;
import java.util.Map;
import jakarta.ws.rs.GET;
import jakarta.ws.rs.Path;
import jakarta.ws.rs.Produces;
import jakarta.ws.rs.core.MediaType;
import org.acme.reservation.inventory.Car;
import org.acme.reservation.inventory.InventoryClient;
import org.acme.reservation.reservation.Reservation;
```

```
import org.acme.reservation.reservation.ReservationsRepository;
import org.jboss.resteasy.reactive.RestQuery;


@Path("reservation")                          ←┐  Sets the path
@Produces(MediaType.APPLICATION_JSON)          │  to /reservation
public class ReservationResource {

    private final ReservationsRepository reservationsRepository;
    private final InventoryClient inventoryClient;

    public ReservationResource(ReservationsRepository reservations,
            InventoryClient inventoryClient) {           ←──────────┐
        this.reservationsRepository = reservations;
        this.inventoryClient = inventoryClient;
    }                                              HTTP GET to
                                                   /reservation/availability
    @GET                                           path invokes this method.
    @Path("availability")                     ←──┘
    public Collection<Car> availability(@RestQuery LocalDate startDate,
            @RestQuery LocalDate endDate) {
        // obtain all cars from inventory
        List<Car> availableCars = inventoryClient.allCars();
        // create a map from id to car
        Map<Long, Car> carsById = new HashMap<>();
        for (Car car : availableCars) {
            carsById.put(car.id, car);
        }

        // get all current reservations
        List<Reservation> reservations = reservationsRepository.findAll();
        // for each reservation, remove the car from the map
        for (Reservation reservation : reservations) {
            if (reservation.isReserved(startDate, endDate)) {
                carsById.remove(reservation.carId);
            }
        }                                   Quarkus creates the instance
    }                                of ReservationResource for us by calling this
        return carsById.values();          constructor, providing the implementations
    }                                      of both the ReservationsRepository and the
}                                   InventoryClient interfaces that we require (as
}                                         they are @Singleton CDI beans).
```

By annotating the class with `@Path("reservation")`, we ensure that Quarkus uses this class to handle all HTTP requests under the /reservation path. The `@Produces(MediaType.APPLICATION_JSON)` ensures that all methods that handle REST calls return a JSON response. This makes Quarkus serialize the result of the method to JSON when returning the HTTP response. It also sets the `Content-Type` header to `application/json`.

The availability method is annotated with the `@GET` and `@Path("availability")` annotations. These annotations establish that the framework invokes this method when an HTTP GET call is made to the /reservation/availability path (the reservation part comes from the value of the `@Path` annotation used on the class).

The two parameters of the method are annotated with `@RestQuery` annotation, meaning that they represent the values of the HTTP query parameters named `startDate` and `endDate`, respectively (matching the names of the variables). The values need to be in the format of `YYYY-MM-DD`.

4.2.2 *Making a reservation*

Now that we have seen how to handle the case where, given a start and end date, we need to return a list of available cars for rent, the next step is to make a reservation of a specific car for a set of dates. This HTTP POST endpoint (because it creates a new reservation) accepts JSON input representing the reservation. The new `Reservation-Resource#make` method handles this endpoint, as shown in the following listing.

> **Listing 4.8 The source of the `ReservationResource#make` method**

```
// import jakarta.ws.rs.Consumes;

@Consumes(MediaType.APPLICATION_JSON)
@POST
public Reservation make(Reservation reservation) {
    return reservationsRepository.save(reservation);
}
```

The method accepts a JSON input, so we use the proper `@Consumes` annotation for this method. It also accepts HTTP POST requests, so we use the `@POST` annotation. It handles the requests under the `/reservation` path inherited from the class-level `@Path` annotation. By simply declaring `Reservation` as a method parameter (without any annotation), we establish that Quarkus deserializes the HTTP request body into an instance of this class. The method only has to save the reservation and return it, thus ensuring that Quarkus serializes it as the HTTP response body in JSON.

4.2.3 *Experimenting with the exposed REST API using the Swagger UI*

Having written all this code, we need a way to exercise it and see how it behaves in practice. It can be done in multiple ways, but we introduce a graphical method using Quarkus's built-in Swagger UI (provided by the `smallrye-openapi` extension) for this section. This UI is available at http://localhost:8081/q/swagger-ui. When accessed and the application still runs in Dev mode, it looks as it does in figure 4.2. The UI shows the two REST endpoints we developed and provides an easy way to test them.

> **NOTE** By default, Quarkus includes this Swagger UI only in the Dev mode. If you would like to have it also in production, you can add the `quarkus` `.swagger-ui.always-include=true` configuration property.

The Swagger UI is a graphical representation of the OpenAPI document available at http://localhost:8081/q/openapi. The `quarkus-smallrye-openapi` extension

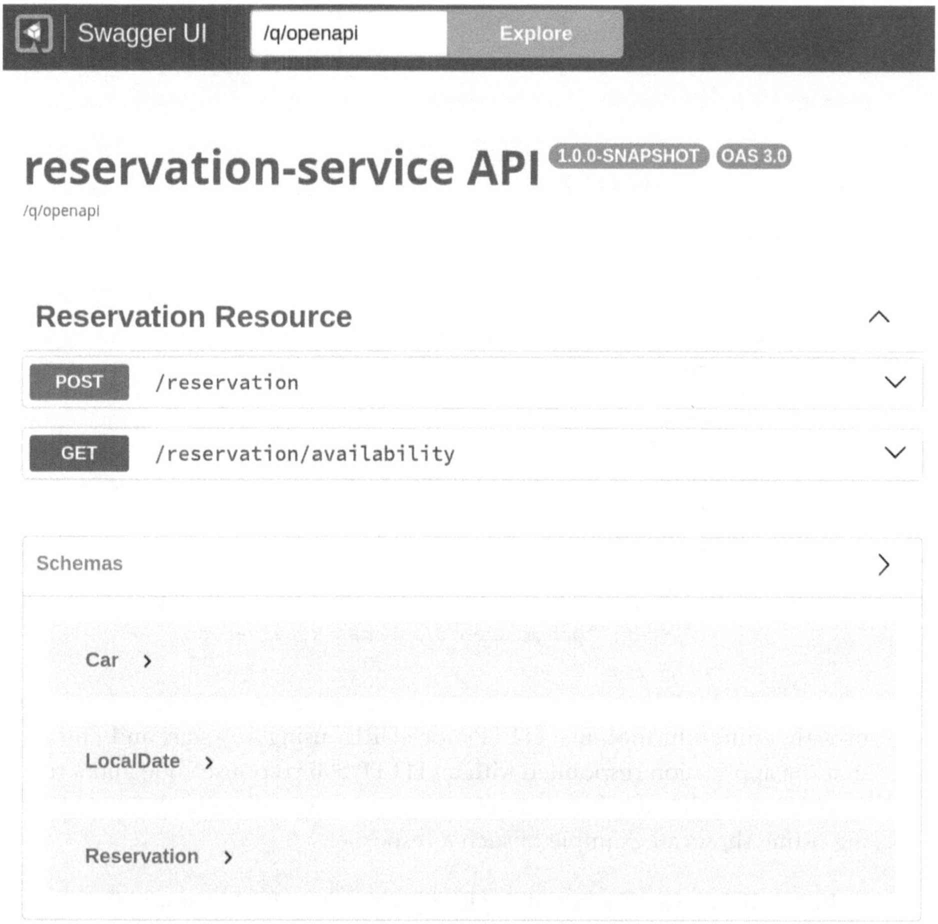

Figure 4.2   Quarkus provides a UI for executing REST operations by using the Swagger UI.

generates this document according to the definition presented by the MicroProfile OpenAPI specification. It is also possible to customize how it is generated. However, that is beyond our scope. If you are interested in how the OpenAPI extension works, you can check the official documentation at https://quarkus.io/guides/openapi -swaggerui.

Listing 4.9 provides a part of the generated OpenAPI document. This part shows some high-level metadata of the service (title and version), as well as the definition of the method for making a reservation (`ReservationResource#make`). You can see that it accepts and produces a JSON format with the corresponding schema to a `#/components/schemas/Reservation` object (which is a representation of the `Reservation` class from our code). You can check the response from http://localhost :8081/q/openapi if you want to see the whole document.

Listing 4.9   The OpenAPI document of the Reservation service

```
---
openapi: 3.0.3
info:
  title: reservation-service API
  version: 1.0.0-SNAPSHOT
paths:
  /reservation:
    post:
      tags:
      - Reservation Resource
      requestBody:
        content:
          application/json:
            schema:
              $ref: '#/components/schemas/Reservation'
      responses:
        "200":
          description: OK
          content:
            application/json:
              schema:
                $ref: '#/components/schemas/Reservation'
```

After trying out the GET /reservation/availability endpoint (either in the Swagger or with a different tool, like HTTPie or cURL) using any start and end dates, we see that the application responded with an HTTP 200 response code and a response body containing all the cars (since there are no reservations yet in the system). The following listing shows an example of such a response.

NOTE   If you want to try out the REST API using cURL, you will find it helpful that the Swagger UI, whenever you execute an operation in its UI, generates and shows an example cURL command that you can copy and paste into your terminal.

Listing 4.10   Example JSON response when no reservations exist in the system

```
[
  {
    "id": 1,
    "licensePlateNumber": "ABC-123",
    "manufacturer": "Toyota",
    "model": "Corolla"
  },
  {
    "id": 2,
    "licensePlateNumber": "ABC-987",
    "manufacturer": "Honda",
    "model": "Jazz"
  },
```

```
  {
    "id": 3,
    "licensePlateNumber": "XYZ-123",
    "manufacturer": "Renault",
    "model": "Clio"
  },
  {
    "id": 4,
    "licensePlateNumber": "XYZ-987",
    "manufacturer": "Ford",
    "model": "Focus"
  }
]
```

To make a reservation for the first car with a start date of `2024-01-01` and end date of `2024-01-05`, we use the `POST /reservation` endpoint with the JSON body shown in the following listing.

Listing 4.11   The JSON request to make a reservation for the car with ID 1

```
{
  "carId": 1,
  "startDay": "2024-01-01",
  "endDay": "2024-01-05"
}
```

The response we get back is also a JSON representing a persisted reservation with the reservation ID set to `1`.

Listing 4.12   The JSON response acknowledging the reservation

```
{
  "id": 1,
  "carId": 1,
  "startDay": "2024-01-01",
  "endDay": "2024-01-05"
}
```

Let's test the Reservation service to ensure we can't reserve the same car for any days in the `2024-01-01` to `2024-01-05` range. We do that by invoking the `GET /reservations/ availabity` endpoint with `2024-01-02` as the start date and `2024-01-04` as the end date (as we previously made a reservation for this same range).

NOTE   For simplicity, we didn't add proper validation in the `/reservation` endpoint, so an actual call to create a reservation would still pass. But the `/availability` endpoint should not mark the car as available.

Listing 4.13   JSON response after reserving the first car

```
[
  {
```

```
    "id": 2,
    "licensePlateNumber": "ABC-987",
    "manufacturer": "Honda",
    "model": "Jazz"
  },
  {
    "id": 3,
    "licensePlateNumber": "XYZ-123",
    "manufacturer": "Renault",
    "model": "Clio"
  },
  {
    "id": 4,
    "licensePlateNumber": "XYZ-987",
    "manufacturer": "Ford",
    "model": "Focus"
  }
]
```

We see that car with ID 1 is missing from this list, as expected.

4.3 Using the REST client

In addition to exposing REST endpoints, Quarkus also makes it very easy to consume REST endpoints. To showcase this capability, we create the Rental service that the Reservation service calls when making a reservation with the starting day equal to today, meaning that the rental starts with the confirmed reservation.

For the time being, the Rental service is a REST endpoint with very simple functionality for rental tracking. In the parent directory, we can create it using this command:

```
$ quarkus create app org.acme:rental-service -P 3.15.1 --extension \
rest-jackson --no-code
```

> **NOTE** Notice that we don't need to provide the full name of the extensions. Quarkus deduces the correct extension if we provide a long enough part of the name to make the selection unambiguous.

To avoid potential port conflicts when running multiple services together, open the src/main/resources/application.properties file and add the configuration property quarkus.http.port=8082.

Once created, we can develop an org.acme.rental.Rental class that represents a simple model of a rental with the code available in the following listing.

> **Listing 4.14 The source code of the** `Rental` **class which models rentals**

```
package org.acme.rental;

import java.time.LocalDate;

public class Rental {
```

```
    private final Long id;
    private final String userId;
    private final Long reservationId;
    private final LocalDate startDate;

    public Rental(Long id, String userId, Long reservationId,
                  LocalDate startDate) {
        this.id = id;
        this.userId = userId;
        this.reservationId = reservationId;
        this.startDate = startDate;
    }

    public Long getId() {
        return id;
    }

    public String getUserId() {
        return userId;
    }

    public Long getReservationId() {
        return reservationId;
    }

    public LocalDate getStartDate() {
        return startDate;
    }

    @Override
    public String toString() {
        return "Rental{" +
            "id=" + id +
            ", userId='" + userId + '\'' +
            ", reservationId=" + reservationId +
            ", startDate=" + startDate +
            '}';
    }
}
```

The `org.acme.rental.RentalResource` is the REST endpoint that initiates a rental request at the `/rental/start` path. It can be composed as demonstrated in the following listing.

Listing 4.15 **The source code of the** `RentalResource` **class**

```
package org.acme.rental;

import io.quarkus.logging.Log;

import java.time.LocalDate;
import java.util.concurrent.atomic.AtomicLong;
import jakarta.ws.rs.POST;
import jakarta.ws.rs.Path;
```

```
import jakarta.ws.rs.Produces;
import jakarta.ws.rs.core.MediaType;

@Path("/rental")
public class RentalResource {

    private final AtomicLong id = new AtomicLong(0);

    @Path("/start/{userId}/{reservationId}")
    @POST
    @Produces(MediaType.APPLICATION_JSON)
    public Rental start(String userId,
                        Long reservationId) {
        Log.infof("Starting rental for %s with reservation %s",
            userId, reservationId);
        return new Rental(id.incrementAndGet(), userId, reservationId,
            LocalDate.now());
    }
}
```

The {} syntax is used to capture the value of the subpaths.

The userId and reservationId parameters match the names in the subpaths of the @Path annotation. Quarkus, therefore, captures the values of these subpaths and populates the parameters from them.

We're using a Quarkus-specific class for logging, which is the recommended approach. You could also instantiate an org.jboss.logging.Logger instance instead, but using static methods is simpler.

Taking a step back, we see how easy it has been to create the various pieces of the microservice architecture we intend to implement. So far, we have bootstrapped a working version of the Reservation and Rental services with a couple of commands and a small amount of clean, simple Java code. The only missing part is implementing the communication layer between reservation and rental to close the loop between them.

The first step to accomplish this task is to define the model for rentals on the reservation side of the communication. As this model is the same as the model used on the rental side, we copy the Rental class into the org.acme.reservation.rental package of the Reservation service.

Next comes the definition of REST-style communication, which we implement in the Reservation service by creating an interface named org.acme.reservation.rental .RentalClient, as demonstrated in listing 4.16. This interface has only one method that takes the user and reservation IDs and returns a rental. The real value Quarkus offers here is that by requiring a few very simple annotations from us, it can provide an implementation of the interface so we don't have to write any tedious HTTP-related code at all.

Listing 4.16   The source code of the `RentalClient` interface

```
package org.acme.reservation.rental;

import jakarta.ws.rs.POST;
import jakarta.ws.rs.Path;

import org.eclipse.microprofile.rest.client.inject.RegisterRestClient;
import org.jboss.resteasy.reactive.RestPath;

@RegisterRestClient(baseUri = "http://localhost:8082")
@Path("/rental")
public interface RentalClient {
```

```
@POST
@Path("/start/{userId}/{reservationId}")
Rental start(@RestPath String userId,
             @RestPath Long reservationId);
}
```

The `@RegisterRestClient` annotation informs Quarkus that this interface consumes a REST endpoint. Quarkus will use the metadata of this interface to provide an implementation of it automatically. The value of `baseUri` is set to the base HTTP URI where our Rental service listens for requests. You would typically provide this value through configuration (or it can even be received dynamically from a service discovery mechanism), but we make it simple for the time being.

This method consumes the `start` REST endpoint of the Rental Service, which is an HTTP POST endpoint, so we annotate the interface method with `@POST`. The called path is constructed from the `@Path` annotations to `/rental/start/`. Also, to make Quarkus populate the HTTP paths that the `start` REST endpoint of the Rental service expects, we annotate the two parameters with `@RestPath`.

Finally, we update the `ReservationResource` to use our new client.

Listing 4.17 Updated source code of the `ReservationResource` class

```java
import org.acme.reservation.rental.Rental;
import org.acme.reservation.rental.RentalClient;
import org.eclipse.microprofile.rest.client.inject.RestClient;

@Path("reservation")
@Produces(MediaType.APPLICATION_JSON)
public class ReservationResource {

    private final ReservationsRepository reservationsRepository;
    private final InventoryClient inventoryClient;
    private final RentalClient rentalClient;

    public ReservationResource(ReservationsRepository reservations,
            InventoryClient inventoryClient,
            @RestClient RentalClient rentalClient) {       ◁──┐  To make Quarkus use
        this.reservationsRepository = reservations;             our RentalClient in the
        this.inventoryClient = inventoryClient;                 ReservationResource,
        this.rentalClient = rentalClient;                       we need to annotate
    }                                                           the constructor
                                                                (injected) parameter
    @Consumes(MediaType.APPLICATION_JSON)                       with @RestClient.
    @POST
    public Reservation make(Reservation reservation) {
        Reservation result = reservationsRepository.save(reservation);
        // this is just a dummy value for the time being
        String userId = "x";                                    ◁──┐
        if (reservation.startDay.equals(LocalDate.now())) {
```

In later parts of the book, where we talk about security, we will use a proper userId.

```
        Rental rental =
            rentalClient.start(userId, result.id);
        Log.info("Successfully started rental " + rental);
    }
    return result;
}
...
}
```

**Starting the rental is simply a matter of
calling the start method of the RentalClient
interface, which makes the remote HTTP call.**

If you now try to invoke Reservation's POST :8081/reservation with a start date of the current date, it will make the call to the Rental service, and you can verify with the log message in the Rental service that it receives the request as expected. Make sure that the Rental service is started (e.g., quarkus dev).

In the next section, we focus on creating the Inventory service, which we then use to properly implement org.acme.reservation.inventory.InventoryClient of the Reservation service, thus replacing the static list implementation we added in listing 4.3.

4.4   *Developing Quarkus applications with GraphQL*

GraphQL is an emerging query language that gives clients the power to ask for exactly what they need without overfetching (receiving data that you don't need) or underfetching (having to execute many queries sequentially to get all the data you need), which helps decrease the number of requests required actually to perform what is needed, and reduces network traffic. This makes GraphQL a good fit for constrained environments like mobile applications.

Depending on how you put it to use, GraphQL can be viewed as an alternative to both SQL (which is more focused on data querying) and REST (which is more focused on APIs and operations). Thanks to statically defined schemas for endpoints, it enables powerful developer tools and easy schema evolution without having to introduce breaking changes.

The backing data storage can be a persistent database, any kind of in-memory data structure, or a combination of both—GraphQL merely defines the querying language. It doesn't assume anything about the source of the data. You can also use GraphQL to create an API that connects multiple completely disparate data sources and exposes a unified view of the data obtained from these sources. In this section, we will show a relatively basic example of our data model derived from a set of Java classes, and we will only store the data inside in-memory data structures. Later, in chapter 7, we will enhance the service further by using a persistent database for storing the exposed data.

The GraphQL schema describes the GraphQL data model. The main components of a schema are types and fields. A GraphQL type, when using GraphQL with a data model defined in Java, most often corresponds to a Java class containing several fields which conform to the fields of that type. When a client asks for data, it specifies which fields need to be fetched.

A client interacts with a GraphQL endpoint by executing so-called GraphQL operations. You can perceive these as rough equivalents of SQL queries or REST methods. GraphQL operations also have a clearly defined contract. They accept parameters and return a particular type. There are three types of operations that clients can execute when communicating with a GraphQL endpoint:

- `Query`—This is an equivalent of a `SELECT` with SQL or a `GET` operation with RESTful endpoints. It allows clients to ask for data and is a read-only operation, so it should not change any data.
- `Mutation`—This is an equivalent of `UPDATE` or `INSERT` in SQL terms and `PUT` or `POST` in REST terms. It's an operation that can also change existing data or add new data. Compared to the SQL equivalents, it can also return some data to the client along with the update.
- `Subscription`—This special query does not return just one response. Instead, the result is a (potentially infinite) stream of responses in which new items can appear over time. You can use this for notifications about events on the data—for example, new orders that arrive in a shop or newly registered users. This is usually implemented using WebSockets.

We won't dive deep into all the features that GraphQL offers. For more information and tutorials, you may visit https://graphql.org.

In Quarkus, the support for GraphQL follows the MicroProfile GraphQL specification. At the time of writing this book, only the server-side components of GraphQL were part of this specification, but work was underway to integrate the client-side APIs. However, Quarkus supports both sides as two separate extensions. They are named `quarkus-smallrye-graphql` and `quarkus-smallrye-graphql-client`. Let's learn how to use them, starting with the server-side extension.

4.5   Car Rental Inventory service

In this section, we create the Inventory service for our car rental project. This service will manage the inventory of cars that are available for rental. It will expose a GraphQL-based API with relevant operations that allow retrieving information about the car inventory and managing it. Later, we will update the Reservation service to use a GraphQL client to obtain the list of cars from the Inventory service.

4.5.1   Exposing the Inventory service over GraphQL

For the GraphQL API that we're about to create, we use a code-first approach, meaning we describe the API with Java code, and the SmallRye GraphQL extension then takes care of translating this model into a GraphQL schema.

To create the skeleton for the project, use the following CLI command in the parent directory:

```
$ quarkus create app org.acme:inventory-service -P 3.15.1 \
--extension smallrye-graphql --no-code
```

To avoid port conflicts when running multiple services together, open the configuration file `application.properties` and add the property `quarkus.http.port=8083`.

TIP You can always refer to the table 4.1, which lists which services run on which ports.

Run the project in Dev mode. Now, create the `org.acme.inventory.model` package for domain model classes, `org.acme.inventory.service` for the GraphQL API, and `org.acme.inventory.database` for the database stub. Let's now add the `Car` class code to the `model` package. Remember, the Reservation service already has a `Car` class, and the plan is that it will be able to exchange information about cars with Inventory service. To make the classes compatible, let's name all fields the same so that their corresponding GraphQL fields will be equal. The code for the `Car` class is shown in the following listing.

> **Listing 4.18   The source code of the `Car` model class**

```
package org.acme.inventory.model;

public class Car {

    public Long id;
    public String licensePlateNumber;
    public String manufacturer;
    public String model;

}
```

We need the `CarInventory` class in the `database` package to serve as our database stub (we will only use in-memory data structures for now). The following listing demonstrates the code for the `CarInventory` class.

> **Listing 4.19   The `CarInventory` class—a database stub for the car inventory**

```
package org.acme.inventory.database;

import org.acme.inventory.model.Car;

import jakarta.annotation.PostConstruct;
import jakarta.enterprise.context.ApplicationScoped;
import java.util.List;
import java.util.concurrent.CopyOnWriteArrayList;
import java.util.concurrent.atomic.AtomicLong;

@ApplicationScoped
public class CarInventory {

    private List<Car> cars;

    public static final AtomicLong ids = new AtomicLong(0);
```

```
@PostConstruct
void initialize() {
    cars = new CopyOnWriteArrayList<>();
    initialData();
}

public List<Car> getCars() {
    return cars;
}

private void initialData() {
    Car mazda = new Car();
    mazda.id = ids.incrementAndGet();
    mazda.manufacturer = "Mazda";
    mazda.model = "6";
    mazda.licensePlateNumber = "ABC123";
    cars.add(mazda);

    Car ford = new Car();
    ford.id = ids.incrementAndGet();
    ford.manufacturer = "Ford";
    ford.model = "Mustang";
    ford.licensePlateNumber = "XYZ987";
    cars.add(ford);
}

}
```

> The framework calls the method annotated with **@PostConstruct** when it instantiates the bean. In our case, we use it to initialize the database stub.

The `@ApplicationScoped` annotation turns this class into a CDI bean that uses the *application scope.* This means that Quarkus creates only one instance of it, and all beans injecting this inventory will share the same car database instance. The `initialData` method, called within the `initialize` method, which Quarkus invokes after the bean is created because of the `@PostConstruct` annotation, stores some cars in the car inventory, so these will always be present after the start of the application. If you want more than just two cars, feel free to add more per your imagination. IDs are automatically generated from the `AtomicLong` increments.

Next, we need to add the `GraphQLInventoryService` class in the `service` package that exposes our model as a GraphQL service. To do so, it utilizes annotations from the MicroProfile GraphQL specification.

Listing 4.20 The `GraphQLInventoryService` exposes the fleet over GraphQL

```
package org.acme.inventory.service;

import org.acme.inventory.database.CarInventory;
import org.acme.inventory.model.Car;
import org.eclipse.microprofile.graphql.GraphQLApi;
import org.eclipse.microprofile.graphql.Mutation;
import org.eclipse.microprofile.graphql.Query;
```

```
import jakarta.inject.Inject;
import java.util.List;
import java.util.Optional;

@GraphQLApi
public class GraphQLInventoryService {

    @Inject
    CarInventory inventory;

    @Query
    public List<Car> cars() {
        return inventory.getCars();
    }

    @Mutation
    public Car register(Car car) {
        car.id = CarInventory.ids.incrementAndGet();
        inventory.getCars().add(car);
        return car;
    }

    @Mutation
    public boolean remove(String licensePlateNumber) {
        List<Car> cars = inventory.getCars();
        Optional<Car> toBeRemoved = cars.stream()
            .filter(car -> car.licensePlateNumber
                .equals(licensePlateNumber))
            .findAny();
        if(toBeRemoved.isPresent()) {
            return cars.remove(toBeRemoved.get());
        } else {
            return false;
        }
    }

}
```

The code is straightforward. The `cars` query retrieves the current list of cars belonging to the fleet, and the `register` mutation serves for registering new cars into the fleet. The `remove` mutation removes cars from the fleet. It returns `true` if a car was removed after invoking it, and `false` otherwise.

4.5.2 *Invoking GraphQL operations using the UI*

Now, let's open the Quarkus GraphQL UI (a slightly modified version of the GraphiQL open source project) and play around by executing various GraphQL operations manually. While the service still runs in Dev mode, open http://localhost:8083/q/graphql-ui/ in your browser. The UI looks like the one presented in figure 4.3. There are three main parts of the page:

- The top-left window is used to write your GraphQL queries.
- The bottom-left window provides values for variables if you use variables in your queries and also for supplying HTTP headers that the query should include.
- The gray window on the right displays the result of operations that you execute.

And there's also the blue Play button that executes the requested operation.

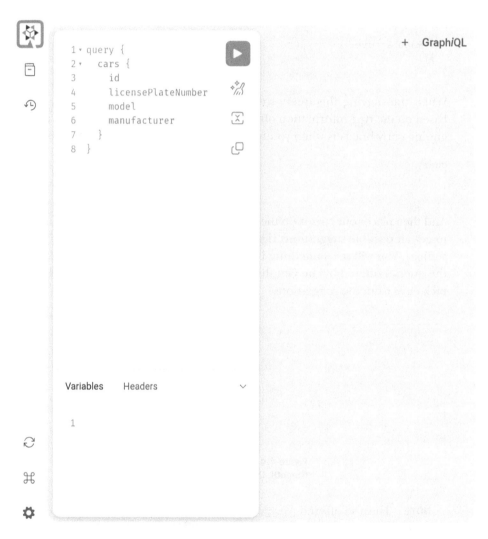

Figure 4.3 GraphiQL is an HTML and JavaScript-based UI for manually executing GraphQL operations.

Now, let's try some queries. Remember that we have a query named cars which is used to retrieve a list of cars currently registered in the fleet. The Car type contains the fields `id`, `licensePlateNumber`, `manufacturer`, and `model`. The query needed to obtain all cars, along with all their fields, is provided in the following listing.

Listing 4.21 A GraphQL query for all fields of all cars in the fleet

```
query {
  cars {
    id
    licensePlateNumber
    model
    manufacturer
  }
}
```

When transferring this query to the UI, note that the UI supports autocompletion based on the type information obtained from the GraphQL schema. It also creates the ending curly brackets when you type opening curly brackets. So, try typing just

```
query {

}
```

And then place your cursor on the empty line in the middle and either press `Ctrl+Space` to get all possible suggestions right away or start typing the word `cars` (just the `c` will suffice). You will see something like this in figure 4.4 because the UI knows about all the queries offered by the GraphQL endpoint. Use the arrow keys and press `Enter` to pick `cars` from the suggestions.

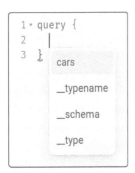

Figure 4.4   After pressing `Ctrl+Space` in the GraphQL UI, you get autocompletion suggestions.

NOTE The also offered __typename, __schema, and __type suggestions represent built-in fields that allow reading metadata about the types in the schema. For example, if you request the __typename field as a subselection of a `Car`, the returned value will be `Car`.

Similarly, by autocompleting the query name, you get suggestions for fields of the `Car` type after pressing `Ctrl+Space` with the cursor in the middle of this unfinished query (or start typing the name of one of the fields):

```
query {
    cars {
        # selected fields from the `Car` type go here
    }
}
```

When the query completes and looks like the one in listing 4.21, press the blue `Play` button to execute it. The result is in JSON format. It looks like the following listing.

Listing 4.22   The result of the `cars` query

```
{
  "data": {
    "cars": [
      {
        "id": 1,
        "licensePlateNumber": "ABC123",
        "model": "6",
        "manufacturer": "Mazda"
      },
      {
        "id": 2,
        "licensePlateNumber": "XYZ987",
        "model": "Mustang",
        "manufacturer": "Ford"
      }
    ]
  }
}
```

Try removing one of the subselection fields from the `cars` query and execute the query again. The result does not include that field.

Now that we've tried a query, let's quickly try a mutation. Recall that a GraphQL mutation is an operation that, unlike a query, can change data, meaning it is not read-only. The mutation that adds a new car into the fleet can look like the one in the following listing. Again, `Ctrl+Space` can autocomplete most of this.

Listing 4.23   The `register` mutation for adding new cars into the fleet

```
mutation {
  register(car: {
    licensePlateNumber: "O123"
    model: "406"
    manufacturer: "Peugeot"
  }) {
    licensePlateNumber
    model
    manufacturer
    id
  }
}
```

We use the mutation word to say this is a mutation, not a query. The register mutation has one parameter of type CarInput (we will explore that shortly), so let's supply the fields to build an object of that type. The mutation not only creates an object but also returns the same object, as we described it in the source code. When the return type is a complex object, it is mandatory to specify which fields we want to fetch from that object. In our example, we fetch all of them, including the automatically generated ID.

After executing, the result looks like the one in listing 4.24. You can see that the mutation echoes back Car while storing it. The result contains the same data that we sent into the operation because we selected all fields from the returned type.

Listing 4.24 The register mutation echoes back the car added to the fleet

```
{
  "data": {
    "register": {
      "licensePlateNumber": "O123",
      "model": "406",
      "manufacturer": "Peugeot",
      "id": 3
    }
  }
}
```

You may now verify that the database contains the added car by executing the cars query again.

TIP You can also find a history of executed queries and mutations in the GraphiQL left menu.

4.5.3 *Reviewing the GraphQL schema*

Recall that GraphQL schema is the contract that the service exposes, and all clients have to adhere to it to be able to communicate with that service. Let's briefly look at the GraphQL schema that the Quarkus GraphQL extension generated from the domain model. Access http://localhost:8083/graphql/schema.graphql, either in your browser or by a terminal command of your choice. The following listing shows the schema of the Inventory GraphQL service.

Listing 4.25 The GraphQL schema of the Inventory service

```
type Car {
  id: BigInteger
  licensePlateNumber: String
  manufacturer: String
  model: String
}
```

```
"Mutation root"
type Mutation {
  register(car: CarInput): Car
  remove(licensePlateNumber: String): Boolean!
}

"Query root"
type Query {
  cars: [Car]
}

input CarInput {
  id: BigInteger
  licensePlateNumber: String
  manufacturer: String
  model: String
}
```

The Car type at the top is an output type. The input counterpart is the CarInput at the bottom of the schema. The GraphQL language makes a strict distinction between output and input types, even when, like in our case, the types are identical (generated from the same Java class). We used the Car class as a parameter of the register mutation, which means the GraphQL extension created an input type, but we also used it as the return type of that mutation; hence, the extension also created the output type.

The type Mutation (the top-level type for mutations, also called Mutation root in proper GraphQL terms) wraps all mutations in our schema, including their parameters and return types. The Query type similarly wraps all queries in our schema. When a type reference is in square brackets, it means a collection of objects of that type. So the [Car] type corresponds to the List<Car> as the return type of the GraphQL-InventoryService#cars method. When a type reference is followed by an exclamation mark, it means that a value for this field is required and must not be null. For inputs, the client has to supply a value; for outputs, the client can expect a value to be always returned, except when an error occurs.

4.5.4   *Consuming the Inventory service using a GraphQL client*

We will now update the Reservation service to use a GraphQL client to obtain the real list of cars in the fleet from the Inventory service instead of using a hard-coded list of cars. So, the Reservation acts as a GraphQL client, whereas the Inventory acts as a GraphQL server. After this exercise, you can find the resulting state of the Reservation service in this book's GitHub repository quarkus-in-action inside the chapter-04/4_5_4/reservation-service directory.

We now need to run the Reservation and Inventory services simultaneously so they can talk to each other. We will only change the Reservation code now so you may run Reservation in Dev mode and Inventory in production mode. But you can run both in Dev mode in parallel if you prefer! This is possible because we specified different default ports for both of them. So the Reservation runs on port 8081 while Inventory runs on port 8083 (see table 4.1 for reference).

Go to the directory of the Reservation service, and let's get started. First, add the GraphQL client extension by executing the following:

```
$ quarkus extension add smallrye-graphql-client
```

We will use a so-called typesafe client, meaning the code will use our domain classes directly. Quarkus also supports *dynamic* GraphQL clients. We will discuss the difference between these two types later. For a typesafe client, we need to add an interface that describes the client-side view of the GraphQL contract it uses to communicate with the server side. Create the GraphQLInventoryClient interface inside the org.acme .reservation.inventory package with the source code presented in listing 4.26.

> **Listing 4.26 The source code of the GraphQLInventoryClient interface**

```
@GraphQLClientApi(configKey = "inventory")
public interface GraphQLInventoryClient extends InventoryClient {
    @Query("cars")
    List<Car> allCars();
}
```

The GraphQLClientApi annotation declares that this interface is a client-side view of a GraphQL API. The configKey parameter assigns a name to this particular GraphQL client. It serves to map the configuration values to this specific client. Any configuration that we will add related to this client will reference it by its name. This allows the definition of multiple GraphQL client APIs with different configuration values.

The InventoryClient interface contains the method allCars, but the GraphQL query exposed by the Inventory service is named cars (listing 4.25). By applying the Query annotation containing the correct name of the query, we instruct the library to execute the correct query when it invokes the allCars method.

The next step is to provide the configuration for our GraphQL client. The only required configuration value is the URL where the client should connect to the server. Add this line to application.properties of the Reservation service:

```
quarkus.smallrye-graphql-client.inventory.url=http://localhost:8083/graphql
```

Notice the word inventory inside the property's key. That refers to the configKey value in the @GraphQLClientApi annotation that we added in the previous step.

Now update the org.acme.reservation.rest.ReservationResource class to actually use the GraphQL-based inventory client instead of the inventory stub InMemory-InventoryClient. Change its constructor, as shown in listing 4.27. By changing the injected type into GraphQLInventoryClient and specifying the name of the client that we want to inject in the @GraphQLClient annotation, we make the Reservation-Resource use a GraphQL client instead of the in-memory client stub. This also means that we can safely remove the stub we used before in class InMemoryInventoryClient.

Listing 4.27 `ReservationResource` **now injecting the** `GraphQLInventoryClient`

```
public ReservationResource(ReservationsRepository reservations,
     @GraphQLClient("inventory") GraphQLInventoryClient inventoryClient,
     @RestClient RentalClient rentalClient) {
   this.reservationsRepository = reservations;
   this.inventoryClient = inventoryClient;
   this.rentalClient = rentalClient;
}
```

One more minor change is needed before we can test it out. Because we use the `Car` class as a return value from the service, Quarkus needs to be able to deserialize it from JSON documents and construct its instances. Therefore, it's necessary to provide a public no-argument constructor in the `Car` class. It can be empty. Add the following constructor to the `org.acme.reservation.inventory.Car` class:

```
public Car() {
}
```

Now we can call the `availability` method and verify that it's using a GraphQL client instead of the `InMemoryInventoryClient`. For instance, with the HTTPie, it can be done as shown in listing 4.28. In the result, you can see the cars come from the Inventory service, as opposed to those hardcoded in `InMemoryInventoryClient`.

Listing 4.28 Calling the reservation availability endpoint

```
$ http :8081/reservation/availability
HTTP/1.1 200 OK
Content-Type: application/json;charset=UTF-8
content-length: 154

[
    {
        "id": 1,
        "licensePlateNumber": "ABC123",
        "manufacturer": "Mazda",
        "model": "6"
    },
    {
        "id": 2,
        "licensePlateNumber": "XYZ987",
        "manufacturer": "Ford",
        "model": "Mustang"
    }
]
```

HOW THE TYPESAFE CLIENT WORKS

In the Reservation service, we used a typesafe GraphQL client. The typesafe client works in a way that internally transforms Java classes into GraphQL types, as we saw with the `Car` class. On the server side, we called a query called `cars` that returns a list of cars (`[Car]` denotes the list in GraphQL terms). The typesafe client looks at all the fields that the `Car` class (in the client-side application) contains and builds an internal representation of the `Car` type from the server side. This representation does not have to be complete. It doesn't have to contain all fields of the target type from the server-side schema. If it had to contain all fields, it would defeat one of the purposes of GraphQL, which is being able to choose which fields to fetch.

When the client API invokes the GraphQL operation, the library converts this invocation into a GraphQL request. In our case, it's the request that obtains the list of cars. The constructed query request looks like this:

```
query {
    cars {
        id
        licensePlateNumber
        manufacturer
        model
    }
}
```

If we left out any of the fields of the `Car` class in the reservation application, then that field would not be part of the selection in the query. When the query is ready, the client sends it to the server over the HTTP protocol. The server responds with the JSON representation of a list of cars currently registered in the fleet. The typesafe client library converts this JSON array into a `List<Car>` returned from the `GraphQLInventory-Client#allCars` method.

DYNAMIC GRAPHQL CLIENT

While a typesafe GraphQL client works directly with model classes, the so-called dynamic client is an alternative to it. Instead of automatically transforming classes to corresponding queries, the dynamic client offers a Domain Specific Language (DSL) that allows the developer to construct GraphQL documents using chained calls of Java methods while making the Java code looks as close as it can be to writing a raw GraphQL document directly. We won't go through a guided example for this one, but to give you a better idea of what the difference is, let's look at a few code snippets that implement an equivalent of the client that we built in the Reservation service. For example, to build the original `cars` query, we could write code in the following listing.

> Listing 4.29 **An example `cars` query with a dynamic GraphQL client**

```
// import static io.smallrye.graphql.client.core.Document.document;
// import static io.smallrye.graphql.client.core.Field.field;
// import static io.smallrye.graphql.client.core.Operation.operation;

Document cars = document(
      operation("cars",
          field("id"),
          field("licensePlateNumber"),
          field("manufacturer"),
```

```
        field("model")
    )
);
```

The resulting `Document` object can then be passed to the client instance and sent over the wire to the target GraphQL service. The response is represented as an instance of the `Response` interface.

Listing 4.30 An example of request execution with a dynamic GraphQL client

```
DynamicGraphQLClient client = ...; // obtain a client instance
Response response = client.executeSync(cars);
JsonArray carsAsJson = response.getData().asJsonArray();
// or, automatically deserialize a List of cars:
List<Car> cars = response.getList(Car.class, "cars");
```

The `Response` object contains all information about the response received from the server, which means the actual data and maybe a list of errors, if any errors occurred during the execution. The data can be retrieved in its raw form as a JSON document. Optionally, it's also possible to automatically deserialize from JSON and receive instances of domain objects.

Typesafe and dynamic clients offer similar features, but their use differs. Typesafe client is easier and more intuitive to use because you use domain classes directly, but with a more complicated GraphQL schema, it might be tricky to properly construct Java counterparts of the GraphQL types in the schema. Also, if you have more operations that work with the same type, but they require fetching a different set of fields from that type, then you will need different Java classes that represent that type, each with exactly the fields that you require. With a dynamic client, this is a little easier because you can simply exclude some fields in the documents that describe the operations.

4.6 *Developing Quarkus services with gRPC*

In previous sections, we learned about REST and GraphQL technologies. This section focuses on gRPC (gRPC Remote Procedure Calls; https://grpc.io), an open source framework for remote process communication that is an excellent match for microservice architectures. Previous experience with gRPC is helpful but not required. We provide a brief overview of the technology for everyone to connect at the same level to explain the gRPC integration in Quarkus.

4.6.1 *Understanding when to use gRPC*

Have you ever implemented a connection to service over HTTP and felt that the limitations of the protocol constricted you? Has latency ever become a real problem for you and your team? Does the JSON format seem like overkill for your needs? Are you looking for something more compact and efficient?

If you find these questions relatable, you may need to check out gRPC. In many real-world cases, projects must keep the latency to a minimum. gRPC facilitates this by using a binary protocol (which is inherently faster than human-readable text-based protocols) and supporting multiplexing (sending multiple requests concurrently over one connection before receiving responses for them), which is faster than the typical HTTP/1 architecture, where requests and responses are serialized one after another.

Figure 4.5 shows the sending of requests and responses over a single TCP connection with and without multiplexing. The first row displays HTTP/1.1, which does not support multiplexing. The second row shows HTTP/2, which does support multiplexing and is used under the hood by gRPC. Notice how multiple requests take less time to fulfill when using multiplexing.

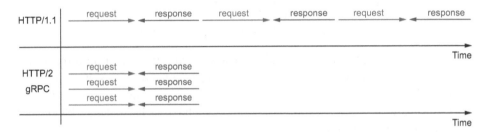

Figure 4.5   Visualizing the value of multiplexing in HTTP2

4.6.2   *Protocol Buffers*

Protocol Buffers specification, also known as protobuf, is a serialization format for typed structured data. It is compact, efficient, and language-independent. Protobuf can use binary and text formats, but the former is way more popular, and thus we focus on it exclusively. Compared to JSON, protobuf messages are smaller and faster to serialize/deserialize. On the other hand, binary messages are not human-readable.

Another critical characteristic of protobuf messages is that they have a schema definition. Users create a special file format called *proto* that describes the schema definition. Different tools then compile the proto file into language-specific code for representing, serializing, and deserializing the protobuf messages.

Let's use the Car example in the Inventory service and analyze how we can represent it in proto (see listing 4.31). The file starts by setting the syntax to proto3, corresponding to the latest protocol buffer version format. The presented options are language-specific and define things like the Java package and how the framework should organize the generated code. Note that besides the Java package, we also define the protobuf package: package inventory, which acts as a namespace for the message(s) defined below. Lastly, the proto file defines the structure of the car message. It specifies each field's type, name, and order (not to be confused with the default value).

The compilation process converts the fields from camel case (using the capital case to separate words) to snake case (using underscore to separate words) to align the code with the Protocol Buffer naming conventions. For example, `licensePlate-Number` is converted to `license_plate_number`.

Listing 4.31 Describing the `Car` model using Protocol Buffers

```
syntax = "proto3";

option java_multiple_files = true;
option java_package = "org.acme.inventory.model";
option java_outer_classname = "InventoryProtos";

package inventory;

message Car {
    string license_plate_number = 1;
    string manufacturer = 2;
    string model = 3;
    int64 id = 4;
}
```

There are multiple ways to compile a proto file, including the `protoc` compiler, build tool plugins, and the `quarkus-grpc` extension. Regardless of the compilation technique, the generated code includes a representation of the `Car` message in Java class accompanied by a builder implementation and methods for serializing/deserializing. Listing 4.32 provides an example of using this generated code. The example shows how we can create an instance of `Car` programmatically and write it to an `Output-Stream`. Note that code uses the builder pattern implemented as part of the generated code and then the `writeTo` method of the `Car` instance that writes it into an `Output-Stream`.

Listing 4.32 An example using the generated protobuf code

```
public void writeCarData(OutputStream os, String licensePlateNumber,
        String manufacturer, String model) throws IOException {
    Car.newBuilder()
        .setLicensePlateNumber(licensePlateNumber)
        .setManufacturer(manufacturer)
        .setModel(model)
        .setId(id)
        .build()
        .writeTo(os);
}
```

4.7 Adding gRPC support to your project

As you might have already noticed from the architectural diagram (figure 4.1), for the demonstration of the gRPC, we add the support for gRPC into the Inventory service to show you the differences to the GraphQL approach. So, if you want to follow the implementation, please execute the examples provided in this section in the `inventory-service` directory.

Message definitions are not the only thing we can define in proto files. We can also define remote service methods. In our case, the generated code includes client and server stubs. The server stubs are the base classes that we can utilize to implement the remote method. The client stubs are classes we can use from the client side to call the remote methods. Quarkus users can use the `quarkus-grpc` extension to generate Java code from their proto files whether they are defining remote methods or not. Let's add this extension to the Inventory service. We can do this by either the CLI as demonstrated in listing 4.33 or manually. The resulting `pom.xml` file contains the dependency shown in listing 4.34.

Listing 4.33   Adding the gRPC extension using the CLI

```
$ quarkus extension add grpc
```

The command adds the dependency shown in the following listing to your `pom.xml`.

Listing 4.34   Adding or verifying the presence of a gRPC extension

```
<dependency>
    <groupId>io.quarkus</groupId>
    <artifactId>quarkus-grpc</artifactId>
</dependency>
```

The next step is to add the proto file `inventory.proto` under the `src/main/proto` directory. Let's use the Protocol Buffer's definition from listing 4.31 as a base. We modify it to a service that adds and removes cars from the inventory. The `Inventory-Service` in listing 4.35 defines two methods—one that sends an `InsertCarRequest` and one that sends a `RemoveCarRequest`. Both methods return a `CarResponse` message representing either the added or the removed car. Note that `Car` is renamed to `InsertCarRequest` and `CarResponse` for styling purposes. This is also convenient as it helps to prevent naming collisions with the code that we introduced in previous sections (e.g., listing 4.18).

Listing 4.35   The Inventory service contract in gRPC (`inventory.proto`)

```
syntax = "proto3";

option java_multiple_files = true;
option java_package = "org.acme.inventory.model";
option java_outer_classname = "InventoryProtos";

package inventory;

message InsertCarRequest {
    string licensePlateNumber = 1;
    string manufacturer = 2;
    string model = 3;
}
```

```
message RemoveCarRequest {
    string licensePlateNumber = 1;
}

message CarResponse {
    string licensePlateNumber = 1;
    string manufacturer = 2;
    string model = 3;
    int64 id = 4;
}

service InventoryService {
    rpc add(InsertCarRequest) returns (CarResponse) {}
    rpc remove(RemoveCarRequest) returns (CarResponse) {}
}
```

Note that we included the `id` field only in the response object but not in the request object (`InsertCarRequest`). IDs are automatically generated, so let's not allow the client to specify it.

The compilation process (`./mvnw clean package`) triggers the `quarkus-grpc` extension. The extension detects the proto file under `src/main/proto` directory and generates Java code under `target/generated-sources/grpc`.

The generated code includes Java classes for the protobuf messages `InsertCar-Request`, `RemoveCarRequest`, and `CarResponse`. It also includes a gRPC client and server stubs. The complete list of generated files can be seen in the output of the tree command available in the following listing.

> **Listing 4.36 The files generated from the proto file definition**

```
target/generated-sources/grpc
└── org
    └── acme
        └── inventory
            └── model
                ├── CarResponse.java
                ├── CarResponseOrBuilder.java
                ├── InsertCarRequest.java
                ├── InsertCarRequestOrBuilder.java
                ├── InventoryProtos.java
                ├── InventoryServiceBean.java
                ├── InventoryServiceClient.java
                ├── InventoryServiceGrpc.java
                ├── InventoryService.java
                ├── MutinyInventoryServiceGrpc.java
                ├── RemoveCarRequest.java
                └── RemoveCarRequestOrBuilder.java
```

If we compiled the proto file using the `protoc` compiler or any tool other than the `quarkus-grpc` extension, the generated code would be the same—with a minor exception. The `MutinyInventoryServiceGrpc` interface is unique to `quarkus-grpc`, and it

represents the `InventoryService` using the SmallRye Mutiny library (https://smallrye
.io/smallrye-mutiny/latest/). Mutiny is a reactive programming library extensively used
in Quarkus. In this case, Mutiny acts as a replacement for the `StreamObserver` API. The
`StreamObserver` API is what the `protoc` compiler uses by default. With Quarkus, it is
commonly replaced with Mutiny, as Mutiny provides a more straightforward API, and
using Mutiny types makes the code more consistent and compatible with what is used by
other Quarkus extensions. Don't worry if you don't understand all the details yet. Chapter 8 focuses on reactive programming and will explain Mutiny concepts in more detail.

4.8   *Implementing a gRPC service using Quarkus*

The `InventoryService` interface is the main point of interest in the generated code.
Implementing this interface is the only thing we need to do to expose the Inventory
service via gRPC. Let's take a closer look at this file. It contains one Java method per
RPC method in the proto file. In our case, it contains both methods for adding and
removing cars to and from the inventory, as shown in listing 4.37. Both methods
return a `Uni` of `CarResponse`. `Uni` (this type comes from Mutiny) represents a single
asynchronous action. It's a stream that emits a single item or a failure.

Listing 4.37   The generated gRPC `InventoryService` interface

```
package org.acme.inventory.model;

import io.quarkus.grpc.MutinyService;

@io.quarkus.grpc.common.Generated(                              The @Generated
    value = "by Mutiny Grpc generator",                         annotation states the
    comments = "Source: inventory.proto")                  ◁─┘ proto source file.
public interface InventoryService extends MutinyService {

    io.smallrye.mutiny.Uni<org.acme.inventory.model.CarResponse>
        add(org.acme.inventory.model.InsertCarRequest request);

    io.smallrye.mutiny.Uni<org.acme.inventory.model.CarResponse>
        remove(org.acme.inventory.model.RemoveCarRequest request);
}
```

Listing 4.38 demonstrates the implementation of the gRPC `InventoryService` provided in a new class `org.acme.inventory.grpc.GrpcInventoryService` that we need
to create in the Inventory service.

> **TIP** If your IDE cannot find the generated classes, you need to mark the
> `target/generated-sources/grpc` directory as sources (or generated sources).

Listing 4.38   Implementing the gRPC Inventory service

```
package org.acme.inventory.grpc;

...
```

```
@GrpcService
public class GrpcInventoryService implements InventoryService {

    @Inject
    CarInventory inventory;

    @Override
    public Uni<CarResponse> add(InsertCarRequest request) {
        Car car = new Car();
        car.licensePlateNumber = request.getLicensePlateNumber();
        car.manufacturer = request.getManufacturer();
        car.model = request.getModel();
        car.id = CarInventory.ids.incrementAndGet();
        Log.info("Persisting " + car);
        inventory.getCars().add(car);

        return Uni.createFrom().item(CarResponse.newBuilder()
            .setLicensePlateNumber(car.licensePlateNumber)
            .setManufacturer(car.manufacturer)
            .setModel(car.model)
            .setId(car.id)
            .build());
    }

    @Override
    public Uni<CarResponse> remove(RemoveCarRequest request) {
        Optional<Car> optionalCar = inventory.getCars().stream()
            .filter(car -> request.getLicensePlateNumber()
                .equals(car.licensePlateNumber))
            .findFirst();

        if (optionalCar.isPresent()) {
            Car removedCar = optionalCar.get();
            inventory.getCars().remove(removedCar);
            return Uni.createFrom().item(CarResponse.newBuilder()
                .setLicensePlateNumber(removedCar.licensePlateNumber)
                .setManufacturer(removedCar.manufacturer)
                .setModel(removedCar.model)
                .setId(removedCar.id)
                .build());
        }
        return Uni.createFrom().nullItem();
    }
}
```

The `@GrpcService` annotation tells Quarkus to manage this class as gRPC service. The class implements the `InventoryService` to provide gRPC operations. It injects the `CarInventory` (an example of field injection as opposed to the constructor injection we used before) to provide access to the data. Then we override the `add` method to implement the add car request handling, which inserts a car into the inventory and sends a response wrapped in Mutiny's `Uni`. The overridden `remove` method similarly removes a car from the inventory.

The `quarkus-grpc` extension takes care of managing the actual gRPC server, and thus no other code is needed. The gRPC service is ready to be used. The best way to try out the implementation is using the Dev mode. The gRPC server starts using port `9000`. It can be accessed using the command-line tools like `grpcurl` (https://github.com/fullstorydev/grpcurl) or the Quarkus Dev UI (http://localhost:8083/q/dev-ui). Since the Dev UI doesn't require us to install anything, we will focus on it for now. Now, a visible gRPC card appears on the main page of the Dev UI, as shown in figure 4.6.

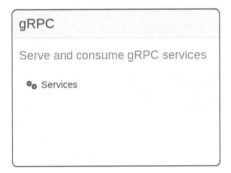

Figure 4.6   The gRPC card in the Dev UI of the Inventory service

The `Services` button takes you to the gRPC service table, which looks like the one shown in figure 4.7. The list contains a health endpoint `grpc.health.v1.Health` and our defined `inventory.InventoryService`. Each service has a button on the right side (it looks like an arrow pointing down), which opens the respective service test form.

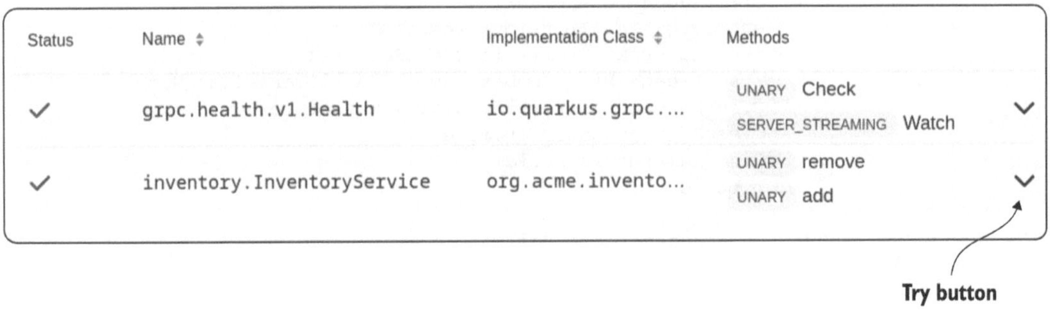

Status	Name ⇕	Implementation Class ⇕	Methods	
✓	`grpc.health.v1.Health`	`io.quarkus.grpc....`	UNARY Check SERVER_STREAMING Watch	⌄
✓	`inventory.InventoryService`	`org.acme.invento...`	UNARY remove UNARY add	⌄

Try button

Figure 4.7   Listing the available gRPC services

If we expand the test form of the `InventoryService` (figure 4.8), we can see that it contains tabs for selecting among all available operations—in our case, just between `add` and `remove`. The input text areas are prepopulated with a blank request messages. For instance, fill in the values for the `add` request and press the `Send` button. The car is now registered in the system.

```
✓        inventory.InventoryService      org.acme.invento...      UNARY  remove      ✓
                                                                  UNARY  add

   remove UNARY      add UNARY
   ─────
{                                              {
  "licensePlateNumber": "IJK123",               "licensePlateNumber": "IJK123",
  "manufacturer": "Mercedes",                   "manufacturer": "Mercedes",
  "model": "SL500"                              "model": "SL500",
}                                               "id": "1"
                                               }

   Reset      Send
```

Figure 4.8   Adding a new car over gRPC using the Dev UI

The in-memory list in the Inventory service now contains the newly persisted car. You can verify it using the GraphQL query returning all cars, as provided in listing 4.21.

The Dev UI makes it easy to try out the service and does not require implementing a client or using external tools like `grpcurl`. More importantly, all changes in the actual implementation take immediate effect, and you can test them without rebuilding and restarting the project. This includes changes to the actual proto file. We advise letting the Dev mode run through the next section to experience the added value of Dev mode firsthand.

4.8.1   Working with gRPC and streams

We just learned the steps of defining protobuf messages and gRPC services, adding gRPC support in the Quarkus project, and implementing a gRPC using a `Uni` to send back a response. To build on that, we can extend the support of the server to send back multiple responses. In this case, we need to prefix the message type in the proto file with the `stream` keyword.

In the same spirit, the client may stream multiple requests. To do that, we need to use the `stream` keyword with the input messages of the RPC methods.

So, we have four distinct classes of gRPC services based on their streaming capabilities:

- *Unary*—The client sends a single request, and the server responds with a single response.
- *Server streaming*—Server returning multiple responses per call.
- *Client streaming*—The client sends multiple requests per call.
- *Bidirectional streaming*—The client and server send multiple requests and responses, respectively.

When we work with a `stream` of gRPC messages, we need to use Mutiny's `Multi` as the input or output type wrapper (for instance, the `InsertCarRequest` message in our case). `Multi` is similar to `Uni` but is capable of emitting multiple (potentially infinitely many) items. Additionally, it emits a completion event to signal the end of the stream.

Let's convert the unary example of adding a new car we created in the Inventory service to bidirectional streaming so that we can add multiple cars over a single connection and directly see how our Quarkus application processes them in the responses. The first step is to update the proto file (`inventory.proto`) and add the `stream` keywords to the `add` method, as shown in listing 4.39.

> **WARNING**   Changing the proto file updates the generated interface in a way that the implementation will no longer compile against it. Quarkus Dev mode, at least in version 3.15, behaves in the way that a hot reload after changing the proto file will still pass, even though the application shouldn't be able to compile until you update the service implementation. If you encounter a compilation error, refer to listing 4.40 for the code updating the `GrpcInventoryService` implementation and restart the application.

Listing 4.39   Adding the stream keywords to the `add` method

```
rpc add(stream InsertCarRequest) returns (stream CarResponse) {}
```

Now simply refresh the Dev UI and see that the `add` method of the `InventoryService` now shows as bidirectional streaming. Figure 4.9 shows how the method is now labeled as `BIDI_STREAMING`.

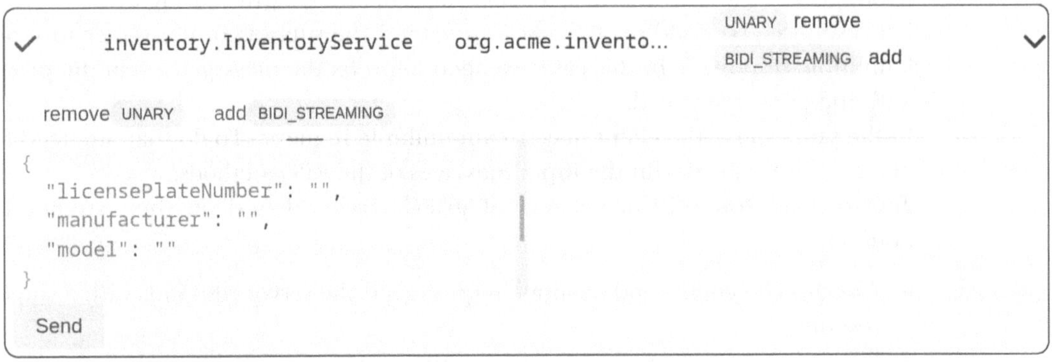

Figure 4.9   The `BIDI_STREAMING` version of the add gRPC method

The `Send` button will not work just yet, as the `GrpcInventoryService` service implementation needs to be aligned. If we pressed it now, we would get an exception.

It should be fairly easy to align the service implementation. We only have to change the implementation of the `add` method, as shown in listing 4.40. The `add` method now accepts a `Multi` of `InsertCarRequest` and produces a `Multi` of `CarResponse`. The implementation performs the same operations as the unary operation before on each `InventoryCarRequest`. First, it maps the received `InsertCarRequest` to the `Car` entity. Then it invokes the (in-memory) persist operation on each mapped car. Lastly, it maps the car to the `CarResponse` streamed back to the client. You can also compare it to the unary version in listing 4.38.

Listing 4.40   `GrpcInventoryService#add` with bidirectional streaming

```
@Override
public Multi<CarResponse> add(Multi<InsertCarRequest> requests) {      ←──────────┐
    return requests
        .map(request -> {
            Car car = new Car();
            car.licensePlateNumber = request.getLicensePlateNumber();
            car.manufacturer = request.getManufacturer();
            car.model = request.getModel();                       The add method
            car.id = CarInventory.ids.incrementAndGet();          accepts and
            return car;                                           produces types
        }).onItem().invoke(car -> {                               wrapped in
            Log.info("Persisting " + car);                        Multi as the
            inventory.getCars().add(car);                         InventoryService
        }).map(car -> CarResponse.newBuilder()                    was regenerated.
            .setLicensePlateNumber(car.licensePlateNumber)
            .setManufacturer(car.manufacturer)
            .setModel(car.model)
            .setId(car.id)
            .build());
}
```

With the implementation in place, our service Dev UI is back in the working state and we can experiment with it as shown in figure 4.10. Note that after adding the first car, a `Disconnect` button appears next to the `Send` button, allowing the client to stop sending requests (by disconnecting the connection). Send as many requests as you feel like and then click the `Disconnect` button. The car pops up in the response window with each sent car.

4.8.2   *Using a gRPC client with Quarkus*

Previous sections have taught you how to set up gRPC in Quarkus to generate code from proto files and implement services using gRPC. The last step is learning how to use Quarkus to consume gRPC services. This section focuses on writing gRPC clients with Quarkus.

In particular, this section consumes the Inventory service already exposed via gRPC through a simple CLI application. For example, we can utilize such an application for the out-of-bounds administration tasks of the Inventory service. All that is

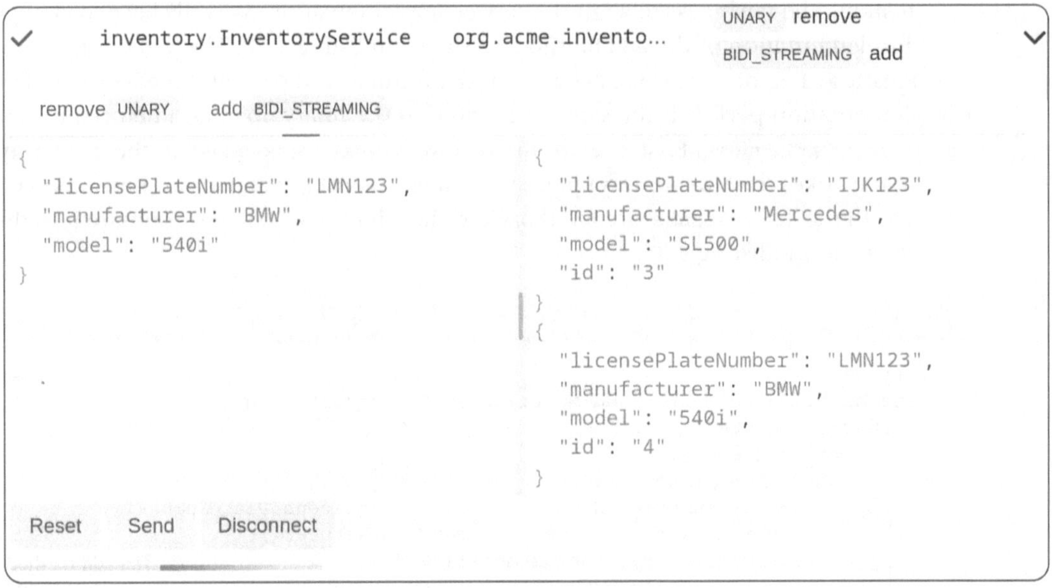

Figure 4.10   Adding multiple cars over a single connection

required is just a Quarkus project with the gRPC extension and the proto file that describes the contract of the exposed Inventory service. Let's start with a unary version of the service that is simpler to consume. We are going to need the unary version of the Inventory service proto file defined in listing 4.35.

Let's create a new `inventory-cli` application with the `grpc` extension. In the parent directory, you can execute the following command:

```
$ quarkus create app org.acme:inventory-cli -P 3.15.1 \
--extension grpc --no-code
```

We can copy the proto file directly from the previous example listing 4.35 to the `src/main/proto/inventory.proto` file. Before we proceed with the client code, we need to define the connection details. The host and port that expose the Inventory service can be specified in the `application.properties` with the addition of these two properties, respectively:

- `quarkus.grpc.clients.{client-name}.host`—The target server host.
- `quarkus.grpc.clients.{client-name}.port`—The target server port.

The `client-name` is the logical name of the client that we use as an identifier in case multiple clients are present. The `application.properties` excerpt in listing 4.41 contains the connection details of the Inventory service that you need to add to the `inventory-cli` configuration file. Note that the `client-name` in the configuration is `inventory`.

Listing 4.41   Configuring the gRPC client in the `inventory-cli`

```
quarkus.grpc.clients.inventory.host=localhost
quarkus.grpc.clients.inventory.port=9000
```

To consume the service, we just have to add the `@GrpcClient` annotation to a field that has one of the generated stubs as type. Listing 4.42 presents a new class, `org.acme` `.inventory.client.InventoryCommand`, which uses a `@GrpcClient` with the logical name `inventory`. The role of the name is to correlate between code and configuration. In this case, the client connects to `localhost:9000`, the host/port combination configured for the name `inventory` in the configuration file `application.properties`.

You probably remember that the result of the `InventoryService` operation is `Uni`, which represents an asynchronous computation. So we need to block our thread if we want the operation to complete before we return from CLI invocation with `await().indefinitely()`, which effectively makes it again a blocking call.

Listing 4.42   Consuming the gRPC service with `InventoryCommand`

```
package org.acme.inventory.client;

import io.quarkus.grpc.GrpcClient;

import org.acme.inventory.model.InsertCarRequest;          Specifies which client should
import org.acme.inventory.model.InventoryService;          be injected according to the
import org.acme.inventory.model.RemoveCarRequest;          configuration

public class InventoryCommand {
                                                           Selects the generated
                                                           service stub to use. In
    @GrpcClient("inventory")                      ◁──┐     our case, it is the
    InventoryService inventory;                   ◁──┘     InventoryService.

        public void add(String licensePlateNumber, String manufacturer,
                    String model) {
        inventory.add(InsertCarRequest.newBuilder()
            .setLicensePlateNumber(licensePlateNumber)
            .setManufacturer(manufacturer)
            .setModel(model)
            .build()
            .onItem().invoke(carResponse ->
                System.out.println("Inserted new car " + carResponse))
            .await().indefinitely();                       ◁──┐
    }                                                          Blocks the thread
                                                               until the operation
        public void remove(String licensePlateNumber) {        completes
        inventory.remove(RemoveCarRequest.newBuilder()
            .setLicensePlateNumber(licensePlateNumber)
            .build()
            .onItem().invoke(carResponse ->
                System.out.println("Removed car " + carResponse))
            .await().indefinitely();
```

```
        }
    }
```

The code in listing 4.42 is perfectly valid, but it does need an entry point to trigger the invocation of the add and remove methods. We need a way to batch-import cars in the inventory from CSV (comma-separated value) files, so let's expose the application as a command line tool. To do so, add the @QuarkusMain annotation to a class that implements the run method of the QuarkusApplication interface. This is all that we need to do, as shown in listing 4.43.

> **NOTE** We don't dive into the command-line applications in this book. But if you are interested in writing CLIs with Quarkus, you can find more information at https://quarkus.io/guides/command-mode-reference.

Listing 4.43 Consuming the gRPC service from the command line

```
package org.acme.inventory.client;

import io.quarkus.grpc.GrpcClient;

import io.quarkus.runtime.QuarkusApplication;
import io.quarkus.runtime.annotations.QuarkusMain;
import org.acme.inventory.model.InsertCarRequest;
import org.acme.inventory.model.InventoryService;
import org.acme.inventory.model.RemoveCarRequest;

@QuarkusMain
public class InventoryCommand
    implements QuarkusApplication {

    private static final String USAGE =
        "Usage: inventory <add>|<remove> " +
            "<license plate number> <manufacturer> <model>";

    @GrpcClient("inventory")
    InventoryService inventory;

    @Override
    public int run(String... args) {
        String action =
            args.length > 0 ? args[0] : null;
        if ("add".equals(action) && args.length >= 4) {
            add(args[1], args[2], args[3]);
            return 0;
        } else if ("remove".equals(action) && args.length >= 2) {
            remove(args[1]);
            return 0;
        }

        System.err.println(USAGE);
        return 1;
    }
```

Marks this class as the main class

Tells Quarkus that this is a Quarkus application

Overrides the main entry point for the Quarkus application

```
    public void add(String licensePlateNumber, String manufacturer,
                    String model) {
        inventory.add(InsertCarRequest.newBuilder()
            .setLicensePlateNumber(licensePlateNumber)
            .setManufacturer(manufacturer)
            .setModel(model)
            .build())
            .onItem().invoke(carResponse ->
                System.out.println("Inserted new car " + carResponse))
            .await().indefinitely();
    }

    public void remove(String licensePlateNumber) {
        inventory.remove(RemoveCarRequest.newBuilder()
            .setLicensePlateNumber(licensePlateNumber)
            .build())
            .onItem().invoke(carResponse ->
                System.out.println("Removed car " + carResponse))
            .await().indefinitely();
    }
}
```

Once built (`./mvnw clean package`), the tool can be used from the command line, as demonstrated in the following snippet. Don't forget to start the Inventory service if it's not already running, so the CLI has a server to connect to.

```
$ java -jar target/quarkus-app/quarkus-run.jar add KNIGHT Pontiac TransAM
```

When executed, the CLI client connects to the Inventory service acting as the gRPC server and inserts a new car. The CLI log prints the following message confirming that it inserted the car:

```
Inserted new car licensePlateNumber: "KNIGHT"
manufacturer: "Pontiac"
model: "TransAM"
```

We could also easily compile the `inventory-cli` application into a native image that we can utilize in various environments even without a JVM. Optionally, as an exercise, you can extend the `inventory-cli` application to support the bidirectional streaming of car additions, whose server side we implemented in section 4.8.1.

4.9 Next steps

In this chapter, we experimented with several communication protocols we can utilize in Quarkus applications. First, we introduced the REST protocol. As we learned, Quarkus integrates the JAX-RS specification through the Quarkus REST project. Next, we looked into the raising alternative called GraphQL that solves the over-fetching and under-fetching problems of REST. For GraphQL, Quarkus utilizes the MicroProfile GraphQL specification through the SmallRye GraphQL extensions. Lastly, we analyzed the gRPC support in Quarkus with the gRPC extension that generated stubs for our implementation utilizing asynchronous types from the SmallRye Mutiny project.

We also created the first services of the Acme Car Rental system—Reservation, Rental, and Inventory—utilizing the mentioned protocols for communications. We also developed an administration CLI application, `inventory-cli`, that acts as a command-line utility managing the car inventory in the Inventory service to which it connects through gRPC.

The subsequent chapters build on top of this base by providing various concepts that represent a requirement for communications handling in modern application deployments like security, testing, fault tolerance, etc.

Summary

- Quarkus makes it trivial to implement and also consume REST-based services.
- Quarkus uses the Quarkus REST project that implements the JAX-RS specification to support REST resources.
- The `smallrye-openapi` extension generates a Swagger API that describes REST resources present in an application and shows them as an HTML page that also allows testing them out directly in the browser.
- Consuming REST resources is possible in a typesafe way through an annotated interface.
- GraphQL is a great way to be more specific about the information a client is requesting from the server, limiting the size of data that travels through the network.
- GraphQL in Quarkus utilizes the MicroProfile GraphQL specification with additions from the SmallRye GraphQL project.
- Quarkus offers two separate GraphQL extensions—for the server and the client side.
- Server-side GraphQL support in Quarkus is provided using the code-first approach, where the developer provides the Java API, and Quarkus generates a schema out of it.
- gRPC is a protocol designed for dealing with the scaling of traditional HTTP-based communications.
- Quarkus simplifies the code generation process of gRPC-related services and manages the low-level gRPC code so users can focus on the business implementations.
- gRPC uses a serialization format named Protocol Buffers. Quarkus generates relevant classes from protobuf files provided by the developer.
- Apart from long-running server applications that listen for requests, it is possible to write command-line applications or executable scripts with Quarkus. This is achieved by creating an entry point class which implements `QuarkusApplication` that is annotated with the `@QuarkusMain` annotation.
- gRPC and GraphQL are both focused on minimizing the network usage, so they are a good fit for cloud deployments where billing is based on network traffic.

Testing Quarkus applications

This chapter covers

- Discovering how Quarkus testing integrates with JUnit
- Developing tests that can execute with a traditional JVM as well as a native binary
- Using testing profiles to run tests with different configurations
- Creating testing mocks of remote services

In chapter 3, we already discussed some aspects of Quarkus application testing, namely the ability to test them continuously using the Dev mode. We also experimented with the Dev Services, which is the ability to automatically run instances of services needed for testing, such as databases or message brokers.

In this chapter, we dive a bit deeper into the capabilities that Quarkus provides for the testing of your applications. We explain the integration of Quarkus with JUnit 5, learn how to execute tests in native mode easily, and how to use testing profiles to execute tests with different configurations in one go. We also look at the facilities for creating mocks of CDI beans that are not suitable to be used directly during test execution. All these features are neatly integrated into Quarkus. We're sure you'll get accustomed to them quickly, saving a lot of time, effort, and nerves compared to traditional testing approaches with different platforms.

For many software developers, writing and executing tests is just a necessary evil (perhaps just to satisfy some company policies). If this is your case, we hope Quarkus's continuous testing has already started changing your mind. Let's see whether we can go even further! For all the practical parts of this chapter, we will be enhancing the Reservation service developed in chapter 4.

5.1   Writing tests

To write tests for your applications, Quarkus comes with its lightweight testing framework based on the JUnit 5 library (https://junit.org/junit5/). This framework takes care of spinning up actual application instances under test and tearing them down after tests finish. Quarkus utilizes this same framework for testing both in JVM mode and in native mode. Most tests work in both modes without changes. Among the facilities that the testing framework offers to test developers are

- Injecting instances of the application's CDI beans directly into a test
- Injecting URLs of the application's endpoints so you don't have to build the URL manually to invoke it
- Integration with Mockito for creating mocks
- Ability to override beans from the application with another implementation
- Testing profiles so that different tests can run against a separate application instance with a different configuration
- Starting and shutting down various services that the application needs (in addition to the Dev Services discussed in chapter 3 and can be used for custom services that Dev Services do not support). This is possible by providing an implementation of the `QuarkusTestResourceLifecycleManager` interface.

NOTE Mocking and the ability to inject CDI beans from the application into the test are unavailable when testing in native mode. This is because while in JVM mode, the testing code runs in the same JVM as the application, native mode tests run as a JVM process communicating with a running prebuilt binary, so the processes are separated and have to communicate over remote protocols, such as HTTP. Application beans can still use CDI injection; this limitation only applies to injecting into the test case itself.

5.1.1   Writing a simple test for the Reservation repository

In this practical part, we develop `ReservationRepositoryTest`, a test inside the codebase of the Reservation service. This test intends to verify that the `InMemory-ReservationsRepository` can properly save a reservation and that it assigns an ID to it. For this test, we use a rather white-box approach that is directly injecting an instance of the `InMemoryReservationsRepository`, rather than communicating with it through a REST endpoint (`ReservationResource`).

One important note before we get to implementing the test: the Reservation service is set to bind to HTTP port 8081 (we added `quarkus.http.port=8081` into `application.properties`), but that's also the default port used by the testing instance during tests. When using Dev mode with continuous testing, these two instances run together and therefore they will clash. To mitigate this, set `quarkus.http.test-port=8181` in the `application.properties` configuration file of the Reservation service. It's also possible to set the port to 0. In that case, Quarkus automatically chooses any free port where the instance can be bound.

Let's create the test. Create a file named `ReservationRepositoryTest.java` inside the `src/test/java/org/acme/reservation` directory (note the `test`, as opposed to `main`), as shown in the following listing.

Listing 5.1 White-box testing of `ReservationsRepository`

```java
package org.acme.reservation;

import io.quarkus.test.junit.QuarkusTest;
import org.acme.reservation.reservation.Reservation;
import org.acme.reservation.reservation.ReservationsRepository;
import org.junit.jupiter.api.Assertions;
import org.junit.jupiter.api.Test;

import jakarta.inject.Inject;
import java.time.LocalDate;
import java.time.temporal.ChronoUnit;

@QuarkusTest
public class ReservationRepositoryTest {

    @Inject
    ReservationsRepository repository;

    @Test
    public void testCreateReservation() {
        Reservation reservation = new Reservation();
        reservation.startDay = LocalDate.now().plus(5, ChronoUnit.DAYS);
        reservation.endDay = LocalDate.now().plus(12, ChronoUnit.DAYS);
        reservation.carId = 384L;
        repository.save(reservation);

        Assertions.assertNotNull(reservation.id);
        Assertions.assertTrue(repository.findAll().contains(reservation));
    }
}
```

To ensure that the Quarkus application gets automatically started and makes all the testing facilities available (for example, CDI injection) we annotate this class with the `@QuarkusTest` annotation. Then we inject an instance of `ReservationsRepository` (which will resolve to the `InMemoryReservationsRepository` singleton in our case).

In the test, we create an instance of `Reservation`, set the reservation to start 5 days from now, end 12 days from now, and supply any car ID (the repository doesn't verify that such a car exists—we don't actually connect to the Inventory service here). Then we save the reservation in the repository and assert that the repository has assigned the reservation a non-null ID, and the repository now contains it.

To execute the test, you can either use the Dev mode and run it via continuous testing (you can enable it by pressing r in the terminal) or use the traditional Maven-based way, where you add a test and then execute it using `./mvnw test`. Both approaches should yield the same result.

NOTE   If your IDE supports running tests directly from the UI, this should generally work too. At a minimum, IntelliJ IDEA works fine.

5.2   *Native testing*

Because Quarkus offers a first-class integration with GraalVM and compiling into native binaries, this support naturally extends to testing as well. It is possible to run the same tests in JVM mode as well as native mode. In many cases, tests will continue working without changes when executed in native mode. There are a few caveats, though. As explained in the introduction to this chapter, mocking and CDI injection (into the test itself) are not supported in native mode tests.

Because native mode tests require compiling a full binary of the application, which takes a lot of time, they also aren't supported for continuous testing. To execute them, one has to execute a separate Maven or Gradle build.

For tests meant to run in native mode, we use the `@QuarkusIntegrationTest` annotation. Tests annotated with `@QuarkusIntegrationTest`, as opposed to `@QuarkusTest`, are executed against a prebuilt result of the Quarkus build, whether it is a JAR, container, or a native binary (remember, we already talked about this in chapter 2). This means that an integration test can also be run in JVM mode, but in that case, the same limitations as for native mode apply (no injection or mocks) because the test runs in a separate JVM from the application. For this reason, it's not very practical to use `@QuarkusIntegrationTest` with JVM mode, and thus integration tests are skipped by default in JVM mode if you generated your project using standard Quarkus tools like the CLI or Maven plugin; they get enabled only when the `native` profile is active. This is controlled by the `skipITs` property that is added to the project model with a default value of `true`. In most cases, the recommended pattern is to use `@QuarkusTest` for tests meant to be used in JVM mode and `@QuarkusIntegrationTest` for native mode, where the integration test case can inherit from a JVM test case and if some particular test methods are not compatible with native mode, they can be marked for skipping in native mode by `@DisabledOnIntegrationTest(forArtifactTypes = DisabledOnIntegrationTest.ArtifactType.NATIVE_BINARY)` annotation.

The diagram in figure 5.1 explains the difference between unit tests, integration tests, native mode, and JVM mode.

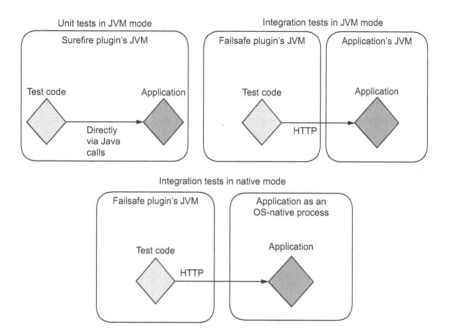

Figure 5.1 The difference between unit tests and integration tests in JVM and native mode

5.2.1 *Writing a test for the Reservation resource*

In this next part, we develop a test that can run both in JVM and native mode. We stick to the described pattern where we have a JVM test class annotated with @QuarkusTest and a test class for native mode that extends that class and is itself annotated with @QuarkusIntegrationTest. The class for the native test is empty and only inherits tests from the JVM test case. If the JVM test can run without changes in native mode, then nothing else is necessary.

In the previous section, we wrote a low-level test for the ReservationRepository, injecting it as a CDI bean. That's why that test can't work in native mode. To develop a test that can work in native mode, we need to go a level higher—we still interact with the ReservationRepository, but this time, it is through a REST endpoint, Reservation-Resource. The communication between the test code and the application under test runs over HTTP protocol. Functionally, the test is very similar, but it looks quite different due to the use of REST instead of CDI.

> **NOTE** As you may remember, methods of the ReservationResource end-point use a REST client and GraphQL client to connect to different services (Rental and Inventory). Our test avoids the need for that. The make method for creating a reservation calls the Rental service only if the starting day of the reservation is today, so we will avoid creating reservations starting today. The availability method needs a connection to the Inventory service, but this

test doesn't use that method. It will be the subject of the next section, where we will substitute the calls to the Inventory service with a mock.

When developing Quarkus tests that invoke REST (or any HTTP-based) endpoints, the *RestAssured* library is recommended, so we will do that. It's an API that significantly simplifies calling HTTP endpoints and verifying the expected results. The testing framework that comes with Quarkus also contains some built-in integration with RestAssured to make it easier to use; it automatically manages the target URLs, so you don't have to specify the URL of the server under test. The new test we're about to create, similar to the ReservationRepositoryTest, creates a reservation, submits it, and then verifies that everything went correctly—an ID was assigned to the reservation, etc.

Because we chose not to include any generated code when we created the Reservation service (the `--no-code` option), we didn't include the RestAssured library that would be present if any tests were generated. So we need to add this dependency into the `pom.xml` in the `reservation-service` directory manually, as demonstrated in the following snippet, before we can utilize this library in the `ReservationRepositoryTest`:

```
<dependency>
  <groupId>io.rest-assured</groupId>
  <artifactId>rest-assured</artifactId>
  <scope>test</scope>
</dependency>
```

The test source of the `org.acme.reservation.ReservationResourceTest` is shown in the following listing.

Listing 5.2   The source code of `ReservationResourceTest`

```
package org.acme.reservation;

import io.quarkus.test.common.http.TestHTTPEndpoint;
import io.quarkus.test.common.http.TestHTTPResource;
import io.quarkus.test.junit.QuarkusTest;
import io.restassured.RestAssured;
import io.restassured.http.ContentType;
import org.acme.reservation.reservation.Reservation;
import org.acme.reservation.rest.ReservationResource;
import org.junit.jupiter.api.Test;

import java.net.URL;
import java.time.LocalDate;

import static org.hamcrest.Matchers.notNullValue;

@QuarkusTest
public class ReservationResourceTest {

    @TestHTTPEndpoint(ReservationResource.class)
    @TestHTTPResource
    URL reservationResource;
```

```
    @Test
    public void testReservationIds() {
        Reservation reservation = new Reservation();
        reservation.carId = 12345L;
        reservation.startDay = LocalDate
            .parse("2025-03-20");
        reservation.endDay = LocalDate
            .parse("2025-03-29");
        RestAssured
            .given()
            .contentType(ContentType.JSON)
            .body(reservation)
            .when()
            .post(reservationResource)
            .then()
            .statusCode(200)
            .body("id", notNullValue());
    }
}
```

Using the `@TestHTTPEndpoint` annotation, we can inject the URL where a particular REST endpoint (in this case, `ReservationResource`) is available during the test run. Similarly to the `ReservationRepositoryTest`, we build an instance of a reservation that doesn't start today (so we don't try to call the Rental service). Then we make a RestAssured request (`RestAssured.given()`) that is converted to an HTTP POST request against the /reservation endpoint, passing our `Reservation` instance as the body in JSON format. Finally, because the response of the /reservation endpoint is a JSON representation of the reservation that we passed earlier, but with an ID already assigned, we verify that the ID did, in fact, get assigned.

Note that the URL injection via `@TestHTTPEndpoint` is not an injection in the CDI sense, so it also works in native mode. This injected URL can then be passed to the `RestAssured` invocations when building requests.

You might now similarly execute this test as in the previous section, either by running a complete test execution (`./mvnw test`) or by running continuous testing in Dev mode.

We have a test that works in JVM mode, so let's create the native mode counterpart. As explained earlier, we can achieve this by simply writing a class that extends the original test and is annotated with `@QuarkusIntegrationTest`. The following listing shows this test class. Let's create a new class, `ReservationResourceIT`, in the same package.

Listing 5.3 `ReservationResourceIT`: the test case that runs in native mode

```
package org.acme.reservation;

import io.quarkus.test.junit.QuarkusIntegrationTest;

@QuarkusIntegrationTest
public class ReservationResourceIT extends ReservationResourceTest {
}
```

Now, if you execute `./mvnw test`, only the JVM tests will run. To have native mode tests also execute, you have to execute `./mvnw verify -Pnative`, which activates the `native` profile. This instructs Quarkus to build a native binary as the build result and execute the `verify` goal, where the `failsafe` plugin picks up and executes integration tests, including our newly created `ReservationResourceIT`. The execution takes longer than usual because of the native binary compilation.

5.3 Mocking

Mocking is a technique used when you need to run a high-level test program that includes components that are not suitable for running in the test environment. This can be due to reasons like budgeting (for example, if a component sends SMS messages, which costs money, and you don't want to spend money on this while testing your product) or because the product needs to access something that is not available in the testing environment or simply for performance purposes, where you use a mock of a remote service to speed things up. The mocked service shouldn't constitute the main target that the test is supposed to verify because then your test would verify the functionality of a mock instead of the production code.

We are going to learn about two mocking approaches that Quarkus's testing framework offers—mocking with CDI beans and the Mockito framework. We also look at practical examples for both methods.

5.3.1 Mocking by replacing implementations

One approach to mocking is to override a CDI bean with another implementation. In CDI terms, this can be achieved by annotating the mock (the implementation that should be used during tests) by `@Alternative` along with `@Priority(1)` annotations. If such bean shares some bean types with the original bean, this ensures that injection points requesting these bean types receive an instance of the mock during tests. Quarkus further simplifies this approach by offering a built-in `@io.quarkus.test` `.Mock` annotation. This CDI stereotype applies the `@Alternative`, `@Priority(1)`, and `@Dependent` annotations when it's placed on a class to provide all required code in a single annotation that defines a mocked CDI bean.

For example, you could mock the `GraphQLInventoryClient` developed in chapter 4 with a bean as code, as in listing 5.4 and as a diagram, as in figure 5.2. Remember, this client is used to retrieve information about all cars from the Inventory service. The shown mock implementation returns a list containing a single hard-coded car. Note that this mock can be used to substitute any implementation of the `GraphQL-InventoryClient` interface, including the GraphQL-based implementation that is generated in the Reservation service.

Listing 5.4   Mock implementation of the `GraphQLInventoryClient`

```
@Mock
public class MockInventoryClient implements GraphQLInventoryClient {
```

```
    @Override
    public List<Car> allCars() {
        Car peugeot = new Car(1L, "ABC123", "Peugeot", "406");
        return List.of(peugeot);
    }
}
```

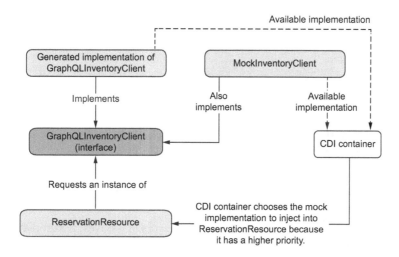

Figure 5.2   Mocking by replacing the implementation with a mock bean

It's enough to place this class somewhere in the sources for the tests (`src/test/java`), and it will be picked up automatically. If you feel like it, you can implement a test that uses this mock to verify that `ReservationResource` behaves correctly when `GraphQL-InventoryClient` returns a single car as an exercise.

> **WARNING**   This is just an example. We don't provide a practical exercise for this mocking approach. In the following section, we will instead use Mockito for mocking out the same bean, so if you added the `MockInventoryClient` to your project, you may have to remove it because it will conflict with the Mockito-based mock.

5.3.2   *Mocking with Mockito*

Another approach to mocking, as opposed to replacing bean implementations with different classes, is to use a mocking framework such as Mockito. *Mockito* offers a toolkit for building mock objects dynamically and defining what behavior they should exhibit when their methods are invoked.

> **NOTE**   Mocking with Mockito, as opposed to using CDI alternatives, is not limited to using only CDI beans. Any object can be replaced with a mock. When used with CDI, the bean has to be of a normal scope, which means `@Singleton` and `@Dependent` beans can't be mocked out (because Mockito

needs to use proxies for such beans, and these two scopes are non-proxyable). All other built-in CDI scopes will work.

Quarkus offers its integration with Mockito in the `io.quarkus:quarkus-junit5` `-mockito` Maven artifact. If you use Mockito in your tests, make sure you import this artifact (with a `test` scope) like this:

```
<dependency>
  <groupId>io.quarkus</groupId>
  <artifactId>quarkus-junit5-mockito</artifactId>
  <scope>test</scope>
</dependency>
```

MOCKING THE INVENTORY CLIENT USING MOCKITO

Let's now add another test for the Reservation service. This test is the most complex and high level of the three we're developing in this chapter. To reiterate, we have the following two tests now:

- `ReservationRepositoryTest#testCreateReservation()`—Saves a reservation into the reservation repository by directly injecting the reservation repository using CDI. This is a white-box test.
- `ReservationResourceTest#testReservationIds()`—Saves a reservation into the reservation repository by calling the `ReservationResource` REST endpoint. This is more of a black-box test. It also supports running in native mode.

The new test (`testMakingAReservationAndCheckAvailability`) that we are going to create in the `ReservationResourceTest` class will do the following:

- Call the `availability` method of the `ReservationResource` to get a list of all available cars for the requested date.
- Choose one of the cars (the first one) and make a reservation for the requested date.
- Call the `availability` method again with the same dates to verify that the car is not returned as available anymore.

We need mocking in this test because calling the `availability` method requires the `ReservationResource` to call the Inventory service. This is normally done with a GraphQL client (the interface `GraphQLInventoryClient`). But in our test, we don't assume that the Inventory service is available for calling. By replacing the GraphQL client with a mock, we ensure that a running Inventory service instance is not required for running the test.

If you also implemented the `MockInventoryClient` from the previous section, it needs to be removed for this test to work correctly, since it also overrides the same implementation that would conflict with the mock we create manually in this section.

> **NOTE** Of course, it is possible to design an integration test suite where multiple services are running simultaneously and can call each other. This is

generally complicated because it involves controlling various applications' life-cycles, resourcing requirements, etc. In this case, we decided to simplify and replace calls to the other service with a mock.

Listing 5.5 shows the relevant code. All this code should be added to the already existing `ReservationResourceTest`.

Listing 5.5 The `testMakingAReservationAndCheckAvailability` test

```java
@TestHTTPEndpoint(ReservationResource.class)
@TestHTTPResource("availability")
URL availability;

@DisabledOnIntegrationTest(forArtifactTypes =
        DisabledOnIntegrationTest.ArtifactType.NATIVE_BINARY)
@Test
public void testMakingAReservationAndCheckAvailability() {
    GraphQLInventoryClient mock =
        Mockito.mock(GraphQLInventoryClient.class);          ◁—— Creates the
    Car peugeot = new Car(1L, "ABC123", "Peugeot", "406");        mocked object
    Mockito.when(mock.allCars())
        .thenReturn(Collections.singletonList(peugeot));
    QuarkusMock.installMockForType(mock,
        GraphQLInventoryClient.class);

    String startDate = "2022-01-01";
    String endDate = "2022-01-10";
    // List available cars for our requested timeslot and choose one
    Car[] cars = RestAssured.given()
        .queryParam("startDate", startDate)
        .queryParam("endDate", endDate)
        .when().get(availability)
        .then().statusCode(200)
        .extract().as(Car[].class);
    Car car = cars[0];

    // Prepare a Reservation object
    Reservation reservation = new Reservation();
    reservation.carId = car.id;
    reservation.startDay = LocalDate.parse(startDate);
    reservation.endDay = LocalDate.parse(endDate);

    // Submit the reservation
    RestAssured.given()
        .contentType(ContentType.JSON)
        .body(reservation)
        .when().post(reservationResource)
        .then().statusCode(200)
        .body("carId", is(car.id.intValue()));

    // Verify that this car doesn't show as available anymore
    RestAssured.given()
        .queryParam("startDate", startDate)
        .queryParam("endDate", endDate)
```

```
        .when().get(availability)
        .then().statusCode(200)
        .body("findAll { car -> car.id == " + car.id + "}", hasSize(0));
}
```

First, we need to inject the URL of the /availability path under the root of the Reservation resource's path with the @TestHTTPResource and the @TestHTTPEndpoint annotations. Next, because we are using mocks in this test, we also need to mark it as skipped when running in native mode.

In the test itself, we create a mock object that implements the GraphQLInventory-Client interface, and we specify that when its allCars() method is called, it should return a hard-coded list of cars (containing only one car in our test). Then, we override the GraphQLInventoryClient CDI bean implementation with our mock in the QuarkusMock.installMockForType static method invocation.

Once we define the mock, we can proceed with the test. We call the availability method to retrieve the list of all available cars. This should return the single Peugeot we hardcoded into the mock of GraphQLInventoryClient. Then we create a reservation object for the returned car and submit this reservation request. The RestAssured invocation also verifies that the created reservation contains the correct carId field. Finally, we call the availability method again and verify that the car with our ID isn't returned anymore. We use a matcher to select from the list of returned cars and then assert that the selection returned an empty list (hasSize(0)).

If you're struggling with the static imports (because your IDE can't figure them out), they are also provided here for your convenience:

```
import static org.hamcrest.Matchers.hasSize;
import static org.hamcrest.Matchers.is;
import static org.hamcrest.Matchers.notNullValue;
```

5.4 Testing profiles

With the way we wrote tests until now, all tests execute against a single instance of the Quarkus application. This approach might not be optimal in all cases for two reasons. First, it might be hard to write the tests properly so that they are isolated and don't affect one another because a full cleanup of the state changes introduced by the test might not be practical or possible. The second reason is that it's impossible to test different configurations—all tests share the same application configuration. For these reasons, Quarkus offers testing profiles. These can be used to organize test cases into groups (profiles) where test cases belonging to the same profile are run together on the same Quarkus instance. That instance is then torn down and replaced by another instance for another test profile. While this increases the time needed to run the whole test suite, it gives the test developer a lot of flexibility.

A test profile can specify its own

- Base Quarkus configuration profile from which configuration values are taken
- Configuration properties overrides on top of the base configuration profile

- Enabled alternatives (beans with an `@Alternative` annotation that should override the original beans)
- `QuarkusTestResourceLifecycleManager` implementations (custom resources that should be started before the test and shut down when they are no longer needed)
- A set of tags (see following discussion)
- Command line parameters (only applicable when the test is a script with a `main` method)

A test profile may declare zero, one, or multiple tags, which allows the filtering of tests to be run in each testing execution. Tags are simple strings. When `quarkus.test .profile.tags` is defined (usually, you will pass it as a system property on the command line) when starting a test run, only those tests that have at least one tag listed by the property will be executed. For example, say test 1 has tags a and b and test 2 has tags b and c. If `quarkus.test.profile.tags` is b, then both tests will run. If the value is c,d, then only test 2 will run, and test 1 will be skipped because it doesn't declare any of the tags c or d. More details are in the Quarkus documentation at https:// mng.bz/5ga1.

A custom test profile is a user-defined implementation of the `io.quarkus.test .junit.QuarkusTestProfile` interface. This interface contains several methods that declare behavior related to the items listed in the previous list. All of them have default implementations, so you can override just the ones you need. A minimal example that only provides some tags and overrides some configuration properties is shown in the following listing.

Listing 5.6 An example implementation of the `QuarkusTestProfile`

```
import io.quarkus.test.junit.QuarkusTestProfile;

import java.util.Map;
import java.util.Set;

public class RunWithStaging implements QuarkusTestProfile {

    // use the staging instance of a remote service
    @Override
    public Map<String, String> getConfigOverrides() {
        return Map.of("path.to.service", "http://staging.service.com");
    }

    @Override
    public Set<String> tags() {
        return Set.of("staging");
    }
}
```

To mark a test to use a specific profile, you can use the `@TestProfile` annotation, as shown in the following listing.

Listing 5.7   Using `@TestProfile` to declare used test profile(s)

```
@QuarkusTest
@TestProfile(RunWithStaging.class)
public class StagingTest {

    @Test
    public void test() {
        // do something
    }
}
```

Given this declaration, the `StagingTest` will have the `path.to.service` property set when it runs. Furthermore, if the `quarkus.test.profile.tags` property is set, it has to contain the tag `staging` to enable this test; otherwise, it will be skipped.

5.5   Next steps

In this chapter, we explored the facilities that Quarkus offers related to testing. It's not only the ground-breaking continuous testing that we introduced in chapter 3. It's also a set of neatly integrated tools on top of JUnit 5 and GraalVM. We learned how to write tests that can be run in native mode out of the box, use CDI injection in tests, create mocks with Mockito, and split tests into isolated groups running with different setup and configuration values.

Now that we have covered the testing aspect, in the next chapter we will focus on another crucial and cross-cutting part of application development—security.

Summary

- Tests for Quarkus applications run both in JVM and in native mode.
- Native mode isn't supported for tests that use mocks or CDI injection into the test itself because the application under test runs in a different OS process than the testing logic.
- Quarkus is tightly integrated with Mockito to allow easy mocking of application classes.
- Mocking is achieved either by replacing a CDI bean with an alternative implementation or by describing the mock's behavior using Mockito DSL.
- Testing profiles organize tests into groups that run with a separate application instance and a potentially different configuration.
- Dev Services, the feature that automatically manages instances of databases, messaging brokers, etc., is supported during tests as well as when developing in Dev mode.

Exposing and securing web applications

6

This chapter covers

- Developing a basic secured web application with HTML
- Creating a more advanced HTMX-based UI
- Propagating the security context for calls between a web application and a REST service
- Exploring other alternatives for frontend development

In this chapter, we focus on two concepts: creating an HTML-based frontend for your application and securing it to require authentication. We already touched security with OIDC and Keycloak a little in chapter 3. We will now apply this concept to the car rental project.

Security, just like testing, is another aspect of software development that is often viewed as a boring but necessary evil and, thus, is often neglected in the early stages of a project. Properly securing an application is generally not an easy task. We will see how Quarkus addresses this and makes security as simple as possible while still providing a high level of flexibility. Changing most security aspects of a Quarkus application is often just a matter of changing a few configuration properties without having to update the code.

143

For the frontend development, Quarkus allows you to choose from many approaches and frameworks. There are pure Java solutions that try to minimize the need to write HTML and JavaScript (like Vaadin and its server-side rendering), but you can also use any framework that runs purely on the client side based on HTML and JavaScript files that you bundle into the application. In this chapter, we present just one of the many approaches that you can take. We will use *Qute* (pronounced as "cute"), a server-side templating engine, and *HTMX*, a client-side toolkit for building responsive web applications that greatly simplifies asynchronous communication with the backend services. While Qute is provided by Quarkus extension and is an integral first-class member of the Quarkus ecosystem, HTMX is a third-party JavaScript-based library completely independent of Quarkus. Nevertheless, we will see that these two frameworks work together very nicely.

> **NOTE** While security and frontend development are generally separate topics, we decided to combine them in this chapter for rather practical purposes because parts of our frontend will require security to be already set up.

The outcome of this chapter will be a new service called Users that exposes a simple HTML frontend allowing logged-in users to view their car reservations and available cars for given dates and create new reservations. Figure 6.1 depicts the architecture of what we will create in this chapter.

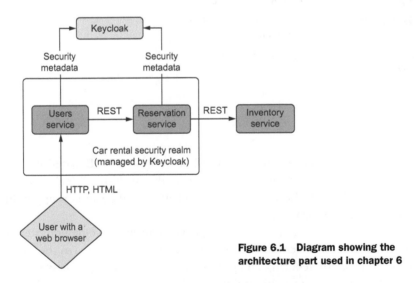

Figure 6.1   Diagram showing the architecture part used in chapter 6

In the practical parts of this chapter, we will use three services:

- The Users service, which we develop here from scratch.
- The Reservation service, which we already developed in chapters 4 and 5, but we will add security features to it now. When the Users service makes REST calls to Reservation service, it propagates the information about the currently logged-in

user (sometimes called "security context") along with these calls, so that the Reservation service knows who's logged in.
- The Inventory service, also developed in chapter 4. We won't make any changes to it now, but it has to be running because it is required by the Reservation service to be able to work with cars and reservations.

The frameworks that we will use for the frontend parts are

- *Qute*—A server-side templating engine designed mostly (but not only) for rendering HTML pages. It comes as a core Quarkus extension.
- *HTMX*—A client-side toolkit for building responsive web applications. It greatly simplifies asynchronous communication with the backend server, sometimes referred to as AJAX (Asynchronous JavaScript And XML). This is achieved by using special HTML elements, and in most cases, it removes or greatly reduces the need to write JavaScript code. It is a third-party open source library, not directly associated with Quarkus, but as you will see, it plays very nicely together with Qute.

Obviously, Qute and HTMX are not the only options you have for creating UI applications with Quarkus. If you're interested in seeing the alternatives, see the appendix C.

Before we actually create the frontend for working with reservations, we will first learn how to secure web applications by creating a very simple HTML page that shows the username of the logged-in user.

6.1 Creating a secured web application

Let's dive right in by creating a new project for the Users service. If you're using the Quarkus CLI, this is the command you will need:

```
$ quarkus create app org.acme:users-service -P 3.15.1 \
--extension qute,rest-qute,oidc,rest-client-jackson,\
quarkus-rest-client-oidc-token-propagation --no-code
```

We're using these extensions:

- `quarkus-qute`—A templating engine that we will use to generate the HTML content.
- `quarkus-rest-qute`—Allows templates processed by Qute to be exposed via a REST endpoint. We will create a REST endpoint that serves HTML resources and provides methods to asynchronously update their contents in the next section.
- `quarkus-oidc`—Used for the security mechanisms. Just as in chapter 3, Keycloak will be used as the OIDC provider.
- `quarkus-rest-client-jackson`—Because the Users service communicates with the REST API exposed by the Reservation service, we need the REST client extension.
- `quarkus-rest-client-oidc-token-propagation`—We need the `@AccessToken` annotation to propagate the OIDC ID token from the Users service to the Reservation service.

NOTE When you run the application in Dev mode, a Dev Services Keycloak instance will automatically start because we've added the `oidc` extension. We will use that for our security concerns later. For now, note that it will slow down the start of Dev mode a bit because the Keycloak container takes a few seconds to start. Live reload only reloads the application itself, though, so don't worry, it won't keep restarting the Keycloak container over and over when you apply changes to the application's code.

6.1.1   Creating a simple HTML page

We start by creating a very simple HTML page that shows the username of the currently logged-in user. Because the application doesn't have configured security just yet, the displayed username will be empty—we aren't required to log in, so the application is called anonymously. As the next step, we will configure the application to require authentication, so only then will the page actually show a username.

We're using the Qute engine to generate the web pages. Qute is a simple but powerful templating engine and comes as a Quarkus extension. It is most commonly used for generating HTML pages, but it's not limited to that. You may use it to generate any kind of document where you require the mixing of a template with injectable parameters. Of course, an example is the best way to show how it works, so let's create a file `src/main/resources/templates/whoami.html` in the `users-service` project, as shown in the following listing.

> **Listing 6.1   The Qute template used for the WhoAmI HTML webpage**

```
<!DOCTYPE html>
<html>
<head>
    <meta charset="UTF-8">
    <title>Who am I</title>
</head>
<body>
<p>Hello {name ?: 'anonymous'}!</p>
<a href="/logout">Log out</a>
</body>
</html>
```

The only Qute-specific part of this template is the `{name}` placeholder. It is replaced by the value of the `name` parameter. This parameter contains the username of the currently logged-in user (we will set this up next). We also specify the name's default value, `anonymous`, if the template doesn't receive any value for this parameter.

We also included a hyperlink that allows a logged-in user to log out. We will implement this functionality later.

To expose an HTML page generated from this template, we use a REST endpoint that produces the HTML content type and uses the `whoami.html` template to generate the output. This is achieved by using the newly created `org.acme.users.WhoAmI-Resource` class, as shown in listing 6.2.

Listing 6.2   The endpoint exposing the WhoAmI template as an HTML page

```
package org.acme.users;

import io.quarkus.qute.Template;
import io.quarkus.qute.TemplateInstance;
import jakarta.inject.Inject;
import jakarta.ws.rs.GET;
import jakarta.ws.rs.Path;
import jakarta.ws.rs.Produces;
import jakarta.ws.rs.core.MediaType;
import jakarta.ws.rs.core.SecurityContext;

@Path("/whoami")
public class WhoAmIResource {

    @Inject
    Template whoami;

    @Inject
    SecurityContext securityContext;

    @GET
    @Produces(MediaType.TEXT_HTML)
    public TemplateInstance get() {
        String userId = securityContext.getUserPrincipal() != null
            ? securityContext.getUserPrincipal().getName() : null;
        return whoami.data("name", userId);
    }
}
```

The `whoami` template injection is automatically matched to the `whoami.html` template based on its name. The injected `SecurityContext` allows us to see the metadata about the currently logged-in user.

The `get` method is a REST resource method that takes the `whoami` template, adds the necessary parameters to it (in this case, just the `name` parameter) and returns it. It is then passed to the `rest-qute` extension that takes the returned `TemplateInstance`, processes it and returns the resulting HTML document as the result of the REST method.

Notice that if there's no active user session, we pass `null` as the value of the `name` parameter, so the template will be rendered using the default value, `anonymous`. Of course, it is also an option to properly handle the default behavior here instead of delegating that to the template.

Now, supposing you have the `users-service` project running in Dev mode, you should be able to open http://localhost:8080/whoami in your browser. Because we don't have security set up yet, you won't be required to log in, and the resulting web page should say:

```
Hello anonymous!
```

The logout link is not usable for now, but we will get it working when we actually enable security for the application.

6.1.2 *Adding security to the application*

Now that we have a simple HTML page, it's time to secure the application so we can see an actual username on the WhoAmI page instead of just anonymous. As already mentioned, we will use Keycloak as the OIDC provider that handles all metadata about registered users. Quarkus will delegate to Keycloak for all authentication purposes. To make things simple, we use a Dev Services Keycloak instance. Remember that Dev Services is the feature of Quarkus that makes development much easier by managing instances of remote services like databases, messaging brokers, and (like in this case) Keycloak as an OIDC provider.

Normally, setting up security for applications is very complicated—when you manage your own Keycloak instance, you have to configure the security realm and manage the list of users. As we're focusing on development aspects in this book, we aim to make it as simple as possible by setting up a Keycloak instance very easily, thanks to Dev Services. This can't be used in production mode, so you will have to manage more things manually there.

One important aspect to note is that we will secure not only the Users service but also the Reservation service. This might sound complicated because you need to manage how both applications use the same Keycloak instance, right? Not really. With Dev Services, the managed Keycloak instance can be easily shared between multiple applications running simultaneously. With the right Dev Services configuration, when you run two or more applications in Dev mode that need a Keycloak instance, Quarkus can automatically create a single Keycloak instance (a single container) shared by all applications. Quarkus will normally boot up a Keycloak container when you start the first application in Dev mode. When you run the next application, it detects that there already is a shared Keycloak instance, and the application will wire itself up to that one instead of starting a new instance.

> **WARNING** With shared Dev Services Keycloak, the Keycloak instance is managed by the first application that started it, so if you stop that one, the Keycloak container will also be stopped, and the other applications using it might stop working properly.

Let's get to it. We already have the quarkus-oidc extension present in the Users service, so Keycloak should already get started and wired up (in Dev mode) properly, along with some sensible default settings for the security realm, so we probably don't need to configure Keycloak itself (but of course, it is possible to customize the Dev Services Keycloak instance via Quarkus configuration properties, if necessary). We will only configure the application. Add the lines in the following listing to the application.properties of the Users service.

Listing 6.3 Security-related configuration in the Users service

```
quarkus.http.auth.permission.all-resources.paths=/*
quarkus.http.auth.permission.all-resources.policy=authenticated
```

```
quarkus.oidc.application-type=web_app
quarkus.oidc.logout.path=/logout
```

Let's go over the individual properties:

- `quarkus.http.auth.permission.all-resources.paths=/*`—Denotes a collection of resource paths (in this case, `/*` means everything) that follow a common authentication policy.
- `quarkus.http.auth.permission.all-resources.policy=authenticated`—Sets the authentication policy for the resource collection.
- `quarkus.oidc.application-type=web_app`—Specifies the application type.
- `quarkus.oidc.logout.path=/logout`—Creates an endpoint that logs the user out (invalidates the active session when called).

Security configuration involves creating collections of resources that share a common authentication policy. In this case, we have only one collection, and we named it `all-resources`. The `paths` attribute is set to `/*`, and `policy` is set to `authenticated`, which means that access to all resources exposed by the application will require authentication. Anonymous access is forbidden. We could also specify more fine-grained policies, like requiring a user to have a specific role.

We choose `web_app` as the application type to say that the preferred authentication method is the so-called Authorization Code Flow, which means that Quarkus redirects any unauthenticated request to the Keycloak URL that allows the user to authenticate (and then the user is redirected back). The other possible type is `service`, which we would generally use for applications that are a set of HTTP (REST) resources rather than a web application; in this case, the preferred authentication mode would be using the `Authorization` HTTP header.

The `quarkus.oidc.logout.path` setting enables an endpoint on the `/logout` path that invalidates the authenticated session, logging the user out when invoked. If you remember the `/logout` hyperlink from the `whoami.html` template, this is exactly where it points.

Because we've changed the configuration of the Dev Services Keycloak for just this one time, we recommend restarting Dev mode completely rather than just letting it perform a live reload. That should make sure all changes are correctly applied. Now, if you refresh the http://localhost:8080/whoami webpage, you are redirected to a screen handled by Keycloak, which asks you to enter your credentials, as shown in figure 6.2.

A Dev Services Keycloak with default configuration contains a user named `alice` with the password `alice`. Enter this into the login form and click the `Sign In` button. If you log in successfully, Keycloak redirects you back to http://localhost:8080/whoami, but as a logged-in user. The page will say:

```
Hello alice!
```

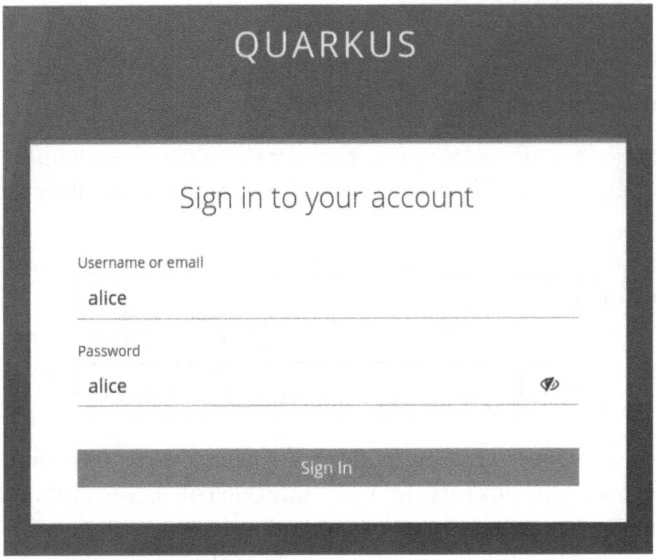

Figure 6.2   Keycloak login screen

NOTE   The default users (`alice` and `bob`) are present by default in a Keycloak instance that was spawned via Dev Services. This set of automatically added users is configurable through the configuration property called `quarkus` `.keycloak.devservices.users`. In production mode, where you would have to manage the instance manually, Keycloak doesn't contain any such users by default. Instead, it offers highly configurable features like user registration forms, activation of accounts through email verification, password resets, blocking existing accounts, etc. The specification of all features that Keycloak provides is out of the scope of this book.

The logout link also works now. You will get logged out if you click it, receiving a screen confirming that. We could specify a different URL where you get redirected after logout, but since all resources of this application require authentication, we don't really have any other reasonable page where to automatically redirect the user because none of them would work after logging out. To log in, manually navigate to http://localhost:8080/whoami in your browser again. This time, try logging in as another user with the included credentials out of the box. As you might have guessed, the username is `bob`, and the password is `bob`. The WhoAmI page should then say:

```
Hello bob!
```

WARNING   If you restart the Keycloak instance (for example, by stopping and restarting the whole Quarkus Dev mode, *not* just a live reload of the application) while you're logged in to the application in your browser, it might happen that after refreshing the page, the browser will again pass the original cookie that identifies the authenticated session but with a new Keycloak instance. This session is not valid anymore; thus, you will get an error (a blank page and a warning in the application's log). To avoid this, we suggest using the logout button before restarting Dev mode. If you don't, you might have to manually tell the browser to forget the `q_session` cookie or wait until the cookie expires (or open a new private window). Session cookies created in Dev mode are valid for 10 minutes by default.

6.2 Creating a UI for managing car reservations

The main goal of this chapter, as we already mentioned, is to create a very simple secured UI in the Users service that makes use of the Reservation service and allows authenticated users to manage their reservations. It allows logged-in users to view the list of reservations, see cars available for renting given a start and end date, and create a reservation by clicking a single button. The resulting application will look like the one in figure 6.3, and will have a header showing the name of the current user.

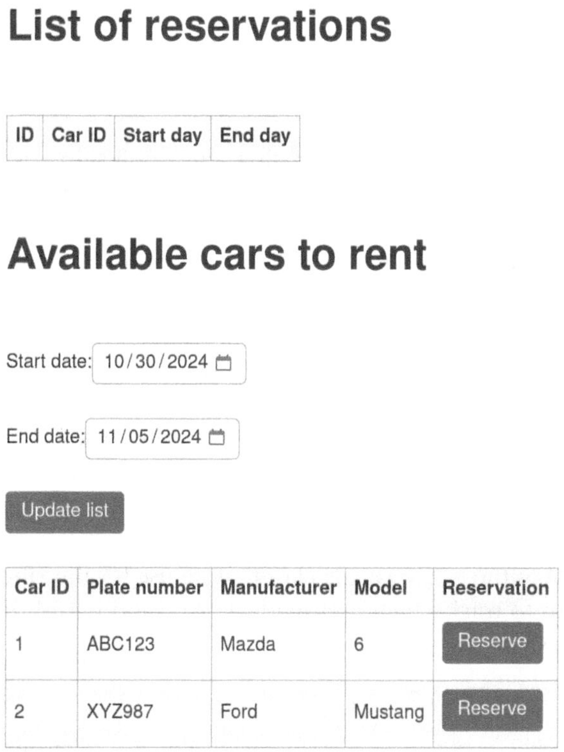

List of reservations

ID	Car ID	Start day	End day

Available cars to rent

Start date: 10/30/2024

End date: 11/05/2024

Update list

Car ID	Plate number	Manufacturer	Model	Reservation
1	ABC123	Mazda	6	Reserve
2	XYZ987	Ford	Mustang	Reserve

Figure 6.3   Reservation management page

Under the `List of reservations` header, there's a table that lists information about all reservations that the current user has made.

Under `Available cars to rent`, you can select a desired start and end date, and after clicking the `Update list` button, the table will be updated to show all cars that are available to be reserved on the selected dates. Each row in the table has a `Reserve` button that creates a reservation for this car and the start/end dates.

The application behaves as a single-page application. Clicking buttons does not lead to reloading the whole page. Instead, it dynamically updates parts of the DOM (Domain Object Model) based on responses to asynchronous HTTP requests. But don't worry, even though we're using asynchronous requests to the backend, we won't need to write a single line of JavaScript code.

6.2.1 *Updates to the Reservation service needed by the Users service*

Let's first enable security for the Reservation service. We make it use a shared Dev Services Keycloak instance together with the Users service when developing both applications on the same machine in Dev mode. Find the directory with the Reservation service project. We need to add the `quarkus-oidc` extension, so either add it into the `pom.xml` manually or use the easier way and execute this CLI command (in the root directory of the `reservation-service` project):

```
quarkus ext add oidc
```

Add the following configuration to the project's `application.properties`:

```
quarkus.oidc.application-type=service
```

`quarkus.oidc.application-type=service` means that the application is a set of RESTful HTTP resources, so the preferred authentication method is the use of the `Authorization` HTTP header rather than a browser cookie.

For simplicity's sake, in this case, we didn't make the authentication mandatory (we did that in the Users service), so there are no `quarkus.http.auth.permission.*` properties. We develop the Reservation service in a way that allows anonymous access. If there is no `Authorization` header on incoming requests, access will be allowed, but the security context will be empty. Thanks to this simplification, you can still call the service's REST endpoints without obtaining and passing an authentication token.

Now that we have set up security for the Reservation service, we can finish some of the things we originally replaced with dummy values inside the `ReservationResource` endpoint.

First, let's add the user ID to the `Reservation` class that we use for the (in-memory) persistence. This will allow us to track which user made a reservation. Add the `userId` field to the `Reservation` class (we use `String` type):

```
public String userId;
```

Let's now focus on the `ReservationResource`. Somewhere at the beginning of the class, inject an instance of `SecurityContext` so that we can access information about the logged-in user:

```
@Inject
jakarta.ws.rs.core.SecurityContext context;
```

> **NOTE** Notice that in CDI, we can mix the field injection that we use for `SecurityContext` together with the constructor injections from chapter 4.

Change the `make` method (it serves to create new reservations) so that it retrieves the current user's name and stores it in the object representing the reservation.

Listing 6.4 Updating the `make` method to include current user's name

```
@Consumes(MediaType.APPLICATION_JSON)
    @POST
    public Reservation make(Reservation reservation) {
        reservation.userId = context.getUserPrincipal() != null ?
            context.getUserPrincipal().getName() : "anonymous";
        Reservation result = reservationsRepository.save(reservation);
        if (reservation.startDay.equals(LocalDate.now())) {
            Rental rental = rentalClient.start(reservation.userId, result.id);
            Log.info("Successfully started rental " + rental);
        }
        return result;
    }
```

We either retrieve the current user's name or set the name to `anonymous` if there's no logged-in user. Either way, we proceed with the reservation.

The UI in the Users service will also be able to list all reservations belonging to the logged-in user, so we need a way to ask the Reservation service for this list. Add the code in the following listing to the `ReservationResource` as a new method.

Listing 6.5 Listing all reservations belonging to the current user

```
@GET
@Path("all")
public Collection<Reservation> allReservations() {
    String userId = context.getUserPrincipal() != null ?
        context.getUserPrincipal().getName() : null;
    return reservationsRepository.findAll()
        .stream()
        .filter(reservation -> userId == null ||
            userId.equals(reservation.userId))
        .collect(Collectors.toList());
}
```

Remember that the `userId` is `null` when no user is logged in. When we filter all reservations to pick the ones belonging to the current user, in this case, we include all reservations in the result (due to the `userId == null` condition). If there's a user logged in, we only include reservations where the `userId` matches the current user.

Now that the Reservation service is secured, it has everything our frontend application needs. Let's next create the actual frontend that manages reservations for users.

6.2.2 Preparing backend parts in the Users service to be used by the UI

The UI in the Users service will need to call the REST endpoints of the Reservation service and also propagate the security credentials of the logged-in user into these calls. The two domain model classes that we need to use are `Car` and `Reservation`, so let's create simplified copies of them in the Users service. In the Users service, create the class `org.acme.users.model.Car`.

Listing 6.6   The `Car` class needed by the Users service

```
package org.acme.users.model;

public class Car {
    public Long id;
    public String licensePlateNumber;
    public String manufacturer;
    public String model;
}
```

And similarly, we create `org.acme.users.model.Reservation`.

Listing 6.7   The `Reservation` class needed by the Users service

```
package org.acme.users.model;

import java.time.LocalDate;

public class Reservation {
    public Long id;
    public String userId;
    public Long carId;
    public LocalDate startDay;
    public LocalDate endDay;
}
```

Again, if you prefer private fields with getters and setters, feel free to use them instead of public fields. It's a matter of taste.

Next, create the interface for the REST client that calls the Reservation service. We saw a REST client interface before in chapter 4, so this should be familiar. The `@AccessToken` annotation is the only new concept in this interface. The REST client is represented by the `org.acme.users.ReservationsClient` class.

Listing 6.8   The `ReservationsClient` class

```
package org.acme.users;

import io.quarkus.oidc.token.propagation.AccessToken;
import org.acme.users.model.Car;
import org.acme.users.model.Reservation;
import org.eclipse.microprofile.rest.client.inject.RegisterRestClient;
import org.jboss.resteasy.reactive.RestQuery;

import jakarta.ws.rs.GET;
import jakarta.ws.rs.POST;
import jakarta.ws.rs.Path;
import java.time.LocalDate;
import java.util.Collection;
```

```
@RegisterRestClient(baseUri = "http://localhost:8081")
@AccessToken                                              ◁─────
@Path("reservation")
public interface ReservationsClient {

    @GET
    @Path("all")
    Collection<Reservation> allReservations();

    @POST
    Reservation make(Reservation reservation);

    @GET
    @Path("availability")
    Collection<Car> availability(
        @RestQuery LocalDate startDate,
        @RestQuery LocalDate endDate);
}
```

> Ensures that the current user's ID token propagates to all calls made by this REST client. It works by adding the token to the Authorization HTTP header.

If you need to refresh your memory on the actual API and implementation of the REST endpoints that we're calling here, go back to the Reservation service and check out the `ReservationResource` class.

6.2.3   Creating the UI using Qute, HTMX, and a REST backend

Now we are ready to create our user interface in the Users service. Let's start with HTMX.

ABOUT HTMX

HTMX is a client-side toolkit for building responsive web applications. Its main goal is to simplify asynchronous communication with the backend server and provide dynamic updates of the pages' contents. Doing this usually requires writing JavaScript code. But HTMX achieves this declaratively with unique HTML attributes. In simpler cases, you won't need to write your own JavaScript at all. The following listing shows a simple example.

Listing 6.9   A simple example of HTMX usage

```
<script src="https://unpkg.com/htmx.org@1.8.4"></script>
<button hx-get="/click" hx-swap="innerHTML" hx-target="#greeting">
    Greet me
</button>
<div id="greeting">
</div>
```

With this piece of pure HTML, you get a `button` and a `div`. When the user clicks the button, HTMX sends an HTTP GET request to the backend server's `/click` endpoint. Then the contents of the `div` element (with the ID `greeting`, as denoted by the `hx-target` attribute) are replaced by the response's body. No JavaScript code is required.

HTMX is a third-party library, so it isn't associated with Quarkus. Nevertheless, some parts of the Qute engine's design were influenced by HTMX to make them work nicely together. More information about HTMX can be found at https://htmx.org.

CREATING TEMPLATES USING QUTE+HTMX AND SERVING THEM

The reservation management page that we're about to create consists of three parts:

- A header containing a title, the current user's name, and a logout button
- A table with all reservations that belong to the logged-in user
- A table listing all cars that are available to rent for the selected dates, and two fields to allow the selection of the start and end dates

Let's create the Qute templates necessary for this page. We use the plural form because we have separate templates for specific parts of the page. Because the most common and basic usage of HTMX, as we just showed in the previous section, is to dynamically replace contents of HTML elements with different HTML content received from the backend server, we create a separate Qute template for each case where we do such upgrades. Namely, we need a template for the following:

- The main page itself (`index.html`).
- Table listing the reservations (`listofreservations.html`).
- Table listing the cars that are available for selected dates (`availablecars.html`).

For each of these templates, we create a REST method that renders a page from that template.

Let's start by implementing the index page. In the `users-service` project, create the new file `index.html` in the `src/main/resources/templates/ReservationsResource` directory. For now, it only contains the header with the username and a logout button, as shown in the following listing.

Listing 6.10   Initial version of the reservation management page

```
{@java.lang.String name}
{@java.time.LocalDate startDate}
{@java.time.LocalDate endDate}

<!DOCTYPE html>
<html>
<head>
  <meta charset="UTF-8">
  <title>Reservations</title>
  <link rel="stylesheet" href="https://cdn.simplecss.org/simple.min.css">
  <script src="https://unpkg.com/htmx.org@1.7.0">
  </script>
</head>
<body>

<header>
  <h1>Reservations</h1>
```

```
<p>For logged-in user: {name}</p>
<a href="/logout">Log out</a>
</header>

</body>
</html>
```

◄ ────┐ The header includes the
      │ name parameter (name
      │ of the logged-in user)
      │ and a logout link.

The first three lines are optional. They constitute a declaration of the parameters this page requires to render, along with their types. If you provide these declarations, the Qute templating engine does its best to ensure the type safety of the template. It also throws an error at build time in the case of the incorrect use of any parameter (for example, if you refer to an attribute that doesn't exist in the class of the parameter). Our page takes three parameters: username and the initial start and end dates (these can be overridden later by the user form). They are used to filter available cars and to create a reservation.

Now we need a REST endpoint that serves this template. In the Users service, create the `ReservationsResource` class in the `org.acme.users` package, as shown in the following listing.

> **Listing 6.11 The REST resource serving the `index.html` page**

```
package org.acme.users;

import io.quarkus.qute.CheckedTemplate;
import io.quarkus.qute.TemplateInstance;
import org.eclipse.microprofile.rest.client.inject.RestClient;
import org.jboss.resteasy.reactive.RestQuery;

import jakarta.inject.Inject;
import jakarta.ws.rs.GET;
import jakarta.ws.rs.Path;
import jakarta.ws.rs.Produces;
import jakarta.ws.rs.core.MediaType;
import jakarta.ws.rs.core.SecurityContext;
import java.time.LocalDate;

@Path("/")
public class ReservationsResource {

    @CheckedTemplate
    public static class Templates {
        public static native TemplateInstance index(
            LocalDate startDate,
            LocalDate endDate,
            String name);
    }

    @Inject
    SecurityContext securityContext;

    @RestClient
    ReservationsClient client;
```

```
@GET
@Produces(MediaType.TEXT_HTML)
public TemplateInstance index(@RestQuery LocalDate startDate,
                              @RestQuery LocalDate endDate) {
    if (startDate == null) {
        startDate = LocalDate.now().plusDays(1L);
    }
    if (endDate == null) {
        endDate = LocalDate.now().plusDays(7);
    }
    return Templates.index(startDate, endDate,
        securityContext.getUserPrincipal().getName());
}
}
```

In this example, we decided to use a slightly different approach to work with templates: checked templates. When you declare a template inside a static class annotated with `@CheckedTemplate`, Qute performs type-safety checks on the template usage during build time. As you can see, instead of passing parameters to the template using the `data` method (which we did in the WhoAmI example), you can declare the template's parameters in a type-safe way as parameters of the method that returns an instance of the template. A method that wants to serve this template can now build an instance of it by calling `Templates.index(parameters…)`. The `index` in the method name corresponds to the name of the template file (`index.html`).

> **NOTE** By default, the template locator looks for a template file with name exactly matching the method name. If you prefer to use underscores or hyphens in the template file names for better readability, you can change the locator strategy by specifying the `defaultName` parameter of the `@CheckedTemplate` annotation. For example, with `defaultName = CheckedTemplate.UNDERSCORED_ELEMENT_NAME`, a method named `indexPage` would look for a template file named `index_page.html`.

The `startDate` and `endDate` parameters are considered optional. If no values are provided, we assume that we're looking for available cars for the timeslot starting tomorrow and ending seven days from today.

With this code in place and Dev mode (of the Users service) running, you may now navigate to http://localhost:8080 to verify that we're on the right track. The page redirects you to the Keycloak instance, which asks you to provide credentials. Remember that it's either `alice` or `bob`, with the password being the same as the username. The page you see after successful login looks like figure 6.4. There is just the header for now. The rest of the page is blank.

Reservations

For logged-in user: alice

Log out

Figure 6.4   Header of the reservation management page

The next step is to list available cars for particular dates, along with the button to create a reservation for the selected car and dates immediately. For that, we need a new template. In the `src/main/resources/templates/ReservationsResource` directory, create a new file `availablecars.html`.

Listing 6.12 Template for the table of available cars

```
{@org.acme.users.model.Car[] cars}              ◁────   For the type-safety checks, declares
{@java.time.LocalDate startDate}                        that the cars parameter is a
{@java.time.LocalDate endDate}                          collection of Car instances
<div id="carlist">
<table>
  <thead>
  <tr>
    <th>Car ID</th>
    <th>Plate number</th>
    <th>Manufacturer</th>
    <th>Model</th>
    <th>Reservation</th>
  </tr>
  </thead>                                        A for loop over the collection of
{#for car in cars}                      ◁────    cars. For each car, we generate
    <tr>                                          an HTML form and a button that
    <td>{car.id}</td>                             creates a reservation.
    <td>{car.licensePlateNumber}</td>
    <td>{car.manufacturer}</td>
    <td>{car.model}</td>                          Defines the action taken upon
    <td>                                          submitting the form—an HTTP
      <form hx-target="#reservations"    ◁────    POST request to /reserve
            hx-post="/reserve">
        <input type="hidden" name="startDate" value="{startDate}"/>
        <input type="hidden" name="endDate" value="{endDate}"/>
        <input type="hidden" name="carId" value="{car.id}"/>
        <input type="submit" value="Reserve"/>
      </form>
    </td>
    </tr>
{/for}
</table>
</div>
```

The `hx-post` attribute on a `<form>` element means that when the user clicks the `Reserve` button, the page sends an HTTP POST request to the specified endpoint (`/reserve`; we will create the actual handling method later). It also adds all values of the form to the request as parameters. In this case, the parameters are all data necessary for creating a new reservation. The `hx-target="#reservations"` attribute specifies that the contents of the response to such request should replace the HTML element with ID `reservations`. Again, we will create this element later; it immediately updates the list of existing reservations after we make a new one.

Now, to show this table of available cars, add a reference to it into `index.html`, along with the simple form that allows you to select the start and end dates for reservations.

The code is in listing 6.13. Place it somewhere inside the `<body>` element, after the end of the `</header>` element.

Listing 6.13   Including the list of available cars in the index page

```
<h2>Available cars to rent</h2>
<form hx-get="/available" hx-target="#availability">
  <p>Start date:<input id="startDateInput" type="date"
                   name="startDate" value="{startDate}"/></p>
  <p>End date:<input id="endDateInput" type="date"
                   name="endDate" value="{endDate}"/></p>
  <input type="submit" value="Update list"/>
</form>
<div id="availability" hx-get="/available"
     hx-trigger="load, update-available-cars-list from:body"
     hx-include="[id='startDateInput'],[id='endDateInput']">
  <!-- To be replaced by the result of calling /available -->
</div>
```

The div that the availablecars.html template populates

The first half of this listing is the form that allows users to select the start and end dates for reservations. The initial value of these two inputs will be the `startDate` and `endDate` parameters passed to the template, but the users can change these values. The `hx-get="/available"` attribute means that when the form is submitted, a GET request is sent to the `/available` endpoint, along with all values from this form as parameters. `hx-target="#availability"` means that when a response is received, the response's body will replace the contents of the element with ID `availability`, not this `<form>` element itself. When the user selects the start and end dates and then clicks the `Update list` button, the page requests a list of cars available in that date range and updates the available cars' table with the received data.

The second part is the table of available cars, populated by the `availablecars.html` template. The `availability` div needs to update its contents in response to three different events. The first is loading the page. We want the table to appear automatically when the page loads in the browser. This triggers the built-in event named `load`, which is why we include `hx-trigger="load"`. The second event is when the user makes a new reservation. We use a custom event named `update-available-cars-list` for that, and we add it to the `hx-trigger` list. We will explain how to trigger this event later. We also have to add a `from:body` modifier to make it work properly (HTMX requirement). The third event triggers a reload of this div when the user submits the form with start and end dates. We already took care of this by the `hx-target="#availability"` attribute in the form element.

When we ask the system for a list of available cars, we need to include the `startDate` and `endDate` parameters in the GET request. The form picks the values from these inputs with IDs `startDateInput` and `endDateInput`. The `hx-include` attribute ensures that the current value of these inputs is included in the request when the user refreshes the table. Careful, we don't want to use the `{startDate}` and `{endDate}` (Qute) parameters of the `index.html` template. These are only the initial values that Qute uses when first rendering the page. If we did, we would ignore potential form updates performed by the user.

Next, we need the template with a table of all reservations. This needs to be in a file named `listofreservations.html` that, similar to the other templates, resides inside the `src/main/resources/templates/ReservationsResource/` directory.

Listing 6.14   Template for showing the list of reservations

```
{@org.acme.users.model.Reservation[] reservations}
<div id="listofreservations">
<table>
  <thead>
  <tr>
    <th>ID</th>
    <th>Car ID</th>
    <th>Start day</th>
    <th>End day</th>
  </tr>
  </thead>
  {#for i in reservations}
    <tr>
    <td>{i.id}</td>
    <td>{i.carId}</td>
    <td>{i.startDay}</td>
    <td>{i.endDay}</td>
    </tr>
  {/for}
</table>
</div>
```

To include this table in the index page, add the code from listing 6.15 to `index.html`. Put it after the end of the `</header>` element containing the logout link.

Listing 6.15   Including the list of reservations in the index page

```
<h2>List of reservations</h2>
<div id="reservations" hx-get="/get" hx-trigger="load">
<!-- To be replaced by the result of calling /get -->
</div>
```

We trigger an update of the `reservations` div as a response to the `load` event to make sure it renders on page load. The other event triggering a refresh of this table is when the user makes a new reservation. You might remember that back in `availablecars.html`, we generated a form for each available car, and the `hx-target` of that form had the value `#reservations` (see listing 6.12), meaning that when the form is submitted (the user makes a reservation request), it will trigger an update of the reservation list.

Now, we need to implement the REST methods for serving the remaining templates and handling the creation of new reservations:

- getReservations—Exposed at the /get endpoint; returns an instance of the listofreservations.html with the list of all the current user's reservations.
- getAvailableCars—Exposed at the /available endpoint; returns an instance of the availablecars.html template. It takes startDate and endDate parameters to narrow down the results.
- create—Exposed at the /reserve endpoint; creates a new reservation and returns the updated list of reservations (the listofreservations.html template), already including the new reservation. It takes the startDate, endDate and carId parameters.

But before we implement these methods, we also need to add factory methods to be able to instantiate the remaining two templates. Remember that we added the listofreservations.html template that takes a collection of reservations and the availablecars.html template that takes a collection of cars, start date, and end date. Update the Templates class (nested inside ReservationsResource) as shown in the following listing.

> **Listing 6.16 Building template instances with type safety**

```
@CheckedTemplate
public static class Templates {
    public static native TemplateInstance index(
                LocalDate startDate,
                LocalDate endDate,
                String name);

    public static native TemplateInstance listofreservations(
                Collection<Reservation> reservations);

    public static native TemplateInstance availablecars(
                Collection<Car> cars,
                LocalDate startDate,
                LocalDate endDate);
}
```

Now add the three mentioned REST methods to the ReservationsResource class, as per the following listing.

> **Listing 6.17 Remaining necessary REST methods to serve all templates**

```
@GET
@Produces(MediaType.TEXT_HTML)
@Path("/get")
public TemplateInstance getReservations() {
    Collection<Reservation> reservationCollection
        = client.allReservations();
    return Templates.listofreservations(reservationCollection);
}
```

```
@GET
@Produces(MediaType.TEXT_HTML)
@Path("/available")
public TemplateInstance getAvailableCars(
        @RestQuery LocalDate startDate,
        @RestQuery LocalDate endDate) {
    Collection<Car> availableCars
        = client.availability(startDate, endDate);
    return Templates.availablecars(
        availableCars, startDate, endDate);
}


@POST
@Produces(MediaType.TEXT_HTML)
@Path("/reserve")
public RestResponse<TemplateInstance> create(
        @RestForm LocalDate startDate,
        @RestForm LocalDate endDate,
        @RestForm Long carId) {
    Reservation reservation = new Reservation();
    reservation.startDay = startDate;
    reservation.endDay = endDate;
    reservation.carId = carId;
    client.make(reservation);
    return RestResponse.ResponseBuilder
        .ok(getReservations())
        .header("HX-Trigger-After-Swap",
            "update-available-cars-list")
        .build();
}
```

> Triggers a custom
> event with the
> HX-specific header

The only new concept here is that we want to trigger a custom event named `update -available-cars-list` when the user creates a new reservation. The call to `/reserve` itself only updates the reservations table (remember the `hx-target="#reservations"` attribute inside `availablecars.html`). Still, we also need to update available cars because, after a successful reservation, that car is no longer available. We trigger this event by adding an `HX-Trigger-After-Swap` HTTP header to the response. This means that after the response is received and the reservations table is updated, we also trigger an update of the list of available cars. This links to the `update-available-cars-list` value inside a `hx-trigger` in `index.html`. Of course, you could think of potentially better solutions than this because, typically, you would want to update both tables simultaneously, whereas here, the table of available cars updates asynchronously after the update of the reservations table. So, it would also be possible to have just one template for both tables and have this REST method return it. Also note that to be able to add headers to the response, we had to wrap the return type in a `RestResponse` and use the `ResponseBuilder` to build the response that contains both the necessary `TemplateInstance` and the header.

6.2.4   *Trying the application*

And that's it. Now let's try it out. Make sure you have all three necessary services running:

- *Users service on* `localhost:8080`—It has to run in Dev mode for now because we didn't set up a Keycloak instance except for the one provided to us by Dev Services.
- *Reservation service (the secured version) on* `localhost:8081`—It also needs to run in Dev mode because it shares a Keycloak instance with the Users service.
- *Inventory service on* `localhost:8083`—It can run in either Dev mode or production mode.

> **NOTE** If you are going to create reservations that start on the current date, you will also need the Rental service on `localhost:8082` because in this case, the Reservation service contacts the Rental service to start a rental. If you refrain from using the current date as a start date, then the Rental service doesn't need to be running.

Now, navigate to http://localhost:8080 and experiment with the application. Use the form in the `Available cars to rent` section to set start and end dates, then click the `Update list` button to refresh the list of available cars on those dates. Once you click the `Reserve` button, a reservation for those dates will appear, and the relevant car will disappear from the list of available cars. This happens via asynchronous HTTP requests, not by reloading the whole page.

We didn't create a way to cancel existing reservations. This is left to the reader as an exercise. You would probably want to achieve this by adding a new column into the first table and a button similar to the `Reserve` button, but it would call a new REST method that deletes a reservation. Support for deleting a reservation also needs to be implemented in the Reservation service!

As another exercise, you might implement a table for rentals, similar to ours for the reservations. This will be very similar to what we did in this chapter, but you need to pull the data from the Rental service.

> **TIP** If you need to undo all your changes and start anew from the original state, trigger a live reload of the Reservation service (press `s` in its terminal window, for example). It will delete all reservations because they are stored in memory inside the application. After reloading the Reservation service and pressing `F5` in your browser, you can start experimenting from scratch.

If you feel that you need more cars for experimenting, feel free to add them in the Inventory service (in the `CarInventory#initialData` method that fills the inventory with initial data) or add them dynamically through the GraphQL or gRPC API (with this approach, they will be lost on restart!). If you don't remember, for GraphQL, you can do this by navigating to http://localhost:8083/q/graphql-ui and executing a mutation similar to the one in the following listing.

Listing 6.18 Adding a car via GraphQL

```
mutation {
  register(car:{
    licensePlateNumber: "123LAMBO"
    model: "Huracan"
    manufacturer: "Lamborghini"
  }) {
    id
  }
}
```

6.3 *Other security features of Quarkus*

Application security is a vast topic, and it would be impossible to cover a large chunk of it in this book. In this section, we will briefly mention some other security features that Quarkus offers. We won't go into details or provide practical examples here. If you are interested in trying some of these, refer to Quarkus quickstarts (https:// github.com/quarkusio/quarkus-quickstarts). This repository contains a lot of example projects, many of which are related to security. Another good starting point for learning more about Quarkus and security is the official Quarkus documentation (https://quarkus.io/guides/security-overview).

- *OIDC*—We used OpenID connect with Keycloak in this chapter, but it's worth mentioning that other OIDC providers are supported. For example, you can connect your application directly to Google's OIDC, allowing users to log in using their Google account. But not only Google. In the same way, at the time of writing, the `quarkus-oidc` extension can also be used with `Apple ID`, `Discord`, `Facebook`, `GitHub`, `LinkedIn`, `Mastodon`, `Microsoft`, `Spotify`, `Strava`, `Twitch` and `X`.

- *Other user management systems*—If you're not using an external provider and want to store and manage user credentials yourself, Quarkus supports retrieving user credentials from storages such as a relational database (either over a raw JDBC connection or using JPA on top of it) or LDAP. There is an extension for JWT (JSON Web Tokens), a modern way to authenticate users where a separate JWT server issues authentication tokens that are then used to authenticate users in various services that support it.

- *CORS protection*—For protection against Cross-Origin Resource Sharing (CORS) attacks, Quarkus provides a filter to check incoming HTTP requests. It is activated by simply adding the `quarkus.http.cors=true` configuration property. It checks the `Origin` header of incoming requests against a list of allowed origins (these are in the `quarkus.http.cors.origins` property). See https://quarkus .io/guides/security-cors for more information.

6.4 Running in production mode

So far, we have developed the Users and Reservation services in a way that they run only in Dev mode because they rely on Quarkus spinning up an instance of Keycloak and providing all the necessary Keycloak configuration (the Inventory service can already run in production mode in the current state because it has no such requirements). In this section, let's see what it takes to be able to run them in Quarkus's production mode. This is the checklist of what is missing:

- Manually run an instance of Keycloak.
- Provide suitable configuration for the `car-rental` security realm in Keycloak.
- Run a PostgreSQL database for more enterprise configuration of Keycloak.
- Enhance the configuration of the two applications to provide the necessary information for connecting to Keycloak. They share the same instance, just like they did in Dev mode.

By default, Keycloak comes with an embedded Java-based H2 database for storing data. However, all changes will be lost on restart since they are kept only in memory. For a production environment, it is recommended to use a more robust database like PostgreSQL. For our example, we will not require to persist Keycloak data, but we will still use PostgreSQL to demonstrate more enterprise-like production configuration.

6.4.1 Running Keycloak and PostgreSQL as containers

We use the Docker Compose (or you may be using Podman Compose; it works the same) project to easily spin up an instance of Keycloak along with an instance of PostgreSQL. We have prepared an entire `docker-compose.yml` file for this. It's located in the book's repository in the directory `chapter-06/production`, along with the file `car-rental-realm.json`, a definition of the Keycloak security realm that the Reservation and Users services will use. A realm created by importing this file is very similar to the realm that Quarkus creates when running Keycloak via Dev Services. The set of users is the same (`alice` and `bob`, where passwords are the same as the usernames), but it also contains the configuration of Reservation and Users services clients.

The `docker-compose.yml` file already contains the logic that makes Keycloak import the realm on startup, as is visible in the following excerpt from the file available in the following listing.

Listing 6.19   Importing a security realm in Keycloak on startup

```
volumes:
    - "./car-rental.json-realm:
➥ /opt/keycloak/data/import/car-rental-realm.json:Z"
command:
    - start-dev
    - --import-realm
```

The first configuration shows the volume (mapping of your filesystem into the container), which mounts the JSON file describing the realm into the container's `/opt/keycloak/data/import` directory. This is where Keycloak looks for realms to import. The second configuration is a command, which is run when the container starts. Here we use `start-dev` to start Keycloak in Dev mode. This simplifies the Keycloak configuration, as we don't need to configure keys and certificates. However, it is not recommended to use this configuration for real production, but it's sufficient for our use cases. We also use the `--import-realm` flag, which tells Keycloak to enable importing of realms in the `import` directory.

To start everything up, go to the `chapter06/production` directory and issue the following command (or with Podman Compose, use `podman-compose`):

```
$ docker compose up

# OR with the -d flag which runs the containers in the background
$ docker compose up -d
```

> **WARNING** Because PostgreSQL takes some time to start, we need to restart Keycloak container if it starts before PostgreSQL is ready. So, the restart in the log is expected.

You can check that the Keycloak started correctly by the following command. Notice that Keycloak also runs on top of Quarkus! This can also give you an idea of how many extensions a real-world Quarkus application can have. Don't bother with the individual extension names. Keycloak 25.0.6 uses older Quarkus version 3.8.5 under the hood, which still uses old extension names. For instance, `resteasy-reactive` in the list is the same extension as `quarkus-rest` (it was renamed starting from Quarkus 3.9):

```
$ docker logs keycloak
...
2024-09-24 11:36:53,073 INFO  [io.quarkus] (main) Keycloak 25.0.6 on JVM
 (powered by Quarkus 3.8.5) started in 13.102s. Listening on:
 http://0.0.0.0:8080. Management interface listening on http://0.0.0.0:9000.
2024-09-24 11:36:53,073 INFO  [io.quarkus] (main) Profile dev activated.
2024-09-24 11:36:53,073 INFO  [io.quarkus] (main) Installed features:
 [agroal, cdi, hibernate-orm, jdbc-postgresql, keycloak, logging-gelf,
 narayana-jta, reactive-routes, resteasy-reactive,
 resteasy-reactive-jackson, smallrye-context-propagation, vertx]
2024-09-24 11:36:53,078 WARN  [org.keycloak.quarkus.runtime.KeycloakMain]
(main) Running the server in development mode. DO NOT use this
 configuration in production.
```

As specified in the `docker-compose.yml` file, Keycloak starts and listens on port 7777. PostgreSQL is not exposed to localhost since it only communicates with Keycloak.

If you want to stop the containers, issue the following command, which stops (if they are running in background) and removes all containers:

```
$ docker compose down
```

6.4.2   *Wiring the services to use Keycloak*

Now we need to configure the Reservation and Users services to be able to connect to our Keycloak instance because when running in production mode, we can't have Quarkus do this for us automatically. Add the configuration in the following listing to `application.properties` in the `reservation-service` directory.

Listing 6.20   Wiring the Reservation service to manually managed Keycloak

```
%prod.quarkus.oidc.auth-server-url=http://localhost:7777/realms/car-rental
%prod.quarkus.oidc.client-id=reservation-service
%prod.quarkus.oidc.token-state-manager.split-tokens=true
```

> **NOTE** The `quarkus.oidc.token-state-manager.split-tokens` is most likely necessary in prod mode because the security realm is configured in a way that the total size of session cookies might exceed 4 kilobytes (a session cookie contains three encrypted tokens: ID, access, and refresh). Some browsers might decide to ignore such cookies, and thus authentication would not work. With this property enabled, Quarkus will split the authentication cookie into three separate cookies, one for each of the mentioned tokens. In Dev mode, the generated security realm is configured to use smaller tokens.

Also, add the configuration in the following listing to the `users-service` directory.

Listing 6.21   Wiring the Users service to manually managed Keycloak

```
%prod.quarkus.oidc.auth-server-url=http://localhost:7777/realms/car-rental
%prod.quarkus.oidc.client-id=users-service
%prod.quarkus.oidc.token-state-manager.split-tokens=true
```

All these properties are prepended with `%prod` prefix, meaning they are only considered when running in production mode, not Dev mode. Dev mode with an automatically managed Keycloak instance is still usable, unaffected by these changes. Also, don't forget to run the Inventory service either in Dev mode or production mode to provide cars for reservations. But now, you can run these two services as in production by running these commands in each of their respective root directories:

```
$ ./mvnw clean package
$ java -jar target/quarkus-app/quarkus-run.jar
```

Feel free to now experiment with the application. Everything should stay very similar to when we were using Dev mode, except you won't be able to do live reloads. In a real-world production environment, this might probably be even more complicated. For example, Keycloak and PostgreSQL can be managed as deployments in a Kubernetes cluster. This section aimed to show you the easiest way to get it running using regular containers.

6.5 Next steps

This chapter combined two critical aspects of application development: security and UI. We decided to incorporate them into a single chapter because they intertwine a lot, especially in smaller applications like the one we are developing in our examples. It's easier to write one with the other.

We used Keycloak as the linchpin of our security solution. Keycloak is very well integrated with Quarkus and offers many security-related features, including user registration, sending verification emails, defining password policies, blocking users, single sign-on for multiple services, and much more. Quarkus uses these features to communicate with the Keycloak instance and delegate user authentication to it. We showed how to easily propagate an ID token between two Quarkus services over a REST client. The receiving instance re-verifies the token's validity by connecting to Keycloak under the hood.

For the UI part, we used a combination of Qute and HTMX. Qute is a core extension of Quarkus, and on the basic level, it's a templating engine that renders HTML fragments on the server side and sends them to the client. HTMX, on the other hand, is a purely client-side library. It's a separate project completely independent of Quarkus, but the Qute extension plays with it very nicely. HTMX greatly simplifies the development of interactive AJAX-based applications that dynamically update their content based on communication with the backend, except that with HTMX (in most cases) you won't need to write any JavaScript code.

In the next chapter, we will return to the backend. We will look at how Quarkus works with databases and how your applications can make use of them.

Summary

- Quarkus's OIDC extension comes with first-class support for Keycloak as the tool for managing almost everything related to securing an application.
- Quarkus also supports OIDC providers such as Google, Apple ID, Facebook, and others.
- With Dev Services, a Keycloak instance is initialized with minimal configuration needed on the user's part (the configuration provides sensible defaults, including some predefined users).
- A Dev Services Keycloak instance can be shared by multiple Quarkus applications running in Dev mode on the same machine.
- Propagating the ID token between services with a REST client is as easy as adding the `quarkus-rest-client-oidc-token-propagation` extension and then adding an `@AccessToken` annotation on the REST client interface.
- In a REST endpoint, you may inject a `SecurityContext` object to inspect the logged-in user.
- Qute is a server-side templating engine for rendering (not only) HTML pages.

- Qute offers (optional) build-time type safety checks on the usage of all Java objects passed into templates.

- HTMX's most basic usage is sending asynchronous HTTP requests to the backend server and then dynamically swapping contents of HTML elements using bodies of received responses. In most cases, you can achieve this without needing to write any JavaScript code.

- The best way to use HTMX with Quarkus is by writing REST endpoints that handle the asynchronous requests dispatched by HTMX and return pieces of HTML code that should replace the relevant parts of the HTML page that the client is viewing.

- The ecosystem of UI frameworks usable with Quarkus is growing. The most notable other frameworks are Renarde and Quinoa (more information about these in appendix C).

Database access 7

This chapter covers

- Learning how to connect Quarkus application to the database
- Introducing Hibernate object-relational mapping with Panache
- Explaining Quarkus approaches to the database access
- Integrating reactive database access to Quarkus applications

Databases. We believe all of us can agree that we must do something with the database at least a few times in our careers. From simple column adjustments to sophisticated migrations, these might become challenging problems to solve. This is why there are a lot of libraries helping us with database access, object-relational mapping (ORM), and migrations whenever we need them.

In the previous chapter, we delegated the user management and credentials storing to the Keycloak server that manages its own persistent store. While this is suitable for user handling, it surely isn't ideal for our custom business data that the car rental system manages. In this chapter, we concentrate on learning how Quarkus manages database access for your applications.

171

This chapter introduces Panache, an API that Quarkus adds on top of the well-known Hibernate ORM framework. Panache implements the active record pattern and provides even further simplification over the ORM provided by Hibernate. However, we don't stop there. As we explain, Panache is also usable with the repository pattern (a repository is a design pattern implemented as a Java object that represents the database table and has methods for interacting with it).

Another very useful feature is using Panache as a REST mapper. This means that you can have REST endpoints with methods for CRUD (create, read, update, delete) operations generated automatically for your entities. We also differentiate databases and connections that your Quarkus applications can utilize, explaining both the traditional SQL databases like PostgreSQL and the NoSQL stores like MongoDB. Switching between SQL and NoSQL is extremely easy, thanks to the abstractions that Panache provides. We also show how to access all these databases reactively.

As usual, the code is available in the `chapter-07` directory of the book source code. We hope you are already interested in how Quarkus handles databases, so let's dive right in.

7.1   Panache

Hibernate (https://hibernate.org) is a very well-known open-source ORM library that you hopefully have already at least heard about. It continues to provide the de facto standard for Java persistence that is also officially standardized via the Jakarta Persistence API [formerly also known as Java Persistence API (JPA)] specification. A lot of materials already exist, including books provided by Manning, that teach you how to access databases with Hibernate ORM. This is why we have different goals here. In this chapter, we focus on the new API called Panache.

Panache, as an idea, came from the very same Hibernate team that wanted to introduce a simplified model for database access. Panache offers a number of different approaches to choose from. In this section, we focus on the active record pattern. We discuss other approaches in the following sections.

7.1.1   Active record pattern

The *active record pattern* aims to encapsulate the operations required for the record manipulation in the database into the record (corresponding to an object in Java) itself! This approach is straightforward. Instead of injecting `EntityManager` as you used to do with traditional Hibernate/JPA practice, you now have the option to include all database access operations in the entity class. How does this work? Let's look at a short example of how Panache works in listing 7.1. The individual operations are either represented as instance methods (e.g., `persist`, `delete`) if you call an operation working on a specific entity, or as static methods of the entity class (`Car` in the example), which serve to perform more general operations on the table corresponding to the entity (e.g., `listAll`, `count`).

Listing 7.1 Panache example of active record manipulation

```
// Assume we have an entity named Car

// persisting into the database called on the object instance
car.persist();

// deleting an entity
car.delete();

// listing all Cars from the database called as a static method
Car.listAll();

// find Car by ID
Car.findById(carId);

// list all blue Cars
Car.list("color", Color.Blue);

// count all cars
Car.count();

// delete Car by ID
Car.deleteById(carId);
```

Panache is based on Hibernate Query Language (HQL), which is an extension of Java Persistence Query Language (JPQL) and allows you to put parts of these languages into the fluent API to build database queries. This allows us to write very readable and maintainable code without the need to write any boilerplate. We use many of the available operations in this chapter, but not all of them. However, because this model provides a fluent API, discovering different options is as simple as pressing the autocomplete button in any modern IDE.

As you may remember, we have only used database stubs in all the car rental services until now. We cannot justify using hardcoded static lists representing production data in any modern application, though. In this chapter, we introduce different database integrations in the respective services of our application. We start by adding a traditional SQL database, PostgreSQL, to the Reservation service.

7.1.2 Getting started with Panache

To be able to use the Panache with the active record pattern approach in our application, we need to do three things:

- Add the relevant configuration for the connection information
- Create our entities
- Make the entities extend the `PanacheEntity` class

PANACHE EXTENSIONS AND APPLICATION CONFIGURATION
As with other functionalities in Quarkus, if we want to use Panache in our Quarkus application, we start by adding a Quarkus extension(s) for it. For Panache, we need

two extensions: `quarkus-hibernate-orm-panache` for Panache itself and a database driver that is specific to the database that our application uses. In our case, it is the `quarkus-jdbc-postgresql` for the PostgreSQL database.

> **NOTE** The JDBC database driver is required for Hibernate Panache to communicate correctly with the underlying database. As we will learn in the following sections, depending on the database you use, you may choose a different driver (e.g., `quarkus-jdbc-mysql`).

If you are not already in the `reservation-service` directory (remember that we start with the current version from chapter 6), change your current directory to it. Now you can execute the command available in listing 7.2 to add required extensions. Of course, you can keep the Dev mode running throughout this chapter. You might notice that the `quarkus-jdbc-postgresql` extension starts a new Dev services instance of the PostgreSQL container for us (e.g., with `docker ps` or by pressing `c` in the Dev mode terminal).

Listing 7.2 Adding extensions required for Panache

```
$ quarkus ext add quarkus-hibernate-orm-panache quarkus-jdbc-postgresql
Looking for the newly published extensions in registry.quarkus.io
[SUCCESS] ✓   Extension io.quarkus:quarkus-hibernate-orm-panache has
  been installed
[SUCCESS] ✓   Extension io.quarkus:quarkus-jdbc-postgresql has
  been installed
```

Or you can add the Maven dependencies directly, as shown in the following listing.

Listing 7.3 Adding extensions required for Panache to `pom.xml`

```
<dependency>
    <groupId>io.quarkus</groupId>
    <artifactId>quarkus-hibernate-orm-panache</artifactId>
</dependency>
<dependency>
    <groupId>io.quarkus</groupId>
    <artifactId>quarkus-jdbc-postgresql</artifactId>
</dependency>
```

Next, as with any other external service, if we want to connect to a database, we must provide the connection configuration specifying its location and how to connect to it (i.e., the URL and the credentials). We first configure the data source as the database to which we are connecting, and then we can optionally provide additional configuration specific to Hibernate. The required configuration for the Reservation service needs to be placed in the `application.properties` as shown in the following listing.

Listing 7.4 The Panache configuration in the Reservation service

```
quarkus.datasource.db-kind=postgresql
quarkus.datasource.username=user
quarkus.datasource.password=pass
%prod.quarkus.datasource.jdbc.url=
➥jdbc:postgresql://localhost:5432/reservation
```

Intentionally defines connection URL only in prod mode to allow Dev services

```
# drop and create the database at startup
quarkus.hibernate-orm.database.generation=drop-and-create
```

We start by defining the database connection information including the driver (db-kind), the username, the password, and the connection URL. Note that we are defining the database URL only in the production mode to allow Dev services to start a PostgreSQL instance for us in Dev mode.

Next, we define Hibernate-specific properties, which in our case is only the database generation strategy. We should also probably mark it to be applicable only in dev and/or test mode, so we don't drop and recreate the database in production. However, for the purposes of our example car rental application, we want to recreate the database with each restart so that we always start in the same state.

This is all that we need to do from the configuration perspective. Next, let's look into how we can define our entities.

DEFINING ENTITIES

An entity in the Panache with the active pattern approach is simply a POJO (plain old Java object) annotated with the @Entity annotation and extending the Panache-Entity class.

To define the Reservation entity in the Reservation service, let's move the Reservation class into the new org.acme.reservation.entity package and modify it like shown in the following listing to update it to a valid Panache entity.

Listing 7.5 The Reservation entity in the Reservation service

```
package org.acme.reservation.entity;

import io.quarkus.hibernate.orm.panache.PanacheEntity;
import jakarta.persistence.Entity;

import java.time.LocalDate;

@Entity
public class Reservation extends PanacheEntity {

    public Long carId;
    public String userId;
    public LocalDate startDay;
    public LocalDate endDay;

    /**
     * Check if the given duration overlaps with this reservation
```

```
 * @return true if the dates overlap with the reservation, false
 * otherwise
 */
public boolean isReserved(LocalDate startDay, LocalDate endDay) {
    return (!(this.endDay.isBefore(startDay) ||
        this.startDay.isAfter(endDay)));
}

@Override
public String toString() {
    return "Reservation{" +
        "id=" + id +
        ", carId=" + carId +
        ", userId='" + userId + '\'' +
        ", startDay=" + startDay +
        ", endDay=" + endDay +
        '}';
}
}
```

And that is all we need. We really just added the `@Entity` annotation, extended the `PanacheEntity` class, and removed our own `id` field. We also provided the `toString` method since we will be printing our entity to the console later.

If you are familiar with JPA, you can see this is an extremely short and concise definition of a database entity. All the usually duplicated code in most entities, including the `id` field, the generation strategy, or the getters and setters, can be omitted because Panache dynamically provides it for us.

> **NOTE** Optionally, instead of extending `PanacheEntity`, you can also extend the `PanacheEntityBase` if you want to define your custom strategy to generate entity IDs (in the same way as generally when using Hibernate with the `@Id` and `@GeneratedValue` annotations).

Notice also that we can keep our fields public. Actually, Panache encourages this approach. So, there is no need to generate a bunch of getters and setters as the JPA specification requires you to do now. Panache will rewrite all direct accesses with the generated getters/setters dynamically for you during build time. If you need to override some getter or setter, you are free to do so. Panache will just use your method instead of the generated one. And you can also still keep the field public. But again, if you prefer private fields, you can use them if you wish (we know this is a combustible discussion topic in the Java community).

Optionally, you can also extend Panache entities with custom business methods that utilize the inherited static methods from the `PanacheEntity` class demonstrated in the example listing 7.1 at the beginning of this section. For instance, imagine you would need a method that returns all reservations for a particular car. This can be easily done as demonstrated in listing 7.6. This method is just an example, but we will use this functionality later in different services.

Listing 7.6   Example business method in the `Reservation` **entity**

```
public static List<Reservation> findByCar(Long carId) {
    return list("carId", carId);
}
```

For more information about the available query options, you may read the Panache guide at https://quarkus.io/guides/hibernate-orm-panache.

7.1.3   Using Panache in the Reservation service

Now we can safely delete the generated stub repository that we created in chapter 4, which is in the `InMemoryReservationsRepository` class. Remove this class. The `ReservationResource` needs to be adjusted as shown in the following listings. Let's start with the fields and constructor in listing 7.7. Because we are moving to the active record pattern, we can remove the `ReservationRepository` field and injection from the constructor.

Listing 7.7   Constructor and field adjustments in `ReservationResource`

```
@Path("reservation")
@Produces(MediaType.APPLICATION_JSON)
public class ReservationResource {

    private final InventoryClient inventoryClient;
    private final RentalClient rentalClient;

    @Inject
    jakarta.ws.rs.core.SecurityContext context;

    public ReservationResource(@GraphQLClient("inventory")
                               GraphQLInventoryClient inventoryClient,
                               @RestClient RentalClient rentalClient) {
        this.inventoryClient = inventoryClient;
        this.rentalClient = rentalClient;
    }

    ...
```

In listing 7.8, we can analyze how active record pattern handling differs from that of the original `ReservationRespository`. The `make` method shows an example of the instance method use with the `reservation.persist()` operation. We can also note the `@Transactional` annotation that executes this method in a transaction as the persist operation requires to save a record into the database. The `allReservations` and `availability` methods demonstrate the use of static methods of the `Reservation` entity inherited from Panache.

Listing 7.8   `ReservationResource` now working with active record pattern

```
@Consumes(MediaType.APPLICATION_JSON)
@POST
@Transactional
```

The POST method must be
executed in a transaction.

```
public Reservation make(Reservation reservation) {
    reservation.userId = context.getUserPrincipal() != null ?
        context.getUserPrincipal().getName() : "anonymous";
    reservation.persist();
    Log.info("Successfully reserved reservation " + reservation);
    if (reservation.startDay.equals(LocalDate.now())) {
        Rental rental = rentalClient
            .start(reservation.userId, reservation.id);
        Log.info("Successfully started rental " + rental);
    }
    return reservation;
}


@GET
@Path("availability")
public Collection<Car> availability(@RestQuery LocalDate startDate,
                                    @RestQuery LocalDate endDate) {
    // obtain all cars from inventory
    List<Cars> availableCars = inventoryClient.allCars();
    // create a map from id to car
    Map<Long, Car> carsById = new HashMap<>();
    for (Car car : availableCars) {
        carsById.put(car.id, car);
    }

    // get all current reservations
    List<Reservation> reservations =
        Reservation.listAll();
    // for each reservation, remove the car from the map
    for (Reservation reservation : reservations) {
        if (reservation.isReserved(startDate, endDate)) {
            carsById.remove(reservation.carId);
        }
    }
    return carsById.values();
}


@GET
@Path("all")
public Collection<Reservation> allReservations() {
    String userId = context.getUserPrincipal() != null ?
        context.getUserPrincipal().getName() : null;
    return Reservation.<Reservation>streamAll()
        .filter(reservation -> userId == null ||
            userId.equals(reservation.userId))
    .collect(Collectors.toList());
}
```

Persisting the reservation into the database

The id field was generated when we persisted this reservation.

Obtains a list of all entities, equivalent to SELECT * FROM Reservation

PanacheEntity.streamAll() needs to get a hint of the entity type because the Java type system can't deduct it directly.

If you are not already running it, then start the Reservation service in Dev mode:

```
$ quarkus dev
```

Since we intentionally didn't define the connection URL to our database in the application.properties for Dev mode, the Quarkus magic kicks in and boots a zero-config PostgreSQL database in a container for us. This container lives only during the lifecycle of the Dev mode execution. Once you stop the Dev mode, the container also stops. Additionally, our Quarkus application is already configured and connected to this PostgreSQL container! You can verify that by pressing c in your Dev mode terminal. If you repeat the calls to make the reservation and get all reservations from chapter 4, they are now propagated into the database.

Now this is impressive—how little code is needed to connect an application to the database. This kind of experience is generally incomparable with any other framework.

If you make a few POST requests to the /reservation endpoint (easily in the Swagger UI provided at http://localhost:8081/q/swagger-ui or in the terminal, just remember to change the dates for the future), you can query the reservations from the database with a GET request to the same /reservation/all endpoint as before.

Additionally, you can also check (with any database connection tool of your liking) that they are persisted in the database. The example utilizing HTTPie and psql (PostgreSQL client) in terminal is available in listing 7.9. Note that the PostgreSQL container-mapped port generates randomly when the container starts, so you need to check which host port your PostgreSQL container is mapped to (use docker ps and check the "PORTS" column). The credentials for the database (set in the configuration) are user:pass. The psql command line utility is totally optional to verify performed operations, so if you don't have it installed, you don't need to install it just for these verifications.

NOTE If you want to make sure that the Dev services database is always reachable on the same, nonrandom host port, specify it using quarkus.datasource .devservices.port=5432 (5432 is the default port used by PostgreSQL, but you can choose a different number). This port on the host will then be forwarded to port 5432 inside the container.

Listing 7.9 An entity persisted in the database

```
# First, persist a new reservation with a POST call
$ http POST :8081/reservation <<< '{
  "carId": 1,
  "startDay": "3333-01-01",
  "endDay": "3333-01-02"
}'

...

# Check that the reservation is available in the application via a GET call
$ http :8081/reservation/all
HTTP/1.1 200 OK
Content-Type: application/json;charset=UTF-8
content-length: 87

[
    {
        "carId": 1,
```

```
          "endDay": "3333-01-02",
          "id": 1,
          "startDay": "3333-01-01",
          "userId": "anonymous"
      }
  ]

  # Connect to the database directly with `psql` CLI, password is `pass`
  $ psql -h localhost -p 39325 -U user \
  -d quarkus -c 'SELECT * FROM Reservation;'
  Password for user user:
     endday   |  startday  | carid | id |  userid
  ------------+------------+-------+----+-----------
   3333-01-02 | 3333-01-01 |     1 |  1 | anonymous
  (1 row)
```

If you are unsure about the name of the tables Hibernate generated for your entities, you can always check the scripts and the entities that the Hibernate extension knows about in the dev UI, as shown in figure 7.1.

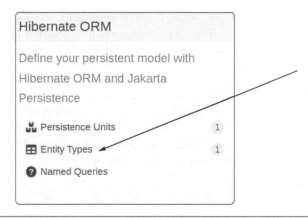

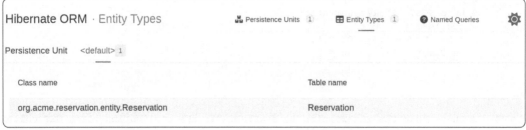

Figure 7.1 Hibernate ORM in the Dev UI: the card allows you to inspect the application's entities, persistence units, and defined named queries.

Now we can also clean the remains of the `ReservationRepository` since the active record pattern replaced it. We can remove the whole `org.acme.reservation.reservation` package. However, this breaks the `ReservationRepositoryTest`. Let's update this test to use the `Reservation` record pattern, which will persist data into a real PostgreSQL database instance that starts with Dev Services for the test execution. Rename the `ReservationRepositoryTest` to `ReservationPersistenceTest` and update the code as demonstrated in the following listing.

Listing 7.10 Updated `ReservationPersistenceTest`

```
package org.acme.reservation;

import io.quarkus.test.junit.QuarkusTest;
import jakarta.transaction.Transactional;
import org.acme.reservation.entity.Reservation;
import org.junit.jupiter.api.Assertions;
import org.junit.jupiter.api.Test;

import java.time.LocalDate;
import java.time.temporal.ChronoUnit;

@QuarkusTest
public class ReservationPersistenceTest {

    @Test
    @Transactional
    public void testCreateReservation() {
        Reservation reservation = new Reservation();
        reservation.startDay = LocalDate.now().plus(5, ChronoUnit.DAYS);
        reservation.endDay = LocalDate.now().plus(12, ChronoUnit.DAYS);
        reservation.carId = 384L;
        reservation.persist();

        Assertions.assertNotNull(reservation.id);
        Assertions.assertEquals(1, Reservation.count());
        Reservation persistedReservation =
            Reservation.findById(reservation.id);
        Assertions.assertNotNull(persistedReservation);
        Assertions.assertEquals(reservation.carId,
            persistedReservation.carId);
    }
}
```

NOTE You might need to clean your project (`./mvnw clean`) after the class rename.

We need to start a transaction again since we persist in an actual database, so we annotate the test with the `@Transactional` annotation. In the test, we perform a real database insert into a Dev Services PostgreSQL database and then a real select from the database to verify that it was persisted. If you now run the test (continuous testing or `./mvnw test`), you can notice that a new instance of PostgreSQL container starts just for the test run. So we have a separate database instance for the Dev mode and for the tests, meaning we can be sure our manual experiments won't conflict with the test executions.

7.2   *Panache repository pattern*

The active record pattern introduced in the previous section is not the right cup of tea (or coffee) for all developers. However, Panache is not constrained only to this model. A very popular alternative is the *repository pattern*. This pattern defines a custom object called the repository, which is responsible for all the database manipulation operations (remember that the active record pattern encapsulated these operations in the record itself). Externalizing manipulation from the record entity classes indeed has benefits (e.g., flexibility or separation of concerns), but eventually, the developer chooses which pattern is more suitable for the application at hand.

> **NOTE** Panache provides both models out of the box. So the choice of the database is orthogonal to the chosen API. We could also have used the repository pattern with the same extensions in the previous section.

We introduce the repository pattern in the Inventory service. Of course, we could again use PostgreSQL, but would we maybe prefer another database? So why we don't use a different one this time? Of course, for Panache, this is not a problem at all. Switching to another database is just a matter of changing the extension for the JDBC driver we include in our Quarkus application.

In the Inventory service, we use another very popular open-source relational database, MySQL, and this time with the repository pattern.

7.2.1   *Utilizing repository pattern with MySQL*

Just like with the active record, we need to do three things to use Panache with the repository pattern:

- Add the required extensions and configuration
- Create the entity classes
- Define the repository class

PANACHE EXTENSIONS AND CONFIGURATION FOR MySQL

We also need two extensions—one for Panache and one for the MySQL JDBC driver. This is exactly the same as with the active record pattern in the previous section. We just utilize a different JDBC driver—this time for MySQL. Changing into the `inventory -service` directory, we can add the extensions either with the CLI or directly to the `pom.xml` as shown in the following listing.

> **Listing 7.11   Adding database extensions to the Inventory service**

```
$ quarkus ext add quarkus-hibernate-orm-panache quarkus-jdbc-mysql
Looking for the newly published extensions in registry.quarkus.io
[SUCCESS] ✔  Extension io.quarkus:quarkus-hibernate-orm-panache has been \
installed
[SUCCESS] ✔  Extension io.quarkus:quarkus-jdbc-mysql has been installed

# or add extensions to the pom.xml manually
<dependency>
```

```
  <groupId>io.quarkus</groupId>
  <artifactId>quarkus-hibernate-orm-panache</artifactId>
</dependency>
<dependency>
  <groupId>io.quarkus</groupId>
  <artifactId>quarkus-jdbc-mysql</artifactId>
</dependency>
```

The configuration is also very similar, but we are connecting to the MySQL database this time. To provide configuration for MySQL, we need to add the properties available in the following listing to the `application.properties` in the Inventory service.

Listing 7.12 Properties required for MySQL connection

```
quarkus.datasource.db-kind=mysql                    ◁──┐  Uses the MySQL driver
quarkus.datasource.username=user
quarkus.datasource.password=pass
%prod.quarkus.datasource.jdbc.url=jdbc:mysql://localhost:3306/inventory

# drop and create the database at startup
quarkus.hibernate-orm.database.generation=drop-and-create
```

If we developed entities in the same way as in the previous sections, it would still work. But we want to utilize the repository pattern in the Inventory service, so the code we need to write is slightly different.

DEVELOPING ENTITIES FOR USE WITH THE REPOSITORY

With the repository pattern, we don't need to do anything special about the created entities. Defining standard JPA entities work as we would expect. So let's use the JPA approach in the Inventory service. We can now modify the `org.acme.inventory.model` `.Car` class as shown in the following listing to make it a valid JPA entity.

Listing 7.13 The `Car` entity

```
package org.acme.inventory.model;

import jakarta.persistence.Entity;
import jakarta.persistence.GeneratedValue;
import jakarta.persistence.GenerationType;
import jakarta.persistence.Id;

@Entity
public class Car {

    @Id
    @GeneratedValue(strategy = GenerationType.IDENTITY)
    private Long id;
    private String licensePlateNumber;
    private String manufacturer;
    private String model;
```

```
    // getters, setters, toString, equals, and hashcode omitted
}
```

We added the @Entity annotation, the id field, and getters/setters/equals/hashcode (not shown in the listing). We used the @Id and @GeneratedValue annotations to define our custom primary key. We could again have extended PanacheEntity to have a numeric ID field generated automatically (such a combination of the active record and repository patterns is supported too), but to show the different approaches, this entity will be a plain JPA entity, so we have to define the ID field ourselves.

> **NOTE** After this change to the Car class, the application won't compile, because we need to adjust the GraphQLInventoryService and the GrpcInventory-Service to use the repository instead of the stubs. We will do this in the next section. Don't be surprised if you download the finished solution for this section that doesn't compile.

CREATING THE REPOSITORY

The last step in using the repository pattern is the actual definition of our repository class that will manage persistent access for cars. This class must implement the PanacheRepository interface providing the record type as the generic parameter. It also needs to be defined as a CDI bean (e.g., with a bean-defining annotation like @ApplicationScoped). We could utilize the already created CarInventory, but since we are creating a repository, it is better to keep class names consistent. Create a new class CarRepository in the new package org.acme.inventory.repository as shown in the following listing.

> **TIP** If you use a primary key of some type other than Long, you will have to implement the PanacheRepositoryBase<Entity, Id> instead of PanacheRepos-itory<Entity>. The second type argument has to be the class that represents the primary key field.

Listing 7.14 The code of the CarRepository class

```
package org.acme.inventory.repository;

import io.quarkus.hibernate.orm.panache.PanacheRepository;
import jakarta.enterprise.context.ApplicationScoped;
import org.acme.inventory.model.Car;

@ApplicationScoped
public class CarRepository implements PanacheRepository<Car> {
}
```

Out of the box, this provides you with the same methods we had at our disposal with the static methods inherited from the active record pattern. As with inheritance in the active record pattern, you can provide your custom methods if needed. An example of a custom business method in the `CarRepository` is demonstrated in listing 7.15. This time, add this method to the `CarRepository`.

```
public Optional<Car> findByLicensePlateNumberOptional(
        String licensePlateNumber) {
    return find("licensePlateNumber", licensePlateNumber)
        .firstResultOptional();
}
```

Our application is now ready to utilize this repository to persist and retrieve rentals from the MySQL database.

7.2.2   *Using the repository pattern in Inventory*

Now that we have the repository in place, we can safely remove the generated stub `CarInventory` (also its `database` package). However, there is one catch. We predefined two cars that populate the inventory with some initial data. It would be good to keep them. There are several ways of how we can do this—e.g., we could use the CDI `@PostConstruct` concept (the method invoked after the bean is created) in the new `CarRepository` or observe the Quarkus startup event. But Panache provides a more elegant solution. We can include a custom `import.sql` SQL script in the `src/main/resources` directory to prepopulate the database. This script automatically executes when Quarkus connects to the database. In our case, it populates the database with our initial data. Of course, in most cases, this is useful only for testing and development. Hence, it is disabled in prod mode by default. So, let's create a new file, `src/main/resources/import.sql`, with the content available in the following listing.

```
INSERT INTO Car (licensePlateNumber, manufacturer, model)
⇒ VALUES ('ABC123', 'Mazda', '6');
INSERT INTO Car (licensePlateNumber, manufacturer, model)
⇒ VALUES ('XYZ987', 'Ford', 'Mustang');
```

Next, we can adjust the `GraphQLInventoryService` and the `GrpcInventoryService` (our exposed APIs) to persist and list the cars from the database. Notice that the methods that modify the database also need to be run in a transaction (`@Transactional`) for the change to be committed to the database.

The `GraphQLInventoryService` needs to replace usages of the `CarInventory` with usage of `CarRepository`. But since we now also have the custom business method that returns `Car` by the license number in the `CarRepository`, we can replace the manual filtering in the `remove` method with the invocation passed directly to the database. The code of the updated `GraphQLInventoryService` is available in the following listing.

Listing 7.17   The `GraphQLInventoryService` modified code

```
@GraphQLApi
public class GraphQLInventoryService {

    @Inject
    CarRepository carRepository;

    @Query
    public List<Car> cars() {
        return carRepository.listAll();
    }

    @Transactional
    @Mutation
    public Car register(Car car) {
        carRepository.persist(car);
        Log.info("Persisting " + car);
        return car;
    }

    @Transactional
    @Mutation
    public boolean remove(String licensePlateNumber) {
        Optional<Car> toBeRemoved = carRepository
            .findByLicensePlateNumberOptional(licensePlateNumber);
        if(toBeRemoved.isPresent()) {
            carRepository.delete(toBeRemoved.get());
            return true;
        } else {
            return false;
        }
    }

}
```

We can now inject the `CarRepository` as a CDI bean. We again need to use `@Transactional` on methods where we want to persist or modify entities. Persisting is done by calling the `persist` method on the repository. In the `remove` method, we also utilize the custom business method we additionally defined in the `CarRepository`.

The code of the `GrpcInventoryService` requires similar modifications. But because we are delegating the invocation of the `persist` method outside the CDI bean (in lambda), and we still need to run it in a transaction, we need to wrap the `persist` invocation in a new transaction created with the programmatic API called `Quarkus-Transaction` (more details later) as shown in listing 7.18. Each `persist(car)` operation runs in its own transaction.

Listing 7.18 The modified code of the `GrpcInventoryService`

```
@GrpcService
public class GrpcInventoryService
    implements InventoryService {

    @Inject
    CarRepository carRepository;

    @Override
    @Blocking
    public Multi<CarResponse> add(Multi<InsertCarRequest> requests) {
        return requests
            .map(request -> {
                Car car = new Car();
                car.setLicensePlateNumber(request.getLicensePlateNumber());
                car.setManufacturer(request.getManufacturer());
                car.setModel(request.getModel());
                return car;
            }).onItem().invoke(car -> {
                QuarkusTransaction.requiringNew().run( () -> {      ◁─── Runs persist()
                    carRepository.persist(car);                          in a transaction,
                    Log.info("Persisting " + car);                       which is
                });                                                      committed
            }).map(car -> CarResponse.newBuilder()                      immediately.
                .setLicensePlateNumber(car.getLicensePlateNumber())
                .setManufacturer(car.getManufacturer())
                .setModel(car.getModel())
                .setId(car.getId())
                .build());
    }
                                                          Runs the whole remove
                                                          method in a single transaction
    @Override                                             committed only when the
    @Blocking                                             method ends.
    @Transactional
    public Uni<CarResponse> remove(RemoveCarRequest request) {   ◁───┘
        Optional<Car> optionalCar = carRepository
            .findByLicensePlateNumberOptional(
                request.getLicensePlateNumber());

        if (optionalCar.isPresent()) {
            Car removedCar = optionalCar.get();
            carRepository.delete(removedCar);
            return Uni.createFrom().item(CarResponse.newBuilder()
                .setLicensePlateNumber(removedCar.getLicensePlateNumber())
                .setManufacturer(removedCar.getManufacturer())
                .setModel(removedCar.getModel())
                .setId(removedCar.getId())
                .build());
        }
        return Uni.createFrom().nullItem();
    }
}
```

We also utilize the injection of the `CarRepository`. The `@Blocking` annotation on both methods tells Quarkus that the method executes a blocking operation (persist or delete) on a database, so it needs to execute on worker thread, which allows blocking. Otherwise, Quarkus won't run it because gRPC defaults to fast event loop threads, which cannot be blocked (more on this in chapter 8).

We could have used a `@Transactional` annotation on the `add` method instead of using the `QuarkusTransaction.requiringNew().run()` method for each car separately. But with this approach, the whole operation would be run in a single transaction, and that transaction would be committed only when the whole stream of cars is processed (and the gRPC stream closed). So we would have a transaction that stays open for a long time, which could easily become a performance bottleneck, and we could also run into a transaction timeout if the stream stayed open for too long (the default transaction timeout is 1 minute). We will explain `QuarkusTransaction` in more detail in section 7.5.2. Of course, if the requirement was to process cars additions in chunks as defined by the stream, we would need to wrap the whole method in a single transaction (and adjust transactions timeouts accordingly).

If you now start the Inventory service in Dev mode (`quarkus dev`), the MySQL container with your development database starts in the background, and your Quarkus application connects to it. If the application starts successfully, we can utilize the exposed GraphQL API—as shown in figure 7.2 in the GraphQL UI—to query all cars and verify

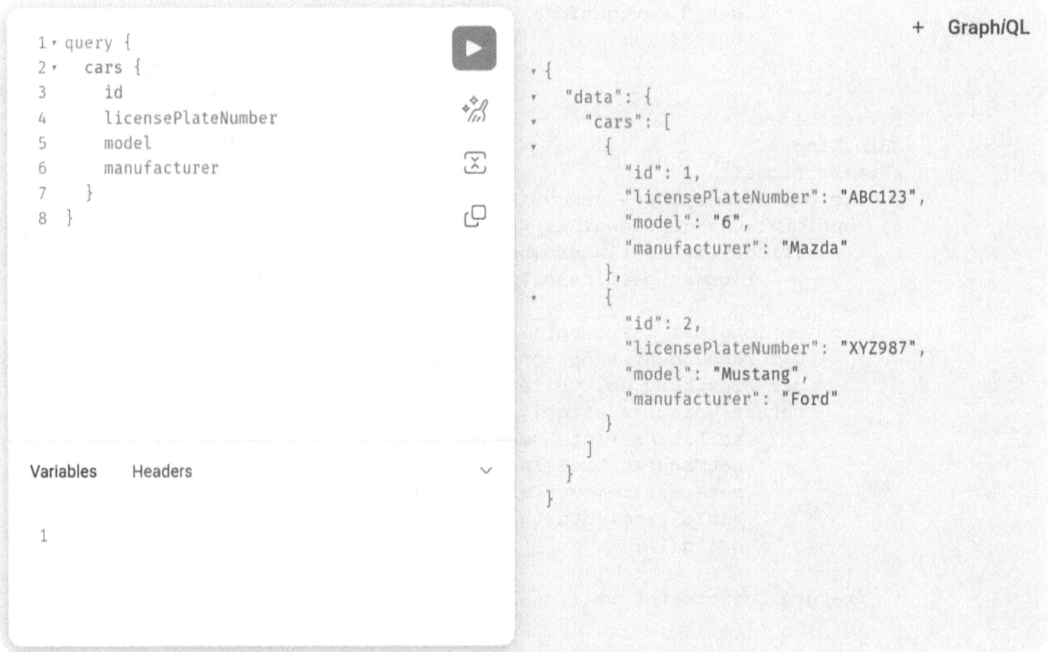

Figure 7.2   Inventory GraphQL query example now pulling the data from the database

that the database was prepopulated with the two cars from `import.sql`. The GraphQL UI is available at http://localhost:8083/q/graphql-ui.

We can now register new cars either through the GraphQL (figure 7.3) or through the gRPC (figure 7.4) exposed APIs.

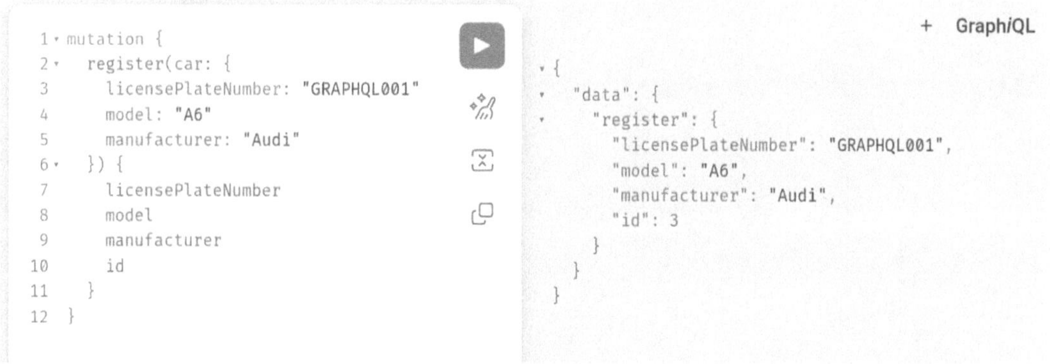

Figure 7.3   Register a car through the exposed GraphQL API

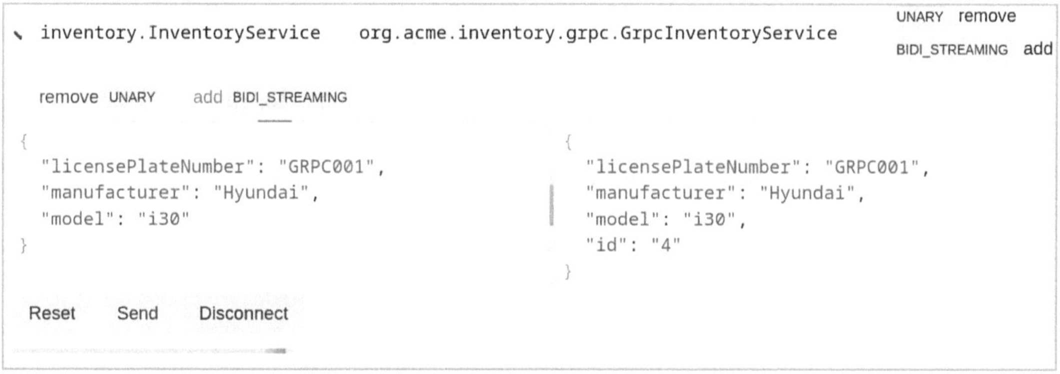

Figure 7.4   Register a car through the exposed gRPC API

Finally, we can verify that both new registrations have been persisted in the database through the GraphQL UI again, as shown in figure 7.5.

But to verify that we actually have the results in the MySQL database, we can also run the following `mysql` CLI command, available in listing 7.19, to list all records from the Car database (credentials are `user:pass` as configured in listing 7.12). Don't forget to replace the port with the actual host port of the MySQL container (use `docker ps` to find out).

Figure 7.5 Verifications of the newly registered cars in the GraphQL UI

TIP The `mysql` tool verification is again optional; feel free to skip it. The `-p` quarkus is the name of the database. When you are prompted for password, it's pass.

Listing 7.19   All cars persisted in the MySQL database (formatted)

```
$ mysql -h localhost -P 38065 --protocol=tcp -u user -p quarkus \
<<< 'SELECT * FROM Car;'
Enter password:
id  licensePlateNumber  manufacturer    model
1       ABC123          Mazda           6
2       XYZ987          Ford            Mustang
3       GRAPHQL001      Audi            A6
4       GRPC001         Hyundai         i30
```

7.3   *Traditional ORM/JPA data access*

Both the active record and the repository pattern provide simplified data access management. However, if you prefer the traditional JPA/Hibernate APIs we have been using in enterprise applications for years, you can still utilize the entire landscape of Hibernate ORM/JPA features in your Quarkus applications.

We don't use pure JPA (without Panache) in our car rental services. However, we want to teach you how to set up your Quarkus application if you wish to do so.

To use Hibernate ORM in your application, you need to add the extensions for the `quarkus-hibernate-orm` and the JDBC driver for the database of your choice. You can develop your JPA entities in the exact same way as in JPA (an example is also provided in the section 7.2.1). One difference from typical JPA applications is that you don't need to include `persistence.xml` in your application if you don't require more advanced configuration. You can configure everything in `application.properties` with the same properties as shown in the previous sections. Of course, if you include the JDBC driver, the Dev services start the database for you in the Dev and test modes.

If you include all steps as described, you can inject the `EntityManager` from the JPA specification as a CDI bean, as shown in the following listing.

Listing 7.20 Standard JPA/ORM data access with `EntityManager`

```
@Path("/users")
public class PersonResource {

    @Inject
    EntityManager em;                            ⟵  Injecting the
                                                     EntityManager

    @POST
    @Transactional
    public void add(String name) {
        Person person = new Person();
        person.setName(name);                        You can use the
                                                     EntityManager as
        em.persist(person);                  ⟵      specified in the JPA.
    }
}
```

7.4 REST Data

A large number of enterprise production applications expose REST APIs that provide CRUD (Create, Read, Update, Delete) operations over an entity in the database. To simplify this tedious and often repeated task, Quarkus provides a set of REST data extensions that expose CRUD operations over Panache entities through the generated JAX-RS resources.

The REST Data extensions include

- `quarkus-hibernate-orm-rest-data-panache`—JDBC with Hibernate ORM.
- `quarkus-mongodb-rest data panache`—MongoDB (NoSQL) with Hibernate ORM.
- `quarkus-hibernate-reactive-rest-data-panache`—Reactive database drivers with Hibernate Reactive.

At the time of writing this book, only the `quarkus-hibernate-orm-rest-data-panache` extension is considered stable. The other two extensions are still considered experimental, and their supported configurations don't cover all the combinations of data access methods that Quarkus supports in general. However, there are REST Data extensions for all varieties that we are discussing in this book (which also corresponds to the most popular user choices), and new combinations might be included in the future.

> **NOTE** Experimental extensions are not guaranteed to be stable, and Quarkus provides them with the intent to collect user feedback. However, REST Data extensions have not been changing frequently in the latest releases, so they may be already considered relatively stable.

Since we haven't covered Hibernate Reactive and Panache with NoSQL databases (like MongoDB) yet, we focus on the `quarkus-hibernate-orm-rest-data-panache` extension in this section. However, we will learn about REST Data modifications for Hibernate Reactive and MongoDB in subsequent sections.

To demonstrate REST Data in action, we include it in the Reservation service, which already provides a subset of CRUD operations over the reservations.

To include REST Data that generate the JAX-RS resource over an entity from the relational database, we need to add three extensions (if not already included):

- The REST Data extension `quarkus-hibernate-orm-rest-data-panache`
- The JDBC driver (e.g., `quarkus-jdbc-postgresql`)
- The REST JSON serialization extension (e.g., `quarkus-rest-jackson`)

You can easily add these extensions to the Reservation service with the command available in listing 7.21. Notice that `quarkus-jdbc-postgresql` and `quarkus-rest-jackson` are skipped because we already added them into Reservation.

> **Listing 7.21   Adding REST Data extensions to the Reservation service**

```
$ quarkus ext add quarkus-hibernate-orm-rest-data-panache \
  quarkus-jdbc-postgresql quarkus-rest-jackson
Looking for the newly published extensions in registry.quarkus.io
[SUCCESS] ✓   Extension io.quarkus:quarkus-hibernate-orm-rest-data-panache
➥ has been installed
  🖘  Extension io.quarkus:quarkus-jdbc-postgresql was already installed
  🖘  Extension io.quarkus:quarkus-rest-jackson was already installed
```

We can reuse the implementation of the `Reservation` entity from listing 7.5 without any additional changes. Next, we only have to define interfaces that denote which Panache entities or repositories should the REST Data extension expose as JAX-RS resources. They are required to extend either the `PanacheEntityResource` interface or, in case of use of the repository pattern, the `PanacheRepositoryResource` interface. Quarkus generates the JAX-RS resources based on these marking files during build time. Since we used the active record pattern in Reservation service, we can define the `ReservationCrudResource` in the `org.acme.reservation.rest` package as shown in the following listing (we need to define a different class name because we already have a `ReservationResource`).

Listing 7.22 The code of `ReservationCrudResource`

```
package org.acme.reservation.rest;

import io.quarkus.hibernate.orm.rest.data.panache.PanacheEntityResource;
import org.acme.reservation.entity.Reservation;

public interface ReservationCrudResource extends
    PanacheEntityResource<Reservation, Long> {
}
```

The extension only requires us to define the entity class and the ID type as type parameters. If you're interested in seeing the declarations of the individual operations, they are in the `io.quarkus.rest.data.panache.RestDataResource` interface (a parent interface of the `PanacheEntityResource`) with a detailed JavaDoc describing each operation. Don't worry about the fact that the default method bodies just throw an exception; they are just placeholders that are overridden with generated code at build time. They are present here so that you, as the application developer, don't have to explicitly override them when declaring an interface that extends `PanacheEntityResource` or `PanacheRepositoryResource`. Also, the extension ignores any additional methods that you might add in your resource interface. However, you can provide customizations for the inherited methods. To do this, you can annotate the REST Data interfaces with these two annotations:

- `@ResourceProperties`—For example, to change the REST path of the resource or if the collection responses return paged results. This annotation should be applied on the REST data interface itself.
- `@MethodProperties`—For example, to define that a particular method is not exposed or to change the path where it is exposed. This annotation should be applied on an overriding method declaration in the REST data interface (if you override a method, don't specify its body, just redeclare it in your interface).

Since the default path of our resource is derived from the class name (i.e., `Reservation-CrudResource`), it is `/reservation-crud`, which is probably not what users of our API would expect, even if it's descriptive. Modify the `ReservationCrudResource` to add the `@ResourceProperties` annotation by customizing the path as shown in the following listing to change the root path on which this generated REST Data endpoint is exposed to `/admin/reservation`.

Listing 7.23 Customizing the `ReservationCrudResource` root path

```
package org.acme.reservation.rest;

import io.quarkus.hibernate.orm.rest.data.panache.PanacheEntityResource;
import io.quarkus.rest.data.panache.ResourceProperties;
import org.acme.reservation.entity.Reservation;
```

```
@ResourceProperties(path = "/admin/reservation")
public interface ReservationCrudResource extends
    PanacheEntityResource<Reservation, Long> {
}
```

If you start the application in Dev mode (if not already running) and go to http://localhost:8081/q/swagger-ui in your browser, you see that the new JAX-RS resource was generated for us, and it now exposes all CRUD operations over the `Reservation` entity. Figure 7.6 presents an excerpt from the Swagger UI showing this new endpoint.

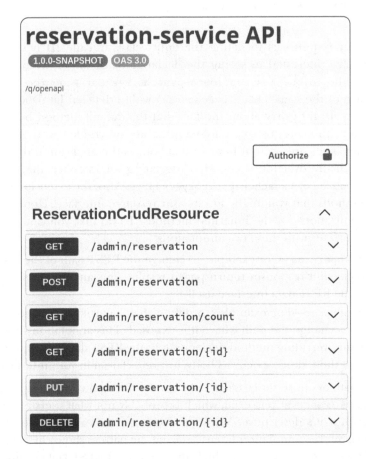

Figure 7.6 Generated REST Data resource in Swagger UI

We will not secure the `/admin/reservation` URL for simplicity. But feel free to utilize what you learned in chapter 6 to secure it yourself as an exercise.

7.5   *Transactions*

Enterprise transactions are surely a topic worth a separate book. Especially in distributed environments like microservices, transactional processing is a complicated problem. We won't dive too deep into the details, but it's important to cover how you need to handle transactions in Quarkus, specifically when used for data access.

Quarkus comes with an integrated transaction manager. If you use any of the extensions that need transactions, they transitively include it for you. If you want to use transactions outside this scope, you might add the `quarkus-narayana-jta` extension to your Quarkus application (Narayana is the name of a project that is an open-source implementation of the transaction manager).

Quarkus provides two ways of handling transactions: declarative and manual.

7.5.1 *Declarative transactions*

Quarkus employs the JTA (Java/Jakarta Transactions API) to denote transactions. We already learned about the `@Transactional` annotation that we used to define transaction boundaries when we were persisting our Car rental entities. This annotation comes from JTA. If you put it on a CDI method, it states that the method runs inside a transaction. The transaction, by default, is started before the method begins, and it's committed or rolled back (depending on the method throwing specified exceptions) when it finishes. The `@Transactional` annotation contains a parameter of type `Transactional.TxType`, which specifies how or if the transaction starts:

- `TxType.REQUIRED`—This is the default. If there is no incoming transaction, start a new one. Join the existing transaction otherwise.
- `TxType.REQUIRES_NEW`—Always execute the method in a new transaction. The framework suspends any existing transaction for the duration of the method execution.
- `TxType.MANDATORY`—The method must be invoked with an already started transaction. Otherwise, it throws an exception.
- `TxType.SUPPORTS`—The method can run both with or without a transaction. If one already exists, join it. If not, run without a transaction.
- `TxType.NOT_SUPPORTED`—The method must be run without transaction. The framework suspends any incoming transaction for the duration of the method execution.
- `TxType.NEVER`—If called within an existing transaction, the framework throws an exception.

The type you choose depends on the use case of the business method. For instance, if the Reservation service would expose an endpoint computing some statistics over all reservations, we don't need to execute this operation in a transaction, so SUPPORTS or NOT_SUPPORTED would be preferred types. However, remember that any operation with transactions (starting or suspending) requires some processing that adds overhead to the method invocation. So it's better not to start transactions when you don't need them.

We can also use this annotation at the class level. It then propagates to all methods. If needed, you can also override the class-level annotation on individual methods.

Furthermore, Quarkus provides the @TransactionConfiguration annotation that you can use to set transaction configuration (e.g., the timeout).

7.5.2 *Manual handling with QuarkusTransaction*

The UserTransaction class, which comes from the JTA, can be easily injected into any CDI bean to utilize the manual management of transactions. However, Quarkus provides a more user-friendly custom API for manual transaction handling in the Quarkus-Transaction class. QuarkusTransaction offers several ways of handling transactions.

The first option of utilization is very similar to the UserTransaction from JTA, where you can manually begin and commit/rollback transactions. But instead of JTA, you can do this with static methods of QuarkusTransaction so you don't need to keep a reference of the user transaction manually. The listing 7.24 provides an example of this API. The begin method also provides an override consuming the BeginOptions instance able to customize some transaction options like the timeout, for example.

Listing 7.24   QuarkusTransaction: manual begin and commit/rollback calls

```
QuarkusTransaction.begin();
// perform operation
result = ...
if (result != null) {
    QuarkusTransaction.commit();
} else {
    QuarkusTransaction.rollback();
}
```

Furthermore, QuarkusTransaction also provides a set of wrappers around Runnable or Callable that execute delegated code in the transaction. The listing 7.25 shows an example of this API. The fluent API allows users to specify the transaction semantic (requiringNew(), joiningExisting(). disallowingExisting(), suspending-Existing()), the transaction timeout, or how to provide an exception handler that can decide whether, in some cases after an exception is thrown, the transaction should still commit successfully.

Listing 7.25   Transaction wrappers provided by QuarkusTransaction

```
QuarkusTransaction.requiringNew().run(() -> {        ◄──┐  Runs a Runnable
    // perform operation                                 │  inside a transaction
});

var txResult = QuarkusTransaction.joiningExisting()
    .timeout(30)
    .exceptionHandler(throwable -> {
        if (throwable instanceof AnyRecoverableException) {
            return TransactionExceptionResult.COMMIT;       Runs a
        }                                                   Callable inside
        return TransactionExceptionResult.ROLLBACK;         a transaction
    }).call(() -> {                                  ◄──┘
```

```
        var result = // perform operation
        return result;
    });
```

7.5.3 Transactions with Panache

In Quarkus, every operation that modifies the database (e.g., persist or update) must execute inside a transaction. Hibernate requires the transaction to propagate the in-memory changes into the downstream database. Quarkus recommends executing transactions at the entry points as we did in our REST resource methods.

Changes made to entities propagate to the database in a batch called *flush*. This is the operation when the framework actually executes SQL statements that have been gathered from the Java-level operations with entities. Hibernate executes a flush at the end of each transaction (before committing it) or before a query. But sometimes it might be useful to perform a flush sooner (e.g., entity or constraints validations). Quarkus provides two methods that force a flush operation:

- `EntityClass.flush()` or `repository.flush()`—Sends current changes to the database
- `entityInstance.persistAndFlush(entity)` or `repository.persistAndFlush (entity)`—Persist and flush in a single method call

These methods throw the `PersistenceException` that you can catch to execute your logic. In every case, use them wisely, as these forms of communication with the database tend to cost a lot of application resources.

7.6 Panache with NoSQL

NoSQL (non-SQL but sometimes also referred to as Not-Only SQL) databases are a newer alternative to relational databases. These databases store the data in different formats than traditional relational databases. There are many types of NoSQL data stores, including key-value, wide column, graph, or document. Quarkus supports many distinct NoSQL databases (MongoDB, Cassandra, Elasticsearch, Neo4j, and Amazon DynamoDB, to name a few) to cover respective users' preferences.

One of the most popular NoSQL databases is MongoDB (https://www.mongodb .com). MongoDB is the most widely used document-based NoSQL database. This is why we will introduce it in the Rental service as our data store.

Quarkus supports MongoDB with its provided API through the `mongodb-client` extension. However, it also provides an integration with the Panache framework that vastly simplifies mapping of the Java objects into MongoDB documents. This means that we can write very similar code to what we did for relational databases. However, Panache stores our entities as documents (represented as JSON) in a NoSQL database this time.

7.6.1   *Utilizing MongoDB with Panache*

If we want to integrate Panache with MongoDB into a Quarkus application, we need to do a few things:

- Add the `quarkus-mongodb-panache` extension and the relevant connection configuration
- Define entity classes
- Make entities extend `PanacheMongoEntity`
- Optionally also define a repository class extending `PanacheMongoRepository` (if using the repository pattern)

PANACHE MONGODB CONFIGURATION

MongoDB comes integrated with Panache in a single extension, so we only need to add the `quarkus-mongodb-panache` extension. Let's now add it to the Rental service (`rental-service` directory), as demonstrated in the following listing.

> **Listing 7.26   Adding `quarkus-mongodb-panache` extension**

```
$ quarkus ext add quarkus-mongodb-panache
Looking for the newly published extensions in registry.quarkus.io
[SUCCESS] ✅   Extension io.quarkus:quarkus-mongodb-panache has been
➡ installed
```

Next, we must configure the connection information in the `application.properties` file. The connection string is the only required property. However, if you don't use the `@MongoEntity` annotation on your entities to specify the name of the database where to map each entity, you also must define the name of the connected database. Listing 7.27 provides an example of MongoDB connection properties. As you might notice, we are again using the prod profile for the connection string, so we have Dev services for MongoDB started in the Dev mode (since in Dev mode, this property is undefined).

> **Listing 7.27   The MongoDB Panache connection information properties**

```
%prod.quarkus.mongodb.connection-string=mongodb://mongo:27017

quarkus.mongodb.database=rental
```

DEVELOPING PANACHE MONGODB ENTITIES

The development is very similar to using Panache with relational databases. The only change is that entities now need to extend a specific MongoDB entity base in the class `PanacheMongoEntity`, or they can also extend the `PanacheMongoEntityBase` if you want to declare your own ID field.

Similarly, if you prefer to use the repository pattern, then you need to create a repository class extending the `PanacheMongoRepository`, or if you also want to change the type of the used IDs, then you need to extend the `PanacheMongoRepositoryBase`.

In the Rental service, we use the active record pattern. We can move the created `org.acme.rental.Rental` class into `org.acme.rental.entity.Rental` to represent our entity and modify it as shown in the following listing.

> **Listing 7.28** The `Rental` Panache MongoDB entity in the Rental service

```
package org.acme.rental.entity;

import io.quarkus.mongodb.panache.PanacheMongoEntity;

import java.time.LocalDate;

public class Rental extends PanacheMongoEntity {

    public String userId;
    public Long reservationId;
    public LocalDate startDate;
    public LocalDate endDate;
    public boolean active;

    @Override
    public String toString() {
        return "Rental{" +
            "userId='" + userId + '\'' +
            ", reservationId=" + reservationId +
            ", startDate=" + startDate +
            ", endDate=" + endDate +
            ", active=" + active +
            ", id=" + id +
            '}';
    }
}
```

We can also remove the original ID field since it is now provided automatically and only keep the `userId` referencing the user owning this rental. We will also soon introduce the handling of rental ends, so we added the `endDate` and the `active` fields.

If you need to change the name of the created collection, the name of the database, or the name of the client, you can add the optional `@MongoEntity` annotation that allows you to change this information. By default, the created collection is named `Rental`, but if we would like to call it `Rentals` (as some teams prefer naming collections in plural), we could do it with the `@MongoEntity` annotation as follows:

```
@MongoEntity(collection = "Rentals")
public class Rental extends PanacheMongoEntity {
```

Now we are ready to persist rentals into the MongoDB NoSQL databases.

Quarkus uses the MongoDB Java driver to serialize Panache entities into MongoDB documents. This conversion uses the Binary JSON (BSON; https://bsonspec.org) formats utilized in MongoDB. So if you need to customize any mapping information, you need to utilize annotations from the `org.bson.codecs.pojo.annotations` package. For instance, if you want to rename a particular field, it is done like this:

```
@BsonProperty("rental-active")
public boolean active;
```

The Rental service won't compile now. But we will fix it the following section.

7.6.2 *Using the Panache MongoDB in Rental service*

We can now extend the Rental service functionality to persist data into MongoDB. Additionally, since we now track the rental state, we can add a few business methods into the `Rental` entity class that we can later utilize in the exposed REST API. Let's add two new methods into the `Rental` class as shown in the following listing.

Listing 7.29   Adding custom business methods to `Rental` entity

```
public static Optional<Rental> findByUserAndReservationIdsOptional(
    String userId, Long reservationId) {
    return find("userId = ?1 and reservationId = ?2",
        userId, reservationId)
        .firstResultOptional();
}

public static List<Rental> listActive() {
    return list("active", true);
}
```

The first method finds a `Rental` with a specific `userId` and `reservationId` if it exists. The second lists all active rentals.

Now we can update the JAX-RS resource in class `RentalResource` to look like presented in the following listing.

Listing 7.30   `RentalResource` with database integration

```
@Path("/rental")
public class RentalResource {

    @Path("/start/{userId}/{reservationId}")
    @POST
    public Rental start(String userId,
                        Long reservationId) {
        Log.infof("Starting rental for %s with reservation %s",
        userId, reservationId);

        Rental rental = new Rental();
        rental.userId = userId;
        rental.reservationId = reservationId;
        rental.startDate = LocalDate.now();
        rental.active = true;

        rental.persist();
```

```
            return rental;
    }

    @PUT
    @Path("/end/{userId}/{reservationId}")
    public Rental end(String userId, Long reservationId) {
        Log.infof("Ending rental for %s with reservation %s",
        userId, reservationId);
        Optional<Rental> optionalRental = Rental
            .findByUserAndReservationIdsOptional(userId, reservationId);

        if (optionalRental.isPresent()) {
            Rental rental = optionalRental.get();
            rental.endDate = LocalDate.now();
            rental.active = false;
            rental.update();
            return rental;
        } else {
            throw new NotFoundException("Rental not found");
        }
    }

    @GET
    public List<Rental> list() {
        return Rental.listAll();
    }

    @GET
    @Path("/active")
    public List<Rental> listActive() {
        return Rental.listActive();
    }
}
```

> Uses the custom method to get the rental from MongoDB

> Uses the custom method to list only the active rentals

MongoDB supports transactions since version 4.0, but their usage is not required, so we omit them for simplicity. This is why we don't have `@Transactional` in this class. In the `end` method, we use our custom business method to find the rental with the provided `userId` and `reservationId`. If it exists, we update the `endDate` and `active` fields and persist the changes in the database. Otherwise, we throw an exception since the rental doesn't exist in our MongoDB database.

Notice that we also removed `@Produces(MediaType.APPLICATION_JSON)` from the `start` method because if we have `quarkus-rest-jackson` as the only REST extension in the project, producing and consuming JSON is implicit. We just wanted to mention that this is possible.

If we now start the Rental service in Dev mode (`quarkus dev`), we can verify that the persisted rentals arc in the MongoDB started with Dev services, as shown in the following listing.

Listing 7.31 Verification of the Rental service functionality

```
$ http POST :8082/rental/start/user1/1
HTTP/1.1 200 OK
```

```
Content-Type: application/json;charset=UTF-8
content-length: 122

{
    "active": true,
    "endDate": null,
    "id": "66f42c220498235e9684db9e",
    "reservationId": 1,
    "startDate": "2024-09-25",
    "userId": "user1"
}

$ http PUT :8082/rental/end/user1/1
HTTP/1.1 200 OK
Content-Type: application/json;charset=UTF-8
content-length: 131

{
    "active": false,
    "endDate": "2024-09-25",
    "id": "66f42c220498235e9684db9e",
    "reservationId": 1,
    "startDate": "2024-09-25",
    "userId": "user1"
}

$ http :8082/rental
HTTP/1.1 200 OK
Content-Type: application/json;charset=UTF-8
content-length: 133

[
    {
        "active": false,
        "endDate": "2024-09-25",
        "id": "66f42c220498235e9684db9e",
        "reservationId": 1,
        "startDate": "2024-09-25",
        "userId": "user1"
    }
]

$ http :8082/rental/active
HTTP/1.1 200 OK
Content-Type: application/json;charset=UTF-8
content-length: 2

[]
```

The result is empty since we don't have any active rentals.

And we can also verify that the document is stored in the MongoDB directly with, for instance, the mongosh command line client (you can find the mapped port with docker ps):

NOTE Just like with relational databases, you can also optionally configure Quarkus to always expose the MongoDB service on a fixed host port (by default the number is chosen randomly on each start). The configuration property is `quarkus.mongodb.devservices.port`. If you set it after the application has already started, you will have to restart Dev mode.

TIP This verification with `mongosh` is again optional. If you don't have it installed, you don't have to install it now.

```
$ mongosh --port 45527 rental --eval "db.Rental.find({})"
[
  {
    _id: ObjectId('66f42c220498235e9684db9e'),
    active: false,
    endDate: ISODate('2024-09-25T00:00:00.000Z'),
    reservationId: Long('1'),
    startDate: ISODate('2024-09-25T00:00:00.000Z'),
    userId: 'user1'
  }
]
```

7.6.3 *Adjusting Reservation service to the Rental service updates*

MongoDB doesn't use a numeric value as the type of the ID field. You might have noticed it in the outputs in the previous section. Now that the `Rental` entity extends the `PanacheMongoEntity`, the ID type has changed to `ObjectId`, which we can mainly interpret as a `String` value that is returned now from our endpoints. Of course, this is not a problem in the Rental service. We didn't interpret the ID manually anywhere, and the Jackson parser can adjust to this change automatically.

However, the problem with the parsing of the `Rental` ID fields arises in the Reservation service that calls the Rental service if the reservation is being made on the current day. We must adjust the Rental JSON parsing in the Reservation service to accommodate this change. Namely, we need to change the type of the `id` field in the `org.acme.reservation.rental.Rental` class to type `String` and adjust the constructor and getter accordingly. The following listing presents this change.

Listing 7.32 Adjustments needed in the Reservation service

```
public class Rental {

    private final String id;

    ...

    public Rental(String id, String userId, Long reservationId,
                  LocalDate startDate) {
        ...
    }
```

```
public String getId() {
    return id;
}


...

}
```

And now we can safely call Rental service from the Reservation service again.

7.7   *Reactive data access*

Reactive programming is a programming paradigm in which users write nonblocking, responsive, asynchronous code based on message passing. We will dive deep into the reactive world in chapter 8, but here we want to look into how you can utilize non-blocking database drivers provided by some databases to integrate the database utilization into your reactive pipelines.

Quarkus uses the Hibernate Reactive project to integrate with different databases supporting reactive drivers. By their definition, "Hibernate Reactive is intended for use in a reactive programming environment like Vert.x or Quarkus, where interaction with the database should occur in a nonblocking fashion. Persistence operations are orchestrated via the construction of a reactive stream rather than via direct invocation of synchronous functions in procedural Java code" (https://hibernate.org/reactive). A stream in Hibernate Reactive is represented as either a `CompletionStage` coming from the JDK or as a `Uni` (single result) or as a `Multi` (multiple results), both of which come from the project called SmallRye Mutiny.

> **NOTE** We will cover SmallRye Mutiny in detail in chapter 8. Here we only need to remember that both `Uni` and `Multi` represent an asynchronously computed single or multiple results, respectively.

Traditional Hibernate ORM and JPA were designed with blocking I/O operations. If you invoke a request to the database, the active thread waits for the response—it's blocked. However, when you write the application reactively, blocking is not allowed, at least not on event loop threads. If your operation needs to block, it must delegate the blocking operation execution to the so-called worker thread, passing the execution back to the event loop thread once the blocking operation finishes. This is what Quarkus with traditional Hibernate ORM does. However, with Hibernate Reactive and reactive database drivers, purely reactive APIs are used, and, in most cases, no blocking operations need to be performed when accessing the database.

You may ask why this is important. And that is an excellent question. The main idea is that reactive code makes your applications more responsive, which is the primary metric that must be scalable in modern applications. But we will cover this in detail in the following chapter. For now, it is only important to learn how to use reactive types with persistence.

Quarkus provides direct integration of Hibernate Reactive, which allows users to utilize the API provided by the library. Quarkus also provides a Panache integration layer on top of this integration to simplify the code users need to write. In the next section, we focus on Panache with Hibernate Reactive.

7.7.1 Using Hibernate Reactive with Panache

As we already learned about Panache, it dramatically simplifies the code for data access for simple data sets. With Hibernate Reactive Panache, we still utilize a very similar model but this time with the reactive programming paradigm and reactive SQL clients. From the development point of view, this boils down to using the Panache-provided methods (either in the entity with the active record or in the repository). Instead of standard types like `E` or `List<E>`, which we had in the blocking version, we now receive results of types `Uni<E>` or `Uni<List<E>>` where `E` is our entity type. This only says that the result in the `Uni<E>` represents an asynchronous computation that completes in the future.

That's enough theory for now (we will focus on reactive programming in the following chapter). Let's change the Reservation service to use Panache with Hibernate Reactive on top of the nonblocking PostgreSQL driver.

PANACHE HIBERNATE REACTIVE EXTENSIONS AND CONFIGURATION

To start, we need to change the extensions that we originally included in the Reservation service. We have to replace the blocking versions of Panache (`quarkus-hibernate-orm-panache`) and PostgreSQL JDBC driver (`quarkus-jdbc-postgresql`) with their reactive counterparts—`quarkus-hibernate-reactive-panache` and `quarkus-reactive-pg-client`—like demoed in listing 7.33, with these commands executed in the `reservation-service` directory. Also, since we utilized REST data in the Reservation service, we need to exchange the `quarkus-hibernate-orm-rest-data-panache` for the reactive version in the `quarkus-hibernate-reactive-rest-data-panache` extension.

> **Listing 7.33 Replacing blocking ORM extensions with their reactive versions**

```
$ quarkus ext remove quarkus-hibernate-orm-panache quarkus-jdbc-postgresql
  quarkus-hibernate-orm-rest-data-panache
Looking for the newly published extensions in registry.quarkus.io
[SUCCESS] ✓  Extension io.quarkus:quarkus-jdbc-postgresql has been
  uninstalled
[SUCCESS] ✓  Extension io.quarkus:quarkus-hibernate-orm-rest-data-panache
  has been uninstalled
[SUCCESS] ✓  Extension io.quarkus:quarkus-hibernate-orm-panache has been
  uninstalled

$ quarkus ext add quarkus-hibernate-reactive-panache
  quarkus-reactive-pg-client quarkus-hibernate-reactive-rest-data-panache
[SUCCESS] ✓  Extension io.quarkus:quarkus-hibernate-reactive-panache has
  been installed
[SUCCESS] ✓  Extension io.quarkus:quarkus-reactive-pg-client has been
  installed
[SUCCESS] ✓  Extension
  io.quarkus:quarkus-hibernate-reactive-rest-data-panache has been
  installed
```

The only required change in the application's configuration is the connection URL string. Other properties remain the same. The configuration in the application .properties of the Reservation service should be changed as shown in the following listing.

Listing 7.34 The Hibernate Reactive configuration

```
quarkus.datasource.db-kind=postgresql
quarkus.datasource.username=user
quarkus.datasource.password=pass
%prod.quarkus.datasource.reactive.url=
➥  vertx-reactive:postgresql://localhost:5432/reservation

# drop and create the database at startup
quarkus.hibernate-orm.database.generation=drop-and-create
```

The only required change from the blocking Panache version ⟵

DEFINING ENTITIES WITH HIBERNATE REACTIVE

The code of our entities is the same as with the blocking versions of the extensions. However, the packages of the classes that our classes extend or implement changed as now they provide the reactive variants. We need to do a few drop-in replacements in files Reservation.java and ReservationCrudResource.java as shown in the following listing. But everything else can stay the same.

Listing 7.35 Replacements of extensions classes with reactive variants

```
// Reservation.java

-import io.quarkus.hibernate.orm.panache.PanacheEntity;
+import io.quarkus.hibernate.reactive.panache.PanacheEntity;

// ReservationCrudResource.java

-import io.quarkus.hibernate.orm.rest.data.panache.PanacheEntityResource;
+import io.quarkus.hibernate.reactive.rest.data.panache.
➥  PanacheEntityResource;
```

7.7.2 *Reservation service updates for Hibernate Reactive usage*

Since we now use reactive types in the Reservation service, we need to adjust our code that communicates with the database to be reactive too. Let's start with the ReservationResource class, which contains most of the required changes. Don't worry if you don't understand everything. We will apply our knowledge with a deeper analysis of reactive programming in chapter 8.

We go over each method of the ReservationResource separately, explaining any additional changes as we go.

We use the Uni type in the return value of the JAX-RS methods to make use of the reactive nature of Quarkus REST. If we return the Uni, the HTTP request suspends until the Uni produces a value (more details in chapter 8). This fits nicely with our reactive access to the database.

RESERVATIONRESOURCE#MAKE

The following listing demonstrates the changes needed in the make method.

Listing 7.36 Reactive changes in `ReservationResource#make`

```
@Consumes(MediaType.APPLICATION_JSON)
@POST
@WithTransaction
public Uni<Reservation> make(Reservation reservation) {
    reservation.userId = context.getUserPrincipal() != null ?
        context.getUserPrincipal().getName() : "anonymous";
    return reservation.<Reservation>persist().onItem()
        .call(persistedReservation -> {
            Log.info("Successfully reserved reservation "
              + persistedReservation);
            if (persistedReservation.startDay.equals(LocalDate.now())) {
                Rental rental = rentalClient
                    .start(persistedReservation.userId,
                        persistedReservation.id);
                Log.info("Successfully started rental " + rental);
            }
            return Uni.createFrom().item(persistedReservation);
        });
}
```

With Hibernate Reactive, if the method returns an Uni, we need to use a custom @WithTransaction annotation to mark the transaction boundary. It behaves the same as the @Transactional in nonreactive code. The transaction boundary just takes into account the asynchronously computed result and the transaction is committed only when the result is available.

The persist method now also returns a Uni<Reservation>, which contains our persisted reservation. With the onItem().call callback, we can define what should happen when we receive the persisted reservation from the database. We execute the same logic as before, but now we also return a new Uni with the persisted reservation to propagate the Reservation as the return value of the make method.

However, we are still not finished. Since the main processing is now nonblocking, even the outgoing Rental service HTTP call can no longer utilize blocking APIs. If you now invoke POST /reservation with the current day, the request fails, with the error message stating BlockingNotAllowedException. We need to also update the return type of the RentalClient#start method to be reactive too, as shown in the following listing.

Listing 7.37 Return type change to nonblocking `Uni` in `RentalClient`

```
@RegisterRestClient(baseUri = "http://localhost:8082")
@Path("/rental")
public interface RentalClient {

    @POST
    @Path("/start/{userId}/{reservationId}")
```

```
Uni<Rental> start(@RestPath String userId,
                  @RestPath Long reservationId);
}
```

This, of course, needs the adjustment in the `ReservationResource#make` method to consume now provided `Uni` return type. This is demonstrated in the following listing.

Listing 7.38   The `ReservationResource#make` method update

```
@Consumes(MediaType.APPLICATION_JSON)
@POST
@WithTransaction
public Uni<Reservation> make(Reservation reservation) {
    reservation.userId = context.getUserPrincipal() != null ?
        context.getUserPrincipal().getName() : "anonymous";
    return reservation.<Reservation>persist().onItem()
        .call(persistedReservation -> {
            Log.info("Successfully reserved reservation "
                + persistedReservation);
            if (persistedReservation.startDay.equals(LocalDate.now())) {
                return rentalClient.start(persistedReservation.userId,
                        persistedReservation.id)
                    .onItem().invoke(rental ->
                        Log.info("Successfully started rental " + rental))
                    .replaceWith(persistedReservation);
            }
            return Uni.createFrom().item(persistedReservation);
        });
}
```

We only need to change the `if` statement for the `rentalClient` invocation to replace the asynchronous response from now reactive invocation of the remote HTTP request to the Rental service with the persisted reservation (the `replaceWith` invocation). This also corresponds to the expected return value of the `make` method.

RESERVATIONRESOURCE#AVAILABILITY

The `availability` method needs similar changes shown in the following listing.

Listing 7.39   Reactive changes in `ReservationResource#availability`

```
@GET
@Path("availability")
public Uni<Collection<Car>> availability(@RestQuery LocalDate startDate,
                                         @RestQuery LocalDate endDate) {
    // obtain all cars from inventory
    List<Car> availableCars = inventoryClient.allCars();
    // create a map from id to car
    Map<Long, Car> carsById = new HashMap<>();
    for (Car car : availableCars) {
        carsById.put(car.id, car);
    }
```

```
    // get all current reservations
    return Reservation.<Reservation>listAll()
        .onItem().transform(reservations -> {
            // for each reservation, remove the car from the map
            for (Reservation reservation : reservations) {
                if (reservation.isReserved(startDate, endDate)) {
                    carsById.remove(reservation.carId);
                }
            }
            return carsById.values();
        });
}
```

The `Reservation.listAll()` method now returns `Uni<List<Reservation>>`. This time we use a different callback method: `onItem().transform`. It receives the list and filters the cars as we did before. The `transform` operation allows us to transform the list of reservations to the collection of available cars within the `Uni` which we can directly return as `Uni<Collection<Car>>` from the `availability` method. We couldn't use the same method in the `make` method before because of the Rental service call, which produces a different result (rental) than what we need to return (reservation).

Similar to before, we also make a blocking call, but this time through GraphQL to Inventory service to collect all cars. We need to make similar changes to the `GraphQL-InventoryClient` (and `InventoryClient`) as we did with REST `RentalClient`. The following listing demonstrates the required changes in both client classes.

Listing 7.40   Return type change in the Inventory service client interfaces

```
@GraphQLClientApi(configKey = "inventory")
public interface GraphQLInventoryClient extends InventoryClient {
    @Query("cars")
    Uni<List<Car>> allCars();
}

public interface InventoryClient {

    Uni<List<Car>> allCars();
}
```

And the `availability` method needs the changes presented in the following listing.

Listing 7.41   Combining the two `Uni` results in the `availability` method

```
@GET
@Path("availability")
public Uni<Collection<Car>> availability(@RestQuery LocalDate startDate,
                                         @RestQuery LocalDate endDate) {
    // obtain all cars from inventory
    Uni<List<Car>> availableCarsUni = inventoryClient.allCars();
    // get all current reservations
    Uni<List<Reservation>> reservationsUni = Reservation.listAll();
```

```
    return Uni.combine().all().unis(availableCarsUni, reservationsUni)
        .with((availableCars, reservations) -> {
        // create a map from id to car
        Map<Long, Car> carsById = new HashMap<>();
        for (Car car : availableCars) {
            carsById.put(car.id, car);
        }

        // for each reservation, remove the car from the map
        for (Reservation reservation : reservations) {
            if (reservation.isReserved(startDate, endDate)) {
                carsById.remove(reservation.carId);
            }
        }
        return carsById.values();
    });
}
```

Here we execute both the call to the Inventory service and the select to the database asynchronously at the same time. Then we use the Uni.combine().all().unis construct to combine the asynchronous results when they are ready. In the defined callback, we execute again the same logic of filtering available cars, and we return it inside a wrapped Uni<Collection<Car>> from the availability method.

RESERVATIONRESOURCE#ALLRESERVATIONS

The last and the simplest method we need to adjust is allReservations. The required changes are in the following listing.

Listing 7.42 **Reactive changes in** ReservationResource#allReservations

```
@GET
@Path("all")
public Uni<List<Reservation>> allReservations() {
    String userId = context.getUserPrincipal() != null ?
        context.getUserPrincipal().getName() : null;
    return Reservation.<Reservation>listAll()
        .onItem().transform(reservations -> reservations.stream()
        .filter(reservation -> userId == null ||
            userId.equals(reservation.userId))
        .collect(Collectors.toList()));
}
```

Unfortunately, we don't have the streamAll method with Hibernate Reactive. We need to use the listAll method and then the transform method to be able to stream the list to filter the reservations based on the user ID as before. We collect the stream back as a list and return it as Uni<List<Reservation>>.

RESERVATIONPERSISTENCETEST

With the main application code now ready, let's move to tests. The ReservationPersistenceTest won't compile since it directly references the Reservation entity (however, the application in Dev mode already starts because our main code compiles!).

We need a more sophisticated rewrite since we need to handle transactions in the reactive code. Quarkus provides a simple helper APIs that are contained in the `quarkus` `-test-hibernate-reactive-panache` extension. Add this extension to the `pom.xml` in test scope:

```
<dependency>
  <groupId>io.quarkus</groupId>
  <artifactId>quarkus-test-hibernate-reactive-panache</artifactId>
  <scope>test</scope>
</dependency>
```

Now we can change the `ReservationPersistenceTest` as demonstrated in the following listing.

Listing 7.43 Reactive invocations in the `ReservationPersistenceTest`

```
@Test
@RunOnVertxContext
public void testCreateReservation(TransactionalUniAsserter asserter) {
    Reservation reservation = new Reservation();
    reservation.startDay = LocalDate.now().plus(5, ChronoUnit.DAYS);
    reservation.endDay = LocalDate.now().plus(12, ChronoUnit.DAYS);
    reservation.carId = 384L;

    asserter.<Reservation>assertThat(() -> reservation.persist(),
        r -> {
            Assertions.assertNotNull(r.id);
            asserter.putData("reservation.id", r.id);
        });

    asserter.assertEquals(() -> Reservation.count(), 1L);
    asserter.assertThat(() -> Reservation.<Reservation>findById(
            asserter.getData("reservation.id")),
        persistedReservation -> {
            Assertions.assertNotNull(persistedReservation);
            Assertions.assertEquals(reservation.carId,
                persistedReservation.carId);
        });
}
```

The `@RunOnVertxContext` annotation is needed for Quarkus to run the test method on the Vert.x (event loop) thread because the main thread wouldn't work with reactive code. This annotation also allows us to use the `TransactionalUniAsserter` that provides an API for assertions on `Uni` results, which we can simply inject into our test. It represents an extension of the base `UniAsserter` that wraps each operation in a new transaction. The asserter provides a similar API as JUnit `Assertions` so the use is pretty similar to normal JUnit usage. This is the recommended way of testing Hibernate Reactive.

Notice also how we can pass information between different asynchronous assertions with the `asserter.putData` and `asserter.getData` methods.

> **NOTE**   The base `UniAsserter` provides more customization options if you need them. You can find more information in the Quarkus documentation (https://quarkus.io/guides/hibernate-reactive#testing).

RESERVATIONRESOURCETEST

The last required change to make the Reservation service reactive is to update the `GraphQLInventoryClient` mock in the `ReservationResourceTest` to provide a newly required `Uni`. Change the test in this class as in the diff presented in the following listing.

Listing 7.44   Mock result adjustment in `ReservationResourceTest`

```
Mockito.when(mock.allCars())
-    .thenReturn(Collections.singletonList(peugeot));
+    .thenReturn(Uni.createFrom().item(Collections.singletonList(peugeot)));
```

The Reservation service now works again as expected—but now with Hibernate Reactive. Feel free to experiment with the available APIs as we did in listing 7.9. If you want a small reminder, you can find all available endpoints at http://localhost:8081/q/swagger-ui when the Reservation service runs in Dev mode. Try to also run the Rental service to verify that the reservation service can start rentals as expected when the starting day is today.

7.8   *Next steps*

In this chapter, we learned how to store application data in a data store with Quarkus. We introduced the new Panache framework built on top of the well-known Hibernate ORM framework to provide simplified API for ORM development.

We differentiated two patterns that users can utilize with Panache: the active record pattern and the repository pattern. We demonstrated the use of both these patterns with relational databases (PostgreSQL and MySQL). We also implemented the NoSQL database (MongoDB) integration in the Rental service. Additionally, we introduced a new REST data framework that significantly simplifies the development of CRUD JAX-RS resources on top of Panache entities.

Furthermore, we illustrated the use of Panache with Hibernate Reactive—a framework that can utilize the nonblocking reactive drivers provided by some databases. We also touched on the reactive programming model. Since Quarkus is built around reactive principles, we will learn how Quarkus applications can utilize reactive development in detail in the next chapter.

Summary

- Panache is a framework providing simplified ORM in Quarkus. It frees the developer from most of the boilerplate code that needs to be written with current data access libraries.

- Panache can be utilized with either the active record or the repository pattern, where both have the same level of expressiveness, and with Panache it is simple to switch between them.
- REST Data is a further simplification for developing JAX-RS CRUD services. It generates the CRUD resources for the specified Panache entities that can be adjusted for user requirements.
- Quarkus can utilize the reactive drivers provided by the database through the Hibernate Reactive library. The application code then uses the reactive, non-blocking, and asynchronous APIs, which makes the applications more scalable and responsive.

Reactive programming

This chapter covers

- Learning what reactive programming is
- Identifying why we want to write reactive code
- Explaining SmallRye Mutiny as the reactive library used in Quarkus
- Analyzing how the reactive paradigm integrates into the Quarkus architecture

We have touched on reactive programming throughout the book since we cannot always avoid it (especially if we want to use Hibernate Reactive). In this chapter, we finally dive into the reactive concepts to understand why you might consider using reactive programming in your applications.

The reactive programming paradigm is an alternative way of writing software programs. In contrast to the imperative model, which executes the program as a sequence of ordered steps, reactive programming focuses on asynchronous executions that notify the caller about the result only when the result computes or an error occurs. In this way, the caller thread is free to do any other work in the meantime and return to the request processing only when there is progress. This means that reactive systems can be more responsive and scalable as the same resources (both software and hardware) can do more work in the same time frame.

This benefit stems mainly from the fact that threads are not blocked while waiting for an I/O operation (a remote service or database call) to finish. Instead of waiting and doing nothing useful, they can be used to process other things. Therefore, your application needs fewer threads to handle the same amount of work, and that's good because thread utilization can be expensive in terms of resources.

8.1 Being reactive

Quarkus is built on top of a reactive engine from the ground up, meaning writing reactive programs is straightforward. However, if you prefer the imperative model, you can still write applications the same way you are used to with imperative code, but you will lose some of the scalability benefits.

Reactive programming is generally considered to be more complex than imperative programming. But if you are willing to write reactive code, in this chapter we explain the transition from the imperative model and the benefits that reactive programming brings to your applications. Note that since JDK 21, we also have virtual threads (project Loom) which provide a solution that allows you to write imperative code while getting similar benefits as reactive. However, there are some limitations to the use of virtual threads, which we will investigate in section 8.5.

Quarkus also allows you to mix both paradigms (actually three if you want to count the virtual threads too). You can actually do this even in the same class, which can significantly help with gradual transition to a reactive programming model.

8.1.1 Handling of I/O operations

The first question you might ask is: why might reactive programming be useful? I/O operations are a great example to demonstrate the distinction between imperative and reactive execution models. Modern applications require I/O, whether to access the database/filesystem, call another service, or process messages from a broker. These operations generally take a long time to complete. In the typical sequential imperative model, these calls represent blocking operations. Each incoming request is assigned to a worker thread from a predefined thread pool that handles it from start to finish, as shown in figure 8.1.

If the request requires I/O operation, the whole thread is blocked. No other work can be done until the I/O operation completes, even if the I/O operation itself delegates to a separate resource (e.g., network device, file system, database). The thread is just idly waiting for the operation to finish. With the move of application workloads to the cloud, having a bigger number of threads to handle concurrent tasks also means higher memory and CPU cycles consumption, which directly translates to higher cloud bills.

With the reactive paradigm, Quarkus allows you to streamline this processing into nonblocking I/O based on an asynchronous event-driven network application

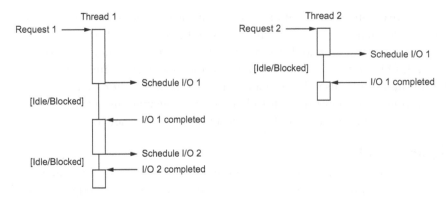

Figure 8.1   Blocking I/O request handling: threads are blocked while waiting for an I/O operation to complete

framework called Netty (https://netty.io). By using only a few eventloop (or I/O) threads that handle concurrent I/O operations, there is no longer a need to delegate each request to a new thread. Instead, I/O interleaves in the same eventloop thread, as shown in figure 8.2.

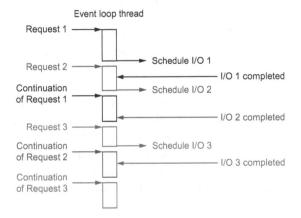

Figure 8.2   Nonblocking I/O request handling: threads don't block while waiting for an I/O operation to complete

Consequently, users must refrain from blocking these eventloop threads for this to function correctly. If you block the eventloop thread for the configured time (2 seconds by default), Quarkus will log a warning. Some operations that are recognized by Quarkus as blocking will throw an exception right away if you attempt to execute them on an event loop thread.

Because scheduled I/O operations don't block the eventloop thread, it may be utilized for other work while the operation progresses. It thus effectively executes operations concurrently in the same thread. If any work needs to block, it is outsourced to a thread from the worker thread pool.

Quarkus automatically deduces whether the method executes on the eventloop or the worker thread depending on the signature of the method. If it's reactive (returning reactive, nonblocking types), it chooses the eventloop thread with the expectation that the method doesn't block it. Conversely, other return types mean that the method is expected to block, so it executes on the worker thread.

Quarkus also provides users with the `@Blocking` and `@Nonblocking` annotations, which, if placed on the method, give Quarkus a hint that the operation needs to execute on the worker (blocking) thread or on the eventloop (nonblocking) thread, respectively. For example, if you need to perform a blocking computation in your reactive pipeline, you can simply put the `@Blocking` annotation on the method that encapsulates this computation, and it will be dispatched to a worker thread.

8.1.2 Writing reactive code

Most developers write their code in the imperative paradigm. When the program starts, the runtime invokes a top-level entrypoint method (e.g., the `main` method in Java) that begins executing declared statements step by step. Conversely, the reactive programming model expresses executions in the form of *continuations*. A continuation defines the code executed when the operation completes. The continuation handles either the successful case (then we have a result available), or it can complete exceptionally, in which case we can handle the received exception. Figure 8.3 shows the difference in executions.

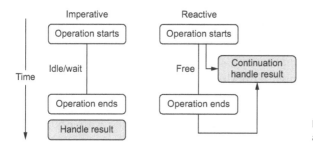

Figure 8.3 Comparison of imperative and reactive code handling

Continuations typically define the same result handling code as in the imperative model. The difference is in when and how it is defined. With step-by-step instructions it is clear that operations handling the result start only when the operation ends (in this case, the processing blocks until the operation ends). Otherwise, we couldn't execute the next operation in the sequence, which requires the result as argument. With reactive programming, we pass the continuation to the operation itself. When the operation ends, the continuation code executes with the result. In other words, our code reacts to the event generated by the end of the operation. The operation invocation is fully asynchronous, and we are free to do any other work in the meantime.

This might sound a lot like an event-driven architecture. And it actually is—however, at a bigger scope, since modern applications need to handle an enormous number of events. These events frequently come from an external source—for instance, user clicks, message retrievals, database updates, or new service version rollout. However, they also include internal concepts like asynchronous operations, I/O requests, or the definitions and executions of reactive pipelines (linking of continuations). Reactive programming thus requires a different way of thinking about the execution flow in the application. In turn, it provides a better scaling and more resilient model that performs better under altering loads.

Let's go over a real-world example to help you understand imperative and reactive handling. Imagine you go into a coffee shop and order a coffee at the counter. With imperative code, you stand at the counter (blocking everyone in the queue behind you) while your coffee is being prepared. Once it's ready, you take it, sit at a table, and enjoy it. In the reactive code, you order your coffee and right away receive a receipt— a promise that you'll get your coffee in the future (sounds like Uni, right?). You will leave the counter and wait for the coffee elsewhere in the shop. You are not blocking anyone else in the queue, so the (coffee) requests are continuously being processed while you wait. Once your coffee is ready, the barista calls you (the notification event saying your result is ready), and you execute your continuation, which is again the operation of picking up the coffee, sitting at the table, and enjoying it. The resulting state is the same, but with the reactive way, you didn't waste any of your or other customers' time with just plain waiting while your coffee was being prepared.

8.2   *Mutiny*

Quarkus uses SmallRye Mutiny as its reactive API exposed to users. Mutiny is a reactive library that provides a set of APIs for nonblocking, event-driven, and asynchronous applications. It implements the Reactive Streams specification, so it comes with integrated *backpressure* (a mechanism that allows consumers to signal producers to slow down the production of items). With Mutiny, user code reacts to events emitted when the result is computed or an error occurs.

> **NOTE** Reactive programming in Quarkus is also usable with Kotlin coroutines, which is outside the scope of this book.

8.2.1   *Reactive streams*

The Reactive Streams specification (https://www.reactive-streams.org) provides an API for the nonblocking asynchronous stream executions with integrated backpressure. Since JDK 9, it is also integrated directly into the JDK as the `java.util.concurrent.Flow` class.

This specification consists of four interfaces:

- `Publisher` is responsible for the publishing of items.
- `Subscriber` is responsible for the consumption of items.
- `Subscription` represents the link between exactly one `Publisher` and one `Subscriber`.
- `Processor` acts as both `Publisher` and `Subscriber`.

The demonstration of the message exchange between the `Publisher` and `Subscriber` is provided in figure 8.4.

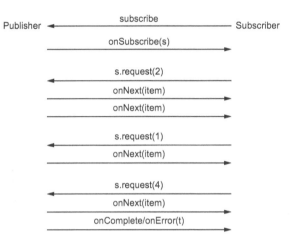

Figure 8.4 The example interaction between Reactive Streams Publisher and Subscriber

In this figure, you can see that the stream processing happens in the following steps:

1 The processing initiates with a call to the `subscribe` method of the `Publisher`, which passes the instance of the `Subscriber`.

2 In turn, the `Publisher` calls the `onSubscribe(s)` method of the `Subscriber` passing in the created `Subscription` object (s) representing the link between them.

3 The `Subscriber` instance then uses the subscription object to request the number of data items it can consume (the `request(n)` method), representing the built-in backpressure. If the `Subscriber` can't catch up with published items fast enough, it can lower the number of requested items to tell the `Publisher` to slow down.

4 After the `request(n)` call, the `Publisher` calls the `onNext(item)` callback on the `Subscriber` n times.

5 This continues until the `Publisher` has no more items to produce or an error occurs, meaning that either `onComplete` or `onError` callbacks are called on the `Subscriber`, respectively.

Even if these interfaces might seem easy to implement at first sight, it is generally not advised to implement them directly in your application as the specification with the associated TCK (Technology Compatibility Kit/Test Suite) is quite complex. Mutiny types implement Reactive Streams APIs (since version 2.0 they implement the JDK `Flow` variants) so you don't have to.

8.2.2 *Mutiny API*

Mutiny provides two main types that represent asynchronously computed results: `Uni` and `Multi`:

- `Uni` represents a single result or failure.
- `Multi` represents a stream of produced results that can be infinite.

As we already learned, both `Uni` and `Multi` receive events when the result computes. One important distinction is that since `Uni` can produce precisely one item or failure, it doesn't represent the full publisher as defined in the Reactive Streams specification. The call to the `subscribe` method is enough to express the initiative to get the result, so it directly triggers the computation. Additionally, it can also handle `null` values, which the Reactive Streams specification prohibits.

Mutiny was built with simplicity in mind. Reactive programming can be complex, so having a simple API is essential. Mutiny provides only the mentioned types: `Uni` and `Multi`. Users utilize these types to define reactive pipelines. The pipeline defines a sequence of applied continuations: each stage of the pipeline runs when the previous part of the pipeline emits an item. In this way, the events (including items) flow through the pipeline. Each stage can change these events, filter/drop some of them, or fire new ones. It is also important to remember that the pipeline only starts once a subscription/subscriber requires it to start (by subscribing to it).

To better imagine how individual stages flow one to another, the visual representation of the pipeline is available in figure 8.5. You may notice the similarity to the Streams flow shown in figure 8.4.

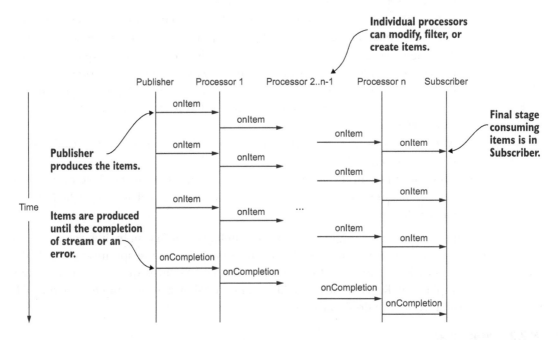

Figure 8.5   The reactive pipeline visualization in Mutiny

Users define the individual stages of the reactive pipelines with a provided fluent API in the Uni and Multi methods. The idea is to use autocompletion in modern IDEs and JavaDoc to determine your needs in a particular stage quickly.

The listing 8.1 provides an example of a reactive pipeline with Mutiny. A complete project that wraps this code in a REST endpoint is available in the chapter-08/ 8_2_2/mutiny-example directory. To run it, just run the project in Dev mode and send a GET request to http://localhost:8080/hello to trigger the pipeline.

Listing 8.1   An example use of the Mutiny API

```
Multi.createFrom().items("a", "b", "c")
    .onItem()
        .transform(String::toUpperCase)
    .onItem()
        .invoke(s -> System.out.println("Intermediate stage " + s))
    .onItem()
        .transform(s -> s + " item")
    .filter(s -> !s.startsWith("B"))
    .onCompletion()
        .invoke(() -> System.out.println("Stream completed"))
    .subscribe()
        .with(s -> System.out.println("Subscriber received " + s));
```

This code executes the following stages in the reactive pipeline:

1 Stage transforming the received items to upper case.
2 Stage that prints the items to the standard output and passes it downstream.
3 Another transformation stage, this time appending a new string.
4 Filter operation that propagates items only if they don't start with "B."

The last two lines define the completion callback, and the subscription with a simple subscriber which is required for the Multi to start producing items.

Executing this pipeline produces the result available in the following listing, where we can differentiate individual items and other events as they flow through the defined pipeline.

Listing 8.2   The result of the Mutiny example code execution

```
Intermediate stage A
Subscriber received A item
Intermediate stage B
Intermediate stage C
Subscriber received C item
Stream completed
```

In the first line, we can see the first intermediate stage hit with the initially produced item "a". The next stage transforms it to "A item" string and since it doesn't start with "B", it is not filtered out. The subscriber thus receives "A item" and prints it on the second line. The intermediate stage for item "b" is filtered later downstream (the subscriber will never receive it) and is listed in line 3. Finally, the case for the produced item "c" is the same as for "a". The completion event fires when the `Multi` has no more items to produce (last line).

8.3 Reactive engine

Reactive programming was essential to the Quarkus design from the beginning. Reactive architecture is one of the core principles of Quarkus. Quarkus runs on top of a reactive core created from components like Eclipse Vert.x (https://vertx.io) and Netty (https://netty.io) to provide a set of features (e.g., nonblocking I/O, eventloop threads, or asynchronous APIs like Mutiny), allowing users to create reactive systems.

However, reactive architecture doesn't require users to write reactive applications. Reactive programming is an optional feature that Quarkus applications are free to utilize but are not required to. It is also possible to mix both blocking and reactive code inside the same application. This is feasible because moving from already reactive code to blocking is possible (as you might remember with, for instance, `.await()` `.indefinitely()`). Conversely, it's not so easy.

Many Quarkus extensions support reactive programming. The extension description typically mentions if it supports reactive APIs (generally encapsulated in Mutiny integration). However, reactive pipelines can be defined and used even without direct integration with other extensions, as we've seen in one of the previous examples (listing 8.1).

8.4 Making Car Rental reactive

The reactive nature of Quarkus already took our path in Car Rental microservices in the reactive direction. In this section, we analyze how we have already utilized the reactive APIs and learn how we can possibly extend their use.

8.4.1 Reservation service

REACTIVE PERSISTENCE

The Reservation service is an excellent example of a reactive service. As we wanted to learn about Hibernate Reactive in chapter 7, we included the `quarkus-hibernate` `-reactive-panache` extension to utilize reactive, nonblocking SQL database drivers. This extension allows mapping the database operations to the reactive streams directly used to map the values returned from the database into the `Uni` or `Multi` types. Listing 8.3 provides an example of such execution. The `persist()` database operation returns a `Uni`, which (when processed) is then passed downstream as a return value of the JAX-RS method.

> Listing 8.3 **Nonblocking version of `ReservationResource#make` method**

```
@Consumes(MediaType.APPLICATION_JSON)
@POST
@WithTransaction
public Uni<Reservation> make(Reservation reservation) {
    ...
```

```
    return reservation.<Reservation>persist().onItem()          ◁─────  The persist
        .call(persistedReservation -> {                                 operation that emits
            ...                                                          an event item when
    });                                                                  the reservation is
}                                                                        persisted in the
                                                                         database.
```

The item emitted by this `Uni` represents the persisted reservation received from the database. We continue the stream execution only when the database operation completes. But we are not blocked while waiting for the database to finish the insert operation. The `make` method is executed on an I/O thread, and then the thread is released to be used by something else while the remote database is processing the persisting. The `onItem` callback is called after the database operation completes and can be potentially executed on a different event loop thread than the one that initially started processing the `make` method.

With Mutiny, it's straightforward to define any operation that should be performed when the database fetches the entity data (the continuation). For instance, if you want to change the entity before we return it from the JAX-RS response, we could chain the `onItem()` calls similarly as demonstrated in listing 8.1.

REACTIVE REST

Since we returned the entities from the database in the JAX-RS methods directly, we also needed to change the signatures of these methods to return Mutiny types. You might remember that another option is to block the created `Uni` results, but that is not reactive. When Quarkus sees the `Uni` as the return type of the JAX-RS method, it automatically runs the method on the I/O thread. In this way, Quarkus is free to serve other requests in the meantime because the method at hand is no longer blocking and will resume the execution of the current request only when the result is available. This follows the same execution model as the one described in section 8.1.1.

As we have learned, Quarkus decides whether the method should run on the non-blocking event loop (I/O) thread or the (possibly blocking) worker thread depending on the method's return value. If the method returns `Uni`, we cannot block it. If we try to do so, Quarkus logs the following warning:

```
WARN  [io.ver.cor.imp.BlockedThreadChecker] (vertx-blocked-thread-checker)
⇒ Thread Thread[vert.x-eventloop-thread-3,5,main]
⇒ has been blocked for 2054 ms, time limit is 2000 ms:
⇒ io.vertx.core.VertxException: Thread blocked
    ...
```

Users can change the thread that executes the operation by annotating the method with the `@Blocking` annotation which tells Quarkus to run the method on the worker (executor) thread instead. The `@NonBlocking` annotation also does the opposite thing for the blocking method (not returning Mutiny types).

You can also use `Multi` in the JAX-RS methods to return a stream of responses. This is particularly useful when streaming data continuously (e.g., logs or binary data) as the server-sent events (SSE) media type.

8.4.2   *Inventory service*

In the Inventory service, we utilized Mutiny and its reactive APIs in the gRPC integration from chapter 4. The gRPC extension generates stubs for our services that already provide Mutiny return types in their method signatures. It doesn't mean they must be used (the extension also generates a blocking service API). However, it is recommended to develop gRPC services with reactive types (which is why we also defaulted to them).

We learned in chapter 4 that the gRPC protocol has an integrated notion of a stream, which we use in the `inventory.proto` file like in the following listing.

Listing 8.4   The `inventory.proto` file showing the stream of requests

```
service InventoryService {
  rpc add(stream InsertCarRequest) returns (stream CarResponse) {}
  rpc remove(RemoveCarRequest) returns (CarResponse) {}
}
```

The gRPC stream naturally maps into the use of the Mutiny type `Multi` as it represents a potentially infinite number of events that come in the form of the `InsertCarRequest` or `CarResponse` items, respectively. In the Java implementation, we define the operations executed when a new request comes in, like in the following listing.

Listing 8.5   The `GrpcInventoryService#add` method

```
@Override
@Blocking
public Multi<CarResponse> add(Multi<InsertCarRequest> requests) {
  return requests
      .map(request -> {
          Car car = new Car();
          car.setLicensePlateNumber(request.getLicensePlateNumber());
          car.setManufacturer(request.getManufacturer());
          car.setModel(request.getModel());
          return car;
      }).onItem().invoke(car -> {
          QuarkusTransaction.requiringNew().run( () -> {
              carRepository.persist(car);
              Log.info("Persisting " + car);
          });
      }).map(car -> CarResponse.newBuilder()
          .setLicensePlateNumber(car.getLicensePlateNumber())
          .setManufacturer(car.getManufacturer())
          .setModel(car.getModel())
          .setId(car.getId())
          .build());
}
```

In this method, we receive a `Multi<InsertCarRequest>` to which we (or, in our case, it's really Quarkus) can subscribe. We define a map operation that changes the received gRPC class into the model class `Car` and passes it downstream. In our continuation, when the mapped `Car` item is produced, we persist it into the database, and we map the same `Car` item into an instance of `CarResponse`, which is returned to stream (`Multi<Car-Response>`) passed back to the caller. The `invoke` operation doesn't change the produced item.

In fact, if you take a closer look at the methods in this class, you might notice that they are not really reactive. Notice the `@Blocking` annotations that we need to use to tell Quarkus that even if the methods return reactive types, we cannot execute them on the eventloop thread because they run database I/O operations (the insert/delete of the car). It is a little strange not to use the Hibernate Reactive here as it would naturally fit into the reactive pipeline. But if we want to demonstrate as many functionalities that Quarkus provides as possible, we need to make compromises.

8.5   *Virtual threads with project Loom*

Reactive programming is generally considered harder to write, maintain, and debug than the imperative programming model that we all learn first. However, the performance of the reactive model (with eventloops) outperforms the imperative programming style in systems with high levels of concurrency and lots of I/O operations.

This is one of the main reasons why the project *Loom* was created. Project Loom, also known as virtual threads, was introduced as a preview feature in JDK 19, and it became generally available in JDK 21. Virtual thread is a thread managed by the JDK that is mapped to the real platform thread called the carrier thread when it runs. Once a blocking operation starts, JDK saves the state of the virtual thread and removes its execution from the carrier thread, letting any other available virtual thread to start executing on that carrier thread. Once the blocking operation completes, the original virtual thread is again eligible to continue its run on carrier thread (not necessarily the same carrier thread).

Virtual threads are more lightweight on resource consumption than platform threads as there is no interaction with the operating system (no system calls or context switches). This allows potentially huge amounts (millions) of virtual threads to be created, whereas a typical system can only handle several thousand regular threads due to the cost they put on the operating system.

The virtual thread model provides similar scalability benefits as reactive programming and an event loop. However, it shields users from using continuations and allows them to write regular imperative code without the burden of actually blocking (expensive) platform threads during runtime. Visually, the execution on virtual threads looks like the one presented in figure 8.6.

Virtual threads do everything in the background, so the users' imperative code doesn't need to change. The platform (JDK) detects the point where you are about to block, and it yields the virtual thread from the carrier thread which allows it to be used by a different virtual thread in the meantime. The performance is then comparable with that of the reactive programming model since the thread utilization is similar.

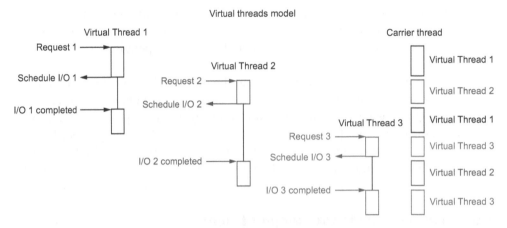

Figure 8.6   Virtual thread execution model with I/O request handling

8.5.1   *Project Loom in Quarkus*

In Quarkus, you might run any method on a virtual thread by simply annotating it with @RunOnVirtualThread annotation. You can also place this annotation on a whole class to make all its methods run on virtual threads.

> **NOTE**   In the book's repository, a full example project demonstrating this is available in the chapter-08/8_5_1/loom-example directory.

```
@GET
@Path("/virtualThread")
@RunOnVirtualThread
public void virtualThread() {
  Log.info("Running on " + Thread.currentThread().getName());
}
```

And calling this method, we can see that we are indeed running it on a new virtual thread every time we call it:

```
... (quarkus-virtual-thread-0) Running on quarkus-virtual-thread-0
... (quarkus-virtual-thread-1) Running on quarkus-virtual-thread-1
... (quarkus-virtual-thread-2) Running on quarkus-virtual-thread-2
```

If you continued running this over and over, you would notice that the ID of the used virtual thread keeps increasing forever and never repeats. This is because virtual threads, unlike platform threads, are not reused. It doesn't make a lot of sense to create pools of reusable virtual threads, simply because they are so cheap to create, start, and destroy (collect). The best practice is to create a new virtual thread for every task where you need it. When the virtual thread finishes its work, it is simply reclaimed by the garbage collector.

You might be asking now: Why do we need to annotate every class we want to run on virtual thread manually? Why isn't there a global flag that would run everything on virtual thread? And those are surely good questions.

8.5.2 Problems with project Loom

Nothing in life is free, and virtual threads are not an exception. They hide a lot of complexity behind the curtain, so they come with a few possible problems.

PINNING OF THE CARRIER THREAD

Pinning happens when the virtual thread cannot be unmounted from the carrier thread when it executes a blocking operation. This essentially blocks the carrier thread too, meaning it cannot execute other virtual threads. This happens in two cases:

- An attempt to unmount the virtual thread happens in a `synchronized` block. This is actually a limitation of the current JDK implementations and might be resolved in the future, but at least in JDK 21, `synchronized` blocks cause thread pinning.
- An attempt to unmount the virtual thread happens when the virtual thread has a native call (through the Java Native Interface) in its stack.

Don't worry if you don't fully understand these concepts. Usually they are not the concern of the end developers. However, they are often utilized in the underlying libraries that your code uses, which means that you might not be able to predict when the pinning can happen.

OVERUSE OF VIRTUAL THREADS FOR COMPUTATIONS

The virtual threads scheduler cannot interrupt a running thread (unless it yields by starting an I/O operation). If you execute long-running CPU-based computations (without I/O operations) on the virtual thread, it might clog up the carrier thread, which is unavailable for other virtual thread executions. This is also called monopolizing.

This brings us to a very important point. Virtual threads, in the same fashion as reactive programming, are only suitable in applications with a lot of I/O operations. If you use them for CPU-bound computations, both reactive programming and virtual threads perform worse than classic imperative programming with platform threads, because they add some overhead and you're not using the main benefit they were introduced for (not blocking expensive threads during I/O operations).

CARRIER THREADS SCALING

If there are too many unscheduled virtual threads (which might be caused by both previous points), the JVM is forced to create new carrier threads. It goes without saying that this brings both CPU and memory overhead. In the worst cases, it can also lead to applications running out of memory.

THREADLOCALS WITH LARGE OBJECTS

Many libraries utilize `ThreadLocal` values to store information. These values are only accessible from the same thread. This holds true also for virtual threads.

The problem arises when the objects stored in `ThreadLocal` are large. When the number of threads used to be small, it wasn't a problem, and these object were often even cached and reused. But with virtual threads, each virtual thread receives its own instance of the thread local object, and so every switch of the virtual thread means a lot of in-memory copying to make sure that each virtual thread has the correct values at all times. All this copying degrades the application's performance. Replacing the usage of thread locals is often not an easy task (e.g., transactions).

JDK proposed a new API called scoped values, that is still in preview in JDK 21 (Java Enhancement Proposal 446), which solves the problems with `ThreadLocal`. However, it will take time until all libraries that rely on it refactor `ThreadLocal` uses to scoped values.

Summarizing the problem overview in this section, we can see that virtual threads are not a silver bullet, but they surely are a great asset. They have their place, but currently, Quarkus cannot rely on project Loom to work correctly in all scenarios, and this is why there is no global flag that would move every execution on virtual thread. You need to explicitly request the execution on the virtual thread with the `@RunOn-VirtualThread` annotation. It will surely take a few years until all libraries used in Quarkus (but also reused in several different frameworks) catch up on all requirements (e.g., pinning or thread locals). So it still makes sense to understand reactive programming since, even if you will not use it directly, it will still be used under the hood to give you the performance benefit comparable to project Loom. Because Quarkus allows you to switch between virtual threads and reactive flawlessly, you can always start with virtual threads and move to reactive programming if you need it.

8.6   *Next steps*

This chapter explains reactive programming. We learned what reactive programming means and why it is advantageous to consider this architecture.

We learned about Quarkus' reactive engine, which makes it easy to start writing reactive applications with Quarkus. However, developers can choose if they want to adapt the reactive paradigm. The transition from imperative programming can even be gradual if needed because Quarkus allows combining both reactive and imperative code in the same application.

Lastly, we explained the project Loom and virtual threads. We showed you how you can use virtual threads in Quarkus and also explained the potential problems that they might bring.

In the next chapter, we learn how to externalize events that are propagated either into our applications or outside of them. We follow up on the reactive concepts explained in this chapter with the reactive messaging—a MicroProfile specification which defines a standard way for the asynchronous message exchange that is defined as the standing pillar of reactive systems.

Summary

- Reactive programming is a programming paradigm in which we write asynchronous, nonblocking, and scalable code based on continuations.
- Reactive programming paradigm might be harder to learn but provides better utilization of resources.
- SmallRye Mutiny is a reactive programming library utilized in Quarkus, providing a simple API which enables writing asynchronous, event-driven applications with integrated backpressure handling.
- Mutiny provides two main types—`Uni` and `Multi`—that contain fluent APIs which build reactive pipelines. You can use autocompletion and JavaDoc to build the pipeline step by step.
- Quarkus has a reactive engine based on Vert.x and Netty, providing a straightforward platform for writing reactive applications. However, a reactive engine doesn't require users to write reactive code, and it is possible to mix both the reactive and imperative code in the same application.
- Quarkus automatically decides whether your code should run on the nonblocking eventloop thread or on the possibly blocking worker thread. This can be adjusted with `@Blocking` and `@NonBlocking` annotations.
- Virtual threads (Project Loom) are lightweight JVM-operated threads that are easy to create in large amounts and are allowed to perform blocking operations without blocking platform threads. But there are still problems that may cause them to limit application performance or even stop its execution if they are not handled correctly.

Quarkus messaging

This chapter covers

- Learning about MicroProfile Reactive Messaging
- Defining Reactive systems
- Utilizing reactive messaging in Quarkus
- Exploring Kafka and RabbitMQ broker integrations in Quarkus
- Reactive messaging in car rental

In the previous chapter, we learned what reactive programming is and why it can benefit user applications. We evaluated reactive programming as a great alternative for applications that have a high resources demand, because they can effectively scale to higher numbers of concurrent requests. But in microservices, where the application consists of many isolated service applications, we also often need a way to let the applications communicate asynchronously without blocking threads while we wait for responses and without coupling the applications together too closely. This is where Quarkus messaging comes in.

In this chapter, we learn about the MicroProfile Reactive Messaging specification that was created with the intent to propagate asynchronous messages between services. This standard provides a simple, unified API that we will also utilize in a newly created Billing service in our car rental application.

We learn about two popular asynchronous messaging alternatives that connect our services: Apache Kafka and RabbitMQ. We will use the MicroProfile Reactive Messaging specification to demonstrate the asynchronous message passing (using the same API for both Kafka and RabbitMQ), which is the base pillar of reactive systems. Additionally, reactive messaging builds on top of the Reactive Streams API, so we can use the Mutiny APIs we experimented with in the previous chapter.

Quarkus messaging represents the MicroProfile Reactive Messaging integration in Quarkus. However, since using this integration doesn't require users to write reactive code, the name of the integration is just Quarkus messaging.

9.1 Car rental messaging integrations

This chapter introduces significant enhancements to the car rental architecture. Figure 9.1 demonstrates everything that we will add and change.

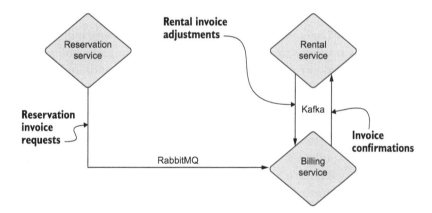

Figure 9.1 The car rental architecture changes incorporating reactive messaging channels

The integrations of Apache Kafka and RabbitMQ providers process messages that represent invoice requests and confirmations processed by the newly created Billing service. For simplicity, the Billing service will not create actual invoices. We just stub the invoice generation and consider it paid after some random time. When we finish this chapter implementation, this newly implemented part of the car rental system will be completely asynchronous and nonblocking.

9.2 Reactive systems

As we learned in the previous chapter, reactive programming utilizes the application resources better than the traditional imperative model. However, it also directly translates to more complicated application architecture and design.

In 2014, a group of independent developers created a document called the Reactive Manifesto (https://www.reactivemanifesto.org). In this document, they described the requirements, which translated to the properties the modern distributed systems should have. These properties are responsiveness, resiliency, elasticity, and message passing. If the system has these properties, it is defined as a reactive system. Putting this together visually, we can see how the properties depend on each other, as shown in figure 9.2.

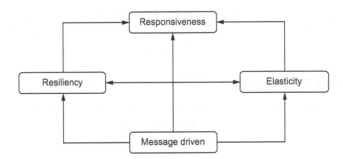

Figure 9.2   The reactive system architecture

- *Responsiveness*—Users expect to measure responses in mere milliseconds. So the application's responsiveness is a building stone of modern enterprise applications. Being responsive means that the system must handle user requests in a timely fashion. It also extends to the ability to identify and deal with failures. Responsiveness is the most important property conditioned by the other properties defined in the manifesto.
- *Resiliency*—The system must be able to stay responsive in case of failures. The application's services should be sufficiently isolated and highly available. In case of a service failure, the transition to another (backup) service should be fast and transparent so the system stays responsive. Users should not notice any service downtime.
- *Elasticity*—Further extends the concept of resiliency, which we can understand as scaling elastic service to zero. Elasticity is the ability to scale the system up and down horizontally (meaning in the number of service instances) depending on the user demand. As modern applications usually deploy in production environments where they pay for the resources only when utilized, it is paramount to scale the services down when they are not needed to run. Conversely, if there is a demand (e.g., during the holiday season), the systems must be able to scale up to stay responsive.
- *Message driven*—Asynchronous message passing represents the base property that enables all the previous properties in the reactive systems. The messages are the only means of communication between individual parts of the application. The system sends the messages to the virtual addresses, meaning that the exact location of the called services is unavailable to the calling service. This

enables seamless integration of resiliency and elasticity into the system. Errors also propagate as messages. Together, this allows reactive systems to be more isolated and loosely coupled. Integrating it also with asynchronicity allows for nonblocking communication that provides concepts like backpressure (the consumer's ability to control the received load).

When the system grows, these properties often become requirements. Reactive system principles need to be integrated into the system design. It is better to do this intentionally from the beginning than to try to add them to an already implemented system.

As an exercise, try to apply these properties to the microservices that we already implemented in the car rental system. What would happen if the Rental service wouldn't be available when the Reservation service tries to call it? You might also want to think about how they compare to the design of the system you are currently working on.

9.3 *MicroProfile Reactive Messaging*

The MicroProfile Reactive Messaging specification was created to standardize the way of defining distributed asynchronous communication. It provides a simple API that the application developers use to propagate messages between CDI beans, which can either produce, consume, or process messages. The messages are propagated through the notion of channels that represent the virtual addresses. These CDI beans are contained to only one application. However, MicroProfile Reactive Messaging defines a service provider interface (SPI) called *connectors* that allows you to plug external services as channels into the application.

9.3.1 *Synchronous vs. asynchronous distributed communication*

A system based on the microservices architecture consists of separated and isolated services that communicate via remote protocols. Many of these systems utilize some form of the synchronous communication protocols. We covered the most frequently utilized protocols for this purpose in chapter 4. These protocols require all parts of the applications to be continuously running to provide fully functional service. In figure 9.3 we see what happens when any of these services or the communication between them fail, which is unavoidable in any production environment.

We can analyze how the failed service error propagates through the calling chain of the services that the original call transmits through. Eventually, if no other service handles the error in a suitable manner (which often cannot be implemented due to the business reasons), the error is received by the original request issuer.

Another option for dealing with the problem of synchronous error propagation is fault tolerance strategies. In fact, there is a separate MicroProfile Fault Tolerance specification that handles these cases. These strategies include retries of the failed requests, timeouts, or circuit breaker implementations. However, all these options directly affect the request times (the time that the system takes to produce the response).

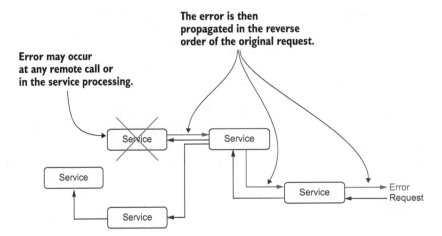

Figure 9.3   The synchronous communication failure propagation in microservices

And, as we learned, responsiveness is the most important property that system should try to achieve in modern production deployments.

> **NOTE**   In this chapter, we focus on reactive systems. Fault tolerance strategies, which are an important concept in the synchronous communications that many applications utilize, are detailed in the following chapter.

With asynchronous message passing, the system doesn't rely on services being always available. Instead, the message replication and delivery guarantees are pushed into the channels themselves. If the called service isn't available, the channel can buffer the messages until the service comes back online and can continue to pull requests from the channel queue. Since the communication is asynchronous, the service that issues the request isn't blocked and can continue processing new requests if needed.

Figure 9.4 demonstrates a failure in a reactive system based on asynchronous message passing. The messages are accumulated in the channel until the receiving service can process them.

In the first step, Service B failed after processing first two messages/requests, so m3 and m4 representing the last two requests are buffered in the asynchronous channel. After this service comes back up, it starts processing messages from the channel again. However, in the second step, Service C also fails, but only after processing message m3. So, now the message m4 is the only one buffered in the second channel, waiting for Service C to restart so it can process it.

9.3.2   *Reactive messaging API*

MicroProfile Reactive Messaging defines an API that connects CDI beans through communication channels. A channel represents a virtual address to which we can send or consume messages. Conceptually, the address represents a unique `string` defined by the user code.

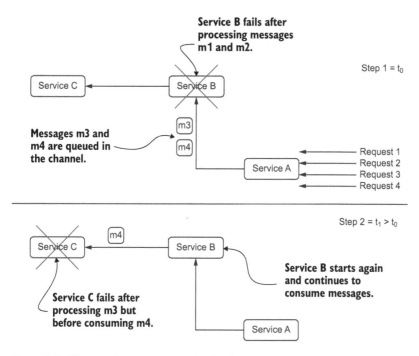

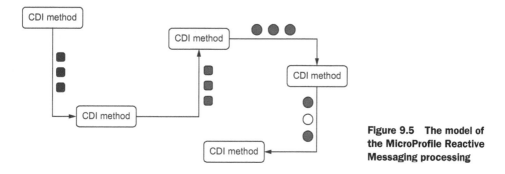

Figure 9.4   The asynchronous communication failure propagation in microservices

The flow of messages is based on the Reactive Streams API that we analyzed in the previous chapter. CDI beans can define multiple methods that either produce, consume, or process messages. In this way, these methods represent either publishers, subscribers, or processors from the reactive streams definitions. Figure 9.5 provides a visual representation of this processing. The CDI methods are methods in one or more CDI beans.

Figure 9.5   The model of the MicroProfile Reactive Messaging processing

The last CDI method acts as a filter on messages, while the others act as processors transforming the received messages. The CDI methods don't have to be all in the same CDI bean. The specification allows only @ApplicationScoped and @Dependent CDI scopes for CDI beans to be used in reactive messaging.

The API conceptually consists of two main annotations: @Outgoing and @Incoming, which are used to either produce or consume messages, respectively. Both annotations take a single String argument that represents the name of the channel from which they are consuming or to which they are producing messages. The use of these two annotations on a method specifies how the method acts in the reactive messaging flow:

- *Producer*—Method annotated with @Outgoing annotation:

```
@Outgoing("channel-name")
public String producer() {
    return "hello";
}
```

- *Consumer*—Method annotated with @Incoming annotation:

```
@Incoming("channel-name")
public void consumer(String payload) {
    System.out.println(payload);
}
```

- *Processor*—Method annotated with both @Incoming and @Outgoing:

```
@Incoming("channel-name")
@Outgoing("channel-name-2")
public String processor(String payload) {
    return payload.toUpperCase();
}
```

The channel is always established only between a single producer and a single consumer with any number of optional processors in between. In other words, for a channel, there is always only one source and one sink. The processors thus also need to communicate through unique channels, which define the order in which the processors apply.

The flow of the reactive stream established through the channel is fully controlled by the implementation of the MicroProfile Reactive Messaging specification. In case of Quarkus, this implementation is the SmallRye Reactive Messaging library. The SmallRye implementation provides many additional features on top of what is required by the specification. For instance, with SmallRye Reactive Messaging, it is possible to broadcast produced messages through a single channel to multiple consumers. Additionally, this implementation also provides several connectors for different external systems that we analyze in the following sections.

The MicroProfile Reactive Messaging specification defines several supported method signatures. Mainly, it also directly supports Reactive Streams types like Publisher or Subscriber and their subclasses. This means that we can directly utilize the SmallRye Mutiny's type Multi we learned about in the previous chapter, which is the preferred way when writing reactive applications in Quarkus because it is a subtype of Publisher. A comprehensive example of reactive messaging use with Mutiny is provided in listing 9.1. It utilizes two channels (ticks and times) that combined produce a timestamp every second for a total of 5 seconds, after which the producer stops producing messages. If you want to try out this application in practice, you can find it as a complete project in the chapter-09/9_3_2 directory; simply run it in Dev mode and observe the application's log after start.

Listing 9.1 MicroProfile Reactive Messaging with Mutiny example

```
@Outgoing("ticks")
public Multi<Long> aFewTicks() {
    return Multi.createFrom()
        .ticks().every(Duration.ofSeconds(1))
        .select().first(5);
}

@Incoming("ticks")
@Outgoing("times")
public Multi<String> processor(Multi<Long> ticks) {
    return ticks.map(tick -> Instant.now().toString());
}

@Incoming("times")
public void consumer(String payload) {
    System.out.println(payload);
}
```

The original producer (aFewTicks method) pushes messages to the ticks channel. The created Multi produces five items representing clock ticks every second. The processor method consumes the messages from the ticks channel and produces transformed items (timestamps) into the times channel. The consumer method is called for every message in the times channel.

Notice the Multi can be used as both the return type and the argument in the processor method. If you now start the Quarkus application containing this code, the consumer method runs five times, once for every message received from the times channel.

9.3.3 *Message acknowledgments*

Acknowledgments provide the means for the consuming services to supply information back to the services that produce messages. For instance, this can be used to propagate an error if the message cannot be processed.

There are two types of strategies that users can choose from for positive acknowledgments (acks) or negative acknowledgments (nacks) processing: explicit or implicit. For most use cases, Quarkus implicitly provides acks or nacks for individual payloads for you.

If you want to manage acks manually, you can explicitly either consume your payload as the Message interface or choose between different strategies using the @Acknowledgment annotation. The Message interface acts as a wrapper around the produced payload, which allows you to explicitly ack or nack the received message by calling the ack() or nack() methods.

The @Acknowledgment annotation controls the strategy for a particular method. It has a single parameter of type Strategy with the following options:

- MANUAL—Strategy requiring explicit ack or nack through provided Message wrapper type.
- PRE_PROCCESING—Messages implicitly acked before the method is entered.
- POST_PROCESSING—Messages implicitly acked (or nacked on exception) after the method finishes.
- NONE—Messages are not acknowledged either explicitly or implicitly. The acknowledgement is handled elsewhere (e.g., different provider).

Processors always send their acks (or nacks) only after their own consumers provide their own ack or nack. In this way, the chain of acks builds in the opposite direction of the direction in which the messages are sent until it reaches the original producer.

For instance, we can control the manual acknowledgments through the Message wrapper as shown in the following listing.

Listing 9.2   A manual acknowledgement example

```
@Incoming("channel-name")
@Acknowledgment(Acknowledgment.Strategy.MANUAL)      ◄─┐  Specifies that
public CompletionStage<Void> consumer(Message<String> message) {     the MANUAL
    if (processMessage(message.getPayload())) {                      strategy should
        return message.ack();                                       be used in this
    } else {                                                        method
        return message.nack(
            new IllegalStateException(
                "Cannot process message " + message.getPayload()));
    }
}
```

The method receives its String payload wrapped in a Message object that it can use to either call the ack() method for the positive acknowledgement or the nack(Throwable) method for the negative acknowledgement.

The @Acknowledgment annotation is not mandatory. The default values of the used strategies differ for the individual combinations of types used in the method signatures. You can find the detailed list of these defaults in the specification. We used implicit acknowledgments in the last example in the previous section (listing 9.1). If the signature directly consumes messages (without the Message<X> wrapper), reactive messaging always automatically acknowledges the received messages in the background (the default value for this signature is POST_PROCESSING).

9.3.4   *Integrating imperative code with reactive messaging*

You might not always be able to move to completely reactive code in all deployed system services. For this reason, MicroProfile Reactive Messaging provides a simple API to bridge the imperative and reactive worlds with the @Channel annotation.

The `@Channel` annotation has two use cases: either to produce messages from imperative code or consume a channel into an instance of `Publisher` through a CDI injection.

To produce a message from an imperative piece of code into a reactive messaging channel, we also need to utilize the `Emitter` class that has a `send` method, as shown in the following listing.

Listing 9.3   An `Emitter` example

```
@Inject
@Channel("requests")
Emitter<String> requestsEmitter;

@POST
@Path("/request")
public String request(String body) {
    requestsEmitter.send(body);
    return "Processing " + body;
}
```

The `@Channel` annotation specifies the channel name to which the emitter sends the asynchronous messages. The `send` method returns a `CompletionStage` that is completed when the message is acknowledged. If the message is never acknowledged, the `CompletionStage` never completes. If the consumer nacks the message, then the `CompletionStage` is completed exceptionally. If we want to wait for the ack or the nack of the message, we can send the message and block the thread until the `Completion-Stage` finishes:

```
requestsEmitter.send(body).toCompletableFuture().join();
```

The second use case of `@Channel` is particularly useful for applications working with server-sent events (SSEs), which push the events from server to clients through an HTTP connection. We can use the `@Channel` annotation to inject instances of Reactive Streams (or `Flow`) `Publisher` or its subclasses as in our case the Mutiny's `Multi`. Consuming the produced ticks from the producer introduced in listing 9.1 into an instance of `Multi` can be done as demonstrated in listing 9.4. This listing also presents the utilization of the `SERVER_SENT_EVENTS` media type in the GET JAX-RS method. This `/consume` endpoint, when called, initializes an SSE connection and pushes all events from the `ticks` `Multi` to the client.

Listing 9.4   Consuming the reactive messaging channel into a `Multi`

```
@Inject
@Channel("ticks")
Multi<Long> ticks;          ⟵⎤  Flow.Publisher can
                               ⎦  also be used here.
@GET
@Path("/consume")
```

```
@Produces(MediaType.SERVER_SENT_EVENTS)
public Multi<Long> sseTicks() {
    return ticks;
}
```

A runnable project demonstrating this code with SSE is available in the `chapter-09/9_3_4/reactive-messaging-example` directory. Try running it and just open the `/ticks/consume` URL in the browser or run one of the following commands. Either way, you can see that the server pushed new data every second:

```
$ http :8080/ticks/consume --stream
$ curl -N localhost:8080/ticks/consume
```

9.4   *Introducing messaging in Reservation*

With what we have learned so far in this chapter, we are now able to include Quarkus messaging in the Reservation service. For now, we will focus only on the semantics in this single service, which we can later transform to remote communication over different protocols supporting asynchronous messaging.

The Reservation service will use reactive messaging to send messages to the Billing service that we haven't created yet. However, we can start integrating reactive messaging in the Reservation by providing a stub for the Billing service that we will create in the following section. This is a good example of how we can develop individual microservices independently. Figure 9.6 provides a visual representation of what we will implement in this section.

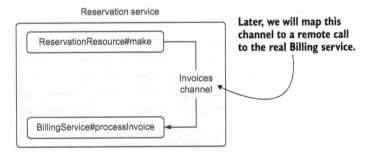

Figure 9.6   The reactive messaging integration in the Reservation service

We start by defining the model for the invoices that we are sending. Let's create a new class `org.acme.reservation.billing.Invoice` as demonstrated in listing 9.5. It contains all the required information that needs to be propagated to the Billing service to create the invoice. As always, you can find the full source code of this class in the book resources `chapter-09` directory.

Listing 9.5 **The code of the** `Invoice` **class**

```
package org.acme.reservation.billing;

import org.acme.reservation.entity.Reservation;

public class Invoice {

    public Reservation reservation;        ◁─┤
    public double price;

    public Invoice(Reservation reservation, double price) {
        this.reservation = reservation;
        this.price = price;
    }

    @Override
    public String toString() {
        return "Invoice{" +
            "reservation=" + reservation +
            ", price=" + price +
            '}';
    }
}
```

Keeps the reservation details, so they can be printed on the invoice

The place where we would like to charge the customer for making a reservation is the `ReservationResource#make` method that creates reservations by persisting them into the database. Before we do that, we should make sure that the customer will be charged for the order. In essence, we can make the request for billing asynchronous, because we can always cancel the reservation later if the invoice isn't paid in time.

Even though we already use several reactive extensions in the Reservation service, none of them uses messaging. We need to add a new extension, `quarkus-messaging`, which we can do with the `quarkus` CLI as shown in the following snippet:

```
$ quarkus ext add quarkus-messaging
```

The `make` method is a JAX-RS POST method, which means that we need to send the message to the reactive channel manually with an `Emitter`, as described in section 9.3.4. The name of the channel is `invoices` as we are sending invoices to the Billing service. Listing 9.6 provides the updated code with relevant parts of the `ReservationResource`. For simplicity, we use a standard rate per day that is applicable to all cars.

NOTE If you run into import conflicts, always use classes from the `org.eclipse` `.microprofile.reactive.messaging` package.

Listing 9.6 `ReservationResource` **producing messages to channel**

```
public static final double STANDARD_RATE_PER_DAY = 19.99;

@Inject
@Channel("invoices")
```

```
Emitter<Invoice> invoiceEmitter;                ←⎯⎯  Injects the Emitter for
                                                      the "invoices" channel
@Consumes(MediaType.APPLICATION_JSON)
@POST
@WithTransaction
public Uni<Reservation> make(Reservation reservation) {
    ...

    return reservation.<Reservation>persist().onItem()
        .call(persistedReservation -> {
            Log.info("Successfully reserved reservation " +
                persistedReservation);

            invoiceEmitter.send(new Invoice(reservation,
                computePrice(reservation)));          ←⎯  Sends the
                                                           asynchronous
    ...                                                    message into the
}                                                          "invoices" channel

private double computePrice(Reservation reservation) {
    return (ChronoUnit.DAYS.between(reservation.startDay,
        reservation.endDay) + 1) * STANDARD_RATE_PER_DAY;
}
```

Since we don't have the Billing service yet, we can create a stub that consumes messages for now and just prints them to the console. Create a new class `org.acme.reservation.billing.BillingService` as demonstrated in the following listing.

Listing 9.7   `BillingService`, a stub for the real Billing service

```
package org.acme.reservation.billing;

import org.eclipse.microprofile.reactive.messaging.Incoming;

import jakarta.enterprise.context.ApplicationScoped;

@ApplicationScoped
public class BillingService {

    @Incoming("invoices")
    public void processInvoice(Invoice invoice) {
        System.out.println("Processing received invoice: " + invoice);
    }
}
```

Creating a new reservation now correctly produces a new asynchronous message to the `invoices` channel, which is then consumed in the `BillingService#processInvoice` method. The following listing shows how we can experiment with this new functionality.

Listing 9.8   Trying Quarkus messaging in the Reservation service

```
$ http POST :8081/reservation <<< '{
  "carId": 1,
```

```
  "startDay": "3333-01-01",
  "endDay": "3333-01-03"
}'

# in the Reservation Dev mode terminal
2024-10-07 17:16:02,834 INFO  [org.acm.res.res.ReservationResource]
 (vert.x-eventloop-thread-4) Successfully reserved reservation
 Reservation{id=1, carId=1, userId='anonymous', startDay=3333-01-01,
 endDay=3333-01-03}
Processing received invoice: Invoice{reservation=Reservation{id=1, carId=1,
 userId='anonymous', startDay=3333-01-01, endDay=3333-01-03},
 price=59.97}
```

The `Emitter#send` method returns a `CompletionStage` that is completed when the produced message is acknowledged. If the message is nacked, the `CompletionStage` is completed exceptionally. To correctly handle the reservation start, we should verify that the invoice request is received by the Billing service, meaning it is acknowledged. We could use the `CompletionStage` directly as shown in the following snippet:

```
CompletionStage<Void> invoiceCS = invoiceEmitter.send(
    new Invoice(reservation, computePrice(reservation)));

invoiceCS.whenComplete((unused, throwable) -> {
    if (throwable != null) {
        Log.errorf("Couldn't create invoice for %s. %s%n",
            persistedReservation, throwable.getMessage());
    }
});
```

This could work, but we are writing a reactive service, so plugging the invoice acknowledgment into the reactive pipeline would be better. With Mutiny, we can do it easily. Mutiny provides the emitter alternative called `MutinyEmitter` that returns a `Uni`. With it, we can update the `make` method as shown in the following listing.

> **Listing 9.9 The `make` method utilizing `MutinyEmitter`**

```
@Inject
@Channel("invoices")
MutinyEmitter<Invoice> invoiceEmitter;          ◁─┐ Injects MutinyEmitter
                                                  │ instead of Emitter
...

@Consumes(MediaType.APPLICATION_JSON)
@POST
@WithTransaction
public Uni<Reservation> make(Reservation reservation) {
    reservation.userId = context.getUserPrincipal() != null ?
        context.getUserPrincipal().getName() : "anonymous";

    return reservation.<Reservation>persist().onItem()
        .call(persistedReservation -> {
```

```
Log.info("Successfully reserved reservation "
    + persistedReservation);

Uni<Void> invoiceUni = invoiceEmitter.send(
    new Invoice(reservation, computePrice(reservation)))
    .onFailure().invoke(throwable ->
        Log.errorf("Couldn't create invoice for %s. %s%n",
        persistedReservation, throwable.getMessage()));

if (persistedReservation.startDay.equals(LocalDate.now())) {
    return invoiceUni.chain(() ->                              ◄─┐
        rentalClient.start(persistedReservation.userId,
            persistedReservation.id)
        .onItem().invoke(rental ->
            Log.info("Successfully started rental " + rental))
        .replaceWith(persistedReservation));
}                                                          Chains the invoice
return invoiceUni                                          acknowledgment to
    .replaceWith(persistedReservation);   ◄─┐              the Rental service
    });                                                        invocation . . .
}                              . . .or replaces the produced invoice
                               ack with a persisted reservation
```

When we use the MutinyEmitter, the send method now returns a Uni. In both return statements, we return the produced invoiceUni to propagate both the success and the failure of invoice creation (later to be replaced by the acknowledgment from the Billing service) asynchronously. On success, we either chain our Rental service call or we simply replace it with the persistedReservation. If the invoiceUni fails, we log the exception with the provided onFailure().invoke handler, and we also propagate this failure from the return statements so the whole request will fail, notifying the user that something went wrong. For now, since we consume messages only in the Reservation service, you can verify this behavior by changing the BillingService#processInvoice method to throw an exception.

Now we have a fully functioning reactive service! The make method is reactive. It guarantees that only if the user pays for the rental (the Billing service acknowledges the invoice request), the rental start request is sent to the Rental service.

Hopefully, this isn't too complicated. Definitely, reactive programming might be a complex programming approach to adapt. But once you get the hang of it, it comes quite naturally. The car rental is now able to process many more reservation requests than it did with the imperative model.

9.5   Connectors

The MicroProfile Reactive Messaging architecture we investigated so far was limited to only one service. However, in the microservices applications we need to be able to communicate with other services. Quarkus consolidates different distributed protocols and projects designed for asynchronous message passing that we can directly integrate into reactive pipelines.

9.5.1   *What is a connector?*

In MicroProfile Reactive Messaging, a *connector* represents an SPI (intended for the implementations, not users) that presents a way to extend the messaging channels to external messaging providers. From the Quarkus user's point of view, the details of a particular provider are abstracted away, and you can switch between them just by changing the configuration. In the application, we define the channels in exactly the same way as in the previous section. The configuration then tells the reactive messaging implementation (SmallRye, in the case of Quarkus) to either push the outgoing messages to the external provider or pull the incoming messages from it. A connector is configured per channel. Figure 9.7 visualizes this concept. The connector represents a boundary of the application that bridges the messages to the remote services while still preserving the reactive messaging (streams) flow.

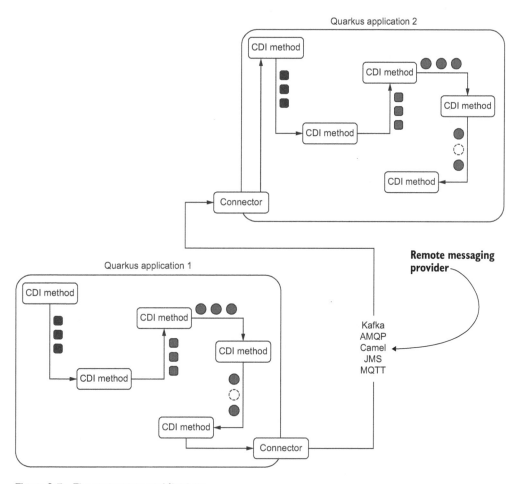

Figure 9.7 The connectors architecture

There are multiple connectors for different remote brokers that users can choose from, including Apache Kafka, RabbitMQ, or JMS (Jakarta Messaging). Of course, they are easily switchable by only changing the application configuration. There is no need to change the reactive messaging code since it is possible to just remap individual channels to a different connector in the configuration.

Users refer to connectors by their names, which are defined by the implementations. In SmallRye Reactive Messaging, they are prefixed with a `smallrye-` prefix following by the underlying technology that the connector bridges (e.g., `smallrye-kafka`, `smallrye-rabbitmq`, or `smallrye-jms`).

9.5.2 *Connector configuration*

Connectors are configured through the standard configuration mechanisms that we learned about in chapter 3. MicroProfile Reactive Messaging specification defines the following formats of configuration properties:

```
mp.messaging.incoming.{channel-name}.{attribute-name}=attribute-value
mp.messaging.outgoing.{channel-name}.{attribute-name}=attribute-value
mp.messaging.connector.{connector-name}.{attribute-name}=attribute-value
```

The configuration of channels (`channel-name`) overrides the global configuration of connectors (`connector-name`). It is important to point out that all configuration for channels is specific to either the `incoming` or the `outgoing` direction. This means that if we use the same channel (`channel-name`) for both producing and consuming of messages (i.e., reactive streams' processor), we need to configure each direction separately, even if they use the same connector.

The only required configuration for each channel is the `connector` attribute, which specifies the name of the connector. However, if you have only one connector extension on the classpath, you don't have to configure it. It is automatically auto-attached to all unconfigured channels. But be careful if you start utilizing any channel in-memory (i.e., you define both the producer and the consumer in the same application); in that case, in-memory connector takes precedence.

Most of the connectors require additional configuration for the external service connections configuration that they need to set up—for instance, the location of the production instance of Kafka or the JMS queue URL.

> **NOTE** The connectors and their respective Quarkus extensions often support Dev Services. So it's preferred to specify connection configuration only for the `prod` profile.

As you probably noticed, the channels we have used so far are not mapped to any connectors (external services). By default, the channels use the in-memory processing (the in-memory connector). In this way, the same reactive messaging concepts apply to local or remote communication, which is easily changeable in the application configuration.

9.6 Quarkus messaging with Kafka connector

We are now ready to introduce the last backend service into the car rental project: the Billing service. As you might remember from the architecture diagram, this service is connected to other backend services purely through nonblocking, asynchronous technologies as demonstrated in figure 9.8. The Billing service is a fully reactive microservice based on asynchronous messaging.

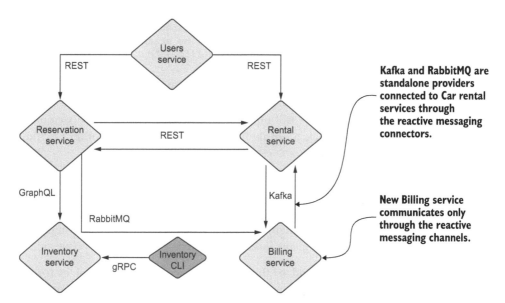

Figure 9.8   The car rental architecture diagram detailing the Billing service integration

Since we have already prepared the Reservation service to send invoices with reactive messaging, let's first focus on the simplest service we created so far, the Rental service. This will allow us to demonstrate how we can start integrating remote messaging from scratch.

The Rental service communicates with the Billing service through an Apache Kafka broker (https://kafka.apache.org). We are not going to cover Kafka internals here, but there is an excellent resource available in the book *Kafka in Action* by Dylan Scott, Viktor Gamov, and Dave Klein (Manning, 2022).

To utilize messaging with Kafka, we need to include a connector that is able to connect to a Kafka broker. SmallRye Reactive Messaging provides such a connector; it's called `smallrye-kafka`.

9.6.1 Kafka integration in the Rental service

As with any other Quarkus functionality, there is an extension that sets up the SmallRye Kafka connector—it's named `quarkus-messaging-kafka`. We can add it to the Rental service with the following command (execute this in the `rental-service` directory):

```
$ quarkus ext add quarkus-messaging-kafka
```

If you now start the Rental service in Dev mode, you'll notice that this extension comes with packaged Dev Services for Kafka broker, whose container is started in the background similarly as the database that the Rental service uses to persist rentals. The following listing shows the log message that details that the Dev Services were started.

Listing 9.10 Dev Services for Kafka started log message

```
INFO  [io.qua.kaf.cli.dep.DevServicesKafkaProcessor] (build-27) Dev
Services for Kafka started. Other Quarkus applications in dev mode
will find the broker automatically. For Quarkus applications in
production mode, you can connect to this by starting your application
with -Dkafka.bootstrap.servers=OUTSIDE://localhost:44131
```

This message also hints that any other Quarkus applications started in Dev mode on the same computer automatically connect to the same Kafka instance, which is very useful for local testing. We will utilize this soon with the Billing service once created. Additionally, we also have a simple flag that we can include if other Quarkus services start in production mode.

> **NOTE** The Kafka Dev Services in fact utilize the Redpanda platform (https:// redpanda.com), which is a more lightweight Kafka-compatible API. However, there are other options, like Strimzi (https://strimzi.io) or kafka-native (https://github.com/ozangunalp/kafka-native), which you can switch to using the configuration (the `quarkus.kafka.devservices.provider` property).

The messages that we send to the Billing service represent invoices for the rentals where users return cars sooner or later than originally reserved through the Reservation service, meaning the price for the rental needs to be adjusted. For this reason, we create a single Kafka topic called `invoices-adjust` to which the Rental service sends invoice messages if such a user case is detected.

First, we need to define the format of the `InvoiceAdjust` messages that the Rental service sends to the Billing service through Kafka. Create a new class `org.acme.rental .billing.InvoiceAdjust`, which looks like the one in the following listing.

Listing 9.11 The `InvoiceAdjust` class

```
package org.acme.rental.billing;

import java.time.LocalDate;

public class InvoiceAdjust {

    public String rentalId;
    public String userId;
    public LocalDate actualEndDate;
    public double price;

    public InvoiceAdjust(String rentalId, String userId,
                    LocalDate actualEndDate, double price) {
```

```
        this.rentalId = rentalId;
        this.userId = userId;
        this.actualEndDate = actualEndDate;
        this.price = price;
    }

    @Override
    public String toString() {
        return "InvoiceAdjust{" +
            "rentalId='" + rentalId + '\'' +
            ", userId='" + userId + '\'' +
            ", actualEndDate=" + actualEndDate +
            ", price=" + price +
            '}';
    }
}
```

Next, we need to set up the emitter that will send the new invoice once the return end date is exceeded. We can update the `RentalResource#end` JAX-RS method as demonstrated in the following listing.

Listing 9.12 `RentalResource` with reactive messaging

```
@Path("/rental")
public class RentalResource {

    public static final double STANDARD_REFUND_RATE_PER_DAY = -10.99;
    public static final double STANDARD_PRICE_FOR_PROLONGED_DAY = 25.99;

    @Inject
    @RestClient
    ReservationClient reservationClient;

    @Inject
    @Channel("invoices-adjust")
    Emitter<InvoiceAdjust> adjustmentEmitter;

    ...

    @PUT
    @Path("/end/{userId}/{reservationId}")
    public Rental end(String userId, Long reservationId) {
        Log.infof("Ending rental for %s with reservation %s",
            userId, reservationId);

        Rental rental = Rental
            .findByUserAndReservationIdsOptional(userId, reservationId)
            .orElseThrow(() -> new NotFoundException("Rental not found"));

        Reservation reservation = reservationClient
            .getById(reservationId);

        LocalDate today = LocalDate.now();
        if (!reservation.endDay.isEqual(today)) {
```

```
        Log.infof("Adjusting price for rental %s. Original " +
            "reservation end day was %s.", rental, reservation.endDay);
        adjustmentEmitter.send(new InvoiceAdjust(
            rental.id.toString(), userId, today,
            computePrice(reservation.endDay, today)));
    }

    rental.endDate = today;
    rental.active = false;
    rental.update();
    return rental;
}

private double computePrice(LocalDate endDate, LocalDate today) {
    return endDate.isBefore(today) ?
        ChronoUnit.DAYS.between(endDate, today)
            * STANDARD_PRICE_FOR_PROLONGED_DAY :
        ChronoUnit.DAYS.between(today, endDate)
            * STANDARD_REFUND_RATE_PER_DAY;
}

    ...
}
```

We first inject the new `ReservationClient` (that we have yet to create) that calls the Reservation service through the exposed REST API and the `invoices-adjust` channel emitter that sends Kafka messages representing invoice adjustments. In the `end` method, we retrieve the reservation from the Reservation service to get the originally promised end day. If the customer returns the car on a different date than promised in the reservation, we charge the customer accordingly.

For simplicity (and because this is not reactive code), the new `ReservationClient` code is omitted here but, with what we learned so far, it shouldn't be hard to implement. Try to implement it as an exercise. Remember that the endpoint which returns the reservation JSON (we only require the `endDay` field) is available at GET `/admin/reservation/{id}`. Note that you also need the `quarkus-rest-client-jackson` extension if you haven't added it to the Rental service before. We added this new class to the `org.acme.rental.reservation` package. If you need a hint on how to implement this, the whole code is available in the `chapter-09/9_6_1` directory of the book resources.

This is all that we need to start sending invoice adjustments from the code perspective. Since `smallrye-kafka` is the only connector on the classpath, Quarkus already configures the `invoices-adjust` channel to be mapped into the `invoices-adjust` Kafka topic and adds required serializers for the `InvoiceAdjust` Kafka record that we send to the Kafka broker. You can see this in the log message when the Dev mode starts:

```
INFO  [io.qua.sma.dep.processor] (build-21) Configuring the channel
 'invoices-adjust' to be managed by the connector 'smallrye-kafka'
INFO  [io.qua.sma.dep.processor] (build-25) Generating Jackson serializer
for type org.acme.rental.billing.InvoiceAdjust
```

However, we don't see the produced messages even though we know now they are produced to the started Kafka Dev service when we send invoice adjustments. Consuming messages from Kafka without reactive messaging is beyond the scope of this book. So, for now, feel free to define an @Incoming consumer for the invoices-adjust channel with which you can verify that the messages are produced correctly. However, if you have experience with Kafka, you can check the Dev Service Kafka with client tools like the example shown in listing 9.13. To test this, you can create the reservation starting today and ending tomorrow and then end the started rental (which ends the rental one day sooner than reserved for). But it would be useful to also verify this message production in an automated test.

> **TIP** This verification is completely optional. The kafka-console-consumer comes from Apache Kafka tools, but if you don't have it already available, you don't need to download it for this example.

Listing 9.13   Consuming the invoices-adjust topic

```
$ ./kafka-console-consumer.sh --bootstrap-server localhost:44131 --topic \
invoices-adjust --from-beginning
{"rentalId":"670d0b2a2074c13ed986936f","userId":"anonymous",
"actualEndDate":"2024-10-14","price":-10.99}
```

9.6.2   Testing messaging with Kafka

Quarkus utilizes the Kafka Companion Java library which is also provided by Small-Rye Reactive Messaging. According to their definition (https://smallrye.io/smallrye-reactive-messaging/4.25.0/kafka/test-companion/) "It is not intended to mock Kafka, but to the contrary, connect to a Kafka broker and provide high-level features". This library provides an easy integration with the already started Kafka Dev Service, which is available during the test execution.

To use the Kafka Companion API, Quarkus provides a wrapper extension quarkus-test-kafka-companion, which can be included in the Rental service in the test scope as demonstrated in listing 9.14. We also include Rest Assured and Mockito, which we are going to use in the new test. Add these dependencies if they are not already present in the Rental service.

Listing 9.14   Rental service test scoped dependencies

```
<dependency>
  <groupId>io.quarkus</groupId>
  <artifactId>quarkus-test-kafka-companion</artifactId>
  <scope>test</scope>
</dependency>
<dependency>
  <groupId>io.rest-assured</groupId>
  <artifactId>rest-assured</artifactId>
  <scope>test</scope>
</dependency>
```

```
<dependency>
  <groupId>io.quarkus</groupId>
  <artifactId>quarkus-junit5-mockito</artifactId>
  <scope>test</scope>
</dependency>
```

Listing 9.15 contains the test source code created in `org.acme.rental.RentalResource-Test` class. You can find the full source code (with all imports) in the `chapter-09/9_6_2` directory of the book resources.

Listing 9.15   The source code of the `RentalResourceTest` test

```
@QuarkusTest
@QuarkusTestResource(KafkaCompanionResource.class)      ◄───┐  KafkaCompanionResource
public class RentalResourceTest {                           │  sets up the test context
                                                            │  and allows us to inject
    @InjectKafkaCompanion                                   │  KafkaCompanion.
    KafkaCompanion kafkaCompanion;

    @Test
    public void testRentalProlongedInvoiceSend() {
        // stub the ReservationClient call
        Reservation reservation = new Reservation();
        reservation.endDay = LocalDate.now().minusDays(1);

        ReservationClient mock = Mockito.mock(ReservationClient.class);
        Mockito.when(mock.getById(1L)).thenReturn(reservation);
        QuarkusMock.installMockForType(mock, ReservationClient.class,
            RestClient.LITERAL);

        // start new rental for reservation with id 1
        given()
            .when().post("/rental/start/user123/1")
            .then().statusCode(200);

        // end the rental with one prolonged day
        given()
            .when().put("/rental/end/user123/1")
            .then().statusCode(200)
            .body("active", is(false),
                "endDate", is(LocalDate.now().toString()));

        // verify that message is sent to the invoices-adjust Kafka topic
        ConsumerTask<String, String> invoiceAdjust = kafkaCompanion
            .consumeStrings().fromTopics("invoices-adjust", 1)
            .awaitNextRecord(Duration.ofSeconds(10));       ◄───┐ The consumption
                                                                │ of Kafka records
        assertEquals(1, invoiceAdjust.count());
        assertTrue(invoiceAdjust.getFirstRecord().value()
            .contains("\"price\":" +
            RentalResource.STANDARD_PRICE_FOR_PROLONGED_DAY));
    }
}
```

This test uses `KafkaCompanion`, which can be easily injected. It first stubs the `ReservationClient` with Mockito, since we can't make the remote REST call to the

Reservation service in our test. Then it creates and ends a new rental through the exposed REST API. Next, it sets up a consumer listener for the `invoices-adjust` Kafka topic to which the `end` method should have pushed the invoice adjustment message (because the mock returns `endDay` one day before today). After that, it can verify that the message is indeed produced to the Kafka broker.

You can execute this test with continuous testing or with

```
$ ./mvnw test
...
[INFO] Tests run: 1, Failures: 0, Errors: 0, Skipped: 0, Time elapsed:
 20.983 s - in org.acme.rental.RentalResourceTest
...
```

The Kafka companion provides a very simple integration testing for our Kafka broker integration, and it proves that we are indeed sending the invoice adjustment messages to the Kafka topic. Now we only need to consume them in the Billing service.

9.7 Quarkus messaging with RabbitMQ

RabbitMQ (https://www.rabbitmq.com) is one of the most popular message brokers. It provides a lightweight platform that supports multiple messaging protocols and also streams (see https://www.rabbitmq.com/docs/streams for the difference). The default protocol is *AMQP* (Advanced Message Queuing Protocol) 0-9-1. The messages are sent and consumed from queues. If you want to learn more about this broker, you can check the *RabbitMQ in Depth* book by Gavin M. Roy (Manning, 2017).

In Quarkus, applications utilize RabbitMQ broker through the SmallRye Reactive Messaging RabbitMQ connector called `smallrye-rabbitmq`. We can use the connector in exactly the same way as the Kafka connector introduced in the previous section since both utilize reactive messaging.

> **NOTE** By default, RabbitMQ utilizes AMQP 0-9-1, which is very different from the latest version AMQP 1.0. RabbitMQ can be configured to use AMQP 1.0 via a separate plugin. SmallRye Reactive Messaging also provides a SmallRye AMQP connector that supports AMQP 1.0.

In this section, we are going to expand the reactive messaging setup in the Reservation service that we prepared in 9.4. Since Quarkus utilizes reactive messaging in the same way whether we use a remote connector to pass messages outside the application's JVM or the built-in in-memory channels, the required changes in the Reservation service are minimal.

As you are probably already used to, our first step is to include the Quarkus extension that brings the `smallrye-rabbitmq` connector. This extension is called `quarkus-messaging-rabbitmq`, and it can be included in the Reservation service as shown in the following listing.

> **Listing 9.16 Adding the `smallrye-rabbitmq` connector extension**

```
$ quarkus ext add quarkus-messaging-rabbitmq
```

In section 9.4, we already prepared the reactive messaging to produce invoices when the reservation is created in the `ReservationResource` class. An excerpt from this class sending the invoices is provided in the following listing.

Listing 9.17   The `invoices` channel utilization

```
@Inject
@Channel("invoices")
MutinyEmitter<Invoice> invoiceEmitter;

...

Uni<Void> invoiceUni = invoiceEmitter.send(
    new Invoice(reservation, computePrice(reservation)))
    ...
```

Similarly to the Kafka connector, if the `smallrye-rabbitmq` connector is the only connector on the classpath, it is automatically configured as the outgoing connector for the `invoices` channel, which is mapped to the `invoices` RabbitMQ exchange, that is bound to a queue.

The RabbitMQ connector extension also provides the RabbitMQ-compatible broker that is started as a Dev Service. In Dev mode, you can now check that the RabbitMQ broker container starts and that our application is already configured to connect to it by pressing `c` in the terminal where the Dev mode runs:

```
messaging-rabbitmq
  Container:        9278e6337d69/funny_beaver
  docker.io/library/rabbitmq:3.12-management
  Network:          e0a206a6-68d4-4c79-8824-c0400be49cf8
  (tc-bzBsu1qw,9278e6337d69) - null:45617->5672/tcp ,null:44267->15672/tcp
  Exec command:     docker exec -it 9278e6337d69 /bin/bash
  Injected config:  - rabbitmq-host=localhost
                    - rabbitmq-http-port=44267
                    - rabbitmq-password=guest
                    - rabbitmq-port=45617
                    - rabbitmq-username=guest
```

The invoices are currently just consumed and printed to the standard output in the `BillingService` class. Since we already have this consumer available, let's investigate how it can consume messages from the RabbitMQ broker. Of course, the `BillingService` class is not yet connected to the RabbitMQ broker since both producer and consumer for the `invoices` channel are in the same application (it uses the in-memory connector). Let's change the name of the incoming channel in the `BillingService` to demonstrate this (listing 9.18).

Listing 9.18   Ranaming incoming channel to `invoices-rabbitmq`

```
@ApplicationScoped
public class BillingService {

    @Incoming("invoices-rabbitmq")
```

```
public void processInvoice(Invoice invoice) {
    System.out.println("Processing received invoice: " + invoice);
}
}
```

The new channel, `invoices-rabbitmq`, and the original channel, `invoices`, are no longer consumed in the Reservation service. Both channels are thus autoconfigured to use the RabbitMQ connector. When the Reservation service starts now in Dev mode (it's also enough just to restart it by pressing the s key), it produces the following log messages stating it is connecting to the `invoices-rabbitmq` and `invoices` channels (they don't need to be in succession):

```
INFO  [io.qua.sma.dep.processor] (build-16) Configuring the channel
 'invoices-rabbitmq' to be managed by the connector 'smallrye-rabbitmq'
INFO  [io.qua.sma.dep.processor] (build-16) Configuring the channel
 'invoices' to be managed by the connector 'smallrye-rabbitmq'
INFO  [io.sma.rea.mes.rabbitmq] (Quarkus Main Thread) SRMSG17036: RabbitMQ
 broker configured to [localhost:45617] for channel invoices-rabbitmq
INFO  [io.sma.rea.mes.rabbitmq] (Quarkus Main Thread) SRMSG17036: RabbitMQ
 broker configured to [localhost:45617] for channel invoices
INFO  [io.sma.rea.mes.rabbitmq] (Quarkus Main Thread) SRMSG17007:
 Connection with RabbitMQ broker established for channel `invoices-rabbitmq`
INFO  [io.sma.rea.mes.rabbitmq] (vert.x-eventloop-thread-6) SRMSG17007:
 Connection with RabbitMQ broker established for channel `invoices-rabbitmq`
INFO  [io.sma.rea.mes.rabbitmq] (vert.x-eventloop-thread-6) SRMSG17000:
 RabbitMQ Receiver listening address invoices-rabbitmq
```

But of course we are only producing messages to the channel derived from the channel declaration in the `ReservationResource` (listing 9.17) which is `invoices`. This means that nothing is received in the consumer method anymore, since it consumes from the channel `invoices-rabbitmq`.

To map the `invoices-rabbitmq` channel to the correct RabbitMQ queue `invoices` we could modify the `@Channel` annotation in the `ReservationResource`, but we can also modify the `application.properties` like presented in listing 9.19, which gives us more flexibility. The `exchange` is the RabbitMQ concept that is responsible for the message routing. It also defaults to channel name if not specified.

> #### Listing 9.19   RabbitMQ queue rename

```
mp.messaging.incoming.invoices-rabbitmq.queue.name=invoices
mp.messaging.incoming.invoices-rabbitmq.exchange.name=invoices
```

When the application now restarts, the `invoices-rabbitmq` channel consumes from the `invoices` RabbitMQ queue. But there is one catch. Since the messages sent to RabbitMQ are encoded as JSON objects (the SmallRye implementation sets the `content_type` property in the message to `application/json`), we can't consume the `Invoice` object in the `@Incoming` method directly, because there is no default mapper that would transform it (as there was with the in-memory channel). However, it is really simple to map this object to the `Invoice` instance again as shown in the following listing.

Listing 9.20 The final version of `BillingService`

```
import io.vertx.core.json.JsonObject;

...

@ApplicationScoped
public class BillingService {

    @Incoming("invoices-rabbitmq")
    public void processInvoice(JsonObject json) {
        Invoice invoice = json.mapTo(Invoice.class);
        System.out.println("Processing received invoice: " + invoice);
    }
}
```

Of course, since we are just printing the invoice to the standard output, we could directly print the received `io.vertx.core.json.JsonObject`. But learning how to easily map the `JsonObject` to the domain objects is surely useful.

> **WARNING** You might need to restart Dev mode if you are renaming the channels created in RabbitMQ Dev Service.

Repeating request for making a new reservation now correctly produces a new invoice message into the RabbitMQ broker, which is then consumed in the `BillingService` and printed to the output. However, now it goes through the RabbitMQ broker.

9.7.1 *Testing messaging with RabbitMQ*

In the RabbitMQ testing, we don't have a similar helper library as we had with Kafka (`quarkus-test-kafka-companion`). We will utilize reactive messaging directly to receive posted message from the `invoice` queue in the test. As you may remember, a Quarkus test is also a CDI bean, so we define the `@Incoming` method similarly as we did in the `BillingService`. In fact, we can move the `BillingService#processInvoice` as is into the newly created test because we will no longer need it in the application itself.

Since we produce messages to RabbitMQ broker asynchronously, we need a mechanism that allows us to wait for the message to be received before we start asserting its contents. For this reason, we use the Awaitility (http://www.awaitility.org) library. You can add it to the Reservation service as the following dependency. The version is imported from the Quarkus BOM, so we don't have to define it in the application's `pom.xml`:

```
<dependency>
  <groupId>org.awaitility</groupId>
  <artifactId>awaitility</artifactId>
  <scope>test</scope>
</dependency>
```

The code of the new `org.acme.reservation.ReservationInvoiceProducerTest` is available in listing 9.21. Create this class in the `src/test/java` directory.

Listing 9.21 `ReservationInvoiceProducerTest` **in the Reservation service**

```
@QuarkusTest
@ApplicationScoped
@TestProfile(ReservationInvoiceProducerTest.RabbitMQTest.class)
public class ReservationInvoiceProducerTest {

    public static final class RabbitMQTest implements QuarkusTestProfile {
    }

    private final Map<Integer, Invoice> receivedInvoices = new HashMap<>();
    private final AtomicInteger ids = new AtomicInteger(0);

    @Incoming("invoices-rabbitmq")
    public void processInvoice(JsonObject json) {
        Invoice invoice = json.mapTo(Invoice.class);
        System.out.println("Received invoice " + invoice);

        receivedInvoices.put(ids.incrementAndGet(), invoice);
    }

    @Test
    public void testInvoiceProduced() throws Throwable {
        // Make a reservation request that sends the invoice to RabbitMQ
        Reservation reservation = new Reservation();
        reservation.carId = 1L;
        reservation.startDay = LocalDate.now().plusDays(1);
        reservation.endDay = reservation.startDay;

        given().body(reservation).contentType(MediaType.APPLICATION_JSON)
            .when().post("/reservation")
            .then().statusCode(200);

        Awaitility.await().atMost(15, TimeUnit.SECONDS)
            .until(() -> receivedInvoices.size() == 1);

        // Assert that the invoice message was received in this consumer
        Assertions.assertEquals(1, receivedInvoices.size());
        Assertions.assertEquals(ReservationResource.STANDARD_RATE_PER_DAY,
            receivedInvoices.get(1).price);
    }
}
```

In this test, we define an `@Incoming("invoice-rabbitmq")` method as a test consumer
that verifies the message is received. The test method just makes an HTTP call for a
new reservation that should produce a new invoice message into the `invoices` channel, and verifies that the consumer method `processInvoice` was called with the correct data. Note that we also added this test into a separate profile so the new test
doesn't conflict with existing tests (the Quarkus test application is restarted).

TIP Always remember to clean your Maven project (`mvn clean`) when you are
removing classes.

We can now delete the `BillingService` as we no longer need it. Actually, we have to delete it because it is also a *sink* (final consumer) for the same channel we use in the test. Also, in `application.properties` we can now prefix the messaging properties with the `%test.` prefix, so they are picked only in the test mode:

```
%test.mp.messaging.incoming.invoices-rabbitmq.queue.name=invoices
%test.mp.messaging.incoming.invoices-rabbitmq.exchange.name=invoices
```

The test can be executed either in the Dev mode by pressing `r` with the focus in the terminal window where the Dev mode is running, or simply by running `./mvnw clean test`. A RabbitMQ broker container is started in the background. The invoice is processed through the queue `invoices` the Reservation service creates once it connects to it.

> **WARNING** `java.util.concurrent.RejectedExecutionException` is expected. We are opening and closing connections to the RabbitMQ broker in quick successions.

9.8   *Car rental Billing service*

Now that we're already producing invoices from both Reservation (RabbitMQ) and Rental (Kafka) services, it's time to create the actual consumer, which is the Billing service.

The Billing service is the last backend service in car rental. It's been a while since we created the last new Quarkus application, but you probably remember that we can simply run the command available in listing 9.22. We also specify the required extensions that we will utilize to start working on billing functionality.

> **Listing 9.22   Creating new Billing service**

```
$ quarkus create app org.acme:billing-service -P 3.15.1 --no-code \
--extension rest-jackson,messaging-kafka,messaging-rabbitmq,mongodb-panache
```

We still want to expose REST API, which is why we need the `rest-jackson` extension. The next two extensions are required because the Billing service consumes asynchronous messages through Kafka and RabbitMQ messaging integrations. The last extension sets up MongoDB database integration.

We implement a simple model that allows persisting of the invoices and exposing them through HTTP. The following code is explained in detail in previous chapters, so we don't dive into specifics. The finished code of the Billing service is available in the `chapter-09/9_8/billing-service` directory.

The final representation of the Billing service can be summarized as

- It has a single `org.acme.billing.model.Invoice` entity (id (`ObjectId`), total-Price (`double`), paid (`boolean`), reservation (`Reservation`)).
- `Reservation` can be a (public static final) inner class containing all parameters (id (`Long`), userId (`String`), carId (`Long`), startDay (`LocalDate`), endDay (`LocalDate`)).
- The `org.acme.billing.InvoiceResource` exposes the sole HTTP GET endpoint at `/invoice` supplying all available invoices.

One last thing is to set up the correct port for the Billing service—which is expected to be running on port `8084`—and the name of the MongoDB database. We can do this in the `application.properties`:

```
quarkus.http.port=8084
quarkus.mongodb.database=billing
```

You should be familiar with all of this code by now. If that's not the case, feel free to revisit previous chapters.

9.8.1   *Messaging in the Billing service*

The Billing service acts as a consumer for the messages coming from the Reservation service through the RabbitMQ queue called `invoices` and also as a consumer for the messages coming from the Rental service through the `invoices-adjust` Kafka topic. Furthermore, it produces asynchronous messages to the Rental service that are also propagated through Apache Kafka via the topic called `invoices-confirmations`. Visual representation of this communication is provided in figure 9.9. It contains the names of the Kafka topics and the RabbitMQ queue, some of which we have already implemented.

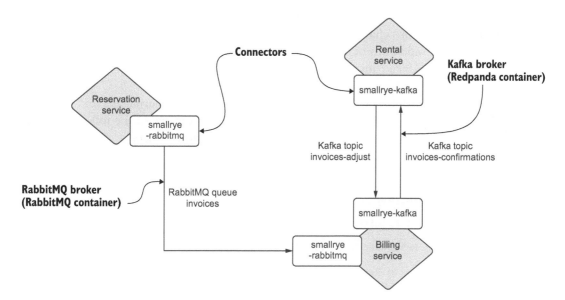

Figure 9.9   The asynchronous messaging architecture in the car rental system

The Kafka topic `invoices-confirmations` contains the messages that the Rental service can use to verify that the reservation/rental has been paid for.

9.8.2   *Consuming RabbitMQ messages from the Reservation service*

When the reservations are created, the Reservation service sends invoice requests to the RabbitMQ queue called `invoices`. To consume these messages in the Billing service, we need to first connect it to the same RabbitMQ broker and implement the consumer that processes the received invoice message and requests the payment.

The connection to the same broker is easy as long as we are using Dev Services since (similarly as with Kafka) any other Quarkus application started in Dev mode on the same machine automatically connects to the Dev Service instance of the RabbitMQ broker started by the first Quarkus application. By starting the Billing service in Dev mode, it automatically connects to the RabbitMQ broker started by the Reservation service or vice versa.

> **WARNING** Remember that the Dev Service needs to be fully started to be discoverable by other Dev modes. Also remember which of the services is owning the Dev Service because if you stop the Dev mode of the owning service, you will break all other Dev modes that depend on the same Dev Service.

We don't need to implement the actual logic that will request payments in our imaginary car rental system. Instead, we will just simply sleep for a random time period after which we consider the invoice paid. After the invoice is paid, we produce a new confirmation message to the new `invoices-confirmations` channel that maps into the Kafka topic.

Because the request payment operation is a blocking process (we need to wait for the user to pay or in our case for the sleep to end), we need to split the processing through one more channel called `invoices-requests`, which allows us to move this blocking operation out of the nonblocking I/O thread. This in-memory channel consumes the produced invoices, requests payments, and sends the confirmation messages if the payment is successful.

We start by defining the consuming message data class `org.acme.billing.data` `.ReservationInvoice` in the Billing service. As demonstrated in the following listing, it is exactly same as the invoice sent from the Reservation service.

Listing 9.23 The `ReservationInvoice` data class

```
package org.acme.billing.data;

import org.acme.billing.model.Invoice;

public class ReservationInvoice {

    public Invoice.Reservation reservation;
    public double price;
}
```

Next we create class `org.acme.billing.InvoiceProcessor` that consumes the `ReservationInvoice` messages (listing 9.24).

Listing 9.24 The source code of the `InvoiceProcessor` class

```
@ApplicationScoped
public class InvoiceProcessor {
```

```
@Incoming("invoices")
@Outgoing("invoices-requests")
public Message<Invoice> processInvoice(Message<JsonObject> message) {
    ReservationInvoice invoiceMessage = message
        .getPayload().mapTo(ReservationInvoice.class);
    Invoice.Reservation reservation = invoiceMessage.reservation;
    Invoice invoice = new Invoice(invoiceMessage.price,
        false, reservation);

    invoice.persist();
    Log.info("Processing invoice: " + invoice);

    return message.withPayload(invoice);
}
}
```

The code of this class is straightforward. We define a processor method `processInvoice` that consumes the invoice messages from the RabbitMQ connector (queue `invoices`). This method receives the `Message` wrapper of the JSON object that represents our message. This wrapper allows us to propagate the ack or nack from the downstream message. This is a safeguard that guarantees we don't lose any invoices because they are always persisted, even in the case some later part of the invoice processing fails.

The `message.withPayload` call creates a new instance of `Message` that takes the metadata and ack/nack from the original `message`. It could also be written as `Message.of(invoice, message::ack, message::nack)` if we would like to be more explicit.

The asynchronous messages in reactive messaging don't automatically trigger live reloads of the Quarkus application running in Dev mode. When you finish your changes, you need to manually restart the application by pressing s in the Dev mode terminal or with an HTTP request.

Because we have connectors both for Kafka and for RabbitMQ on the classpath (`smallrye-kafka` and `smallrye-rabbitmq` extensions), we need to also configure which connector should be used for the `invoices` channel in `application.properties`:

```
mp.messaging.incoming.invoices.connector=smallrye-rabbitmq
```

If you now tried to start a new reservation, you would not see anything happening in the Billing service because we didn't configure the `invoices-requests` channel consumer yet.

Let's implement the payment request processing. Create a new class `org.acme.billing.PaymentRequester` as shown in the following listing.

> **Listing 9.25 The source code of the `PaymentRequester` class**

```
@ApplicationScoped
public class PaymentRequester {

    private final Random random = new Random();
```

```
@Incoming("invoices-requests")
@Outgoing("invoices-confirmations")
@Blocking
public InvoiceConfirmation requestPayment(Invoice invoice) {        ◁─────────
    payment(invoice.reservation.userId, invoice.totalPrice, invoice);

    invoice.paid = true;
    invoice.update();
    Log.infof("Invoice %s is paid.", invoice);

    return new InvoiceConfirmation(invoice, true);
}

private void payment(String user, double price, Object data) {
    Log.infof("Request for payment user: %s, price: %f, data: %s",
        user, price, data);
    try {
        Thread.sleep(random.nextInt(1000, 5000));
    } catch (InterruptedException e) {
        Log.error("Sleep interrupted.", e);
    }
}

/* uncomment in order to consume confirmation here
@Incoming("invoices-confirmations")
public void consume(InvoiceConfirmation invoiceConfirmation) {
    System.out.println(invoiceConfirmation);
}
*/
}
```

> **We are executing a blocking operation in this method, so we must make sure it executes on the worker thread.**

The `@Blocking` annotation is required because of the sleep, not because of invoice update (remember that we are not using transactions with MongoDB). The processor sleeps for a random period between 1 and 5 seconds to simulate payment operations. After the sleep is done, it produces an `InvoiceConfirmation` message to the `invoices-confirmations` channel.

We can also see that this blocking method uses normal types even if we are in the reactive messaging channel pipeline. With Quarkus messaging, you don't have to use reactive types (`Uni`, `Multi`, `Message`) if you don't want to.

Lastly, we need the data class called `InvoiceConfirmation` that we can send to the Rental service. Create this class in the `org.acme.billing.data` package.

Listing 9.26 The `org.acme.billing.data.InvoiceConfirmation` class

```
package org.acme.billing.data;

import org.acme.billing.model.Invoice;

public class InvoiceConfirmation {

    public Invoice invoice;
    public boolean paid;
```

```
    // all-arg constructor, toString
}
```

The information on whether the invoice is paid or not is also contained in the invoice itself. But for the demonstration of the processor, we want to showcase returning a different data class than the one that is received.

The `invoices-confirmations` channel is not mapped into any connector for now. If you would like to test the functionality, you can uncomment the `consume` method in the `PaymentRequester` to see the invoices printed to the console when you create new reservations in the Reservation service.

9.8.3   Producing confirmations to the Rental service

As demonstrated in figure 9.9, we are expected to produce the invoice confirmations to the Rental service once the payment is processed. After the last section, we are already producing messages into the `invoices-confirmations` channel. To send them to Apache Kafka, we need to configure this channel to use the `smallrye-kafka` connector.

If you are not already running the Rental service in Dev mode, start it. Depending on whether the Billing service is already running, either Rental service now automatically connects to the started Redpanda (Kafka) container or vice versa. However, we recommend starting the Billing service first so it manages Dev Services both for RabbitMQ and for Kafka. It makes it easier for us to manage the Dev Services instances if the origin is in the same Dev mode.

It would be good to stop a while now and think about how much effort and how many tedious tasks the Quarkus's Dev mode takes off our shoulders. Simply by running in Dev mode, Dev Services automatically wire three of our services through two separate remote brokers that we don't need to manage. Can you think about how long it would take you to create this setup manually?

Now that both services are connected to the same Kafka instance, changing the production of the invoice confirmation to be sent to Kafka is as simple as setting the connector for the `invoices-confirmations` channel in the `application.properties` of the Billing service. Remember to also remove the optional consumer in the `Payment-Requester#consume` method if you opt to implement (uncomment) it, since we can't consume in two sinks:

```
mp.messaging.outgoing.invoices-confirmations.connector=smallrye-kafka
```

Note the `outgoing` keyword in the configuration. This is important since we are producing messages to Kafka.

The Billing service is now acting as a real invoice processing service. The last missing functionality is to integrate it also with the Rental service.

9.8.4   *Rental service invoice confirmations*

The Rental service communicates with the Billing service in two ways. It consumes the invoice confirmations for created reservations, and it produces the invoice adjustment requests. All of this communication utilizes the Apache Kafka broker.

If the Rental service runs in Dev mode, it is already connected to the same Kafka instance as the Billing service. We can start integrating the invoice confirmations.

Because all of our invoice processing is asynchronous, we verify that the customer paid for the rental only when the rental is ending. At that point, we also request any invoice adjustments if the original rental isn't ended on the perceived day.

We start by adding the `paid` attribute to the `Rental` entity, which we can use to track the payment confirmations. Modify the `org.acme.rental.entity.Rental` class as demonstrated in listing 9.27. The rest of the class doesn't need any changes.

Listing 9.27   Adding the `paid` attribute to the `Rental` entity

```
public class Rental extends PanacheMongoEntity {

    public boolean paid;
    ...

    @Override
    public String toString() {
        return "Rental{" +
            "paid=" + paid +
            ", userId='" + userId + '\'' +
            ", reservationId=" + reservationId +
            ", startDate=" + startDate +
            ", endDate=" + endDate +
            ", active=" + active +
            ", id=" + id +
            '}';
    }
}
```

We can start consuming messages from the `invoices-confirmations` topic in the Kafka broker. Create a new class `org.acme.rental.invoice.InvoiceConfirmation-Service` as shown in the following listing.

Listing 9.28   `InvoiceConfirmationService` consuming messages from Kafka

```
@ApplicationScoped
public class InvoiceConfirmationService {

    @Incoming("invoices-confirmations")
    public void invoicePaid(InvoiceConfirmation invoiceConfirmation) {
        Log.info("Received invoice confirmation " + invoiceConfirmation);

        if (!invoiceConfirmation.paid) {
            Log.warn("Received unpaid invoice confirmation - "
                + invoiceConfirmation);
```

```
        // retry handling omitted
    }

    InvoiceConfirmation.InvoiceReservation reservation =
        invoiceConfirmation.invoice.reservation;

    Rental.findByUserAndReservationIdsOptional(
            reservation.userId, reservation.id)
        .ifPresentOrElse(rental -> {
            // mark the already started rental as paid
            rental.paid = true;
            rental.update();
        }, () -> {
            // create new rental starting in the future
            Rental rental = new Rental();
            rental.userId = reservation.userId;
            rental.reservationId = reservation.id;
            rental.startDate = reservation.startDay;
            rental.active = false;
            rental.paid = true;
            rental.persist();
        });
    }
}
```

This consumer method first performs a check that tests if the invoice is really paid and, if not, it logs a warning message. Retrying of the failed payments is beyond the scope of our example application. Next, we check if the rental covered by this invoice has already started by looking it up in the database. If it is already persisted, then it has started without payment. In this case, we can just mark it as paid. If it is not in the database, then we received the invoice confirmation before the start of the rental. We can then persist it here as it represents an already paid rental.

We don't need to block in this method (`@Blocking`) even though we execute database operations, since MongoDB, which we use in the Rental service, by default doesn't use transactions.

We also need the data classes that can be mapped to the received invoices. To save some space, let's create a class `InvoiceConfirmation` in the `org.acme.rental.invoice` `.data` package that contains all data classes. Notice that we are not parsing all the data that is sent in the invoice:

- `InvoiceConfirmation` (invoice (`Invoice`), paid (`boolean`))
- inner class `Invoice` (paid (`boolean`), reservation (`InvoiceReservation`))
- inner class `InvoiceReservation` (id (`Long`), userId (`String`), startDay (`LocalDay`))

The full source code of this class is available in the `chapter-09/9_8_4` directory. We renamed the reservation class to `InvoiceReservation` so it can't be confused with the `Reservation` data class we use in the `ReservationClient`. But also note that the field must be named as *reservation* to correctly parse sent confirmations from the Billing service. We also included `toString` methods for each class.

Now we can adjust the `RentalResource` class to take into account already confirmed rentals. The following listing details the `start` method changes that now need to check if the rental for a selected reservation is already persisted because the invoice confirmation was received before, or if the new rental needs to be started as before.

Listing 9.29   `RentalResource#start` accommodating invoice confirmations

```
@Path("/start/{userId}/{reservationId}")
@POST
@Produces(MediaType.APPLICATION_JSON)
public Rental start(String userId,
                    Long reservationId) {
    Log.infof("Starting rental for %s with reservation %s",
        userId, reservationId);                              Tries to find the rental
                                                             in the database
    Optional<Rental> rentalOptional = Rental
        .findByUserAndReservationIdsOptional(userId, reservationId);

    Rental rental;
    if (rentalOptional.isPresent()) {
        // received confirmed invoice before
        rental = rentalOptional.get();
        rental.active = true;          If found, updates
        rental.update();               the active attribute
    } else {
        // rental starting right now before payment
        rental = new Rental();
        rental.userId = userId;
        rental.reservationId = reservationId;
        rental.startDate = LocalDate.now();
        rental.active = true;
        rental.persist();              If not found, persists a
    }                                  new record that will be
    return rental;                     paid for in the future
}
```

The `end` method is simpler. We check that the rental is paid, otherwise, we let the customer know that there is a problem. The payment error processing is left out for simplicity.

Listing 9.30   `RentalResource#end` verifying payments

```
public Rental end(String userId, Long reservationId) {
    ...

    Rental rental = Rental
        .findByUserAndReservationIdsOptional(userId, reservationId)
        .orElseThrow(() -> new NotFoundException("Rental not found"));
```

```
    if (!rental.paid) {
        Log.warn("Rental is not paid: " + rental);
        // trigger error processing
    }

    Reservation reservation = reservationClient
        .getById(reservationId);
    ...
}
```

It was a lot of code, but we are now correctly handling the invoice confirmations in the Rental service. If you wish to take this a bit further, you can write tests that verify the correct scenario handling as an exercise. In every case, you can try the functionality now by creating a reservation with the start day equal to today and with the one in the future. In both cases, all rentals (`GET :8082/rental`) are eventually updated as paid.

The last missing piece is to consume invoice adjustments sent from the Rental service in the Billing service if the customer returns the car on an unexpected date. The Rental service is already sending these messages to the Kafka topic called `invoices -adjust`, which we implemented in section 9.6.1.

By now, you should know what needs to be done in the Billing service to consume these messages. So if you feel like it, try it first yourself as an exercise. You can always look back to this section if you need.

In the Billing service, we will save the adjustment invoices into a separate MongoDB collection. Let's create a new entity (that `extends PanacheMongoEntity`) class `Invoice-Adjust` in the `org.acme.billing.model` package. We also recommend adding the `toString` method since we will use this entity in some log messages:

- `InvoiceAdjust (id (ObjectId), rentalId (String), userId (String), actual-EndDate (LocalDate), price (double), paid (boolean))`

This time, we keep all the attributes that the Rental service sends for the tracking purposes in the Billing service. The invoice adjustments are the sole responsibility of the Billing service. The Rental service doesn't need to be involved in the payment processing after it sends the adjustment message.

The processing of the invoice adjustment is similar to the invoice processing. We can add the new method `requestAdjustment` the `PaymentRequester` as presented in the following listing.

Listing 9.31 `PaymentRequester#requestAdjustment` **method**

```
@Incoming("invoices-adjust")
@Blocking
@Acknowledgment(Acknowledgment.Strategy.PRE_PROCESSING)
public void requestAdjustment(InvoiceAdjust invoiceAdjust) {
    Log.info("Received invoice adjustment: " + invoiceAdjust);

    payment(invoiceAdjust.userId, invoiceAdjust.price, invoiceAdjust);
    invoiceAdjust.paid = true;
```

```
    invoiceAdjust.persist();
    Log.infof("Invoice adjustment %s is paid.", invoiceAdjust);
}
```

We also changed the acknowledgment strategy to `Acknowledgment.Strategy.PRE_PROCESSING` in order not to block the producer waiting for payment to be processed.

Lastly, we need to configure the new `invoices-adjust` channel to pull messages from the Kafka broker. Add the following configuration properties to the `application.properties` file in Billing service:

```
mp.messaging.incoming.invoices-adjust.connector=smallrye-kafka
mp.messaging.incoming.invoices-adjust.auto.offset.reset=earliest
```

The `earliest` offset allows us to reload unprocessed messages from Kafka in case of crashes.

The Billing service is now able to consume invoice adjustments. Feel free to experiment a little with the provided APIs. Try creating reservations starting today and in the future. Also try to set the rental end date in the future and end it manually in the Rental service to see the adjustment processing in the Billing service.

The log statements nicely demonstrate the flow of asynchronous messages. When you create a reservation, you can see in the Billing service how the payment is being processed.

So why would you choose to implement your application with reactive messaging? The whole payment backend processing is asynchronous and extremely reliable. Try to push several reservations in quick succession or try to stop any service (that is not owning the Dev Service instances!) and push some messages to other running services. Rental service is a good choice because it is at the end of the message chain. Use the start day in the future because Reservation also calls Rental via HTTP if the start day is today. This shows the nice comparison to asynchronous message passing in this scenario. You will see that both RabbitMQ and Kafka keep track of unprocessed (not yet acknowledged) messages. When the Rental service comes back up, it can still process the messages that were sent while it was down.

9.9   *Next steps*

This chapter introduced the MicroProfile Reactive Messaging specification together with the SmallRye Reactive Messaging library. We defined the reactive systems and their properties that are becoming necessary for any modern enterprise application with the asynchronous message passing as the base pillar of such systems.

Next, we investigated the APIs provided by the MicroProfile Reactive Messaging specification. We learned about connectors and how they allow us to connect to different messaging providers.

Lastly, we created a new Billing service that communicates with the Reservation service through the RabbitMQ broker via the AMQP 0-9-1 protocol. It also exchanges asynchronous messages with the Rental service through the Apache Kafka platform.

There was a lot of coding in this chapter. However, it was fun! We learned that plugging in a reactive pipeline as a connection between two Quarkus services is rather easy. With two annotations (`@Incoming` and `@Outgoing`), a little bit of configuration, and the power of Dev services, you can write reactive services with ease.

Summary

- The reactive manifesto defines reactive systems as applications that are responsive, elastic, resilient, and based on asynchronous message passing.
- MicroProfile Reactive Messaging is a specification defining a simple API for asynchronous message passing based on reactive streams. Messages flow through channels defined as methods in CDI beans annotated with the `@Incoming` and `@Outgoing` annotations.
- Quarkus uses the SmallRye Reactive Messaging library that implements the specification, but it also provides useful features that are not in the specification yet.
- In Quarkus, you can also utilize blocking APIs for messaging integrations, even if the specification is called Reactive Messaging.
- Connectors are SPI bridges that allow production and consumption of messages from remote services as, for instance, Kafka or RabbitMQ broker.
- SmallRye Reactive Messaging connectors are packaged in separate extensions. They also provide Dev Services for the remote brokers, which are the connector bridges.
- Applications started in Dev mode automatically connect to the remote brokers started as Dev Services even if the Dev Service belongs to another application running in Dev mode.

Part 3

Quarkus in the cloud and beyond

We have explored the different tools and frameworks that can be used for building Quarkus applications. But some pieces of the puzzle are still missing. How do you deploy it? How do you monitor it? How do you scale it? Cloud environments are pretty much a necessity for deploying modern applications nowadays. In the last part of the book, we will explore how Quarkus gets you ready to deploy your application in the cloud.

We will start gently by exploring some generic patterns that systems should follow to be ready to be deployed in production and handle today's requirements. Then, we will see how to actually deploy the Acme Car Rental application in a Kubernetes or OpenShift environment.

The last chapter will be somewhat different: we will show how to create a custom Quarkus extension. This might be useful if you decide to use Quarkus with a framework that isn't integrated in the Quarkus ecosystem yet. Doing this will require some more advanced knowledge of the inner workings of Quarkus, but don't worry, we will guide you through it!

Cloud-native
application patterns

10

This chapter covers

- Introducing the MicroProfile set of specifications for cloud-native Java applications
- Monitoring the status and health of applications
- Collecting and visualizing application metrics
- Tracing requests within and across services
- Adding fault tolerance capabilities to applications

We've repeated multiple times that Quarkus is a framework for building cloud-native applications. But what does it mean exactly? What are the characteristics of cloud-native applications? What are the patterns that are commonly used to build them?

In this chapter, we'll answer these questions and show you how to implement these patterns in Quarkus applications. We also look into the related tools Quarkus offers to make these integrations easier. In the next chapter, we will expand on what we learn here by actually deploying the full Acme Car Rental in the cloud and seeing how all these functionalities neatly work together.

The main characteristics that we discuss in this chapter are

- *Health*—Applications should expose information about their health so that various kinds of their problems can be detected (either by a human operator or automatically). An application is unhealthy if some of its components or external connections don't work as needed—for example, if a database connection isn't working, a deadlock is detected, or the memory heap is full. Human operators or automated tools can then respond to this information and take appropriate action, such as restarting the application.
- *Metrics*—Metrics are similar to health checks in that they convey information about the status of an application. However, unlike health checks whose outcome is binary (good or bad), metrics are numeric values. They can tell how much memory is used, how many threads in a thread pool are usually busy, how many requests are being processed per minute, and so on. You may create automated alerts for metrics—for example, to receive an email when an application's memory usage exceeds a certain threshold.
- *Tracing*—Tracing allows you to follow (visually) a request as it flows through multiple components and services. This is useful for troubleshooting purposes and can help to find performance bottlenecks.
- *Fault tolerance*—Fault tolerance allows applications to gracefully deal with failures. For example, they can retry a request to a failing external service instead of propagating the failure to the caller.
- *Service discovery*—Service discovery is a way of dynamically finding the location of services that your application needs to interact with, allowing you to decouple the location of those services from your configuration. This makes deployments more robust and adaptable to changes.

> **NOTE** Health, metrics, and tracing (and also logging) are very often together called *observability*. This term refers to characteristics of an application that make it possible to observe its state while it's running.

The practical sections of this chapter focus on updating the Inventory service to add the capabilities that were outlined in the bulleted list.

But first, we should talk about MicroProfile. MicroProfile is a set of specifications that define a programming model for building cloud-native Java applications, including the aforementioned capabilities. We have already worked with a few MicroProfile specifications in previous chapters, such as the REST Client, GraphQL, and OpenAPI, and we explore more of them in this chapter.

> **NOTE** Health, Tracing, Metrics, and Fault Tolerance are part of MicroProfile APIs. Service Discovery is not part of it at the time of writing but may well be in the future.

10.1   MicroProfile, SmallRye, and Quarkus

As mentioned, MicroProfile (https://microprofile.io) is a set of specifications. It belongs under the Eclipse Foundation umbrella, and it's a community-driven effort. All specifications are available as open source on GitHub (under the Eclipse organization: https://github.com/eclipse/).

Under the MicroProfile umbrella, you will actually find two sets of specifications. The first set is the so-called MicroProfile platform. Just like the Jakarta EE platform, this is a set of specifications that are released together under a single version number (each specification has its own versioning, though, and a platform release bundles a particular set of specification versions together).

The second set is the individual specifications that aren't part of the platform, usually referred to as "standalone" specifications. This includes, for example, the GraphQL specification that we've already used in previous chapters.

At the time of writing, Quarkus 3.15 aligns with this MicroProfile 6.1, with one exception (Metrics, we will discuss this in the relevant section later).

The MicroProfile 6.1 platform contains the following specifications:

- Telemetry 1.1
- OpenAPI 3.1
- REST Client 3.0
- Config 3.1
- Fault Tolerance 4.0
- Metrics 5.1
- JWT Authentication 2.1
- Health 4.0

Quarkus 3.15 also supports the following standalone specifications:

- LRA 2.0
- GraphQL 2.0
- Context Propagation 1.3
- Reactive Messaging 3.0
- Reactive Streams Operators 3.0
- OpenTracing 3.0

Quarkus's compatibility with each specification is verified using a so-called *Technology Compatibility Kit* (TCK). This is a set of tests that verify that the implementation behaves as specified. The TCKs are provided as part of the MicroProfile specifications, and Quarkus runs them as part of its own build.

10.1.1   What is SmallRye?

SmallRye (https://smallrye.io) is a set of implementations of the MicroProfile specifications. We said that Quarkus is also a MicroProfile implementation, so this begs for a bit of explanation. Each SmallRye project implements one of the MicroProfile specifications. Quarkus then provides an extension per each SmallRye project that integrates the SmallRye implementation into Quarkus and allows you to use it in your applications.

The Quarkus extension makes sure that the project is well integrated into the overall Quarkus architecture—for example, by providing relevant `quarkus.*` configuration properties and by contributing some related logic into the build-time application initialization mechanism.

SmallRye implementations also provide various additional features on top of the specifications, which they implement with the target of specifying them in the future. Users can thus choose if they want to align purely with the specification (gaining easier portability between implementations) or experiment with additional features provided by the SmallRye implementations.

10.2 *Monitoring application health*

In cloud deployments (and in computing in general), all kinds of things can go wrong. A network connection can fail; a database can become unavailable; a disk can fill up. It's important to be able to detect these problems and react to them. MicroProfile Health is one of the tools that you may use for this. It allows you to expose information about the status of your application via an HTTP endpoint. That endpoint can then be periodically monitored by various tools. For example, in a Kubernetes deployment, it typically serves as the endpoint for the Kubernetes liveness, readiness, and startup probes. These probes run periodically (in configured intervals), and when the application reports problems, Kubernetes can react to that, for example, by restarting the pod or refraining from sending traffic to it until health problems are resolved.

The implementation of MicroProfile Health in Quarkus is SmallRye Health (integrated in the `smallrye-health` extension).

With SmallRye Health, there are five different kinds of health checks:

- *Liveness*—This is usually used as the target of Kubernetes liveness probes. When an application's liveness check fails, it signifies that the application has had an error it is not expected to recover from, like running out of memory or detecting a deadlock. Kubernetes reacts by restarting the pod.
- *Readiness*—This is usually used as the target of Kubernetes readiness probes. When a readiness check fails, it signifies that the application is not ready to receive traffic—for example, because a required database connection isn't working or because the application has detected that the amount of current active tasks is above a certain threshold. Kubernetes will react by holding off sending further traffic to the pod until the condition is resolved.
- *Startup*—This is usually used as the target of Kubernetes startup probes. The startup check should start passing when the application is initialized and ready to start receiving traffic. This check is only used during the initial startup of the

application, and after it passes once, it is not called anymore—the liveness and readiness checks take over its responsibility.

- *Wellness*—This is actually not a part of the MicroProfile Health specification but is added as an extra feature by SmallRye Health. The wellness check conveys potential health problems that might affect the application but are not severe enough to warrant a restart or a traffic hold-off. This can be useful for reporting data to custom monitoring tools or manual monitoring by human operators.
- *Custom health groups*—These are any custom user-defined health groups (types of checks) that can have arbitrary use. They are also not yet defined in the MicroProfile Health specification.

10.2.1 *Monitoring the health of car rental*

Let's see some ways to monitor the health of the car rental applications. We start by verifying the functionality of the Inventory service's database connection—this is a check that Quarkus provides by default, so it is very easy. After that, we will learn how we can add a custom health check.

DATABASE CONNECTION HEALTH CHECK

When your application uses a JDBC data source, Quarkus automatically adds a readiness health check that verifies that the database connection is working. When the database is unavailable, the readiness check fails, saying that the application can't process requests right now. Let's try it out with the Inventory service with its MySQL connection.

Navigate to the `inventory-service` project's directory and add the `quarkus -smallrye-health` extension:

```
$ quarkus extension add smallrye-health
```

Run the `inventory-service` project in Dev mode. This automatically starts a MySQL database instance via Dev Services as a container.

To see the health check's status, we have two options. One is to view the Health UI, which is part of the Dev UI. Navigate to it either by opening http://localhost:8083/ q/dev-ui in a browser or by pressing the d key in the terminal window where you started the application. In the Dev UI, locate the card titled `SmallRye Health` and click the `Health UI` link inside that card (see figure 10.1).

In the Health UI, you will see a health check with a title `Database connections health check` with a status `UP`, just like in figure 10.2. There is probably also at least one other check that is related to the gRPC server which is embedded in the application. This page shows all health checks together, regardless of their type.

Let's also try to access the check via the HTTP endpoint directly. Open http:// localhost:8083/q/health, either via a browser or your favorite command-line tool. You should see the raw JSON output of all health checks, like in listing 10.1.

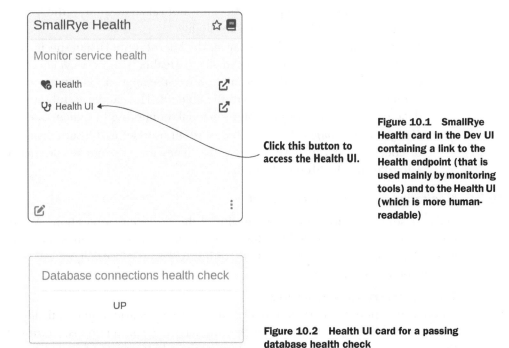

Figure 10.1   SmallRye Health card in the Dev UI containing a link to the Health endpoint (that is used mainly by monitoring tools) and to the Health UI (which is more human-readable)

Figure 10.2   Health UI card for a passing database health check

Listing 10.1   JSON output from the endpoint for health checks

```
{
  "status": "UP",
  "checks": [
    {
      "name": "gRPC Server",
      "status": "UP",
      "data": {
        "grpc.health.v1.Health": true,
        "inventory.InventoryService": true
      }
    },
    {
      "name": "Database connections health check",
      "status": "UP",
      "data": {
        "<default>": "UP"            ◁─── Each data source is listed separately.
      }                                   We have only one data source, and
    }                                     it is named "<default>".
  ]
}
```

NOTE   http://localhost:8083/q/health returns all checks grouped by their type. You can also append either /live or /ready to access only the liveness or readiness checks, respectively. There are also separate endpoints for startup (/started), wellness (/well), and health groups (/group).

NOTE The following container restart works by default in Podman, but if you are using Docker, Docker assigns a new port after the container starts again, which is +1 to the original port. In that case, you need to fix the MySQL Dev service to a particular port with the `quarkus.datasource.devservices.port` config property. E.g., `quarkus.datasource.devservices.port=3306` to fix it on the default MySQL port, but any free port will do the same.

Now let's deliberately crash the database. Use your container runtime tooling to find the ID of the running MySQL container and stop the container. For example, with Docker:

```
$ docker ps --format "{{.ID}} {{.Image}}"
775bdc6785c2 docker.io/library/mysql:8.4

$ docker stop 775bdc6785c2
```

Now request the health check again. If you do it in the Dev UI, the card of the check turns red, as shown in figure 10.3. You might need to refresh the page twice to get this particular error.

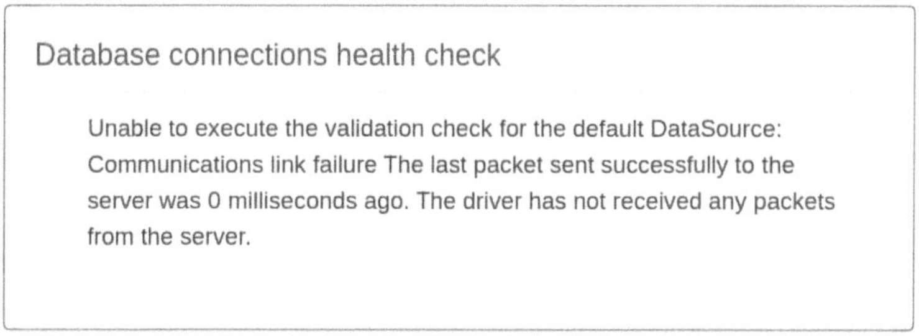

> Database connections health check
>
> Unable to execute the validation check for the default DataSource: Communications link failure The last packet sent successfully to the server was 0 milliseconds ago. The driver has not received any packets from the server.

Figure 10.3   Health UI card for a failing database health check displays the error message related to the failure.

On the HTTP endpoint, you will see the equivalent in raw JSON, as shown in listing 10.2. The gRPC check was omitted from this listing for brevity.

Listing 10.2   JSON output with a failing database check

```
{
  "status": "DOWN",
  "checks": [
    {
      "name": "Database connections health check",
      "status": "DOWN",
      "data": {
        "<default>": "Unable to execute the validation check for the
➥ default DataSource: Communications link failure\n\nThe last packet
➥ sent successfully to the server was 0 milliseconds ago. The driver has
➥ not received any packets from the server."
```

```
        }
      }
      ...
   ]
}
```

To bring the database back up, execute the following command (replace the container ID with the same that you used earlier):

```
$ docker start 775bdc6785c2
```

The health check should now pass again.

CUSTOM HEALTH CHECK

Now let's add a custom health check to the Inventory service. We will use a very simple wellness check that shows a status of "DOWN" if it is detected that the car inventory is empty. An empty inventory does not necessarily mean that the application itself is broken, but it surely is a sign that something is wrong, so a wellness check is probably the correct type for this check. Add the class that implements the check; it will be named CarCountCheck and reside in the org.acme.inventory.health package.

Listing 10.3   Wellness check reporting DOWN if the inventory is empty

```
package org.acme.inventory.health;

import io.smallrye.health.api.Wellness;
import jakarta.inject.Inject;
import org.acme.inventory.repository.CarRepository;
import org.eclipse.microprofile.health.HealthCheck;
import org.eclipse.microprofile.health.HealthCheckResponse;

@Wellness
public class CarCountCheck implements HealthCheck {

    @Inject
    CarRepository carRepository;

    @Override
    public HealthCheckResponse call() {
        long carsCount = carRepository.findAll().count();
        boolean wellnessStatus = carsCount > 0;
        return HealthCheckResponse.builder()
            .name("car-count-check")
            .status(wellnessStatus)          ← Sets the status to UP if
            .withData("cars-count", carsCount)    there is at least one car
            .build();                        ← Reports the number of
    }                                           cars as additional data
}
```

After your application starts up, there should actually be two cars imported automatically, so the check should pass, as you can verify by viewing the Health UI or calling http://localhost:8083/q/health/well (the `/well` suffix means that you only want to see wellness checks). The output should look like the following listing.

Listing 10.4   JSON output of the wellness check

```
{
    "status": "UP",
    "checks": [
        {
            "name": "car-count-check",
            "status": "UP",
            "data": {
                "cars-count": 2
            }
        }
    ]
}
```

To make the check fail, you need to delete both cars from the database. You may use either the GraphQL endpoint at http://localhost:8083/q/graphql-ui/ or the gRPC CLI that we created in chapter 4. For the CLI, navigate to the `inventory-cli` project's directory, make sure the project is built (`quarkus build` or `./mvnw package`), and execute

```
$ java -jar target/quarkus-app/quarkus-run.jar remove ABC123
$ java -jar target/quarkus-app/quarkus-run.jar remove XYZ987
```

Now request the wellness check again. You should see the output shown in the following listing.

Listing 10.5   The wellness check when the inventory is empty

```
{
    "status": "DOWN",
    "checks": [
        {
            "name": "car-count-check",
            "status": "DOWN",
            "data": {
                "cars-count": 0
            }
        }
    ]
}
```

If you want to re-add the initial two cars into the database, force a hot reload by pressing s in the terminal where the Inventory service is running.

10.3   Application metrics

Metrics provide additional insight into the well-being of a running application. Compared to health checks, which have a binary outcome (up or down), metrics are numeric values and thus can be used for various other purposes (e.g., for plotting charts and generating aggregate statistics).

The typical usage of metrics in cloud deployments is to have applications periodically report their metrics to a central monitoring system, such as Grafana, which then can plot graphs for visualization and raise automatic alerts when certain defined thresholds are exceeded—for example, if an application starts using too much memory or its response time becomes too high.

Generally, we can distinguish two kinds of metrics: framework metrics and application-specific (business) metrics. Framework metrics are usually provided by the runtime automatically, and they track general information about the running application, such as

- Number of requests received by the application per time unit
- Heap memory consumption
- Number of active database connections
- Time that it takes to handle one request
- Occupancy of threads in a thread pool
- Number of messages waiting in a queue to be processed

Business metrics are provided by the application itself and usually track something specific from the domain of the application. For example, in a web shop, you might want to track the number of orders placed per time unit.

10.3.1   Micrometer

The recommended way to work with metrics in Quarkus is to use the Micrometer extension. *Micrometer* (https://micrometer.io) is a library that provides a common API for working with metrics, and it supports submitting metrics to many different monitoring backends, such as Prometheus, Graphite, SignalFX, or Datadog.

The MicroProfile 6.1 platform, which Quarkus 3.15 aligns with, contains the MicroProfile Metrics 5.1 specification. Quarkus supports only MicroProfile Metrics 4.0. This is the only exception to Quarkus's compatibility with the MicroProfile platform. The reason is that the Quarkus developers have decided to use a slightly different approach, which is to prefer the Micrometer extension as the default way of working with metrics. There is a built-in SmallRye Metrics extension that is compatible with MicroProfile Metrics 4.0, but it's not recommended and it will be removed in a future release. Instead, the Micrometer extension is preferred as the way forward.

10.3.2   Metric types

Micrometer supports the following types of metrics:

- *Timer*—Measures the time that it takes to execute a certain operation and generates a histogram of the measured times.

- *Counter*—A simple counter that can only be incremented; it counts the number of occurrences of a particular event.

- *Gauge*—A single numeric value that can change in any direction over time. An example would be the heap memory usage of the application.

- *Distribution summary*—A histogram of numeric values, just like a timer but not necessarily tied to time-related measurements.

Counters and gauges are single-value metrics, while timers and distributions consist of multiple values. By default, they contain three values: `max` for the maximum value, `count` for the number of values, and `sum` for the sum of all values. They can also be configured to, for example, publish individual percentiles.

> **NOTE** In the context of Micrometer, and in its documentation, the term "meter" is more commonly used than "metric." On the other hand, in the MicroProfile space, "metric" is the more common term. We will use the term "metric" in this book.

10.3.3 Metric dimensionality

To allow for more flexibility in querying and generating useful insights from metrics, they can be dimensional. This means that a metric is not only identified by its name but also by a set of key-value pairs called tags. Metrics that are related to each other can share the same name but have different tags. For example, to count the HTTP requests coming to a server, you can have a set of counters under the name `http_requests` with the following tags:

- `method`—The HTTP method used for the request, such as `GET` or `POST`
- `path`—The path of the request, such as `/api/orders`
- `status`—The status code of the response, such as `200` or `404`

Each unique combination of tag values is associated with a separate counter. With this naming strategy you can, for example,

- Query the number of requests for a particular HTTP method by aggregating together all values where the `method` tag contains the desired method name.
- Query the number of requests for a particular path that resulted in a particular status code by aggregating all metrics where both the `path` and `status` tags have the desired values.

You will see that this is what Quarkus does for most of its built-in metrics, but of course it's possible (and recommended) to add dimensions to your business metrics too, when applicable. When choosing appropriate dimensions for your metrics, bear in mind that to be useful for querying purposes, they should have a low cardinality (number of unique values). For example, using a user ID as a dimension is not a good idea, because an ID is unique for each user.

10.3.4 The programming model

We mentioned two types of metrics—framework and business (application-specific)—and that framework metrics are built in to the runtime, so they don't need any coding, only configuration. So how do we work with business metrics; how can we collect them?

With the Micrometer library and Quarkus, there are two possible approaches: imperative (programmatic) and declarative (using annotations). The annotation-based approach is much easier and less verbose; on the other hand, the imperative approach is more flexible and allows for some more advanced use cases.

To declare a simple counter metric with an annotation, you only need to put a `@io.micrometer.core.annotation.Counted` annotation on a method of a CDI bean:

```
@Counted(name = "orders", description = "Number of orders placed")
public void orderPlaced(OrderDetails details) {
    // order processing logic
}
```

This will automatically register a counter metric named `orders` and attach an interceptor to your method; that interceptor will take care of incrementing the counter's value by 1 whenever the method is called.

To achieve the equivalent using the imperative approach, you would need to do the following. The `MeterRegistry` imports from the `io.micrometer.core.instrument` package:

```
@Inject
MeterRegistry meterRegistry;

public void orderPlaced(OrderDetais details) {
    // order processing logic
    meterRegistry.counter("orders").increment();
}
```

The method `meterRegistry.counter(…)` has a get-or-create semantic, so it will automatically create a counter of the given name if it doesn't exist yet and then return it. The `MeterRegistry` is the global registry of all metrics that are present in your application and allows dynamically adding and removing metrics.

> **NOTE** In the previous example, we didn't specify the description of the metric. If you want to do that, you need to use the `Counter.builder(…)` method to create the metric manually with all its associated metadata and then register it in the registry. This needs to happen just once, before any updates to the metric start happening. For example, you may do this inside a `@PostConstruct` method of a `@Singleton` bean (a `@Singleton` is a CDI bean that creates only one instance, and that instance is created automatically immediately when the application starts).

10.3.5 *Prometheus and Grafana*

Now that we have explained the programmatic side of collecting metrics, we need to discuss what happens to them after they are collected. Generally, metrics from running applications are periodically fed into a monitoring system that stores them, processes them, and allows humans to query them, potentially also by visualizing them in a dashboard. There are many monitoring systems available; one of the most popular solutions in the cloud-native world are *Prometheus* (https://prometheus.io) and *Grafana* (https://grafana.com). This is the combination that we will use in this book.

Prometheus is an engine for collecting, storing, and querying metrics. Grafana is a dashboarding tool that can query the metrics from Prometheus and display them in a dashboard.

Prometheus works by periodically scraping metrics from the application; that means it periodically makes HTTP requests to an application's endpoint. Prometheus defines a certain format that the endpoint needs to return. In the context of Quarkus, this endpoint is served by the `micrometer` extension and is available (by default) at `/q/metrics`. The endpoint contains a separate line for each metric value.

The complete architecture of a deployment with Prometheus and Grafana is shown in figure 10.4.

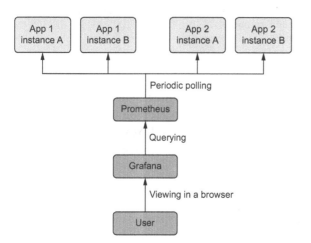

Figure 10.4 Typical deployment for monitoring metrics with Quarkus, Prometheus, and Grafana

10.3.6 *Monitoring metrics of car rental*

Enough theory: let's jump to the practical part and collect some metrics related to the Inventory service. First, let's look at metrics that Quarkus provides out of the box and how to visualize them with Grafana, and then we will create some custom ones.

The first thing that we need to do is add the `quarkus-micrometer-registry` `-prometheus` extension, which provides the Micrometer integration with the format intended for Prometheus. Go to the `inventory-service` directory and run:

```
$ quarkus extension add micrometer-registry-prometheus
```

From now on, whenever you start the application, it collects and exposes some metrics. Let's try it out. Start the application in Dev mode. Then call the /q/metrics endpoint that presents all registered metrics along with their values. If you're using HTTPie, you can do it as follows:

```
$ http :8083/q/metrics # same as curl http://localhost:8083/q/metrics
```

Another option is to open the Dev UI and click the Prometheus link inside the card titled Micrometer metrics.

In the output, you will see a lot of metrics (it should be well over 100 lines). These are all the metrics that Quarkus collected by default when Micrometer is enabled. Some lines are prefixed with # TYPE; these are metadata lines that describe the type of the metric (counter, gauge, etc.). Some lines are prefixed with # HELP; these are metadata lines that show the description of the particular metric, if it has one. Metrics that don't start with # are the actual metric data.

As just one example, the following listing shows lines that are related to the metric describing how long the JVM process has been running.

> **Listing 10.6   The process.uptime metric in the Prometheus output**

```
# HELP process_uptime_seconds The uptime of the Java virtual machine
# TYPE process_uptime_seconds gauge
process_uptime_seconds 128.22
```

VISUALIZING IN GRAFANA

Now that we have some metrics, let's visualize them in Grafana, because reading them in the raw form is not very convenient. To run Prometheus and Grafana, we have prepared a Docker Compose file that should set up everything you need, and we won't dive into the details about how this is all configured. You can find the file in the Git repository as chapter-10/docker-compose-files/docker-compose-metrics.yml. Start it by executing the following:

```
$ docker compose -f docker-compose-metrics.yml up
```

If everything succeeds, Grafana is available at http://localhost:3000 and Prometheus at http://localhost:9090. We don't need to look into the Prometheus UI; Prometheus runs just to serve as the metric storage engine that is used under the hood by Grafana. Now open your browser and navigate to http://localhost:3000. At the login screen, use admin as both the username and the password. If you are asked to change the password, you can press the Skip button to ignore this prompt.

Open the main menu on the left, and click Dashboards to view a list of dashboards that are currently registered in Grafana. See figure 10.5 for a screenshot of the main menu.

> **NOTE**   To make the screenshots more suitable for the book, we are using the light theme of Grafana. The default theme is dark, so your UI might look different. To switch to the light theme, open the main menu, click Administration,

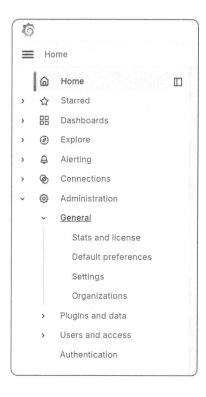

Figure 10.5   Navigating the main menu in Grafana

then `General`, then `Default preferences`; then select `Light` from the `Interface theme` selector and hit the `Save` button.

In the list of dashboards, there should be one dashboard named `Inventory service`. Click it to open it. For this example, we have prepared for you a dashboard that contains three metrics:

- *Car registrations*—A line chart with the number of cars that have been added to the inventory using the GraphQL endpoint (the `register` mutation). We haven't implemented this metric yet, so the chart probably isn't showing any data right now.
- *Process uptime*—A single-value panel that shows the value of the `process.uptime` metric that we saw earlier.
- *Process CPU usage*—A line chart showing the values of the `process.cpu.usage` metric over time.

A screenshot of the `Inventory service` dashboard is shown in figure 10.6.

All the charts get updated automatically over time. Grafana is configured to query Prometheus for the current data every 10 seconds, and this is the same interval that Prometheus is configured to query the application.

Try playing around with the dashboard. For example, in the top-right corner, there is a dropdown allowing you to select the time range from which you want to see data.

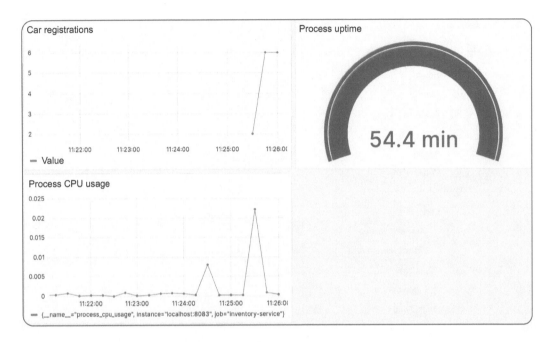

Figure 10.6   The Inventory service dashboard in Grafana

The default is Last 5 minutes, but you can select any time range in the past (if there's data for it).

Existing visualizations can be rearranged with your mouse. New visualizations can be added under the Add button in the top-right corner. Grafana knows which metrics are exposed by your application, so it will offer you a list that you can choose from. If you choose a multidimensional metric, the generated chart will contain multiple data series, one for each combination of tags. An example of such metric is jvm_memory_ used_bytes that contains the size of used memory in each JVM memory pool (Eden space, Old gen, Survivor space, etc.) separately. As an exercise, you may try to create a visualization of the jvm_memory_used_bytes metric that might look like figure 10.7. Under the options of the time series, select the unit to let Grafana know how to convert the values automatically to something more convenient—like bytes(SI), for instance.

CUSTOM METRICS

Now let's get back to the metric for car registrations. This is not a built-in metric provided by Quarkus out of the box; we have to define it manually. As we already discussed, for application-specific metrics, we have two approaches: programmatic (using the MeterRegistry object) and declarative (with annotations). Given that in this case it's just a matter of counting the invocations of a single method, we can use the annotation approach.

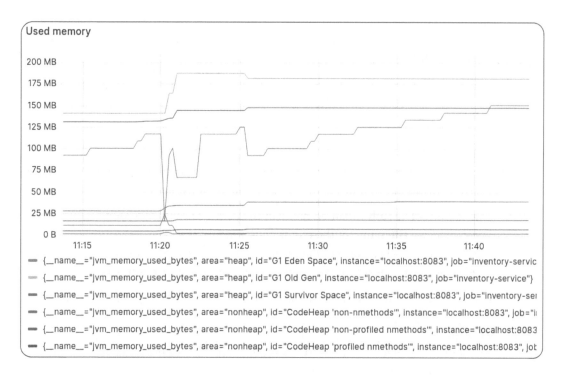

Figure 10.7 Visualizing JVM memory usage in Grafana

Open the class with the GraphQL endpoint for managing the inventory, `org.acme` `.inventory.service.GraphQLInventoryService`. Now simply annotate the `register` method with

```
@Counted(description = "Number of car registrations")
```

The correct import for this annotation is `io.micrometer.core.annotation.Counted`. And that's it. But before you call the `/q/metrics` endpoint to view it, you have to call the `register` method at least once, because the counter is registered lazily when the owning bean is first instantiated. Open the GraphiQL UI at http://localhost:8083/ q/graphql-ui/ and execute the following mutation:

```
mutation {
  register(car:{
    licensePlateNumber: "123"
  }) {
    id
  }
}
```

The metric should now appear in the /q/metrics endpoint as well as start showing some actual values in the Grafana chart. In the /q/metrics endpoint output, it looks like the following:

```
method_counted_total{
class="org.acme.inventory.service.GraphQLInventoryService",
exception="none",
method="register",
result="success"} 1.0
```

It's actually a multidimensional metric. Every counter created via a @Counted annotation will correspond to multiple data series. The dimensions are

- class—The fully qualified name of the class where the counted method resides
- method—The name of the counted method
- exception—The name of the exception that was thrown from the counted method
- result—The result of the counted method (success or failure)

Feel free to experiment with these dimensions in the Inventory service dashboard.

10.4   *Tracing*

One of the challenges of microservices is the complexity of the flows between multiple services. A single HTTP request from a client might trigger a relatively large chain of invocations between services. When something goes wrong in that chain (be it a failure or a performance problem), it's not exactly easy to trace the flow of the request and find out where the problem is.

This is where distributed tracing comes in. Distributed tracing allows users to follow the flow of a request inside the components of a single service (allowing you to see which methods are invoked), as well as between services, and visualize it for easier troubleshooting. You can see not only where the request goes but also how long each part of the processing takes, so it's easier to spot performance problems too.

This is achieved by adding a unique identifier to each request: a trace ID. Each incoming request into a system corresponds to one trace. A trace consists of spans, where a span represents a single unit of work within a trace. A span typically corresponds to a method invocation when tracing the inside of a single service. It can also be a database invocation or a remote request when tracing communication between services. Just like a trace, each span also has its unique ID. Spans are typically nested, so they form a tree. An example of a trace is shown in figure 10.8.

This is a simple example that only involves a single application. It is a trace from a single invocation of a REST operation that adds a new product definition into a shop. From the screenshot, it is easy to deduce that the trace ID in this case is ed9889a. The trace consists of three spans: the root span (the first line in the table) represents the REST call, and then there are two database calls. One is a SELECT to generate the

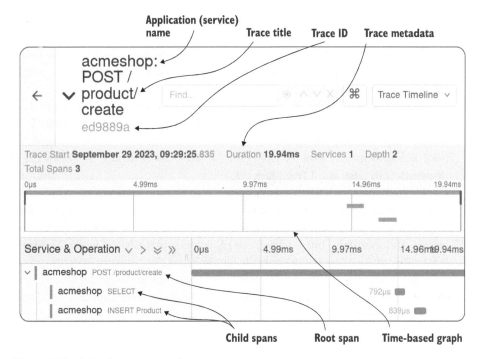

Figure 10.8   A simple trace example

next ID from a database sequence; the other one is the actual INSERT of the new product definition.

The trace ID is propagated between services (only those that support distributed tracing, of course), so that it is possible to correlate spans from different services that belong to the same trace. This adds a requirement on the underlying protocol to support passing this metadata. For instance, the HTTP protocol propagates traces using the HTTP headers.

Now that we know that individual services are instrumented to generate span data, how are spans collected and visualized? This depends on the tracing library and the chosen visualization tool. In our case, we will be using *OpenTelemetry* as the tracing library, which is currently the most popular tracing library in the cloud-native world. Quarkus has first-class support for OpenTelemetry. For visualizing the traces, we will use *Jaeger*—the tool from which the example screenshot in figure 10.8 is. Let's now talk briefly about OpenTelemetry.

10.4.1 *OpenTelemetry*

OpenTelemetry (https://opentelemetry.io), commonly referred to as OTel for short, is a collection of various tools and APIs that are used to collect and export telemetry data from applications. OpenTelemetry doesn't only cover tracing. It also has capabilities for collecting metrics and logs, but these were not yet considered ready and stable, and thus not supported by Quarkus at the time of writing this book, so we will focus only on the tracing part.

Usage of OpenTelemetry in the context of cloud-native Java applications is further specified by the MicroProfile Telemetry specification. Quarkus is an implementation of this specification.

OpenTelemetry was conceived by merging two former projects: OpenTracing and OpenCensus. It is a vendor-neutral and programming language-agnostic. It provides a common protocol (named OTLP) for exporting telemetry data from applications to a tool named OpenTelemetry Collector, which then centrally processes the data and forwards it to a backend (e.g., Jaeger).

Usage of an OpenTelemetry collector is in most cases optional. Application frameworks may support exporting telemetry data directly to a backend without going through an OpenTelemetry Collector. For smaller-scale deployments, this is easier to set up and maintain, but for larger deployments, it is advised to use an OpenTelemetry Collector, because it can centrally add features like filtering, batching, and retrying in case of failures. In our practical examples, we will be using Jaeger, which supports receiving OTLP data directly from applications, so we won't actually need to use a separate collector (even though it is possible).

Figure 10.9 depicts the tracing topology using a collector.

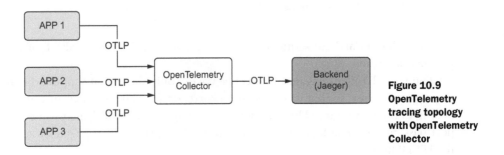

Figure 10.9 OpenTelemetry tracing topology with OpenTelemetry Collector

Figure 10.10 depicts the tracing topology without a collector, where the backend directly communicates with the target services.

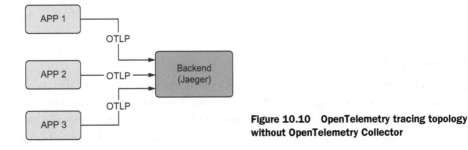

Figure 10.10 OpenTelemetry tracing topology without OpenTelemetry Collector

10.4.2 *Adding tracing capabilities to car rental*

Let's try to add tracing to our car rental application. In this exercise, we use three existing services (Users, Reservation, and Inventory) to show how tracing works between multiple services. We don't add any new business functionality, and there are zero changes to the application code—everything is achieved by simply adding the OpenTelemetry extension to each of these services. The solution, as always, can be found in the `chapter-10/10_4_2` directory in the book's git repository.

Go to the root directories of all the mentioned services (`users-service`, `reservation-service`, and `inventory-service`) and add the `quarkus-opentelemetry` extension for each of them:

```
$ quarkus extension add opentelemetry
```

RUNNING JAEGER

Now that we've added the extension, Quarkus will automatically start collecting tracing data. But to be able to store and visualize the data, we need Jaeger. We will make use of the fact that, in recent versions, Jaeger supports receiving OpenTelemetry data directly without needing a separate collector. We have again prepared a ready-to-use docker-compose file that starts everything. The file can be found as `chapter-10/docker-compose-files/docker-compose-tracing.yml` in the git repository. It's really short, so we will also include it here in the following listing.

Listing 10.7 The docker-compose file to start Jaeger

```
version: "3.7"
services:
  jaeger-all-in-one:
    image: docker.io/jaegertracing/all-in-one:1.62.0
    ports:
      - "16686:16686" # Jaeger UI
      - "4317:4317"   # OTLP receiver
```

It's actually just a single container that contains Jaeger. The OpenTelemetry collector is conveniently omitted since Jaeger includes everything we need. You can see that the Jaeger UI is exposed on port `16686`, and the OpenTelemetry Collector listens on port `4317` for incoming data. What's convenient is that `localhost:4317` is also the default export target for the OpenTelemetry Quarkus extension, so we don't need to configure anything in our applications.

Start the docker-compose file by running

```
$ docker compose -f docker-compose-tracing.yml up
```

Since we are running only one container, we can also run it using the container runtime (Podman, Docker, etc.) directly—for example, with Docker:

```
$ docker run --rm -p 16686:16686 -p 4317:4317
 docker.io/jaegertracing/all-in-one:1.62.0
```

But since we will later use it with other services, we will stick to a Docker Compose file.

GENERATING SOME TRACING DATA AND VISUALIZING IT

Now it's time to start the three applications (Users, Reservation, and Inventory) in Dev mode. After that, we'll access the Users service by opening http://localhost:8080 in a browser. After logging in as `alice` with the same password, you should see the familiar UI of the Users service from chapter 6, with some cars available for reservation. The difference is that this time, by opening this page, we have generated some tracing data.

Let's go to the Jaeger UI at http://localhost:16686 and see what we can find. In the left-hand menu, you see a dropdown item with services that Jaeger knows about—services that have submitted some tracing data. There should be four services: `users-service`, `reservation-service`, `inventory-service`, and `jaeger-all-in-one` (which is an internal service that traces requests to Jaeger itself and is always present), as shown in figure 10.11.

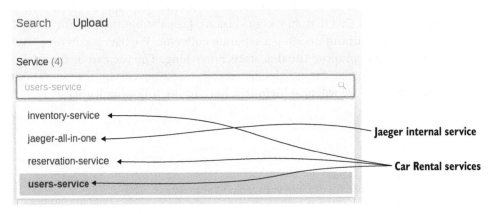

Figure 10.11   Jaeger UI—service dropdown

> **NOTE**   If you can't see all four, it is possible that some services haven't submitted their data yet. Data is collected periodically, so perhaps a refresh in a few seconds will fix it.

By selecting a service from this list and clicking the `Find Traces` button below, we ask Jaeger to show us all known traces that involve that service. Select the `users-service` and click `Find Traces`. Depending on how many HTTP requests you've made to the Users service, your results may look a bit different, but you should be able to find a set of three traces that look like those in figure 10.12.

These three separate traces correspond to what had to be done to render the entry page at http://localhost:8080.

The first trace from the bottom corresponds to the GET request itself that was made by your browser to the Users service. This request was handled by simply rendering the `index.html` page, which was returned to the browser. That's why it contains only one span. If you click that trace and then open the single span, you will see the tags added to

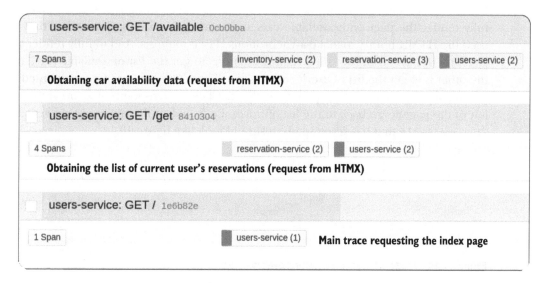

Figure 10.12   Jaeger UI—traces

that span (figure 10.13). Here you can see various metadata for the request, such as the client's IP address, response's content length, status code, etc.

Figure 10.13   Jaeger UI—trace tags

But the server simply sending the HTML page isn't everything that was necessary to fully render the page with available cars and user's reservations. Remember that we used the HTMX library to make asynchronous HTTP requests. And to fully render the page, there have to be two such requests. One is to get the list of available cars, and the other is to get the list of user's reservations. These two requests are represented by the first two traces from the top in figure 10.12. Click the left-pointing arrow at the top left of the page to go back to the list of traces. Let's look at the trace `users-service:` `GET /available` that has seven spans: it should look like figure 10.14.

Figure 10.14   Jaeger UI—trace for getting available cars

This trace corresponds to the request to the `/available` endpoint exposed by the Users service that was performed by the browser and the HTMX code. See the file `src/main/resources/templates/ReservationsResource/index.html` in the Users service if you need to refresh your memory.

To render the table of available cars, multiple services had to be involved (Reservation and Inventory as well); that's why you can see spans from three services inside the trace. After clicking the trace, you will see a graph showing the spans, their relationships, and a time axis, as shown in figure 10.15.

We explain each span and what it represents, going from top to bottom:

1 The `GET /available` span is the AJAX request made by the browser to `localhost:8080/available`.

2 The second GET span corresponds to the client part of the request made by the Users service to the Reservation service. After opening the tags of the span, you should see that the `url.full` tag shows `http://localhost:8081/reservation/availability?` followed by date arguments.

3 The third span is the server-side part of that request—it was generated by the Reservation service. Again, look through the tags to see what exactly was actually called.

4 This span corresponds to a database call made by the Reservation service to obtain a list of reservations from its PostgreSQL database instance. In the `db.statement` tag, you can see the whole SQL query.

5 Client-side span of the GraphQL request that the Reservation service made to the Inventory service to obtain the list of cars in the inventory.

6 Server-side span created for the HTTP request received by the Inventory service.

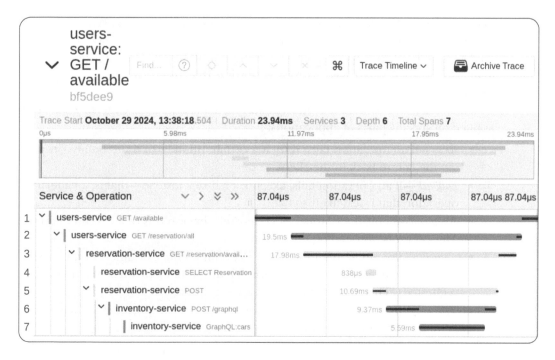

Figure 10.15   Jaeger UI—graph of spans from calling the car availability endpoint

7 Span for the GraphQL operation itself. You can see that the Inventory service created two spans: one for the received HTTP request itself and one for the `cars` GraphQL query that was executed while handling the request.

We highly recommend you spend some time exploring the spans and their metadata to get an understanding of what piece of work each span corresponds to.

We have only looked at spans that are generated automatically by Quarkus, but you can generate custom spans for all kinds of operations. For example, any method of a CDI bean can be marked with a `@io.opentelemetry.instrumentation .annotations.WithSpan` annotation so that any invocations of the bean will be recorded as spans. For more complex scenarios, it is also possible to inject an instance of `io.opentelemetry.api.trace.Tracer` to generate any custom spans programmatically using a builder API.

10.5 Fault tolerance

In distributed systems, we very often have to deal with unexpected failures. If the system is not built with fault tolerance in mind, a single failure can easily have a cascading effect and bring down large parts of the system. *Fault tolerance* is a feature of a system that allows it to continue working with as little impact as possible when some of its components face failures. For this reason, Quarkus implements the MicroProfile

Fault Tolerance API. MicroProfile Fault Tolerance (https://mng.bz/JYDv) is a specification and an annotation-based Java API that allows developers to build more resilient applications. For Quarkus, the implementation of these strategies is provided by the `quarkus-smallrye-fault-tolerance` extension that brings in the SmallRye Fault Tolerance library.

Fault tolerance is achieved through various fault tolerance patterns that can be applied on specific parts of applications:

- *Retry*—If an operation fails, retry it a certain number of times before propagating the failure back to the client.
- *Fallback*—If an operation fails, execute a fallback instead—that is, an alternative operation that is less likely to fail.
- *Bulkhead*—Limit the number of concurrent invocations of a certain operation. This prevents overloading the system.
- *Circuit breaker*—If an operation fails a certain number of times, stop reattempting it for some amount of time (instead, throw an error when the operation is requested). This helps to prevent cascading failures.
- *Timeout*—If an operation takes too long, abort it. This prevents the system from getting stuck and unresponsive.

Everything is achieved declaratively using annotations, so the API is very easy to use and doesn't pollute business code with fault tolerance logic. SmallRye Fault Tolerance also offers an imperative (programmatic) API, but we don't discuss that in this book. You can find more about it in the official SmallRye documentation (https://mng.bz/wJ9Q).

10.5.1 Adding fault tolerance to car rental

Let's add some fault tolerance capabilities to car rental. We keep it simple and only add two fault tolerance policies; both apply to calls from the Reservation service to the Inventory service when the Reservation service requests the list of available cars to be able to return a list of cars available for the given dates (we're talking about the `/availability` endpoint of the Reservation service). We assume that the Inventory service can be unavailable at times, and we allow some time for it to come back up before failing the `/availability` request; this is achieved using a retry policy. We also add a fallback policy in case the Inventory service is down for too long and the retry policy gives up—in that case, we return an empty list of cars available for the given dates, instead of throwing an exception.

RETRY POLICY

Start by adding the `smallrye-fault-tolerance` extension to the Reservation service:

```
$ quarkus extension add smallrye-fault-tolerance
```

We are adding the extension to the Reservation service, not the Inventory service. This is because fault tolerance policies apply to the client side of the request, not the server side; we want the Reservation service to be resilient to failures of the Inventory service. The Inventory service can have its own fault tolerance policies—for example, for accessing the database—but that's not our goal here.

Open the `reservation-service` directory in your IDE and then open the `ReservationResource` class. Annotate the `availability` method with

```
@Retry(maxRetries = 25, delay = 1000)
```

The correct import is `org.eclipse.microprofile.faulttolerance.Retry`. This way, we have established a retry policy that makes the `availability` method get re-executed up to 25 times, with a 1-second delay between each attempt. The method uses a REST client internally to call the Inventory service, which is the most likely place for the failure to happen. If all 25 attempts fail, only then the failure propagates back to the client. This also means that when the Inventory service is down, the `availability` method will wait for up to 25 seconds before failing the request.

> **WARNING** When using the `@Retry` annotation, make sure that the method is idempotent, meaning it can be executed multiple times without causing inconsistencies (side effects). This generally shouldn't be a problem if it only accesses transactional resources, because each invocation starts a new transaction, which is then rolled back on failure. Nevertheless, you should be careful when you use `@Retry` on methods that modify any data in a nontransactional manner. When writing the retryable method, you don't know when and how many times it will be executed.

Now let's try this out by calling the `/availability` endpoint while the Inventory service is down. Run the Reservation service but **not** the Inventory service. Call the `/availability` endpoint, for example, by opening the Swagger UI at http://localhost :8081/q/swagger-ui (invoking the `/reservation/availability` operation). Or simply call the endpoint directly by sending a GET request to

```
http://localhost:8081/reservation/availability?
endDate=3333-01-03&startDate=3333-01-01
```

Change the dates to anything else if you want. The dates aren't important right now.

If the Inventory service isn't running, the request will hang for up to 25 seconds, during which you have time to bring the Inventory service up (we suggest Dev mode, as always). If 25 seconds isn't enough, feel free to tinker with the arguments in the `@Retry` annotation and increase that time. After the Inventory service is up, the request will succeed. If it doesn't come up during that time, the request will fail.

FALLBACK POLICY

Let's take it a step further by adding a fallback policy. We will tell the `Reservation-Resource` that when the Inventory service is unavailable for more than 25 seconds, it should return an empty list of cars available for the given dates instead of returning an error.

NOTE As you might have guessed, the retry policy has a higher priority than the fallback policy, so the fallback policy (returning an empty list) will come into effect only after all configured retries have failed.

Add the new method to the `ReservationResource` that serves as the fallback for the `availability` method, as shown in listing 10.8. The parameters and return type of the fallback need to be the same as in the original method.

Listing 10.8   Fault tolerance availability fallback

```
public Uni<Collection<Car>> availabilityFallback(LocalDate startDate,
                                                 LocalDate endDate) {
    return Uni.createFrom().item(List.of());
}
```

Annotate the original `availability` method to use the fallback:

```
@Fallback(fallbackMethod = "availabilityFallback")
```

The correct import is `org.eclipse.microprofile.faulttolerance.Fallback`.

Now let's try this out by, again, calling the `availability` endpoint while the Inventory service isn't running. After the configured retries have been exhausted, the call returns, but this time with an empty list of cars. Again, if you don't feel like waiting 25 seconds, adjust the numbers in the `@Retry` annotation as you wish.

10.5.2 *Alternative fault tolerance approaches*

HYSTRIX

Hystrix (https://github.com/Netflix/Hystrix) is a fault-tolerance library developed by Netflix. It is no longer in active development, but the MicroProfile Fault Tolerance specification was heavily inspired by it.

ISTIO

Istio (https://istio.io) is a service mesh implementation for Kubernetes. It provides tools for managing observability, traffic management, and security for applications deployed in Kubernetes clusters. It can also be used to add fault tolerance patterns. Compared to using the MicroProfile Fault Tolerance specification, the fault tolerance policies are applied at the service mesh level—that is, by injecting proxy containers, called sidecars, next to application pods.

Moving the fault tolerance logic to this level has its advantages as well as disadvantages. The main advantage is the centralization of the fault tolerance policies configuration and the possibility of changing them dynamically without having to rebuild the application. The main disadvantage is that you lose the ability to apply policies on a per-method basis. It's also harder for applications to watch the status of the fault tolerance components because they are exposed on a higher level.

10.6 Service discovery

Another challenge that is commonly faced in cloud deployments is discovering the location of other services. Given that instances of a service can be dynamically created and destroyed and that their IP addresses are not known in advance, it may be necessary to use a service discovery mechanism to allow services to find one another. In Kubernetes in particular, this is usually not very difficult, because Kubernetes employs the notion of services, where a service is a logical abstraction that groups a set of pods and provides network access to them. Using the service name as the URL when establishing a connection to another service, automatically connects you to that service. It also optionally provides load balancing between service instances to evenly spread the load between its instances. This is handled on the Kubernetes level. The communication is depicted in figure 10.16.

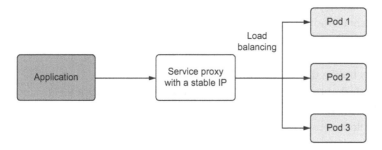

Figure 10.16 **Communication between pods via a Kubernetes service proxy**

However, if you can't or don't want to use the Kubernetes service discovery mechanism, Quarkus provides SmallRye Stork, a library that implements an abstraction over different service discovery mechanisms, allowing you to easily swap between them. Kubernetes is one of the supported underlying mechanisms too, so you can use it together with Stork if you want the flexibility of switching to a different mechanism (for example, Consul).

At the time of writing, Stork supports the following mechanisms:

- Consul
- DNS
- Kubernetes
- KNative
- Eureka
- Composite (a combination of multiple mechanisms)
- Static list (a hardcoded list of URLs)
- Custom mechanism implemented as a Java class

Stork also provides configurable load balancing strategies to more evenly spread the load between multiple instances. We won't dive into Stork here, since our production will be in Kubernetes/OpenShift. This section is just to let you know the basic concept. For more information about Stork, visit https://smallrye.io/smallrye-stork.

10.7   Next steps

In this chapter, we learned about patterns that are commonly used when running microservices in cloud environments. One of the most important aspects is observability (which includes health checks, metrics, logging, and tracing), because when running in the cloud, monitoring how the applications are working is generally more complex than with traditional server-based deployments where everything can be found in one place. Luckily, Quarkus offers tools to make all observability components easier.

We explored health checks using the MicroProfile Health specification. These serve not only for manual monitoring but fit in well with probes built into Kubernetes, meaning they allow automatic restarts of unhealthy pods or the means to detect if the application is ready to process requests, etc.

We also learned about metrics and the Micrometer project and how to visualize them as charts in Grafana. Metrics grant insight into application behavior and are used for troubleshooting performance problems or simply for collecting statistics about how users utilize the application.

We also learned about distributed tracing and how to use OpenTelemetry to collect tracing data from applications and visualize it in Jaeger. Distributed tracing is useful for troubleshooting problems that span multiple services, because it allows us to see the whole picture of what happens in the system when processing requests. It also allows us to see how long each service took to process each operation, so we can identify the performance bottlenecks.

Then we learned about how to apply fault tolerance patterns to make applications more resilient to failures in other services they depend on, because failures in complex cloud deployments are very hard to avoid. Using the MicroProfile Fault Tolerance utilities mitigates the impact of such failures.

We also briefly mentioned service discovery mechanisms that are used in cloud deployments to allow services to find one another without having to hardcode the addresses of other services.

Summary

- MicroProfile is a set of specifications for building cloud-native applications in Java.
- MicroProfile Health provides a way to expose health checks for applications over HTTP endpoints. Health check types are liveness (whether the application can continue to run), readiness (whether the application can accept requests at the moment), startup (whether the application has finished initializing), wellness (for reporting less serious problems that don't require immediate automated action), and custom health groups. Wellness and custom health groups are added by SmallRye on top of the MicroProfile Health specification.

- Quarkus provides some health checks out of the box (for example, whenever you use a data source, a readiness check is automatically created for it) and allows you to create your own custom health checks by implementing the corresponding `HealthCheck` interface.

- Health checks are monitored by calling an HTTP endpoint. For development purposes, Quarkus also offers a way to view the status of health checks in the Dev UI.

- Micrometer is a library for collecting metrics from Java applications. It offers a declarative and an imperative API and supports a wide variety of backends to export the metrics to. One of the most popular solutions is to use Prometheus for storing metrics and Grafana for their visualization and alerting.

- Metrics with Micrometer are defined either by using annotations or programmatically. They use dimensions (tags) to allow for more advanced querying and aggregation.

- Quarkus also provides some metrics out of the box. For example, whenever you use a data source, metrics can be automatically created for it, if you specify a configuration property for it.

- OpenTelemetry is a collection of tools and APIs for collecting telemetry data from applications. In this book, we focus on its distributed tracing capabilities. Distributed tracing allows you to trace requests as they flow in a distributed system and visualize the traces to understand the performance of the system and to debug problems.

- Jaeger is one of the popular tools for visualizing distributed tracing data. A trace consists of spans, which represent individual operations. Spans inside a single trace form a tree structure.

- Fault tolerance is the ability of a complex system to limit the impact of failures in its components. With Quarkus, this is achieved by using various fault-tolerant patterns declared via annotations from MicroProfile Fault Tolerance API. The patterns include Retry, Fallback, Bulkhead, Circuit Breaker, and Timeout.

- SmallRye Stork is a project that allows you to decouple your services and avoid hardcoding addresses of services that another service depends on. It's an abstraction over different service discovery mechanisms, and it allows you to easily switch between them without changing your application's code.

- Stork also provides client-side load balancing, allowing a more even spread of the load among multiple instances of a service.

Quarkus applications in the cloud

After completing chapter 10, we are finished with the development of the car rental microservices. Now it's time to move from Dev mode to production. This chapter explores several deployment scenarios ranging from a local test environment with Docker to a fully deployed system in the public cloud.

More and more applications are moving to cloud environments. This is the general direction that the software industry has been heading toward for years now. It allows for more flexibility, scalability, reliability, and in some cases also significant cost savings. In previous chapters, we focused on the program aspects (capabilities of the application itself) needed for cloud deployments—mainly observability and reliability, and how Quarkus makes it all very easy. In this chapter, we focus on the operational aspects: once your application is written, how do you deploy and manage it? Quarkus has a plethora of tools and integrations to make this easy. We start by running our car rental services in Quarkus production mode and then continue with their containerization; then we deploy the full Acme Car Rental system to the cloud.

11.1   *Car rental production*

Let's first repeat what our production system precisely consists of. Throughout the book, we have developed five car rental microservices: Reservation, Rental, Inventory, Users, and Billing services. Apart from the five car rental microservices and additional Inventory CLI, we also have ten containers that are either started as Dev Services (e.g., PostgreSQL or RabbitMQ) and three services that we need to start manually (e.g., Jaeger, which we tackled in chapter 10). Figure 11.1 describes everything we need to run for our Acme Car Rental system production to function properly.

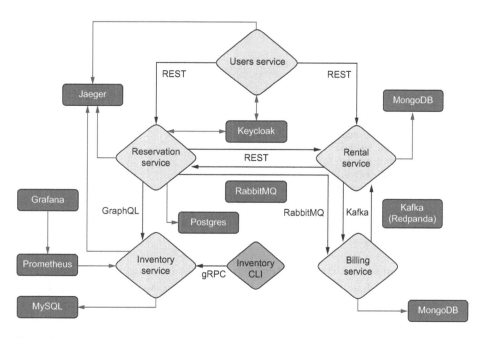

Figure 11.1   The Acme Car Rental production with Dev Services

To run a full Acme Car Rental deployment on your system with Dev mode and Dev Services, follow these simple steps:

1   Go into the chapter-11 directory of the book resources.
2   Start containers that don't have Dev Services:

```
$ docker compose -f docker-compose-files/docker-compose-observability
    .yml up
```

This starts the first three containers: Jaeger, Prometheus, and Grafana.

3 In a new terminal, navigate to the `chapter-11/11_1/users-service` directory and start Dev mode (`quarkus dev`). Dev Services start the Keycloak container.

4 In a new terminal, navigate to the `chapter-11/11_1/reservation-service` directory and start Dev mode (`quarkus dev`). Dev Services start PostgreSQL and RabbitMQ containers.

5 In a new terminal, navigate to the `chapter-11/11_1/rental-service` directory and start Dev mode (`quarkus dev`). Dev Services start MongoDB and Redpanda containers.

6 In a new terminal, navigate to the `chapter-11/11_1/inventory-service` directory and start Dev mode (`quarkus dev`). Dev Services start the MySQL container.

7 In a new terminal, navigate to the `chapter-11/11_1/billing-service` directory and start Dev mode (`quarkus dev`). Dev Services start the second MongoDB container for Billing service.

Wow, that's a lot of services currently running! For verification, the following listing shows all containers running in addition to the five Dev modes of our car rental services.

Listing 11.1   All containers running in local car rental production

```
$ docker ps --format "table {{.ID}} {{.Image}}"
CONTAINER ID IMAGE
7d4658f259ab mongo:7.0
d0caf5187c48 mysql:8.4
52489ddf21cd vectorized/redpanda:v24.1.2
dc31b4601d6d mongo:7.0
d932c9b333f3 rabbitmq:3.12-management
b598310b3d8a postgres:14
c33189b9d7c5 quay.io/keycloak/keycloak:25.0.6
4239b3d592c5 jaegertracing/all-in-one:1.62.0
b764b014e18c prom/prometheus:v2.54.1
7ed1bbd494cc grafana/grafana:11.2.2
```

Now we can verify that the system is running by opening `http://localhost:8080` in any browser that redirects us to Keycloak, where we can log in (`alice:alice` or `bob:bob`) and land on our main page. You can make a few reservations if you feel like it and see how all of our five microservices propagate messages.

It is relatively easy to get the 15 services (5 applications and 10 supporting containers) running locally. However, in production, we won't be able to use Dev Services. So next we need to externalize our Dev Services and run individual containers manually.

11.1.1 *Externalizing providers for independent deployment*

Externalizing every provider we use in Acme Car Rental is relatively simple. We need to extract the containers from listing 11.1 to a Docker Compose file. This file is too long to be inlined in the book, so the full version is available in the book resources at

`chapter-11/docker-compose-files/docker-compose-infra.yml`. The local production deployment changes as demonstrated in figure 11.2.

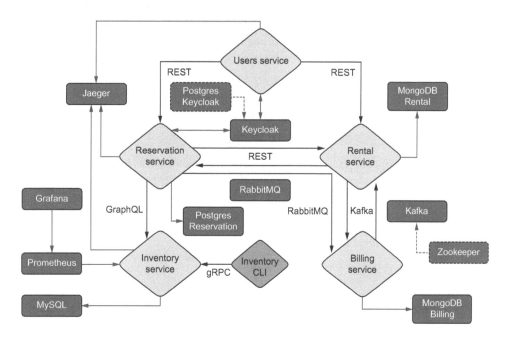

Figure 11.2   The Acme Car Rental production with all dependent services

You might notice that it starts more containers than we had with the Dev Services
since the production versions of our infrastructure services sometimes require additional resources. This happens in two cases:

- We replace Redpanda with the Strimzi Kafka platform. This is because the Red-
  panda container didn't work well in OpenShift at the time of writing (Open-
  Shift has stricter security requirements). This version of Kafka also requires the
  Zookeeper service (https://zookeeper.apache.org) for its metadata management.

- The Keycloak production deployment uses a real PostgreSQL database instead
  of an in-memory one.

NOTE   By the time of the final production of this book, an alternative Kafka
platform deployment had been introduced that doesn't require Zookeeper.
Instead, it uses the Raft protocol (Apache Kafka Raft; KRaft) to consolidate
metadata into the Kafka itself. At the time of writing, this technology was still
considered experimental.

Overall, this brings us to 12 containers. They can all be started and managed together
by running

```
$ docker compose -f docker-compose-files/docker-compose-infra.yml up
```

Sometimes, not all containers stop when you kill this process. In such case, run

```
$ docker compose -f docker-compose-files/docker-compose-infra.yml down
```

which stops and removes all defined containers. For verification, listing 11.2 again provides the overview of all running infrastructure containers. This time we include names instead of container IDs because we are able to provide names for our containers in the `docker-compose` file.

Listing 11.2   Infrastructure Docker containers run through Docker Compose

```
$ docker ps --format "table {{.Names | printf \"%-20s\"}} {{.Image}}"
NAMES                IMAGE
keycloak             quay.io/keycloak/keycloak:25.0.6
kafka                quay.io/strimzi/kafka:latest-kafka-3.8.0
zookeeper            quay.io/strimzi/kafka:latest-kafka-3.8.0
postgres-keycloak    postgres:14
mongodb-rental       mongo:7.0
rabbitmq             rabbitmq:3.12-management
postgres-reservation postgres:14
jaeger               jaegertracing/all-in-one:1.62.0
mongodb-billing      mongo:7.0
prometheus           prom/prometheus:v2.54.1
mysql                mysql:8.4
grafana              grafana/grafana:11.2.2
```

Now we can proceed to the hard part. We need to provide all the configuration that the Dev Services handled manually. We take this opportunity to also prepare our services for the scenario where they won't all run on a local, single machine. Let's review all car rental services to see what changes we must make.

USERS SERVICE

The Users service calls the Reservation service to get and create reservations. The location of the Reservation resource is currently hardcoded in the `org.acme.users` `.ReservationsClient` interface, as shown in the following listing.

Listing 11.3   The original code of `ReservationsClient` in Users service

```
@RegisterRestClient(baseUri = "http://localhost:8081")
@AccessToken
@Path("reservation")
public interface ReservationsClient {
...
```

Hardcoding the URL in the annotation was the quick and easy approach, but it won't really work in production. We will have to configure the REST client using regular Quarkus configuration mechanisms to have more flexibility. Change the `Reservations-Client` as demonstrated in the following listing.

Listing 11.4 `ReservationsClient` **update with the configuration key**

```
@RegisterRestClient(configKey = "reservations")
@AccessToken
@Path("reservation")
public interface ReservationsClient {
...
```

Now we can adjust the configuration file `application.properties` to utilize the newly defined configuration key:

```
quarkus.rest-client.reservations.url=http://localhost:8081
```

> **NOTE** It's also possible to override the REST client's URL without specifying a custom config key—the default config key is the fully qualified name of the interface. In that case, the property would be `quarkus.rest-client."org` `.acme.users.ReservationsClient".url`. However, this might not be ideal since you need to remember to change this configuration in case the package or name of the class changes.

The Users service also utilizes Keycloak for authentication. We already created the Keycloak prod mode setup in chapter 6, so we can reuse it here. In the `application` `.properties`, we can find the following configuration that connects to the Keycloak started on `localhost:7777`:

```
%prod.quarkus.oidc.auth-server-url=http://localhost:7777/realms/car-rental
%prod.quarkus.oidc.client-id=users-service
%prod.quarkus.oidc.token-state-manager.split-tokens=true
```

Hardcoded `localhost` won't obviously work in the cloud, but we will keep it like this for now while we're still running everything locally.

RESERVATION SERVICE

The Reservation service calls the Rental service to start rentals. We have the same problem with the hardcoded REST client URL, so change the `org.acme.reservation` `.rental.RentalClient` as follows:

```
- @RegisterRestClient(baseUri = "http://localhost:8082")
+ @RegisterRestClient(configKey = "rental")
```

Add the following configuration:

```
quarkus.rest-client.rental.url=http://localhost:8082
```

The Reservation service was also prepared for the production Keycloak in chapter 6. The properties are the same as those in the Users service. It also manages its own PostgreSQL database, and it connects to RabbitMQ. First, let's review the PostgreSQL configuration we added in chapter 7:

```
quarkus.datasource.db-kind=postgresql
quarkus.datasource.username=user
quarkus.datasource.password=pass
%prod.quarkus.datasource.reactive.url=
⇨vertx-reactive:postgresql://localhost:5432/reservation
```

> **TIP** Storing credentials in the `application.properties` is not the best idea. However, it is the easiest for our use case. In the real production deployment, you could externalize this configuration in many ways (different config locations, environment variables, system properties, Kubernetes secrets).

Notice that, except for the last property, we can define all other properties without the `%prod.` prefix since they are applicable in any mode (we use the same credentials as Dev Service). However, the last `%prod.quarkus.datasource.reactive.url` should be defined only in prod mode if we want Dev Services to start in Dev mode (if the URL is defined, it turns off Dev Services).

RabbitMQ only requires connection information to the broker, which is also defined only in prod mode to keep the Dev Services working. Add the following configuration to the `application.properties` file of the Reservation service:

```
%prod.rabbitmq-host=localhost
%prod.rabbitmq-port=5672
%prod.rabbitmq-http-port=15672
%prod.rabbitmq-username=guest
%prod.rabbitmq.password=guest
```

RENTAL SERVICE

The last REST client we need to adjust is in the Rental service's `org.acme.rental.reservation.ReservationClient`. The changes are the same as in the previous two services, so we summarize them in the following snippet:

```
- @RegisterRestClient(baseUri = "http://localhost:8081")
+ @RegisterRestClient(configKey = "reservation")

# In application.properties
+ quarkus.rest-client.reservation.url=http://localhost:8081
```

We utilize MongoDB to store the created rentals. The Rental service also sends and receives data from the Kafka broker. To get the MongoDB and Kafka connections set up, add the following configuration (also only in prod mode to keep Dev Services):

```
%prod.quarkus.mongodb.connection-string=mongodb://localhost:27017
%prod.kafka.bootstrap.servers=localhost:9092
```

INVENTORY SERVICE

The Inventory service exposes the GraphQL UI we used to access from the Dev UI. Dev UI isn't available in prod mode, but the GraphQL UI can still be added explicitly.

To make the GraphQL UI available in production mode, add the following config property, and it will again be available on http://localhost:8083/q/graphql-ui:

```
quarkus.smallrye-graphql.ui.always-include=true
```

The Inventory service only utilizes the MySQL database, which is similar to the Reservation service integration with PostgreSQL integrated through Hibernate with Panache. We already added this to the Inventory service in chapter 7, but just in case:

```
quarkus.datasource.db-kind=mysql
quarkus.datasource.username=user
quarkus.datasource.password=pass
%prod.quarkus.datasource.jdbc.url=jdbc:mysql://localhost:3306/inventory
```

The Inventory service also contains some starting data that we load into the database with the `import.sql` script in Dev mode. Since it would be helpful for us to begin with some cars available in the DB also in prod mode, we can add this configuration that will load this SQL script also in prod mode:

```
quarkus.hibernate-orm.sql-load-script=import.sql
```

The default behavior is that in Dev mode, `import.sql` is used (if it exists). In prod mode, loading SQL scripts is disabled by default, so here we explicitly enabled it by setting the file name. If we wanted to disable it in Dev mode, we would set `%dev` `.quarkus.hibernate-orm.sql-load-script=nonexistent-file`.

BILLING SERVICE

The Billing service is the most complex since it connects to RabbitMQ, Kafka, and its instance of MongoDB. But it's not something we can't manage:

```
%prod.quarkus.mongodb.connection-string=mongodb://localhost:27018
%prod.kafka.bootstrap.servers=localhost:9092
%prod.rabbitmq-host=localhost
%prod.rabbitmq-port=5672
%prod.rabbitmq-http-port=15672
%prod.rabbitmq-username=guest
%prod.rabbitmq.password=guest
```

Note that we need to change the MongoDB port to `27018` so it doesn't conflict with the MongoDB instance of the Rental service (which runs on port `27017`).

This is all that we need to adjust and configure to get the Acme Car Rental production running. We can now follow these steps to run Docker Compose and start our services in prod mode:

1 Change your current directory to `chapter-11` directory.

2 Start containers for remote providers:

```
$ docker compose -f docker-compose-files/docker-compose-infra.yml up
```

3 Open the following directories, each in a new terminal, and run `quarkus build` (`./mvnw clean package`) followed by `java -jar target/quarkus-app/quarkus -run.jar`:

a `chapter-11/11_1_1/users-service`

b `chapter-11/11_1_1/reservation-service`

c `chapter-11/11_1_1/rental-service`

d `chapter-11/11_1_1/inventory-service`

e `chapter-11/11_1_1/billing-service`

Congratulations! This is our complete Acme Car Rental production running on your system. Together, these 17 services provide the functionality we've implemented throughout the book.

> **WARNING** The configuration of dependent services is purposely simplified to ease the full system deployment (e.g., Keycloak's `start-dev` command for easy realm integration), and it shouldn't be used in real production systems. We focus on writing Quarkus applications in this book, so we don't have the space to cover much of the details of all dependent services.

Feel free to experiment with the system as you like (the UI, which belongs to the Users service, is at `http://localhost:8080`, and you can log in as `alice` with the same password). Next, we move to the containerization of our car rental services as a required step before we can move all of this workload to the cloud.

11.2 *Building and pushing container images*

We already touched on the containerization of Quarkus applications in chapter 2 when we explained the Dockerfiles generated by default when you create a new Quarkus application. However, Quarkus also provides five extensions that provide automation of the image building and pushing. It supports the following technologies:

■ *Jib*—Extension `quarkus-container-image-jib`. *Jib* (https://github.com/Google ContainerTools/jib) is a tool that provides fast, reproducible, and daemonless (without the Docker daemon) image builds compatible with Docker and *OCI* (Open Container Initiative—https://opencontainers.org; outside the scope of this book). It automatically splits the application into several layers, doing the same thing as we saw with the generated Dockerfiles. It moves your Quarkus application dependencies (`target/lib` folder) to a separate layer with the expectation that the dependencies don't change as often as the application, which allows faster image rebuilds. Note that Docker (or Podman) is still needed if you build the image, because Jib registers the built image with it to make the image available in your local registry.

■ *Docker*—Extension `quarkus-container-image-docker`. This extension uses the generated Dockerfiles in the `src/main/docker` directory to perform normal Docker builds.

- *Podman*—Extension `quarkus-container-image-podman`. Same as previously described Docker but uses Podman for the image builds.

- *BuildPack*—Extension `quarkus-container-image-buildpack`. *Buildpacks* (https://buildpacks.io) are a toolset that transforms an application's source code into a runnable image. It automatically detects everything your application needs to run. Quarkus utilizes the Docker daemon for the actual build. While there are buildpack alternatives to Docker, this extension only supports Docker as of the time of writing. It also purposely doesn't define the default base build image, so the user needs to provide it manually through the configuration

```
quarkus.buildpack.jvm-builder-image=... # JAR
quarkus.buildpack.native-builder-image=... # native
```

- *OpenShift*—Extension `quarkus-container-image-openshift`. This extension uses OpenShift-specific binary builds. Such a build takes your built artifact (and dependencies) and uploads it to the OpenShift cluster. OpenShift then builds the application image automatically in the OpenShift build system. This is also called *s2i* (source to image). From the user's point of view, you don't need to do anything. The extension generates everything required for your s2i build to complete successfully.

These are the choices of the underlying technology that builds the images with your Quarkus application. The manipulation with all of these extensions is the same.

11.2.1 Building images with Quarkus without extensions

We don't need to add the extensions mentioned previously to our Quarkus application to start building images. Quarkus CLI `quarkus` already ships with built-in commands that we can use. For instance, to create an image with Jib, you can use the command in the following listing that we can test—for example, in the Reservation service.

> **NOTE**   This functionality also works with the Maven plugin (`./mvnw quarkus :image-build`) but not with Gradle. Maven supports adding dynamic dependencies, but Gradle doesn't. The CLI works in both cases because it implements a workaround for Gradle (which is not applicable when running a Gradle task directly).

> **Listing 11.5   Build image using Jib (in Reservation service)**

```
$ quarkus image build jib

...

[INFO] [io.quarkus.container.image.jib.deployment.JibProcessor] Starting
⮡ (local) container image build for jar using jib.
...
[INFO] [io.quarkus.container.image.jib.deployment.JibProcessor] Created
⮡ container image <username>/reservation-service:1.0.0-SNAPSHOT
⮡ (sha256:<sha>)
```

The `quarkus image build` command takes one of the five arguments that correspond to the available containerization options: `jib`, `docker`, `podman`, `buildpack`, and `openshift`. `openshift` requires a connection to the OpenShift cluster and the manifests (that are generated by either `openshift` or `kubernetes` extensions). We will come back to OpenShift builds later in this chapter.

If we want to push the built image, we can do it with `quarkus image push`. It uses the `docker.io` registry (Docker Hub) by default. In the background, this is a standard `docker push`, so if your local username is the same as your Docker username and you're authenticated, this will work out of the box. We will explain how to change these defaults soon.

11.2.2 *Building and pushing images with Quarkus extensions*

We can also add any containerization extensions mentioned previously directly to our Quarkus projects. In that case, we can integrate the building of the images directly in our build pipeline (both Maven and Gradle).

For instance, let's add the `quarkus-container-image-docker` extension to the Reservation service. For example, with `quarkus` CLI:

```
$ quarkus ext add quarkus-container-image-docker
```

The following instructions are the same for all four container extensions. To build the image, we can use the `quarkus` CLI (`quarkus image build`) or specify the configuration property `quarkus.container-image.build=true`. The property is a standard Quarkus configuration, so if we define it in `application.properties` we create an image with every application build. More preferably, we should only set it on the command line build command to apply it only when we need to build the image as shown in the following listing.

> **Listing 11.6   Build image with included extension in Reservation service**

```
# same as ./mvnw clean package -Dquarkus.container-image.build=true
$ quarkus image build
...
[INFO] [io.quarkus.container.image.docker.common.deployment.CommonProcessor]
➥ Starting (local) container image build for jar using docker
...
[INFO] [io.quarkus.container.image.docker.deployment.DockerProcessor]
➥ Built container image <username>/reservation-service:1.0.0-SNAPSHOT
```

> **TIP** If you are using Podman, use the `quarkus-container-image-podman` extension and build the image with `quarkus image build podman`.

Similarly, if you want to push the created image, the CLI command is `quarkus image push` or the property is `quarkus.container-image.push=true`. Utilizing it during the application build will push the image to the `docker.io` registry by default, as shown in listing 11.7. Note that this only works if your local username aligns with your Docker Hub name.

Listing 11.7 Pushing an image using the included extension

```
# same as ./mvnw clean package -Dquarkus.container-image.push=true
$ quarkus image push
...
[INFO] [io.quarkus.container.image.docker.common.deployment.CommonProcessor]
 No container image registry was set, so 'docker.io' will be used
[INFO] [io.quarkus.deployment.util.ExecUtil] The push refers to
 repository [docker.io/<username>/reservation-service]
...
[INFO] [io.quarkus.container.image.docker.common.deployment.CommonProcessor]
 Successfully pushed docker image
 <username>/reservation-service:1.0.0-SNAPSHOT
```

If you include multiple containerization extensions in the same Quarkus application (in the same build configuration or profile), Quarkus won't allow you to build or push images. But if you have such a use case, you can add the `quarkus.container-image` `.builder` configuration property, which defines which of the extensions should be used (e.g., `docker` or `jib`).

If you are logged into the Docker Hub, you can see that the image was pushed to https://hub.docker.com. You may need to push to a different registry, or the username on your local system doesn't match the username you chose on Docker Hub. So, let's look into how we can change the specifics of the created images.

11.2.3 Image customizations

Another very popular alternative to Docker Hub, which we also use for our services in this book, is Quay (https://quay.io). The following listing demonstrates the individual configuration properties that change the parameters of the created images.

Listing 11.8 Customizing images created with Quarkus container extensions

```
quarkus.container-image.registry=quay.io # defaults to docker.io
quarkus.container-image.group=quarkus-in-action # defaults to username
quarkus.container-image.name=reservation-service # defaults to artifactId
quarkus.container-image.tag=1.0 # defaults to project version
quarkus.container-image.image=registry/username/image-name:tag
```

Note that `quarkus.container-image.image` takes precedence in case of conflicts. In the previous case, the produced image would be `registry/username/image-name:tag`. Another useful property is `quarkus.container-image.additional-tags`, which allows you to create multiple tags from the same image build. Quarkus also enables you to override the connection information to the registry with `quarkus.container-image` `.[username|password|insecure]` if needed.

11.2.4 Pushing car rental images to quay.io

We are now ready to create our production images. For the rest of this chapter, we will be deploying our car rental services to cloud platforms. For some of these use cases, we must have images of our services publicly available. For the actual deployments, you can either build and push your own images for all five of our services, or use the provided ones (deployed under quay.io/quarkus-in-action namespace, https://quay .io/organization/quarkus-in-action). Therefore, the following steps are optional. If you decide to skip pushing your own images, you can jump straight to section 11.3.

Now let's demonstrate how to push the images to your own quay.io registry. To be able to do this, you need to create an account at https://quay.io. An account with the free tier should be sufficient. Later, when logging in using the docker login command, we recommend using the encrypted CLI password stored in your filesystem as a file that you can download from your profile page. Figure 11.3 shows where you can find this at the site, but note the exact instructions may change in the future.

Docker CLI Password

The Docker CLI stores passwords entered on the command line in **plaintext**. It is therefore highly recommended to generate an an encrypted version of your password to use for docker login.

CLI Password: Generate Encrypted Password

Figure 11.3 The quay.io encrypted CLI password UI

One more important thing to note is that the quay repositories that you push to should be public to allow OpenShift to pull from them without additional configuration. You can find this under the image Settings → Repository Visibility.

For the following tasks, if you use the prepared solutions from the chapter-11 of the book's resources, all projects have quarkus.container-image.group set to quarkus -in-action. You will have to either change this directly in all the relevant application .properties files or always pass the -Dquarkus.container-image.group=<your-quay -org> parameter to override it with your own quay.io organization or username.

The following series of steps allow us to deploy the Reservation service to the quay.io:

1 If you haven't already, add the quarkus-container-image-docker extension:

```
$ quarkus ext add quarkus-container-image-docker
```

2 Add the following configuration to the application.properties:

```
quarkus.container-image.registry=quay.io
# replace below with your quay.io group!
quarkus.container-image.group=quarkus-in-action
quarkus.container-image.tag=1.0.0
```

3 Log in to the `quay.io`:

```
$ docker login quay.io
```

4 Build and push the image:

```
./mvnw clean package -Dquarkus.container-image.build=true
-Dquarkus.container-image.push=true

# or

# build JAR artifact
$ quarkus build --clean

# build and push the image in the same command
$ quarkus image push --also-build
```

After the command finishes, we can find the pushed image in our Quay account (in the reference repository, it is at https://quay.io/repository/quarkus-in-action/reservation-service). Don't forget to make the image public in the `Settings` → `Repository Visibility` menu!

If you are pushing your images, follow the same steps for all remaining car rental services. Otherwise, you can use the provided set of images available at https://quay.io/organization/quarkus-in-action. When you finish, your quay.io organization/account should look like presented in figure 11.4 (and contain five image repositories).

REPOSITORY NAME ↓	LAST MODIFIED	QUOTA CONSUMED	ACTIVITY
quarkus-in-action / users-service	10/17/2024	185.12 MiB	
quarkus-in-action / reservation-service	10/17/2024	206.67 MiB	
quarkus-in-action / rental-service	10/17/2024	217.73 MiB	
quarkus-in-action / inventory-service	10/17/2024	270.61 MiB	
quarkus-in-action / billing-service	10/17/2024	217.57 MiB	

Figure 11.4 The final deployed car rental images at https://quay.io/organization/quarkus-in-action

Now we are ready to consume these images in our production environments. If you want to test our complete production car rental system, we provide `docker-compose -car-rental.yml` (inside `chapter-11/docker-compose-files`) containing all car rental services and infrastructure. Together, that takes it to 17 containers. If you've pushed your own images, change the referenced image names (organization id) in this file accordingly. Once you're ready, you can start car rental production with a single command, as demonstrated in the following listing.

Listing 11.9   Running car rental production with Docker Compose

```
$ docker compose -f docker-compose-files/docker-compose-car-rental.yml up
```

Give it a few minutes to start since it can take a while. Once all containers initialize, you can verify you see 17 containers as shown in listing 11.10. You can also test the functionality of our system at http://localhost:8080.

Listing 11.10   Car rental containers in full production with Docker Compose

```
$ docker ps --format "table {{.Names |  printf \"%-20s\"}} {{.Image}}"
NAMES                  IMAGE
users-service          quay.io/quarkus-in-action/users-service:1.0.0
reservation-service    quay.io/quarkus-in-action/reservation-service:1.0.0
rental-service         quay.io/quarkus-in-action/rental-service:1.0.0
billing-service        quay.io/quarkus-in-action/billing-service:1.0.0
keycloak               quay.io/keycloak/keycloak:25.0.6
kafka                  quay.io/strimzi/kafka:latest-kafka-3.8.0
inventory-service      quay.io/quarkus-in-action/inventory-service:1.0.0
zookeeper              quay.io/strimzi/kafka:latest-kafka-3.8.0
mongodb-rental         mongo:7.0
postgres-keycloak      postgres:14
jaeger                 jaegertracing/all-in-one:1.62.0
mysql                  mysql:8.4
rabbitmq               rabbitmq:3.12-management
postgres-reservation   postgres:14
prometheus             prom/prometheus:v2.54.1
grafana                grafana/grafana:11.2.2
mongodb-billing        mongo:7.0
```

If some containers don't stop when you stop your Docker Compose process, run `docker compose -f docker-compose-files/docker-compose-car-rental.yml down`, which removes all containers defined in the file.

11.3 *Kubernetes and OpenShift integration*

Now that we have all services ready to be deployed to the cloud, we can start with the operations "fun"! We know many developers (including authors) don't like writing long YAMLs to operate their applications in clouds, and Quarkus understands this too. In this section, we explain how Quarkus simplifies the deployment to platforms like Kubernetes and OpenShift (a Red Hat-branded version of Kubernetes that we will use for our deployments), which will allow us to experiment with the deployment of the car rental system in these various platforms later in this chapter.

11.3.1 Generating Kubernetes resources

Since writing long YAML is a tedious and error-prone task, Quarkus provides extensions to do this work for us in the background. It utilizes a library called *Dekorate* (https://dekorate.io) that generates Kubernetes manifests. It generates sensible defaults for modern Java applications and provides easy customization options (e.g., with properties or annotations). Additionally, the generated manifests can be combined with predefined ones (if you have resources you need to deploy together).

Quarkus generates Kubernetes manifests with the following extensions that target three leading platforms:

- `quarkus-kubernetes`—Original Kubernetes
- `quarkus-openshift`—OpenShift-specific manifests
- `quarkus-knative`—Serverless platform (see section 11.5)

We will look into each of them in this chapter. These extensions generate resources in the `target/kubernetes` directory (or `build/kubernetes` for Gradle). The names of the generated files are derived from the name of the extension that created them (e.g., `kubernetes.yml`). The generated manifests are complete Kubernetes resources, so we can directly apply them to the target cloud cluster. Quarkus can even apply these resources automatically for you.

If we also include any of the image extensions we learned about in section 11.2, the generated manifests will be automatically adjusted to point to our built (and/or pushed) images. This hugely simplifies the integration with the target Kubernetes platform, as the images often need to be available before we can apply manifests.

11.3.2 Customizing generated manifests

The sensible defaults are a great start, but we often need to tweak the generated resources for our specific deployments. Quarkus does this through configuration properties. Quarkus extensions allow you to customize almost every aspect of the Kubernetes resources they generate. The list is too long for the book, but the following are a few examples of often-utilized configurations (parts written in capital letters are placeholders that you should replace with names of your choice):

```
# The application resource type
quarkus.kubernetes.deployment-kind=Deployment|StatefulSet|Job|CronJob

# The number of replicas
quarkus.kubernetes.replicas=5

# The namespace for the resources
quarkus.kubernetes.namespace=custom-namespace

# Annotations to add to the resources
quarkus.kubernetes.annotations.ANNOTATION_KEY=annotation-value

# Labels to add to the resources
quarkus.kubernetes.labels.LABEL_KEY=label-value
```

```
# Environment variables, env-var-key translates to ENV_VAR_KEY variable
quarkus.kubernetes.env.vars.ENV_VAR_KEY=env-var-value

# Volume mounts
quarkus.kubernetes.mounts.MOUNT_KEY.name=name-of-the-volume-to-mount
quarkus.kubernetes.mounts.MOUNT_KEY.path=/path/where/to/mount
```

You can find the complete list of customization options in the Quarkus documentation (https://quarkus.io/guides/all-config; search for `kubernetes`, `openshift`, or `knative`).

All of the `quarkus.kubernetes` properties represent standard Quarkus configuration properties and are processed when the image and manifests are being built. Changing them later (when deploying the manifests to Kubernetes or even overriding them on the application's command line during start) won't have any effect.

The generated manifest can also be enhanced by already-existing manifests that you, as the application developer, provide. This is useful if you already have some manifests you must base on or apply for your application to function correctly. An example can be a database that deploys together with the Quarkus application (which we will see in the next section). We can do this by placing a file named `kubernetes.yml` (or `openshift.yml`, `knative.yml`, or their JSON variants) to the `src/main/kubernetes` directory. When such file is detected during build, Quarkus combines it with the manifest generated by the relevant extension.

With Quarkus' Kubernetes extensions, we have an excessive arsenal of functionalities at our disposal. So let's see it in action!

11.3.3 *Deploying Quarkus applications on Kubernetes*

Since our car rental application is highly complex, we will stick to one service deployment for now and explain it in more detail, and later return to the entire system deployment by the end of the chapter (section 11.6) with slightly less detail. We chose the Inventory service since its only external dependency is the MySQL database. Feel free to experiment with other services in these sections if you want a small challenge.

> **NOTE** This and the following section (OpenShift) are optional. We don't cover the Kubernetes cluster setup or describe how to download the `kubectl` tool. But if you would like to experiment, we recommend lightweight clusters like *Kind* (https://kind.sigs.k8s.io), *K3s* (https://k3s.io), or *Minikube* (https://minikube.sigs.k8s.io/docs). Some online (often paid) Kubernetes platform is also an option.

> **NOTE** In the following section, we will rewrite the changes from this section (deploying to Kubernetes) by using OpenShift instead. If you prefer just using OpenShift, skip to 11.3.4.

Let's start by adding the `quarkus-kubernetes` extension to the Inventory service project. Change your working directory to the `inventory-service` subdirectory and execute the following `quarkus` command or add it directly to `pom.xml`:

```
$ quarkus ext add kubernetes
```

We now generate Kubernetes manifests whenever we build the Inventory service:

```
$ quarkus build
```

The build generates two new files in the `target/kubernetes` folder called `kubernetes.yml` and `kubernetes.json`. Both files represent the same Kubernetes resources. We stick to YAML since it's more commonly used for Kubernetes resource definitions. We cannot fit the whole file here, so listing 11.11 contains only the essential parts of it. You can find it for reference in the book resources in the `chapter-11/kubernetes/kubernetes-default.yml` file.

Listing 11.11   Simplified version of the generated `kubernetes.yml`

```
apiVersion: v1
kind: Service
  ...
spec:
  ports:
    - name: grpc
      port: 9000
      protocol: TCP
      targetPort: 9000
    - name: http
      port: 80
      protocol: TCP
      targetPort: 8083
---
apiVersion: apps/v1
kind: Deployment
  ...
spec:
  ...
    spec:
      containers:
        - env:
            ...
          image: quay.io/quarkus-in-action/inventory-service:1.0.0
          imagePullPolicy: Always
```

The default configuration generates three Kubernetes resources: *Service* (network exposure), *Deployment* (declarative application definition), and *ServiceMonitor* (Prometheus operator scrape configuration). Notice that our configuration from the Inventory service has been propagated to the individual parts of the manifest. For instance, under the Service definition, we can find the following target port configuration, which correctly points to ports 9000 and 8083 on which we run the Inventory service (it was detected that gRPC is used in the application, so an entry to expose the port 9000 was automatically added).

The most important part of the Deployment resource definition is the location of the image. Quarkus Kubernetes already read the configuration of the Inventory service and correctly set the target image identifier to the one that the application is configured to produce and push to quay.io.

All generated resources contain a lot of additional configurations, like various annotations, labels, or the number of replicas (spawned pods). Notice also the automatic addition of liveness, readiness, and startup probes that point to the endpoints exposed by the `smallrye-health` extension we added in chapter 10.

MANUAL DEPLOYMENT WITH KUBECTL

The generated file is already ready to be deployed to Kubernetes. However, the Inventory service needs a working connection to the MySQL database. For simplicity, we already provided a ready-to-deploy MySQL Kubernetes manifest in `chapter-11/kubernetes/mysql.yml`. We could now apply the MySQL resources followed by the generated manifest of the Inventory service, but there is still one more catch. We hardcoded the location of the MySQL database to localhost in `application.properties`:

```
%prod.quarkus.datasource.jdbc.url=jdbc:mysql://localhost:3306/quarkus
```

In Kubernetes, our MySQL runs at `mysql://mysql:3306` (defined by the Service resource), so we must change this configuration when we deploy to the Kubernetes cluster. With the Quarkus Kubernetes extension, we can do it through the environment variable configuration. We can add the oneliner from the following listing to the Inventory service's `application.properties`.

Listing 11.12   Changing the location of the MySQL database in Kubernetes

```
quarkus.kubernetes.env.vars.quarkus-datasource-jdbc-url=
➥ jdbc:mysql://mysql:3306/inventory
```

Since the ServiceMonitor resource, which is generated by default, works only with the deployed Prometheus operator (which we will not be using in our examples), we can also add the following configuration property to skip its inclusion in the generated Kubernetes manifest. Our Prometheus instance will run in its own container and will be configured with the locations of the services, so we don't need the operator:

```
quarkus.kubernetes.prometheus.generate-service-monitor=false
```

When you now rerun the build in the `inventory-service` directory, the regenerated manifest contains the `QUARKUS_DATASOURCE_JDBC_URL` environment variable correctly set to the URL of MySQL in Kubernetes.

We are now ready to deploy the Inventory service to Kubernetes. Normally, it would be a two-step process: deploy MySQL and then Inventory. But as mentioned in the previous section, the Quarkus Kubernetes extension allows combining existing manifests with the generated ones. We just need to copy the `mysql.yml` manifest and save it as `inventory-service/src/main/kubernetes/kubernetes.yml`, and Quarkus will take care of the rest. Rerunning the build will produce one combined manifest that contains both the Inventory service and MySQL. Now we can deploy both services with a single command, as shown in listing 11.13. Since MySQL might be slow to start, we can expect a few restarts of the Inventory service. We use a simple `port-forward` command to expose our service on port `8083`.

Listing 11.13   Applying generated Kubernetes manifest

```
$ kubectl apply -f inventory-service/target/kubernetes/kubernetes.yml
service/mysql created
service/inventory-service created
deployment.apps/mysql created
deployment.apps/inventory-service created             Verifies the pods are
                                                      created and running
$ kubectl get pods                               <───┘
NAME                                READY   STATUS    RESTARTS      AGE
inventory-service-77f997bf47-4d5hf  1/1     Running   1 (68s ago)   72s
mysql-58664f58fc-zr2v9              1/1     Running   0             72s

$ kubectl port-forward inventory-service-77f997bf47-4d5hf 8083:8083
Forwarding from 127.0.0.1:8083 -> 8083
```

We can now access the running Inventory service at http://localhost:8083/q/graphql -ui or check its logs with `kubectl logs deployment/inventory-service`. Except for having to define YAML for the MySQL resources (which would be most likely provided for us in the actual production environment), we have a working instance of our application running in Kubernetes without writing a single line of YAML!

AUTOMATING KUBERNETES DEPLOYMENTS

We already saw in the previous section how we can automate image pushing with the application build. The Quarkus Kubernetes extension extends it also to the (re)application of generated manifests. With a single build time flag `quarkus.kubernetes .deploy=true`, we can, in one command,

1 Build our Quarkus application and its image.
2 Push the built image to the registry.
3 Apply/reapply the generated manifest to the Kubernetes cluster.

This significantly simplifies the general development workflow. So let's try it in the Inventory service. We need to do two things before this flag can work: log into an image registry (if you're not logged in already) and configure the Kubernetes namespace.

Log into a Docker registry like quay.io. If you followed the previous section, you should still be logged in. If not, you can do it with `docker login quay.io`. To configure the Kubernetes namespace, we can utilize the Kubernetes extension's configuration, which we must add to `application.properties`. Use the name of your namespace:

```
quarkus.kubernetes.namespace=default
```

Now we can run the following command, which builds the Inventory service, builds its image, pushes the image to quay.io, and redeploys our manually deployed Inventory service to Kubernetes:

```
$ ./mvnw clean package -Dquarkus.kubernetes.deploy=true
```

Note that this command doesn't include the MySQL services. But that is also intended since we typically deploy dependent services once, and only make changes to our application. You can also check your quay.io to see the new version of the deployed image. As an exercise, make some changes and rerun the previous command to see that they propagate to the latest version of your deployment in Kubernetes.

The Quarkus Kubernetes extension is compelling. We only touched the surface (see https://quarkus.io/guides/deploying-to-kubernetes for the full reference guide). Many configurations can plug into the generated manifests that simplify real Kubernetes work. Next, we move to OpenShift, which gives us access to even more options.

11.3.4 *Deploying Quarkus applications on OpenShift*

Openshift (https://mng.bz/7pVy) is a Red Hat-branded version fork of Kubernetes that provides additional features, easier management, and (opinionated) better usability. Most of the features we covered for Kubernetes in the previous sections apply also to OpenShift. We decided to focus on OpenShift because it comes with new resources, intuitive UI, and, most importantly, a free public OpenShift instance called Sandbox that you can use for your testing. You don't need to install almost anything (besides the client-side tool, `oc`) on your local systems to experiment with Quarkus on OpenShift!

In this section, we also focus on the deployment of a single service (Inventory) in more detail, and we will get back to deploying the whole system with less detailed explanations in 11.6. The exercise in this section is also optional. Section 11.6.1 provides the instructions for setting up OpenShift Sandbox environment. You might choose to use Sandbox also here, but if you would like to try OpenShift on your local system, you can use the *OpenShift Local* (https://mng.bz/mGg2). OpenShift Local provides functionality similar to Minikube for Kubernetes. No matter which option you choose, you must have the `oc` (OpenShift client) executable locally available (see the instructions in 11.6.1).

We continue with the Inventory service that we already prepared for Kubernetes deployment. The Quarkus OpenShift extension (`quarkus-openshift`) is an alternative that provides the same functionality for OpenShift. Let's remove Kubernetes and add OpenShift extension in the `inventory-service`:

```
$ quarkus ext remove kubernetes
Looking for the newly published extensions in registry.quarkus.io
[SUCCESS] ✔   Extension io.quarkus:quarkus-kubernetes has been uninstalled
$ quarkus ext add openshift
[SUCCESS] ✔   Extension io.quarkus:quarkus-openshift has been installed
```

However, if you try to build the Inventory service now, it will fail because, as you might remember, the OpenShift extension is also an alternative to image build extensions (section 11.2). For this reason, we also need to remove the Docker image extension, or we can provide the following configuration to use openshift by default (add it to the Inventory service configuration):

```
quarkus.container-image.builder=openshift
```

The OpenShift extension behaves similarly to Kubernetes, but in addition to the original Kubernetes files (`kubernetes.yml|json`), which didn't change, it also generates files called `openshift.yml` and `openshift.json`. All files are in the same directory (`target/kubernetes` for Maven or `build/kubernetes` for Gradle). Let's focus on `openshift.yml`. The following two listings show a simplified version of the generated `openshift.yml` part by part. The full version is available for reference in the `chapter -11/openshift/openshift-default.yml` file of the book resources.

> **Listing 11.14   Simplified version of the generated `openshift.yml`**

```yaml
---
apiVersion: v1
kind: Service
  ...
  name: inventory-service
  ...
---
apiVersion: image.openshift.io/v1
kind: ImageStream
  ...
  dockerImageRepository: registry.access.redhat.com/ubi8/openjdk-21
  ...
---
apiVersion: image.openshift.io/v1
kind: ImageStream
  ...
  name: inventory-service
  namespace: default
spec:
  dockerImageRepository: quay.io/quarkus-in-action/inventory-service
  ...
```

This first part starts with the Service definition, which is the same as in `kubernetes .yml`. The following two resources are called *ImageStream*. ImageStream is a custom OpenShift resource that provides an abstraction over container images. This will be important later as we can use it to redeploy our application automatically. There are two defined ImageStreams: one for JDK and one for our Inventory service image. They are utilized by the *BuildConfig* resource, which we can see in the following listing.

Listing 11.15   Continuation of the simplified generated `openshift.yml`

```
---
apiVersion: build.openshift.io/v1
kind: BuildConfig
  ...
  name: inventory-service
  namespace: default
spec:
  output:
    to:
      kind: ImageStreamTag
      name: inventory-service:1.0.0-SNAPSHOT
  source:
    binary: {}
  strategy:
    sourceStrategy:
      from:
        kind: ImageStreamTag
        name: openjdk-21:1.20
---
apiVersion: apps/v1
kind: Deployment
  ...
  name: inventory-service
  namespace: default
spec:
  ...
    spec:
      containers:
        ...
          - name: JAVA_APP_JAR
            value: /deployments/quarkus-run.jar
          image: quay.io/quarkus-in-action/inventory-service:1.0.0
          imagePullPolicy: Always
```

This is where OpenShift excels. The BuildConfig configuration defines a s2i build of the Inventory service based on the JDK image we saw in listing 11.14. We can understand JDK-based s2i for our applications in this way:

1 We build a JAR locally.
2 The JAR is pushed to OpenShift.
3 OpenShift builds the application Docker image in the OpenShift build.
4 The new image is run as a deployment.

From our perspective, we build the project, and OpenShift takes care of everything else. The last part, the *Deployment,* is the resource that puts everything together. It defines the `inventory-service:1.0.0` quay.io image as the image it runs from. However, it also automatically redeploys our application when there is an image change in the `inventory-service:1.0.0-SNAPSHOT` ImageStreamTag that is produced by the Build-Config. So every time we trigger a s2i build, it automatically redeploys the deployment.

MANUAL DEPLOYMENT WITH GENERATED OPENSHIFT.YML

Similarly as with Kubernetes, the generated `openshift.yml` would deploy the Inventory service right away, but we would still miss the MySQL connection. We can also include the `mysql.yml` manifest in the `src/main/kubernetes` directory to fix it. It just has to be named `openshift.yml` as every file in this directory is applied to the resource of the same name. We can simply rename `kubernetes.yml` to `openshift.yml` in this directory without additional changes.

Furthermore, since we now use the OpenShift extension, we must also adjust the configuration that creates the environment variable which points to MySQL in `application.properties`. Since we also don't use a Prometheus operator, we can also disable the ServiceMonitor creation. We can also create an OpenShift custom resource called *Route*, which exposes our deployment to the outside world. Also, we must remove or adjust the Kubernetes namespace to correspond to our project in OpenShift if it differs:

```
# Remove the Kubernetes configuration from the previous section
-quarkus.kubernetes.env.vars.quarkus-datasource-jdbc-url=
  jdbc:mysql://mysql:3306/inventory
-quarkus.kubernetes.prometheus.generate-service-monitor=false
-quarkus.kubernetes.namespace=default

quarkus.openshift.env.vars.quarkus-datasource-jdbc-url=
  jdbc:mysql://mysql:3306/inventory

quarkus.openshift.prometheus.generate-service-monitor=false

# Expose created service to the world
quarkus.openshift.route.expose=true
```

After building the application and manifests, we can now directly apply the generated `openshift.yml` (remember that you first need to log in the same terminal where you run these commands), which produces several resources with the `oc` tool, as follows:

```
$ oc apply -f inventory-service/target/kubernetes/openshift.yml
```

Now we can verify that the Inventory service runs in Openshift with

```
$ oc get pods
NAME                                     READY   STATUS    RESTARTS       AGE
inventory-service-856cd84dc9-stpx5       1/1     Running   1 (82s ago)    93s
mysql-7bc9d5b4b4-tzbzs                   1/1     Running   0              93s

$ oc get routes
NAME   HOST/PORT   PATH   SERVICES   PORT   TERMINATION   WILDCARD
inventory-service   <your-url>   inventory-service   http   None
```

OpenShift also comes with a bundled web console. If you don't know where it runs, you can find it with the command

```
$ oc whoami --show-console
```

It looks as presented in figure 11.5.

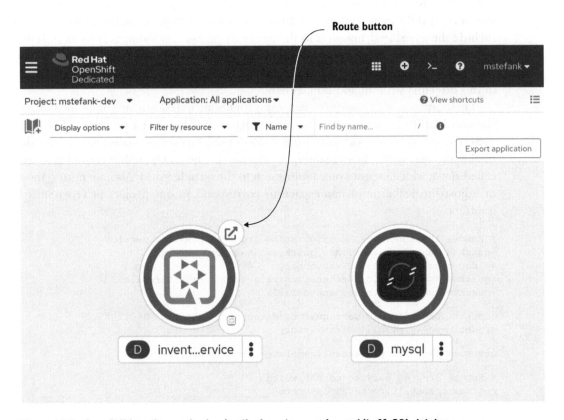

Figure 11.5   OpenShift's web console showing the Inventory service and its MySQL database

We can navigate to the exposed Inventory service route URL by going to `<your-url>` or clicking the route button as shown in figure 11.5. Change the path to `http://<your-url>/q/graphql-ui`, and you will see the familiar UI of the Inventory service now running in OpenShift! We didn't configure SSL, so the route exposes HTTP (`http://`). Routes might open on HTTPS instead, so we need to adjust it.

> **TIP** Modern browsers might come with a preconfigured *HSTS* (HTTP Strict Transport Security) that forces HTTPS. To work around this policy, you can configure your browser to turn off this setting, but you can also open HTTP URLs in an incognito window.

AUTOMATING OPENSHIFT DEPLOYMENT WITH S2I

We've prepared the BuildConfig resource to trigger application redeploy when the s2i build finishes. However, because we configured `quarkus.container-image.*` properties, Quarkus automatically picks them to align generated manifests to point to the deployed image. If we want to utilize the image built with s2i, we need to remove them. To remove the need to have them specified whenever we build or push images (if we decide to do so again), we can define a custom `s2i` configuration profile that removes these properties (listing 11.16).

Listing 11.16   The `s2i` profile removing container image properties

```
%s2i.quarkus.container-image.registry=
%s2i.quarkus.container-image.group=
%s2i.quarkus.container-image.tag=
```

If you now regenerate `openshift.yml` with the `s2i` profile active, it points to the `inventory-service:1.0.0-SNAPSHOT` image, which corresponds to the ImageStream-Tag produced by our BuildConfig. To trigger the s2i build, we can run the following command that sets the required flags to use our new config profile (in addition to the `prod` profile) and to trigger an s2i build:

```
$ ./mvnw clean package -Dquarkus.profile=prod,s2i
  -Dquarkus.openshift.deploy=true
```

This will take a minute. In the terminal, you see the running OpenShift s2i build consuming logs from OpenShift (it can also be found in the OpenShift web console under the "Builds" menu). You can follow how it builds the final Inventory service image.

> **TIP**   To remove all deployed resources from OpenShift at any point if you get stuck, just run `oc delete all --all`.

After it finishes, you will see a different pod replaced our original pod (note the suffix of the `inventory-service` pod). We can also see the pod in which OpenShift performed the build of our image, which is now completed:

```
$ oc get pods
NAME                                   READY   STATUS      RESTARTS   AGE
inventory-service-1-build              0/1     Completed   0          63s
inventory-service-5999884d6d-4t18z     1/1     Running     0          15s
mysql-7bc9d5b4b4-tzbzs                 1/1     Running     0          3m39s
```

Our OpenShift workflow is now complete. In section 11.6 we look into what we need to do to get the full car rental deployment running in OpenShift. But the hard part is now over. If you understand these basic OpenShift concepts, we can start our journey to get our production running in OpenShift.

11.4   Kubernetes and OpenShift clients

So far, we have utilized various management tools (`kubectl` or `oc`) that have allowed us to manage our Kubernetes or OpenShift platforms. While there are other ways to deploy Quarkus applications (e.g., OpenShift UI or `oc new-app` command), they all require manual steps. Quarkus also allows us to define our deployment workflow in Java directly in the Quarkus application. For this reason, Quarkus provides two extensions—`quarkus-kubernetes-client` and `quarkus-openshift-client`—that integrate *Fabric8* client (https://github.com/fabric8io/kubernetes-client). The Fabric8 library provides programmatic access to the Kubernetes and OpenShift REST API.

These extensions allow us to inject (with CDI) an instance of either `Kubernetes-Client` or `OpenShiftClient`. They provide a custom *DSL* (domain-specific language) for accessing Kubernetes or OpenShift, respectively. We don't dive into details here since this is specific to your cloud platform. But, for example, if we would like to list all running pods in our OpenShift instance from the last section (`oc get pods --field -selector status.phase=Running`), we can do it as shown in the following listing.

Listing 11.17 Example usage of the `quarkus-openshift-client` extension

```
@Inject
OpenShiftClient openShiftClient;

@GET
@Path("/pods")
public List<Pod> pods() {
    return openShiftClient.pods().inNamespace("mstefank-dev")
        .withField("status.phase", "Running").list().getItems();
}
```

This DSL provides access to the complete Kubernetes/OpenShift API. If we chose to, we could write our full deployment pipelines and processing in Java with Quarkus cloud client extensions. Compared to the traditional approach with generated manifests and CLI tools, it allows more flexibility, but it is also likely to be more complicated and require more code.

11.5 *Serverless application with Quarkus*

At the beginning of the book, we introduced Quarkus as a framework for microservices and serverless applications. So far, we have covered microservices extensively, but we only touched a little on Quarkus's serverless story. It was intentional, since Manning has a separate book, *Serverless Java in Action*, focusing on all available Quarkus' serverless integrations. For this reason, the coverage of this topic here is reduced to demonstrating the very basics of how to start with Quarkus serverless, but we won't dive into deeper details.

11.5.1 *Serverless architecture*

Serverless architecture consists of smaller application deployments that can independently scale up or down depending on user demand. This application scaling means that we can adjust the running application resources according to the user requests, which means that we don't need to pay for unused resources (when there is no demand). When the demand is high, the serverless platform automatically spins up new instances, and when the traffic decreases, it can stop some instances to scale the application down again.

Naturally, application scaling extends to the scale to zero functionality where there are no instances of a particular application running. When a user request comes in, the serverless platform starts a new instance of the user application that can handle the request (aka cold start). The application's startup time adds to the handling time of the (first) request, which means that the serverless application must start fast (nobody would like to wait several dozens of seconds for a page load).

This is where "serverless" comes in, since many traditional servers are big and slow to start. Especially in Java, the platforms were designed to run for months (or years) at the time, so starting in a few minutes or consuming a few GBs of memory was fine. Java was less popular for serverless models. But technologies like Quarkus have started to change that. Quarkus's focus on low memory footprint and ahead-of-time compilation makes it possible to write Java serverless applications. Compilation to GraalVM native images extends this even further to make even smaller and faster-to-start applications. Since serverless applications typically don't run for long (by default, 1 minute; see later discussion), native binaries are an excellent fit for serverless application deployment. As we already saw with Quarkus, creating a native executable is just a matter of a build time flag.

11.5.2 *Funqy*

There are several serverless platforms (aka *FaaS*, Function as a Service) on the market (e.g., Knative, AWS Lambda, Google Cloud Functions, Azure Functions). Each provides its own Java API that can be utilized in your Quarkus application. But each API is different, meaning using such API locks your application to a particular platform.

Quarkus's serverless strategy is based on the library called *Funqy*. Funqy provides a unified API that abstracts all FaaS platforms mentioned earlier. It represents a very simple API that we can use to develop Quarkus serverless applications.

> **NOTE** Funqy—in the way we use it in this book—is exposed through HTTP in a similar way to REST services. But it doesn't serve as a replacement for REST. It doesn't expose all REST features. But if you need complete REST, you can still use Funqy together with the REST extensions provided by Quarkus.

The core of the API consists of an annotation called `@Funq`. It defines a method that the extension invokes when the user calls the function. The following listing presents an example of this API.

Listing 11.18 The example use of the Funqy API

```
import io.quarkus.funqy.Funq;

public class Function {
```

```
@Funq
public String process(String input) {
    return "Processed: " + input;
}
}
```

We can also use POJOs (plain old Java objects) as inputs/outputs (they need to have a default constructor and getters+setters), use reactive Mutiny types, or use dependency injection. But that's it. This simplicity allows us to port this kind of function to different FaaS providers without problems because Quarkus takes care of the various integrations.

11.5.3 *Car statistics application with Knative*

In this section, we develop a new but totally optional service called `car-statistics` that we deploy as a serverless function with Knative. We chose Knative as the easiest platform to utilize since it is preinstalled already in the OpenShift Sandbox (refer to 11.6.1 for setup instructions) in its Red Hat-branded product version called OpenShift Serverless. It calls our deployed Inventory service using GraphQL to return some statistics of currently tracked cars. Since a service like this doesn't need to run all the time, it's a perfect target for serverless because at times when we don't need the data, we don't need to keep the application running.

> **NOTE** The development part in this section is optional. If you're using the OpenShift Sandbox, you can start right away. If you're using custom OpenShift or Kubernetes, you must install Knative manually (https://knative.dev/docs/install/).

Let's create a new Quarkus `car-statistics` application:

```
quarkus create app org.acme:car-statistics -P 3.15.1 --extension \
funqy-http,smallrye-graphql-client,openshift --no-code
```

We need three extensions—Funqy API, GraphQL client to call the Inventory service, and OpenShift integration for seamless Knative deployment to Openshift. Open the project in the IDE.

We start by copying the `org.acme.reservation.inventory` package (three classes) from the Reservation service to the `org.acme.statistics.inventory` package in `car-statistics` since the logic of calling the Inventory service through its exposed GraphQL API is the same. Feel free to implement it from scratch as an exercise. You can always verify it with the code in the Reservation service.

Regarding configuration, we need to add the configuration properties in the following listing to `application.properties`.

Listing 11.19 The `car-statistics` configuration

```
# Needed to generate Knative resources
quarkus.kubernetes.deployment-target=knative
```

```
# Inventory service URL on localhost
quarkus.smallrye-graphql-client.inventory.url=http://localhost:8083/graphql
# Inventory service location in OpenShift
quarkus.knative.env.vars.quarkus-smallrye-graphql-client-inventory-url=
➥http://inventory-service/graphql

# Needed to configure where Knative pulls the image
quarkus.container-image.registry=
➥image-registry.openshift-image-registry.svc:5000
quarkus.container-image.group=<your-openshift-namespace>

# Max concurrent requests to a single pod
quarkus.knative.revision-auto-scaling.container-concurrency=2
```

> **TIP** If you're using the prepared solution from the book's resources, don't forget to change the `quarkus.container-image.group` to your OpenShift namespace.

The `quarkus.kubernetes.deployment-target` comes from the underlying Kubernetes extension (since Knative is not specific to OpenShift). It specifies what resources Quarkus generates. The possible values include `kubernetes`, `openshift`, `knative`, `minikube`, and `kind` or any combination of these values. We also need to configure the name of the image included in the generated Knative resources. Since we will utilize s2i, we point it to the internal OpenShift registry and your namespace/project. But this could also be configured to the external image we could pull. Lastly, we configure the maximum concurrent requests per single pod/container. It also allows us to try scaling to multiple application instances if there are three or more concurrent requests.

We can now create our Funqy function. Create a new class `org.acme.statistics` `.CarStatistics` as presented in the following listing.

Listing 11.20 The code of the `CarStatistics` class using Funqy API

```
package org.acme.statistics;

import io.quarkus.funqy.Funq;
import io.smallrye.graphql.client.GraphQLClient;
import io.smallrye.mutiny.Uni;
import jakarta.inject.Inject;
import org.acme.statistics.inventory.GraphQLInventoryClient;

import java.time.Instant;

public class CarStatistics {

    @Inject
    @GraphQLClient("inventory")
    GraphQLInventoryClient inventoryClient;

    @Funq
    public Uni<String> getCarStatistics() {
```

```
        return inventoryClient.allCars()
            .map(cars -> ("The Car Rental car statistics created at %s. " +
                "Number of available cars: %d")
                .formatted(Instant.now(), cars.size())));
    }
}
```

Now we can test our function in Dev mode. You will also need a running instance of the Inventory service (Dev mode is sufficient). When ready, call `http://localhost:8080/getCarStatistics` to get these simple car statistics:

```
$ http :8080/getCarStatistics
HTTP/1.1 200 OK
Content-Type: application/json
content-length: 102

"The Car Rental car statistics created at 2024-10-17T17:30:31.762233088Z.
➥ Number of available cars: 2"
```

11.5.4 *Car statistics Knative deployment*

The final step is to push our function to the cloud. We use the OpenShift Sandbox that comes with Knative preinstalled. With Quarkus, we can do this in a single command:

```
$ ./mvnw clean package -Dquarkus.knative.deploy=true
```

This command triggers an s2i build of our `car-statistics` application that we configured our Knative function to point to in listing 11.19. You can verify this in the generated `knative.yml/json` files in the `target/kubernetes` directory.

  After the s2i build finishes, we can see the `car-statistics` Knative service deployed in our OpenShift instance, as shown in figure 11.6.

  You can now freely call the exposed route to get back the statistics of our currently tracked cars—for example, by clicking the route button or by `http`:

```
$ http http://<your-route>/getCarStatistics
...
"The Car Rental car statistics created at 2024-10-22T14:25:25.257426983Z.
➥ Number of available cars: 2"
```

By default, we have the scale-to-zero functionality enabled. If you don't call our `car-statistics` Knative application for 1 minute, Knative automatically scales it to zero replicas by stopping the running pod instance. Figure 11.7 demonstrates this scenario.

  But if we now access the exposed route again (in the browser or terminal), a new pod is started and handles our request! Notice how fast it is (only a few seconds). Remember, this is still Quarkus in JVM. It could be even faster if we compiled `car-statistics` to native. You can easily try this; it's just a matter of adding `-Dnative` to the build command of the `car-statistics` application. The native build will take longer, but then the startup will be extremely quick.

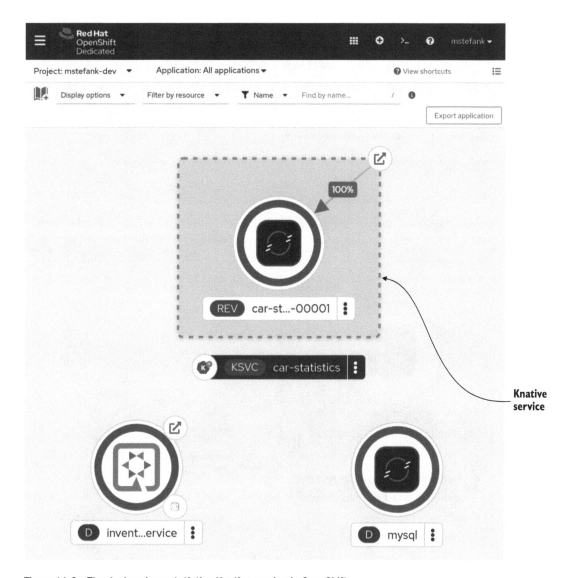

Figure 11.6   The deployed car-statistics Knative service in OpenShift

As an exercise, try to invoke the deployed function with two or more concurrent requests to see how the car-statistics application scales up when it is not able to keep up with the requests load (if you know how to make concurrent requests; e.g., repeating calls in three concurrent loops). When you call it concurrently, you can see multiple pods being created as shown in figure 11.8. If executing concurrent requests is hard because the application is too fast to respond, just add an artificial Thread .sleep into the getCarStatistics method to slow down the response.

Figure 11.7   The car-statistics Knative deployment scaled to zero

Figure 11.8 The car-statistics scale up with multiple concurrent requests

TIP   This is easier to do from the service autoscaled to 0 (cold start).

This is the serverless magic. We are running our `car-statistics` application only when we have requests, saving resources when we don't need to call it.

11.6   *Deploying car rental in the cloud*

We are now finally ready to deploy our car rental application to the cloud! With everything we learned so far, you'll see this will not be very hard to do. We use the Open-Shift Sandbox that we learn how to set up in the following section. The Sandbox is a free, testing, development-targeted, and shared OpenShift cluster with 14 GB of RAM and 40 GB storage for 30 days. It also comes with everything we need for our deployment preinstalled.

11.6.1   *Setting up OpenShift Sandbox*

To start with OpenShift Sandbox, navigate to https://dn.dev/rhd-sandbox and click the `Start your sandbox for free` button, as shown in figure 11.9.

Create your
OpenShift
cluster.

What is the Developer Sandbox?

The Developer Sandbox for Red Hat OpenShift provides you with 30 days of no-cost access to a shared cluster on OpenShift, an enterprise-grade Kubernetes-based platform. Get instant access to your own minimal, preconfigured OpenShift environment for development and testing, hosted and managed by Red Hat.

Figure 11.9   OpenShift Sandbox landing page

It redirects you to authenticate with your Red Hat Developer account. If you don't already have one, you can create it. It is completely free and doesn't need credit card information.

After you log in, you land in the Hybrid Cloud Console, where you need to click the `Get started` button. Afterward, you can see the `Launch` button for OpenShift that opens your OpenShift (figure 11.10).

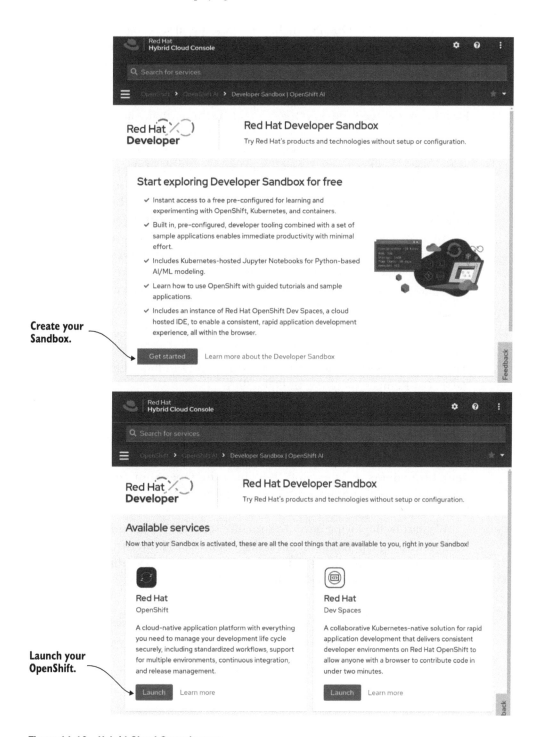

Create your Sandbox.

Launch your OpenShift.

Figure 11.10   Hybrid Cloud Console page

We are now in the OpenShift. In Sandbox, we always log in with the *DevSandbox* account into the *<your-username>-dev* project (namespace). After you log in (by clicking the DevSandbox button), you land in the OpenShift UI (figure 11.11).

For now, we focus on the top-right corner, where we can find the relevant tools and information that we need to log in to this OpenShift also from local machines. For local login, we need the oc (OpenShift client) tool, that you can download from the question mark button, as shown in figure 11.12.

Download the binary for your local system and put it into an executable path. To utilize the oc tool to log in on your local system, we need the login command for this particular OpenShift cluster. On the last page, you can also see the Copy login command button, which would take you to the login command, but there is also a more straightforward way: opening your profile in the top-right corner (figure 11.13).

After you click the Copy login command button, a new browser tab again asks you to authenticate with a DevSandbox account. Then click the Display Token button on the next page, which takes you to the actual token page, also presented in figure 11.13. Copy the oc login … command and paste it into your local terminal:

```
$ oc login --token=TOKEN --server=SERVER
Logged into "SERVER" as "<username>" using the token provided.
```

The oc tool is now connected to your OpenShift sandbox! Let's now deploy the full Acme Car Rental system to your OpenShift.

11.6.2 *Car rental infrastructure deployment with OpenShift Sandbox*

Acme Car Rental in OpenShift presents challenges similar to those we overcame for the local Docker Compose production deployment. We will still deploy all 17 car rental containers to OpenShift, but since the OpenShift communication specifics are different (i.e., we are no longer on localhost), we need to adjust our services accordingly.

We start by deploying our infrastructure services. We provided a single, more than 3,000-lines-long OpenShift manifest that deploys all 12 infrastructure services we need in one step. You can find it in the chapter-11/car-rental directory and run it with the oc tool as presented in the following listing.

> **Listing 11.21   Deploying dependent car rental services in OpenShift**

```
$ oc apply -f car-rental/car-rental-dependent-services.yml
```

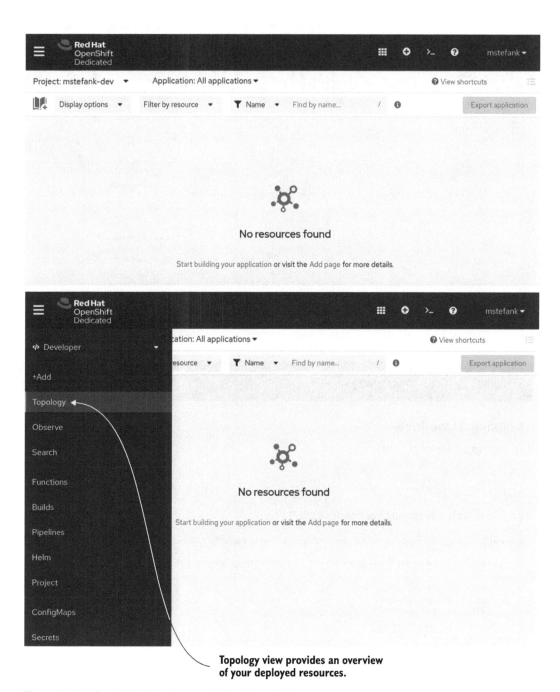

Topology view provides an overview
of your deployed resources.

Figure 11.11   OpenShift UI/web console (Topology view)

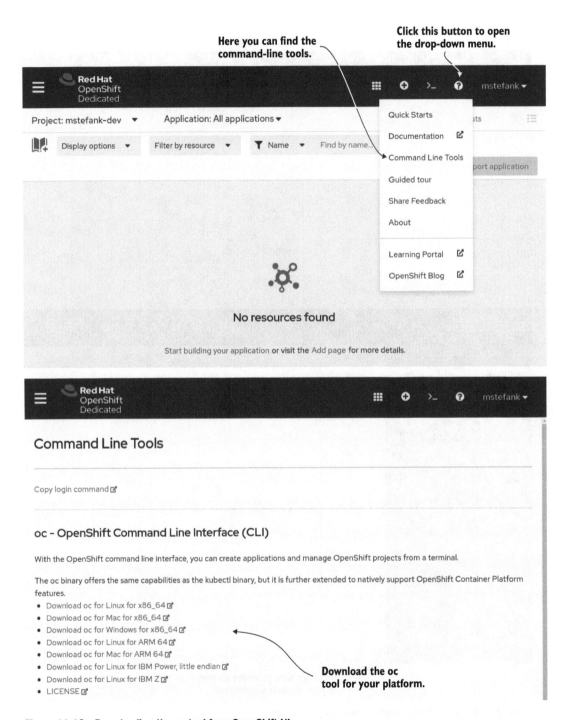

Figure 11.12   Downloading the oc tool from OpenShift UI

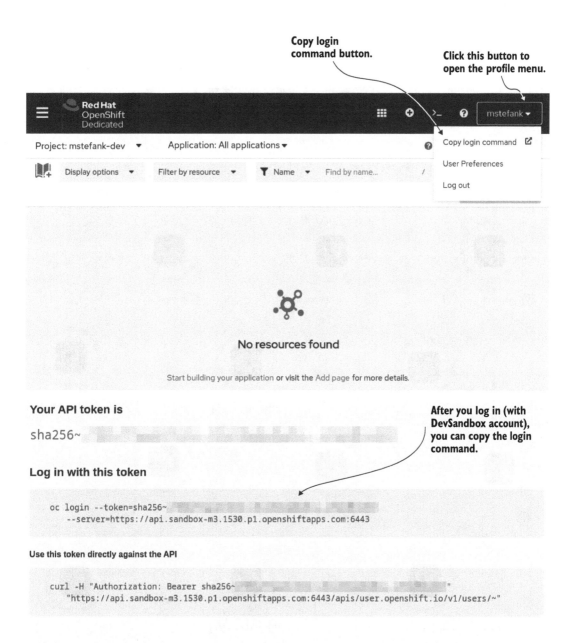

Figure 11.13 Copy the login command from the OpenShift UI for local login

After the command finishes, you can check the OpenShift console that shows all deployed containers running. Figure 11.14 presents a (reorganized) view of the finished deployment.

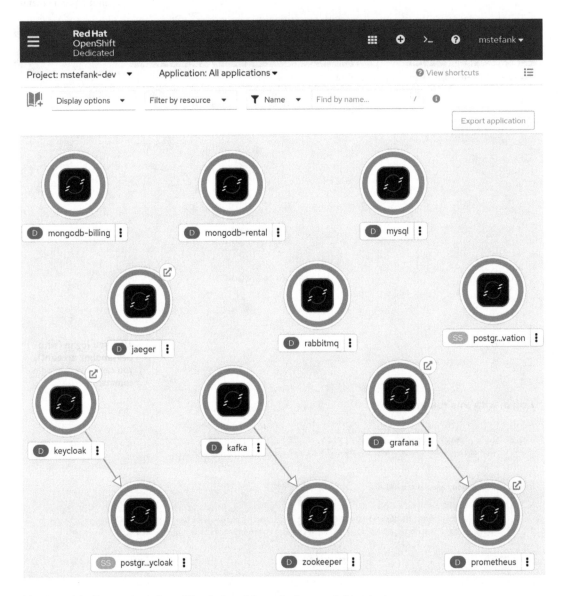

Figure 11.14   Reorganized view of the deployed dependent car rental services

Except for the 12 infrastructure services that you can see in the figure, we also created four *ConfigMaps* (Kubernetes configuration resources) that host various configuration files for them. You can check them in the `ConfigMaps` tab.

Now we are ready to start deploying our Quarkus Car rental services. If you need to remove all created resources at any point, the following listing shows how you can do it with the `oc delete` command utilizing the same manifest.

> **Listing 11.22   Deleting all created resources with manifest**

```
$ oc delete -f car-rental/car-rental-dependent-services.yml
```

ConfigMaps are specific resources, which means they are not removed even with `oc delete all --all`. However, when deleting using the manifest as demonstrated in listing 11.22, ConfigMaps defined in the manifest will get deleted too.

11.6.3   *Car rental services deployment with OpenShift Sandbox*

We've come to the final stage of our deployment. Only the five Quarkus car rental services remain to be deployed to the OpenShift Sandbox. We go step by step over all services, utilizing the features explained in section 11.3.4 to deploy them all to OpenShift Sandbox.

The first thing we need to do is to add the `quarkus-openshift` extension. Run the following `quarkus` command in all Quarkus Car rental services. It might already be in Inventory service if you followed the previous sections:

```
$ quarkus ext add openshift
```

In each service, we also need to apply the same minimum configuration as we did in the Inventory service. Namely, choose `openshift` as the image builder extension, define the `s2i` profile that removes the container image specifications, remove the ServiceMonitor creation, and expose a public route, so we can access our services from outside OpenShift:

```
%s2i.quarkus.container-image.registry=
%s2i.quarkus.container-image.group=
%s2i.quarkus.container-image.tag=

quarkus.container-image.builder=openshift
quarkus.openshift.prometheus.generate-service-monitor=false
quarkus.openshift.route.expose=true
```

As in the OpenShift/Kubernetes environment, Deployment resources communicate with each other via the Service resources that assign hostnames, so we need to adjust the URL locations of our services—remove all `localhost` references as they don't work in OpenShift.

NOTE   Quarkus car rental services generate Service resources such that container ports (808x) are mapped to port 80 externally, which means that we need to call (for example) the Reservation service using `reservation-service:80` instead of `reservation-service:8081`. 80 is also the default HTTP port, so it can be omitted, and you can simply use `reservation-service` (just the name of the Service resource) for the URL. You can also configure the target port with the `quarkus.openshift.ports."http".host-port` configuration property.

As we learned in 11.3.2, we can utilize the configuration options of the `quarkus-openshift` extension which allow us to define the environment variables that propagate to the generated manifests to override the configuration hardcoded in the images (inside `application.properties`). Let's adjust the configuration files in the individual car rental services, as demonstrated in the following snippets.

USERS SERVICE

In OpenShift, we must configure the applications that use Keycloak to access it through its publicly exposed route because any browser's request accessing our application is redirected to this URL (and thus a URL based on a Service reference wouldn't work). You can find the Keycloak's route with `oc get routes`. The Reservation service is exposed on port 80, configured by its generated Service resource. We also need to adjust the Jaeger URL for OpenTelemetry traces:

```
# TODO: Don't forget to insert your Keycloak route here
quarkus.openshift.env.vars.quarkus-oidc-auth-server-url=
➥http://<your-keycloak-route>/realms/car-rental
quarkus.openshift.env.vars.quarkus-rest-client-reservations-url=
➥http://reservation-service
quarkus.openshift.env.vars.quarkus-otel-exporter-otlp-endpoint=
➥http://jaeger:4317
```

TIP   Even if you're using the prepared solutions from the book's GitHub repository, in this case you have to manually update the `quarkus.openshift.env.vars.quarkus-oidc-auth-server-url` because this property is specific to each reader's deployment, and we can't provide a value that will work for everybody. Obtain the route using `oc get route keycloak` after you have deployed the resources from the `car-rental-dependent-services.yml` file.

RESERVATION SERVICE

Reservation is a little more complex. We need to change the URLs for Inventory and Rental services, PostgreSQL database, Keycloak (again using your own route the same way as in the Users service), Jaeger, and RabbitMQ:

```
quarkus.openshift.env.vars.quarkus-smallrye-graphql-client-inventory-url=
➥http://inventory-service/graphql
quarkus.openshift.env.vars.quarkus-rest-client-rental-url=
➥http://rental-service
quarkus.openshift.env.vars.quarkus-datasource-reactive-url=
```

```
⇒vertx-reactive:postgresql://postgres-reservation:5432/reservation
# TODO: Don't forget to insert your Keycloak route here
quarkus.openshift.env.vars.quarkus-oidc-auth-server-url=
⇒http://<your-keycloak-route>/realms/car-rental
quarkus.openshift.env.vars.quarkus-otel-exporter-otlp-endpoint=
⇒http://jaeger:4317
quarkus.openshift.env.vars.rabbitmq-host=rabbitmq
```

RENTAL SERVICE

Similarly, in the Rental service, we need to adjust the locations for the Reservation service, MongoDB, and Kafka.

```
quarkus.openshift.env.vars.quarkus-rest-client-reservation-url=
⇒http://reservation-service
quarkus.openshift.env.vars.quarkus-mongodb-connection-string=
⇒mongodb://mongodb-rental:27017
quarkus.openshift.env.vars.kafka-bootstrap-servers=kafka:9092
```

INVENTORY SERVICE

If you followed section 11.3.4, Inventory is already ready for the OpenShift deployment. But we still need to update the Jaeger URL for telemetry. We can now also remove the provided MySQL manifests from `src/main/kubernetes` since MySQL is deployed with dependent services:

```
quarkus.openshift.env.vars.quarkus-otel-exporter-otlp-endpoint=
⇒http://jaeger:4317

# Needed only if you didn't follow previous OpenShift deployment
quarkus.openshift.env.vars.quarkus-datasource-jdbc-url=
⇒jdbc:mysql://mysql:3306/inventory
```

BILLING SERVICE

Lastly, the Billing service needs to adjust URLs for its MongoDB, Kafka, and RabbitMQ, as shown in the following snippet. Since we don't need to deal with port conflicts, MongoDB exposes port 27017, the default MongoDB port:

```
quarkus.openshift.env.vars.quarkus-mongodb-connection-string=
⇒mongodb://mongodb-billing:27017
quarkus.openshift.env.vars.kafka-bootstrap-servers=kafka:9092
quarkus.openshift.env.vars.rabbitmq-host=rabbitmq
```

We can start deploying these services to the OpenShift Sandbox. For each service, we either need to use the s2i build to create images in the OpenShift sandbox or use `oc apply` with the pushed images (either the ones provided by authors or the ones pushed by you). Feel free to reread 11.3.4 if you need a reminder of how we can deploy Quarkus to OpenShift. In every case, remember to log in with your `oc` tool as shown in 11.6.1 before you continue.

For our convenience, since this is a lot of repeating commands, we created shell and bat scripts that automate these tasks in all car rental services at the same time (adjust the following commands for Windows by replacing / with \ and `.sh` with `.bat`). These scripts should be executed from a directory that contains all car rental services (e.g. `chapter-11/11_6_3` or `acme-car-rental` root directory).

If you get stuck, you can remove all deployed services with `oc delete all --all`. Note that this doesn't remove created ConfigMap objects (for this, you need to run `oc delete -f car-rental/car-rental-dependent-services.yml`).

DEPLOYING CAR RENTAL SERVICES WITH S2I

As we learned in 11.3.4, we can trigger s2i builds with the `-Dquarkus.openshift.deploy=true` flag included in the build command. The entire deployment consists of two steps:

1. Change the directory to the individual service—`cd users-service`
2. Build with s2i—`./mvnw clean package -Dquarkus.profile=prod,s2i -Dquarkus.openshift.deploy=true` (or `quarkus build` with the same flags)

Alternatively, you can deploy all car rental services together with the `deploy-car-rental-s2i.sh/bat` script in the `car-rental` directory. This script needs to run from a directory that contains all car rental services—for instance, `chapter-11/11_6_3`:

```
# If executed from chapter-11/11_6_3
$ ../car-rental/deploy-car-rental-s2i.sh
```

Note that this script takes a few minutes since it runs all tests and runs s2i builds. But after it finishes, you will have deployed a complete Acme Car Rental system to OpenShift!

DEPLOYING CAR RENTAL SERVICES WITH MANIFESTS

To manually apply generated OpenShift manifests, we need to execute the following sequence of commands in every car rental service:

1. Build the project—`quarkus build` or `./mvnw clean package` to rebuild the manifests. If you want to push your custom images, then also run `quarkus image push` and make sure you've also defined the `quarkus.container-image.group` in all five projects to point at your own quay.io organization. If you use the value `quarkus-in-action`, OpenShift will use the reference images that the authors provided with this book, and thus your deployment will reflect your local changes in manifests but not in the application code that will run in OpenShift.
2. Apply the generated manifest using `oc apply -f target/kubernetes/openshift.yml`.

As this is, again, quite a tedious task, we provide `deploy-car-rental-oc.sh` script in the `chapter-11/car-rental` directory that automates it. There is also `deploy-car-rental-oc.bat` for Windows users. If ran from `chapter-11/11_6_3` directory:

```
# If executed from chapter-11/11_6_3
$ ../car-rental/deploy-car-rental-oc.sh
```

Alternatively, we have provided a manifest called `car-rental-full.yml` that deploys the full Acme Car Rental system in one step. It consumes all prepared images from the `quay.io/quarkus-in-action` organization and also deploys the complete system infrastructure. Just remember that you still need to change the Keycloak URL to point to your cluster (it will be the same as before; you just need to change the project name in the provided example URL). Search for two TODOs in this file. When Keycloak URL is correct, you can deploy all our services with a single command:

```
$ oc apply -f car-rental/car-rental-full.yml
```

> **NOTE** If Users and Reservation services start before Keycloak, you can restart them with arrows in the Details menu of their Deployment.

Whether we use s2i or manual manifests, when the scripts finish, the final Acme Car Rental production runs in the OpenShift Sandbox! Figure 11.15 presents our final deployed project running in the cloud.

To tear it down, run the following set of commands:

```
$ oc delete -f car-rental/car-rental-full.yml # delete car rental resources
$ oc delete all --all # clean remaining build resources (if you used s2i)
```

This is the entire Acme Car Rental system that we developed throughout the book in action! Together, 17 containers are now running in the cloud. Quarkus puts all building blocks in place to develop, test, and deploy our Quarkus microservices with such an ease and fun that we hope you now want to try it in your projects!

11.7 Next steps

In this chapter, we learned how to use Quarkus to package our applications into Docker images and how to easily deploy them in various deployment environments. We defined the full Acme Car Rental production deployment as 17 applications, of which 5 are Quarkus car rental services and 12 are infrastructure-supporting services such as Kafka or Prometheus.

We explained how we can build and deploy Docker images to public registries as quay.io both manually and declaratively with extensions. We were then able to run car rental production locally with Docker Compose.

The Quarkus cloud-native integrations excelled when we started deploying the car rental to cloud management platforms. We learned how Quarkus's Kubernetes and OpenShift extensions simplify the deployment of images to the cloud. We also learned about serverless technology and how Quarkus extensions (like Funqy) make switching from microservice to serverless deployment easy.

Lastly, we focused on the OpenShift Sandbox deployment, combining all knowledge accumulated in this chapter to deploy Acme Car Rental production in various ways (s2i, manifests). Looking at the full deployment of 17 services working in unison is undoubtedly a good reward for everyone following the book's development. This is Quarkus in action!

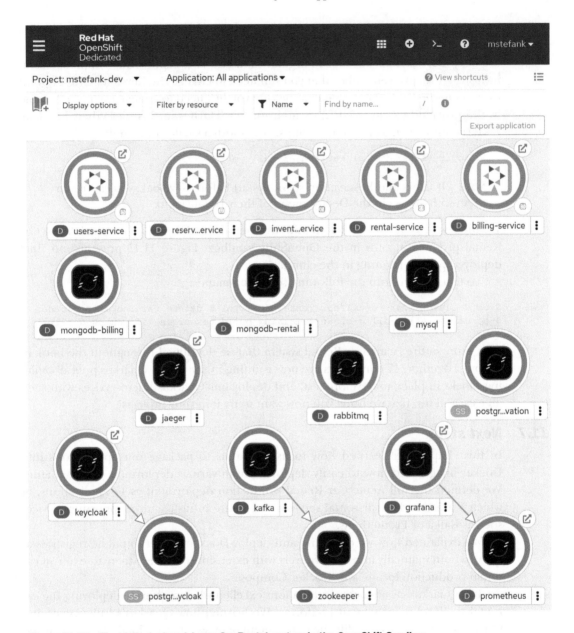

Figure 11.15   **Final fully deployed Acme Car Rental system in the OpenShift Sandbox**

Summary

- Acme Car Rental production consists of 17 services, where 5 are Quarkus services we develop throughout the book.

- Quarkus provides five image-building options (Jib, Docker, Podman, BuildPack, and OpenShift). Quarkus CLI allows us to build and push images without requiring extensions, but extensions provide a way to integrate image processing into the build pipeline.

- Quarkus can generate all required Kubernetes, OpenShift, or Knative resources (manifests) without the need to develop them manually. All of these extensions provide configuration hooks that can customize the final generated resources, which allows us to keep deployment specifications in the configuration.

- The OpenShift extension provides two options of deployments: s2i and manual manifest application. S2i is an OpenShift-specific mechanism that builds an image in the OpenShift provided copy of a locally packaged application (JAR or native).

- Serverless strategy in Quarkus focuses on the Funqy library. Funqy provides a very simplified API interoperable with many different FaaS platforms.

- OpenShift Sandbox is a free OpenShift cluster that anyone can utilize for development and test purposes. Because of the Quarkus cloud-native integrations, the full Acme Car Rental production deployment rollout to this platform can be fully automated.

Custom Quarkus
extensions

In the last chapter of this book, we look at Quarkus extensions. You already know that Quarkus is a framework that is built on top of a set of extensions. An extension is usually a set of features related to a specific technology that makes it easy to integrate it in your Quarkus application.

Let's note right away that creating Quarkus extensions is an advanced topic, and many Quarkus users will not need it. But if you still decide to try it, it will give you a much deeper understanding of how Quarkus works internally, especially the build-time and runtime split. In this chapter, we will create a relatively simple example extension, and explain the necessary theoretical concepts.

It is also important to note that when you want to use a specific library in a Quarkus application, it's not generally necessary to have a dedicated Quarkus extension for it, but in many cases it can make usage of the library in Quarkus applications much easier. In the following section, we discuss a set of possible things that an extension might do to facilitate building Quarkus applications using a specific library.

> **TIP** If you ever decide to create a new Quarkus extension, and you believe that it might be useful for others, you can have it published in the Quarkiverse (https://quarkiverse.io, https://github.com/quarkiverse). We already discussed this at the end of chapter 2. That also means that before you actually decide to write a new extension, you should check the Quarkiverse to see if someone has already created a similar one!

12.1 Motivation to create custom extensions

This section provides a nonexhaustive list of features that an extension might provide. The appropriate features needed for an extension for a specific library depend on the particular library. After finishing this chapter, you might get even more ideas about what an extension might do.

12.1.1 Initialization

When your applications need to use a library that requires some initialization steps, you can delegate the initialization to an extension. That way, the application's code can be cleaner and more focused on the business logic. Furthermore, the initialization might require using something from Quarkus APIs, like adding an extra HTTP interface (on a different port than regular HTTP traffic), in which case it has to be done in an extension.

12.1.2 Build-time steps and bytecode generation

As we discussed back in chapter 1, Quarkus achieves a fast startup partly thanks to moving some initialization steps to build time and executing them only once, instead of doing the same thing every time the application starts. If you want to make use of this and do some initialization work during build, you need to do it in an extension.

As an example, let's consider the GraphQL (server-side) extension that scans application classes for GraphQL operations and model classes (anything that affects the schema). It generates the corresponding GraphQL schema definition at build time. The extension then saves the schema into the packaged application. This speeds up the application startup because the schema doesn't have to be computed again. It is serialized in the application in the form of optimized recorded bytecode that, when executed, directly instantiates the schema object. The bytecode doesn't need to look at the model classes again. All the necessary information is already contained in the recorded bytecode.

To illustrate how the recorded bytecode works, imagine a class that is used as a GraphQL type, as in listing 12.1. The `@Name` annotation changes the type names in the generated schema.

Listing 12.1   An example Person type used in GraphQL schema

```
@Name("MyPersonType")
public class Person {
  @Name("BirthDate")
  public Date dateOfBirth;
}
```

The relevant code that scans the application for GraphQL types might look similar to the following listing (this is not an excerpt from the real code of the SmallRye GraphQL extension, but just highly simplified pseudocode to ease the understanding of the concept):

Listing 12.2   The pseudocode of the GraphQL extension type processing

```
public GraphQLType createGraphQLType(String clazz) {
    ClassInfo classInfo = annotationIndex
        .getClassByName(DotName.createSimple(clazz));
    AnnotationInstance nameAnnotation = classInfo.annotation(Name.class);
    String typeName = nameAnnotation != null ?
        nameAnnotation.value() : classInfo.simpleName();
    GraphQLType graphQLType = new GraphQLType(typeName);
    for (FieldInfo field : classInfo.fields()) {
        AnnotationInstance nameAnnotation = field.annotation(Name.class);
        String fieldName = nameAnnotation != null ?
            nameAnnotation.value() : field.name();
        Type fieldType = field.type();
        GraphQLField field = new GraphQLField(fieldName, fieldType);
        graphQLType.addField(field);
    }
    return graphQLType;
}
```

The `createGraphQLType` takes a class name and turns it into a `GraphQLType`. It first determines the type name from either the `@Name` annotation or the class name as a fallback. Then it iterates over all fields and for each field, it also finds out the correct field type and adds it to the parent GraphQL type.

Given the `Person` class from listing 12.1, the corresponding piece of recorded bytecode that gets packaged into the application will look like the one in listing 12.3. The code is presented in the decompiled form from the generated `.class` file.

Listing 12.3   Decompiled bytecode produced by the example GraphQL extension

```
GraphQLType graphQLType = new GraphQLType("MyPersonType");
GraphQLField field = new GraphQLField("BirthDate", Date.class);
graphQLType.addField(field);
```

You can see that there are no `if` or `for` statements or any use of Java reflection. All the necessary information gathered during build is already contained in this bytecode. The bootstrap of the application is thus much faster.

Apart from recording bytecode as a means of transferring information from build time to runtime, many Quarkus extensions also generate custom bytecode. For example, the CDI (ArC) extension generates bytecode to save individual beans' metadata (which would otherwise need to be collected with reflection during the application start).

12.1.3 Configuration

An extension can extend the configuration model of Quarkus. This means that it can add new configuration properties in the `quarkus.*` namespace. You might ask why is this necessary, and it's a valid question. After all, you can always use any regular properties as defined by MicroProfile Config, which the extension can still use directly. One key difference is that the Quarkus-managed configuration model supports distinguishing between build-time and runtime properties. If your property configures something that needs to be known and acted upon during the build but is unnecessary at runtime, then it's better to use the Quarkus configuration model and declare this property as build-time-only. If a user then tries to override the value of this property during application startup, they will receive a warning describing it as a build-time property and stating that it can't be overridden at runtime. It was already acted upon during the build, so changing it now would potentially lead to inconsistencies.

As examples of a build-time-only properties, we could mention all properties that the Swagger (OpenAPI) extension declares. An example is `quarkus.swagger-ui.title`, which controls the title of the generated HTML page with the API description, or `quarkus.swagger-ui.theme`, which controls the UI's look-and-feel theme. Because Quarkus generates the Swagger UI at build time, the extension can store already pregenerated HTML files in the built application. It's not possible to change these properties at runtime (when the application starts—let alone changing them dynamically even later). If you still do try to override this configuration, it has no effect other than that Quarkus gives you a warning in the log.

On the other hand, an example of a runtime property is `quarkus.http.port`, which denotes the port that the main HTTP interface is listening on. This can be defined also when the application starts. Binding to a port is not something that can be done at build time. You can't serialize and somehow package an open socket into a JAR file. Neither does it make much sense to fix the port at build time already, making it impossible to change later. Therefore, Quarkus doesn't read or act upon this property's value during build.

12.1.4 Dependency injection

An extension can provide various CDI beans that can be injected into your application. For example, the RESTEasy Client extension makes it possible to inject instances of your REST clients (the interfaces that you annotate with `@RegisterRestClient` etc.), because it scans (at build time) your application for these interfaces and generates a CDI bean for each of them.

If needed, you can also access all beans, modify their behavior, or supply new beans for your extension users. It's also possible to define synthetic beans where the CDI beans metadata is not derived from an implementation class but is provided in the code of the Quarkus extension that registers them. For instance, this is useful for integrating libraries that don't support CDI since we can still align them with the Quarkus development model in the extension integration.

12.1.5 Dev mode shutdown hooks

An extension may or may not need to make additional changes to assure its integration works properly in Dev mode. For example, if the library holds some resources like network connections or open files, then during a hot reload, these resources need to be properly cleaned up and closed to prevent various kinds of resource leaks. Quarkus provides a mechanism that allows extensions to register shutdown hooks that get called during the shutdown of the Quarkus application and also during the shutdown phase of a hot reload, meaning the extension can align for individual Quarkus modes accordingly.

12.1.6 Dev Services

If you use a library that requires some external service to be running (e.g., a database) and you want to be able to provide your own Dev Services implementation to allow Quarkus to automatically manage container-based instances of this service, guess what: you need a Quarkus extension. Quarkus provides an API for extensions which allows them to manage these containers. It also provides the necessary tools for enabling the extension to additionally inject the connection details into the application's configuration (so the extension users don't have to provide them manually).

12.1.7 Dev UI

The extension is also able to provide any form of graphical user interface to be included in the Dev UI. Each extension receives its own card in the main panel, and its content is up to the extension developer. You can imagine adding any form of information (e.g., beans count in Arc), a testing playground (e.g., GraphiQL or gRPC console), or even operations that change the behavior of your extension (e.g., manually executing some operations in the database that a configured datasource points to). The possibilities are endless.

12.1.8 Native mode

The usage of native mode brings its own set of problems. For example, if the application runs in the native mode and uses reflection, all classes accessed reflectively need to be registered in advance (so that the native image builder includes the class's reflection metadata in the binary). While an application may by itself register its own classes for reflection by applying the @RegisterForReflection annotation, a Quarkus extension may make this easier for application developers, because it can detect and automatically register what classes need to be registered for reflection. Library developers know what kind of code their users write with their library, so encapsulating this configuration in the Quarkus extension is often easier for everyone.

12.2 Extension concepts and structure

In this section, we explain the basic concepts you need to know to be able to actually write, build, and test extensions.

We won't dive too much into the details, because this is a very complicated subject. You can find all available options in the official Quarkus documentation (https://quarkus.io/guides/writing-extensions).

12.2.1 Modules

An extension typically consists of two Maven modules. One is the deployment module, which contains the code that is needed at build time. The other is the runtime module, which has all the necessary runtime dependencies. The deployment module has a dependency on the runtime module, so everything that will be available at runtime is also available during build but not vice versa.

The runtime and deployment modules are usually wrapped in a single parent Maven module. It is also possible to have more modules under the parent—for example, a module with integration tests.

12.2.2 Processors and recorders

Most build-time logic executes in a class called a *processor*. Processors always reside in the deployment module. An extension can have one or more processors. A processor contains *build steps*. A build step is a method annotated with the @BuildStep annotation that consumes and produces *build items* (more on these in a bit). It can also call a *recorder* to record some bytecode that should be present in the built application. A recorder is a class that resides in the runtime module, acting as a kind of bridge between the build-time and runtime parts of the extension. Recorders' methods contain code with the actual runtime logic, but, when called during the build, instead of normally invoking this code, they record its bytecode, so that it can be re-executed at runtime. Any object that is constructed in a processor and passed to a recorder is recorded as bytecode (an optimized sequence of steps needed to build exactly this instance) and included in the packaged application, so the recorded object is easily constructible at runtime. The processor receives back a proxy object representing the runtime value. This proxy object can be passed to other processors (build steps), and they can then use it to record other objects that depend on it.

Some Quarkus extensions also generate new bytecode or modify existing bytecode directly, without using a recorder. For that, they make use of a tool called *Gizmo*. Gizmo (https://github.com/quarkusio/gizmo) is a project that provides an API for generating and manipulating JVM bytecode. A typical use case for this is reducing runtime usage of Java reflection by generating bytecode that directly invokes a method instead of using reflection to find and invoke it.

12.2.3 Build items

Build items are objects that are passed between build steps. They are the main means of communication between various processors that make up an extension or even across processors from different extensions. Each build step can consume one or more build items and produce one or more build items. This way, build steps with their consumed and produced build items constitute a graph of actions that are executed at build time.

For example, there is a built-in class `AdditionalBeanBuildItem` that can be produced by a processor (from any extension, including your own) that wants to register a new CDI bean. This build item is then consumed by a processor from the `quarkus-arc` extension that takes the bytecode recording steps needed to make the bean available. Another example would be `FilterBuildItem`, which tells the Vert.x HTTP extension to apply a specific filter to every HTTP request that the application receives. The Vert.x HTTP extension consumes this build item and, again, records the necessary bytecode to wire up the filter. So if you wanted to add some custom auditing of all incoming requests, then you would probably do it by producing this build item in a processor within your own Quarkus extension.

For further illustration about how processors, build steps, and recorders are related, see figure 12.1.

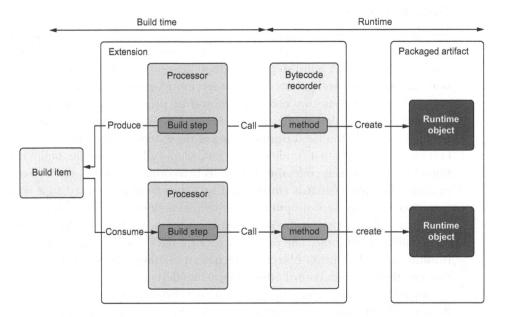

Figure 12.1 The relationships between build-time processing components and how they translate to runtime

A very common use-case for processors is to scan the application classes. For that, a processor can consume the `ApplicationIndexBuildItem`, which includes an index of the application classes in the *Jandex* format. Jandex is a tool for indexing Java classes in a way that their metadata can be queried efficiently, without having to actually load the class into the JVM. This is used in almost all core Quarkus extensions, because it allows them to search for usage of a particular library in the application, validate the usage, generate some initialization bytecode, and store a precomputed model of the usage into the built artifact.

For reference, Quarkus provides the full list of available build items at https://quarkus.io/guides/all-builditems.

12.3   Creating an extension

In this section, we create a Quarkus extension from scratch. It is a very simple extension that exposes an extra HTTP endpoint. This endpoint will return some basic metadata of the application: its name, version, and the set of runtime dependencies (i.e., the set of Maven artifacts that are on the classpath at runtime). The metadata will be exposed as a JSON document with three fields: `name` (a string), `version` (a string), and `dependencies` (an array).

> **NOTE**   A rather similar extension—called `info`—is available in Quarkus itself, but we will do it a bit differently and make it simpler. The official extension also doesn't expose the runtime dependencies.

12.3.1   Creating the project

To generate the scaffolding of the project, just like for application projects, you can use the Quarkus CLI or the Quarkus Maven plugin.

If you prefer to use the CLI:

```
$ quarkus create extension org.acme:metadata-extension -P 3.15.1
```

If you prefer the Maven plugin:

```
$ mvn io.quarkus:quarkus-maven-plugin:3.15.1:create-extension
 -DgroupId=org.acme -DextensionId=metadata-extension
```

Now we can review what was created by the chosen tool. You can see a multimodule Maven project with two submodules (`runtime` and `deployment`), which correspond to the modules discussed earlier. It also contains an `integration-tests` module, which we won't use in this chapter.

12.3.2   Extending the configuration model

Because our extension aims to expose an HTTP endpoint, it is probably useful to make the path to that endpoint configurable. Let's add a configuration object that extends the Quarkus's configuration model to allow our users to configure the path.

As we already discussed, configuration can be marked to be available at build time, at runtime, or at both. In our case, the path is something that we can act upon during the build (when registering the handler during build, we specify the path to it), so let's mark it as build-time only. We can therefore create it in the `deployment` module. Open the `deployment` module's code in your IDE and add the `MetadataExtensionConfig` class in the `org.acme.metadata.extension.deployment` package, as shown in the following listing.

Listing 12.4   The configuration object for the Metadata extension

```
package org.acme.metadata.extension.deployment;

import io.quarkus.runtime.annotations.ConfigPhase;
import io.quarkus.runtime.annotations.ConfigRoot;
import io.smallrye.config.ConfigMapping;
import io.smallrye.config.WithDefault;

@ConfigRoot(phase = ConfigPhase.BUILD_TIME)      ←── The configuration
@ConfigMapping(prefix = "quarkus.metadata")          values are available
public interface MetadataExtensionConfig {           at build time only.

    /**
     * The path to the metadata endpoint.
     */
    @WithDefault("/metadata")
    String path();
}
```

We set the prefix to `quarkus.metadata` so the full configuration key the users can set is `quarkus.metadata.path` (unless you specify it explicitly, the key consists of the prefix followed by the method name converted to kebab case). Note that every configuration entry also must have a JavaDoc entry, which is used to generate documentation.

With this class in place, we have extended the Quarkus configuration model. The new property named `quarkus.metadata.path` is not used anywhere yet. We will do that later when registering the HTTP handler that handles this path. But first we have to implement the handler itself.

12.3.3   Creating the HTTP handler

Let's create the HTTP handler that handles the user requests to the `/metadata` endpoint (or whatever other path the application configures it to be). We use a very basic plain HTTP handler based on the Vert.x API (since Vert.x is the HTTP engine used almost everywhere in Quarkus). For that, we need to declare our extension dependency on the Vert.x HTTP extension.

As with everything in Maven, dependencies are transitive, so when our extension declares a dependency on the HTTP layer, then any application using our extension will also receive the HTTP layer. We have to add the deployment part of the extension to our `deployment` module and the runtime part to the `runtime` module. So add the contents of listing 12.5 into `deployment/pom.xml` and the contents of listing 12.6 into `runtime/pom.xml`.

Listing 12.5 The deployment dependency on the Vert.x HTTP extension

```xml
<dependency>
  <groupId>io.quarkus</groupId>
  <artifactId>quarkus-vertx-http-deployment</artifactId>
</dependency>
```

Listing 12.6 The runtime dependency on the Vert.x HTTP extension

```xml
<dependency>
  <groupId>io.quarkus</groupId>
  <artifactId>quarkus-vertx-http</artifactId>
</dependency>
```

Now we can create the HTTP handler's class. We will pass a prepared `String` with all the metadata that we gathered at build and store it in the handler. Add the `MetadataHandler` class as presented in listing 12.7 into the `org.acme.metadata.extension.runtime` package. It has to be in the `runtime` module. This is important; the handler will be used as runtime.

Listing 12.7 HTTP handler serving the metadata

```java
package org.acme.metadata.extension.runtime;

import io.vertx.core.Handler;
import io.vertx.ext.web.RoutingContext;

public class MetadataHandler
    implements Handler<RoutingContext> {          // Implements the Vert.x HTTP handler interface

    private final String data;

    public MetadataHandler(String data) {          // Stores the prepared metadata
        this.data = data;
    }

    @Override
    public void handle(RoutingContext ctx) {
        ctx.response().putHeader("Content-Type",
            "application/json");
        ctx.end(data);
    }
}
```

The class needs to implement the `Handler<RoutingContext>` interface to override the `handle` method. It stores the received data `String` in the field to return it once a request is received as a JSON object.

12.3.4 *Creating the recorder*

Now let's create the recorder that takes care of recording the code needed to instanti-ate the handler at runtime. Add the `MetadataExtensionRecorder` class as shown in the following listing into the same package in the `runtime` module.

Listing 12.8 The recorder for the Metadata extension

```
package org.acme.metadata.extension.runtime;

import io.quarkus.runtime.annotations.Recorder;
import io.vertx.core.Handler;
import io.vertx.ext.web.RoutingContext;

@Recorder
public class MetadataExtensionRecorder {
    public Handler<RoutingContext> createHandler(String data) {
        return new MetadataHandler(data);
    }
}
```

There is nothing complicated about this code. We just create the `MetadataHandler` instance with the provided data. But because this happens in a recorder, the actual steps to create the `Handler<RoutingContext>` are recorded as bytecode and serialized into the application. The `data` String will be computed at build time (we will imple-ment this in a bit), so it is inlined into the recorded bytecode and not recomputed during application start.

12.3.5 *Creating the processor*

The last missing piece that connects it all is the processor. The extension generator tool already created a processor class (`MetadataExtensionProcessor` in the `deployment` module), so we can add a build step to it. This build step is shown in listing 12.9 (you can check the correct imports in `chapter-12/12_3_5` directory in book's resources).

Listing 12.9 The build step in the `MetadataExtensionProcessor`

```
@BuildStep
@Record(ExecutionTime.STATIC_INIT)
RouteBuildItem createRoute(MetadataExtensionRecorder recorder,
                           ApplicationInfoBuildItem info,
                           AppModelProviderBuildItem appModel,
                           MetadataExtensionConfig config) {
    ObjectNode json = JsonNodeFactory.instance.objectNode();    ◁── Creates the
    json.put("name", info.getName());                                metadata object
    json.put("version", info.getVersion());
    ArrayNode dependenciesArray = json.putArray("dependencies");
    ApplicationModel applicationModel = appModel
        .validateAndGet(new BootstrapConfig());
    applicationModel.getRuntimeDependencies().forEach(dep -> {
```

```
        dependenciesArray.addObject()
                .put("artifact-id", dep.getArtifactId())
                .put("group-id", dep.getGroupId());
    });
    Handler<RoutingContext> handler = recorder          Instantiates the handler
        .createHandler(json.toString());                through the recorder
    return new RouteBuildItem.Builder()                 Registers the route with the handler
            .handler(handler)                           and produces it as a build item
            .route(config.path())
            .build();                          Sets route path
}                                              from configuration
```

The arguments of this method contain our defined `MetadataExtensionRecorder` (a recorder) and `MetadataExtensionConfig` (a configuration object belonging to this extension). Additionally, the `ApplicationInfoBuildItem` is a build item that is produced by Quarkus to provide information about the application (name and version) to various extensions that need it. Similarly, `AppModelProviderBuildItem` provides information about the Maven dependencies of the application. We use it to fill the `dependencies` field of the metadata. Quarkus takes care of finding the right values for all these parameters.

In the build step method, we first create our metadata JSON object filling in the details extracted from provided build items. Next, we call the recorder to create the handler instance passing in the produced JSON. Remember that it actually records the bytecode of this operation. Finally, we can produce a new `RouteBuildItem` creating our new HTTP endpoint exposed at the path configured by our property. This build item is later consumed by the `vertx-http` extension, which takes care of registering the route on the HTTP server that it manages.

We should also briefly explain the `STATIC_INIT` execution time that we used in the `@Record` annotation. There are two execution times for the recorded bytecode: `STATIC_INIT` and `RUNTIME_INIT`. `STATIC_INIT` is always executed before `RUNTIME_INIT`. But the main difference is that in native mode, `STATIC_INIT` bytecode executes during the image build and the result is recorded into the image. In JVM mode, both `STATIC_INIT` and `RUNTIME_INIT` execute when the application boots, and the only difference between them is that `STATIC_INIT` executes first. Thus using `STATIC_INIT` (where it's possible) makes no difference in JVM mode, but it makes the application start even faster in native mode. However, not all operations are possible to execute in `STATIC_INIT` (for example, opening sockets). Generally, `STATIC_INIT` should be preferred in cases where it's possible and `RUNTIME_INIT` in other cases. Refer to the Quarkus documentation for a more detailed explanation.

Note that we calculated the metadata (the resulting JSON document) at build time (in a processor). The result is recorded into the application, and it doesn't have to be recomputed during application start. While this particular example won't make a big difference in the startup time, it demonstrates the general concept of build-time initialization that is one of the core concepts around which Quarkus is built.

12.3.6 *Trying out the extension*

To try out the extension, we need to build it (`quarkus build` or `mvn install`, the Maven wrapper is not generated in extensions) and then add it to any Quarkus application. It has to be installed because we need to reference it in other projects, meaning `mvn package` is not sufficient in this case. You can try it with any of the car rental applications that we created earlier or with your own application that you've written. For example, let's add it to the Inventory service, which we used the most in our examples. Add the following dependency to the `inventory-service/pom.xml`:

```
<dependency>
  <groupId>org.acme</groupId>
  <artifactId>metadata-extension</artifactId>
  <version>1.0.0-SNAPSHOT</version>
</dependency>
```

Then build and run the application as normal, in Dev or production mode. You can see that our extension is included in the extension list once your Quarkus application starts:

```
INFO  [io.quarkus] (Quarkus Main Thread) Installed features: [...,
➥ metadata-extension, ...]
```

When it's running, invoke http://localhost:8083/metadata (or a different port than 8083 if you're using different application), and you will see a large JSON document that looks something like the following listing.

Listing 12.10   The output of the metadata endpoint

```
{
  "name": "inventory-service",
  "version": "1.0.0-SNAPSHOT",
  "dependencies": [
    {
      "artifact-id": "metadata-extension",
      "group-id": "org.acme"
    },
    {
      "artifact-id": "quarkus-vertx-http",
      "group-id": "io.quarkus"
    },
    {
      "artifact-id": "quarkus-credentials",
      "group-id": "io.quarkus"
    }
# ... and many more dependencies
```

To verify that the `quarkus.metadata.path` configuration property allows you to configure the path to the endpoint, shut the application down and restart it (or just restart if you are using Dev mode), but add `quarkus.metadata.path=/some-other-path` either to its `application.properties`, or as a system property (`-Dquarkus.metadata.path=/some-other-path`). The metadata endpoint should now be available on the new path instead of `/metadata`. The old path will now return a 404 error.

12.4   Testing an extension

The Quarkus extension generator tool also created a unit test class for the extension in the `deployment` module. The test class is called `MetadataExtensionTest` but doesn't actually contain any tests for now. There's also `MetadataExtensionDevModeTest`, which we would use if we wanted to test the Dev mode capabilities of the extension, but we don't need to do it here. Let's add a simple test to the `MetadataExtensionTest` class that verifies that the metadata endpoint works. We use REST Assured, just like we did when we were testing other HTTP endpoints of the applications we developed before.

> **NOTE**   Quarkus extensions normally require an application to serve a purpose. However, the Quarkus testing framework allows us to create unit tests for extensions without any application (or, more precisely, with an empty application that is still able to boot up all the functionality provided by the used extensions). But of course, extensions generally only make sense together with applications, so you can provide some application classes and resources to the test, and it will run with them.

First, add the REST Assured dependency to the `deployment` module's `pom.xml`. The scope should be `test` to make sure we don't package the library in the final application:

```
<dependency>
  <groupId>io.rest-assured</groupId>
  <artifactId>rest-assured</artifactId>
  <scope>test</scope>
</dependency>
```

Now change the generated `writeYourOwnUnitTest` test method inside the `MetadataExtensionTest` class.

Listing 12.11   Testing the metadata extension

```
// Start unit test with your extension loaded
@RegisterExtension
static final QuarkusUnitTest unitTest = new QuarkusUnitTest()
    .setArchiveProducer(() -> ShrinkWrap.create(JavaArchive.class));

@Test
public void writeYourOwnUnitTest() {
    RestAssured.when().get("/metadata")
        .prettyPeek()
        .then()
        .statusCode(200)
        .contentType("application/json")
        .body("name", equalTo("metadata-extension-deployment"))
```

```
        .body("version", equalTo("1.0.0-SNAPSHOT"))
        .body("dependencies", not(emptyArray()));
}
```

This test simply calls the metadata endpoint and logs the returned JSON object to the console. It also checks the status code and content type of the response. The reported `name` and `version` in this special case will match the artifact ID and version of the `deployment` module of the extension because Quarkus actually starts an empty application for the test. If you try to execute this test now, it will pass. The definition of the application that is booted up for the test is in the `unitTest` static field inside this class. Quarkus allows you to customize this application by adding whatever application classes you want to it, and many other customization options, but in this case, we just want an empty application that only contains the metadata extension.

As the final code we write in this book, let's add one more test which will verify that if users change the `quarkus.metadata.path` configuration, the extension correctly moves our endpoint. Create a new test class `MetadataExtensionConfigTest` in the same package, as shown in the following listing.

Listing 12.12   The source code of the `MetadataExtensionConfigTest`

```
package org.acme.metadata.extension.test;

import io.quarkus.test.QuarkusUnitTest;
import io.restassured.RestAssured;
import org.junit.jupiter.api.Test;
import org.junit.jupiter.api.extension.RegisterExtension;

import static org.hamcrest.Matchers.emptyArray;
import static org.hamcrest.Matchers.equalTo;
import static org.hamcrest.Matchers.not;

public class MetadataExtensionConfigTest {

    @RegisterExtension
    static final QuarkusUnitTest unitTest = new QuarkusUnitTest()
        .overrideConfigKey("quarkus.metadata.path", "/some-other-path");

    @Test
    public void testMetadataConfigPathChange() {
        RestAssured.when().get("/some-other-path")
            .prettyPeek()
            .then()
            .statusCode(200)
            .contentType("application/json")
            .body("name", equalTo("metadata-extension-deployment"))
            .body("version", equalTo("1.0.0-SNAPSHOT"))
            .body("dependencies", not(emptyArray()));
    }
}
```

This new test executes the same logic as the previous one, but this time it calls our application on `/some-other-path` endpoint instead of `/metadata`. We pass the configuration override to the started empty Quarkus application through the JUnit5 extension (`@RegisterExtension`). Feel free to check other available methods of `QuarkusUnitTest` class that allow you to redefine many aspects of the Quarkus application under test.

If you now run the build in the metadata extension project, all tests should pass:

```
$ quarkus build
...
[INFO] Results:
[INFO]
[INFO] Tests run: 3, Failures: 0, Errors: 0, Skipped: 0
```

12.5 Next steps

In this chapter, we introduced the concepts related to Quarkus extensions, including how to create, use, and test them.

We discussed all the different things that an extension can do to enhance applications that use the extension. We explained how an extension can extend Quarkus configuration, how it can utilize bytecode recording, and the build-time initialization concepts.

We also created a simple extension that adds a metadata endpoint to Quarkus applications. This endpoint returns some basic information about the application, such as its name, version, and the list of runtime dependencies. We created two simple unit tests that verify that the created endpoint returns the expected data and that our custom configuration property can be used to change the path of the endpoint.

Summary

- Quarkus extensions are typically created to make the use of a library in Quarkus applications easier and more concise.
- Extensions can do many things, such as adding HTTP endpoints, registering custom CDI beans, doing build-time initialization work, recording bytecode, registering metadata for compiling to native image, managing Dev Services instances, or adding functionalities into the Dev UI.
- The Quarkus CLI or Maven plugin can create a project skeleton for a new extension.
- Configuration related to an extension is represented by annotated interfaces.
- Configuration properties can be marked as build-time-only, runtime-only, or both (available in both phases).
- An extension usually consists of two Maven modules, `deployment` and `runtime`. At runtime, Quarkus applications utilizing the extension use only the `runtime` artifact (it's available on the classpath). The `deployment` artifact is used only during the build and its classes are not included in the final artifact.

- A processor is a class containing build steps. Build steps consume and produce build items and can call recorders to record bytecode.
- Build steps often use the Jandex index to scan the application classes and their annotations to avoid the necessity to do this via reflection at runtime.
- A build item represents the means to pass data between different build steps (regardless of whether they are in the same or different extensions).
- A recorder is a class that records bytecode which needs to be available at runtime. Recorded bytecode can either be marked STATIC_INIT or RUNTIME_INIT. In native mode, the STATIC_INIT bytecode executes during the image build and the result is recorded into the image. In JVM mode, both STATIC_INIT and RUNTIME_INIT execute when the application boots.

appendix A
Alternative languages and build tooling

We decided to choose both Java and Maven as the most utilized JVM programming language and build tool, respectively. However, Quarkus has a large user base that prefers Kotlin and Gradle. In this appendix, we detail how you can set up and use them both with your Quarkus applications.

A.1 Gradle

Gradle is utilized in a very similar way to the Quarkus Maven plugin. All operations are just mapped to Gradle tasks.

A.1.1 Creating Quarkus Gradle projects

We can create a Quarkus application project based on Gradle in three ways: the quarkus CLI, the Quarkus Maven plugin, and the graphical starter interface (https://code.quarkus.io).

CREATING GRADLE APPLICATIONS WITH THE QUARKUS CLI
We only need to specify the --gradle flag when we generate the project:

```
$ quarkus create app org.acme:quarkus-gradle --gradle
```

CREATING GRADLE APPLICATIONS WITH THE MAVEN PLUGIN
Gradle doesn't provide a way to generate a project from the command line as Maven does. But we can utilize the same Quarkus Maven plugin with the full GAV to also generate Gradle projects:

```
$ mvn io.quarkus.platform:quarkus-maven-plugin:3.15.1:create \
    -DprojectGroupId=org.acme \
    -DprojectArtifactId=quarkus-gradle \
    -DbuildTool=gradle
```

CREATING GRADLE APPLICATIONS WITH CODE.QUARKUS.IO
Simply choose `Gradle` in the `Build Tool` menu, as shown in figure A.1.

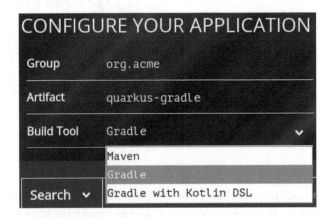

Figure A.1   code.quarkus.io
Gradle build tool

A.1.2   Quarkus with Gradle

The `quarkus` CLI will work exactly the same as with Maven. After all, that's its purpose. If you prefer to work with Gradle tasks directly, you can list all available operations with

```
$ ./gradlew tasks
```

The `io.quarkus` plugin adds the Quarkus-specific tasks. Notable examples are

```
# Dev mode, --console=plain is needed to make Dev mode commands work
$ ./gradlew --console=plain quarkusDev

# Extensions
$ ./gradlew listExtensions
$ ./gradlew listCategories
$ ./gradlew addExtension
$ ./gradlew removeExtension

# Images
$ ./gradlew imageBuild
$ ./gradlew imagePush
```

But Quarkus with Gradle also defines some operations that the Maven plugin doesn't have. For instance, `./gradlew quarkusTest` runs the continuous testing mode, which is just continuous testing without starting Dev mode.

You can find more information on Quarkus usage with Gradle at https://quarkus .io/guides/gradle-tooling.

A.2 *Kotlin*

Kotlin is the second most popular JVM language after Java. Its community is still growing. Quarkus aims to provide first-class support for Kotlin.

Quarkus currently supports Kotlin 2.0.10 because it needs to include some of the Kotlin core libraries (all defined in Quarkus BOM). Using the same version is recommended, but if you need to, it is possible to override it.

To generate a Kotlin project with Quarkus, we can simply add the `kotlin` extension. In Gradle, there is also `gradle-kotlin-dsl` build tool option in the CLI, Maven plugin, and the generator site.

When Kotlin is enabled during project creation, the generated starting code (for example, `GreetingResource` class for `quarkus-rest` extension) is also generated as Kotlin classes (in cases where the particular extensions support generating Kotlin starter code).

A.2.1 *Kotlin allOpen*

By default, Kotlin marks all classes generated by the Kotlin compiler as `final`. This doesn't work with many extensions that generate proxies (e.g., REST or Arc). So Quarkus configures the `all-open` option to mark classes that should stay nonfinal. The following snippet shows an excerpt from a Quarkus project using Kotlin and Gradle `build.gradle` file:

```
allOpen {
    annotation("jakarta.ws.rs.Path")
    annotation("jakarta.enterprise.context.ApplicationScoped")
    annotation("jakarta.persistence.Entity")
    annotation("io.quarkus.test.junit.QuarkusTest")
}
```

For now, you need to configure any additional annotations manually, but Quarkus will most likely generate the required configuration for `allOpen` option automatically in the future.

A.2.2 *Kotlin coroutines*

Here is the list of extensions that support Kotlin coroutines: `rest`, `rest-client`, `messaging`, `scheduler`, `smallrye-fault-tolerance`, `vertx`, and `websockets-next`. There is also the `io.smallrye.reactive:mutiny-kotlin` module for Mutiny integration. More information can be found at https://smallrye.io/smallrye-mutiny/latest/ guides/kotlin/.

A.3   *Other languages*

In the Quarkus main repository, there is a `quarkus-scala` extension that supports Scala 2. In Quarkiverse, there are extensions for Scala 3 (`quarkus-scala3`) and Groovy (`quarkus-groovy`).

appendix B
Tools installations

All tools we use in this book evolve, so all we can provide here is a snapshot of their installation instructions at the time of this writing. Make sure to always double-check the official documentation (linked in all sections) when you read this appendix.

B.1 Quarkus CLI

The official documentation can be found at https://quarkus.io/guides/cli-tooling.

The Quarkus CLI can be installed with the following package managers:

- *SDKMAN!*—(https://sdkman.io) Linux/macOS
- *Homebrew*—(https://brew.sh) Linux/macOS
- *Chocolatey*—(https://chocolatey.org) Windows
- *Scoop*—(https://scoop.sh) Windows
- *JBang*—(https://www.jbang.dev) Linux/macOS/Windows

For instance, with SDKMAN!:

```
$ sdk install quarkus
```

Or with Chocolatey:

```
PS C:\> choco install quarkus
```

To verify you have the Quarkus CLI installed, you can run

```
$ quarkus --version
3.15.1
```

B.2   *Maven*

The official documentation can be found at https://maven.apache.org/install.html.

As a reminder, all projects generated by the Quarkus Maven plugin, the Quarkus CLI, or code.quarkus.io also contain a Maven wrapper, so you don't need to install Maven manually to work with them (the correct version will be downloaded automatically). Obviously, to generate a project with the Quarkus Maven plugin in the first place, you do have to install Maven.

The operating system package managers very often provide Maven binaries. It's worth checking whether your operating system has this option.

To install Maven manually, follow these steps:

1   Download the binary Maven archive from https://maven.apache.org/download .cgi.

2   Unzip the downloaded archive—for instance:

```
$ unzip apache-maven-3.9.9-bin.zip
```

3   Add the apache-maven-3.9.9/bin folder to the PATH environment variable.

To verify you have Maven installed, you can run

```
$ mvn -v
Apache Maven 3.9.9 (8e8579a9e76f7d015ee5ec7bfcdc97d260186937)
Maven home: /path/to/maven
Java version: 21.0.2, vendor: Eclipse Adoptium, runtime: /path/to/jdk
Default locale: en_US, platform encoding: UTF-8
OS name: "linux", version: "6.11.3", arch: "amd64", family: "unix"
```

B.3   *GraalVM*

The official documentation can be found at https://mng.bz/5gj1.

The required version of GraalVM or Mandrel is 21. We recommend either Mandrel or GraalVM Community Edition (CE), but if you have access to GraalVM Enterprise Edition (EE) you can also use it.

1   Download or install the GraalVM distribution.

Either download the archive, or you can use package managers:

– *Mandrel*—Available at https://github.com/graalvm/mandrel/releases

– *GraalVM CE*—Available at https://github.com/graalvm/graalvm-ce-builds/ releases

– *SDKMAN!*—Available at https://sdkman.io/jdks/#graalce

– *Homebrew*—Available at https://github.com/graalvm/homebrew-tap

– *Scoop*—Available at https://github.com/ScoopInstaller/Java

For instance, with the SDKMAN!:

```
$ sdk install java 21-graalce
```

2 Set the GRAALVM_HOME environment variable to the installation directory. For instance:

```
$ export GRAALVM_HOME=$HOME/Development/mandrel/
```

On macOS, point GRAALVM_HOME to the Home subdirectory:

```
$ export GRAALVM_HOME=$HOME/Development/graalvm/Contents/Home/
```

On Windows, use the control panel, but note that installing GraalVM with scoop will do this for you.

3 *Optionally* set the JAVA_HOME also to the GRAALVM_HOME:

```
$ export JAVA_HOME=${GRAALVM_HOME}
```

4 *Optionally* add GRAALVM_HOME/bin to PATH:

```
$ export PATH=${GRAALVM_HOME}/bin:$PATH
```

To verify you have GraalVM (or Mandrel) installed:

```
$ echo $GRAALVM_HOME
/path/to/graalvm

# only for GraalVM CE/EE
$ $GRAALVM_HOME/bin/native-image --help

GraalVM Native Image (https://www.graalvm.org/native-image/)
...
```

B.4   HTTPie

The official documentation can be found at https://httpie.io/docs/cli/installation.
There are several ways of installing HTTPie:

- *Python*—All operating systems:

```
python -m pip install --upgrade pip wheel
python -m pip install httpie
```

- *Homebrew*—macOS:

```
brew update
brew install httpie
```

- *MacPorts*—macOS:

```
port selfupdate
port install httpie
```

- *Chocolatey*—Windows:

```
PS C:\> choco install httpie
```

- *Linux Package Manager*—Various Linux distributions:

```
# Debian and Ubuntu
curl -SsL https://packages.httpie.io/deb/KEY.gpg | sudo gpg --dearmor -o
    /usr/share/keyrings/httpie.gpg
echo "deb [arch=amd64 signed-by=/usr/share/keyrings/httpie.gpg]
    https://packages.httpie.io/deb ./" | sudo tee /etc/apt/sources.list
    .d/httpie.list > /dev/null
sudo apt update
sudo apt install httpie

# Fedora
dnf install httpie

# Snapcraft (Linux)
snap install httpie

# Arch Linux
pacman -Syu httpie

# FreeBSD
pkg install www/py-httpie
```

To verify you have HTTPie installed, you can run

```
$ http
usage:
    http [METHOD] URL [REQUEST_ITEM ...]
...
```

appendix C
Alternatives for developing frontend applications with Quarkus

We used Qute and HTMX to develop a frontend for our application in chapter 6, but this is obviously not the only way to create frontend applications with Quarkus. Let's explore some of the alternatives. This is obviously not an exhaustive list; there are already more options, and new ones will probably arise. We will focus on the two prominent alternatives that are receiving some support from the Quarkus community itself and thus can be expected to stay relevant for usage with Quarkus.

C.1 Quinoa

Quinoa is a Quarkus extension whose goal is to ease development, building, and deploying of single-page web applications. It is compatible with any framework that uses NodeJS for building (React, Angular, Vue, etc.). You quickly get a full-stack Quarkus single-page application and benefit from all the Quarkus eco-system (full-stack dev mode, GraphQL, REST endpoints, messaging, etc.).

At the time of writing, the `quarkus-quinoa` extension was a Quarkiverse extension. Quarkiverse was explained at the end of chapter 2 (section 2.7.5).

More information about Quinoa can be found in the official documentation: https://mng.bz/nRMg.

C.2   *Renarde*

Quarkus Renarde is a new server-side rendered Web Application framework based on Quarkus. Its main role is to bind together Qute, Hibernate, and RESTEasy Reactive by creating a concise MVC (Model-View-Controller) layer over them. It also provides tooling to deal with forms, validation, routing, and security.

See https://mng.bz/oKpr for more information.

index

RELATED MANNING TITLES

Kubernetes Native Microservices with Quarkus and MicroProfile
by John Clingan and Ken Finnigan

ISBN 9781617298653
328 pages, $59.99
December 2021

Spring in Action, Sixth Edition
by Craig Walls

ISBN 9781617297571
520 pages, $59.99
January 2022

Spring Start Here
by Laurentiu Spilca
Foreword by Victor Rentea

ISBN 9781617298691
416 pages, $49.99
September 2021

*Spring Microservices in Action,
Second Edition*
by John Carnell and Illary Huaylupo Sánchez

ISBN 9781617296956
448 pages, $59.99
May 2021

For ordering information, go to www.manning.com